JUSTICE AS A VIRTUE

Justice as a Virtue

A Thomistic Perspective

Jean Porter

WILLIAM B. EERDMANS PUBLISHING COMPANY
GRAND RAPIDS, MICHIGAN

Wm. B. Eerdmans Publishing Co.
2140 Oak Industrial Drive N.E., Grand Rapids, Michigan 49505
www.eerdmans.com

22 21 20 19 18 17 16   1 2 3 4 5 6 7

ISBN 978-0-8028-7325-5

Library of Congress Cataloging-in-Publication Data

Names: Porter, Jean, 1955- author.
Title: Justice as a virtue : a Thomistic perspective / Jean Porter.
Description: Grand Rapids, Michigan : William B. Eerdmans Publishing Company, [2016] |
    Includes bibliographical references and index.
Identifiers: LCCN 2016024702 | ISBN 9780802873255 (pbk. : alk. paper)
Subjects: LCSH: Thomas, Aquinas, Saint, 1225?-1274. | Justice (Virtue) | Virtues.
Classification: LCC B765.T54 P68 2016 | DDC 172/.2—dc23
    LC record available at https://lccn.loc.gov/2016024702

For Joseph Blenkinsopp

Beati qui esuriunt et sitiunt justitiam:
quoniam ipsi saturabuntur

Contents

Preface   ix

Acknowledgments   xii

1. **Justice as a Virtue**   1

   Preliminary Considerations   7

   The Theoretical Framework   17

   The Virtues as Normative Ideals   31

   An Overview of the Virtue of Justice   44

   Reason, Revelation, and Justice   51

2. **Virtues and Vices of the Will**   59

   The Will as a Causal Principle   63

   The Will as the Principle of Voluntary Actions   73

   Habits of the Will   85

   Justice as a Perfection of the Will   104

3. **Justice as a Moral Ideal**   115

   Justice, Equality, and Right   116

   Equality, Right, and Obligation   131

   Justice, Practical Reason, and First Principles   146

   The Common Good, Political Rule, and the Ideal of Equality   161

4. **From Ideal to Law** 171

Norm, Precept, and Act 173

Justice and the Moral Emotions 187

Norms of Nonmaleficence 204

The Place of Discernment in the Activities of Justice 219

5. **The Perfections of the Will** 229

Reason and the Virtues 231

Value, Morality, and Perfections of the Will 238

Commitment and Regard, Two Aspects of Justice 257

Conclusion 269

Bibliography 274

Name Index 282

Subject Index 285

Preface

A little over ten years ago, I completed a theory of the natural law, derived largely although not exclusively from the work of Thomas Aquinas. As I worked through the interpretative and theoretical issues raised by that project, it became clear to me that Aquinas's theory of the natural law is incomplete without the theory of virtue that accompanies it. The virtues represent the full and appropriate development of natural human capacities, exercised in the context of an admirable and satisfying way of life. They are therefore the touchstones for any theory of the natural law, which presupposes some account of the normative significance of human nature. At the same time, the virtues presuppose rational insights into the true end of human life and the ways in which we can, or should, pursue that end, and Aquinas, together with many of his interlocutors, identifies the natural law with the first principles that lie behind these insights. Clearly, we cannot separate Aquinas's theories of the natural law and virtue, as if these were two disparate ways of thinking about morality. Just as the natural law and the virtues are two distinct but complementary principles of the human act, so Aquinas's theory of morality offers an integrated account of these two aspects of the moral life.

The close interconnection between natural law and virtue is nowhere more evident than in Aquinas's account of justice. While Aquinas and our own contemporaries have very different conceptions of justice, they would agree that justice is distinctively associated with objective standards for equity, fairness, and obligation, formulated in terms of stringent rules. Yet Aquinas also claims that justice is a virtue, not just in the attenuated sense of a disposition to perform just actions, but in the same robust way that temperance and courage are virtues. As such, justice represents a full and appropriate development—a perfection, in other words—of the capacity that it informs, the will. To put the point in somewhat anachronistic terms, justice is the characteristic virtue of the human person as an autonomous, rational agent, whose lawful acts are the highest expressions of freedom. At the same time, for Aquinas rational freedom is not the aim of the virtue of justice. Rather, justice is quintessentially the virtue of the individual in relation to others. It is a stable disposition of rational love, and it moves the agent to render to each that which is his or her right.

This book is a study of the virtue of justice as Aquinas presents it in the *Summa theologiae*, developed in such a way as to bring out the contemporary significance of his account. As I hope to show, a close study of Aquinas's account of justice offers unexpected insights into many different aspects of his overall theory of morality, including his views on the foundations of moral judgment and his treatment of the norms of nonmaleficence. At the same time, his account of justice, along with the theory of virtue that it presupposes, represents a key part of a cogent theory of morality that deserves consideration on its own terms. I believe that Aquinas's overall account of justice and the virtues is the true theory of morality, or as near to a true theory as we can ever come, but I will not try to make a conclusive case for that view in this book. My aim is simply to present an interpretation of Aquinas's account of justice and virtue that is persuasive as a reading of Aquinas, while at the same time making the best case I can for the theory of morality implied by that account.

In order to complete this book, I have had to place certain constraints on this project. The first has already been implied. That is, this is a study in Aquinas's account of justice as presented in his final, comprehensive synthesis of his thought, the *Summa theologiae*. I do not attempt to trace the development of Aquinas's thought on justice and related topics, nor do I try to offer an overview of all that he says about justice in his extensive writings. My aim is to reconstruct the unified theory that underlies his treatment of justice, the virtues, and the will in one particular text, and I do not try to examine Aquinas's other writings on these topics in any systematic way.

Second, I do not attempt to bring Aquinas into conversation, so to speak, with the two modern authors whose views are most relevant to his own, namely, David Hume and Immanuel Kant. In each case, we find intriguing points of contact between Aquinas and a modern thinker, together with deep disagreements. I have bracketed both thinkers, partly in order to keep this book within manageable bounds, but more fundamentally because the differences among these three authors are too deep to allow for a quick treatment, developed in the context of another project. Aquinas, Hume, and Kant hold three different views of causality, and their respective accounts of moral agency, freedom, and accountability cannot be understood, much less compared, unless their fundamentally different conceptions of change and agency are taken into account. That would be a worthwhile and fascinating project, but it is a project for another day.

Acknowledgments

This book is an extensively revised version of the Stone Lectures, which I delivered at Princeton Theological Seminary, October 3–11, 2011. I also delivered a shorter version of the same lectures as the Jellema Lectures at Calvin College, Grand Rapids, Michigan, April 3–4, 2012, and I delivered a paper on a related subject as a plenary address at the Central Meeting of the Society of Christian Philosophers, Hendrix College, Conway, Arkansas, March 23, 2012. I am not sure that this book would have existed at all without the incentives that these invitations gave me to formulate my thoughts on Aquinas's account of justice. At any rate, anything I might have written on this subject would have been much poorer without the many questions and comments that I received on these occasions, and I am grateful to all those who participated. Special thanks are due to Iain Torrance, Matthew Halteman, and Aaron Simmons for extending invitations to these events, and to them and their colleagues for their warm, generous hospitality.

Following on these initial formulations, this book went through more revisions than I like to remember. I am grateful to the University of Notre Dame, which granted me a sabbatical for the academic year 2012–13, during which time I finished a draft of the book. I have also benefited immeasurably from conversations with colleagues and students on justice, virtue, and related topics. My colleague Jerry McKenny has been an invaluable conversation partner, as well as a good friend. He commented on portions of this manuscript, but by the time the manuscript was finished enough for comments, our many conversations on morality and the will had already shaped my thought in innumerable ways. In addition, he and I taught a doctoral seminar on Aquinas, Kant, and the will in the fall of 2014, just as I was beginning the last phase of writing, and I benefited greatly from his insights and those of our students. I also want to thank my students in a doctoral seminar

"Theories of Justice," which I taught at Notre Dame in the fall of 2011, for stimulating conversations on contemporary philosophical theories of justice. Finally, thanks to Craig Iffland, who commented on portions of this book and provided bibliographic assistance and comments and many illuminating conversations on Aquinas, justice, and contemporary moral theology; and to John Bolin, John Hare, and Russell Hittinger for ongoing conversations—not to say arguments—on justice, virtue, and eudaimonism. My work, and my life, would be much poorer without these students, colleagues, and friends.

At some points, I draw on articles that have been published elsewhere, and I use them with permission of the editors of the original publications:

"Justice, Equality, and Natural Rights Claims: A Reconsideration of Aquinas's Conception of Right," *Journal of Law and Religion* 30.3 (2015): 446–60.

"Choice, Causality, and Relation: Aquinas's Analysis of the Moral Act and the Doctrine of Double Effect," *American Catholic Philosophical Quarterly* 89.3 (Summer 2015): 479–504.

"Moral Passions: A Thomistic Interpretation of Moral Emotions in Non-human and Human Moral Animals," *Journal of Moral Theology* 3.2 (June 2014): 93–108.

"Why Are the Habits Necessary? An Inquiry into Aquinas's Moral Psychology," *Oxford Studies in Medieval Philosophy* 1 (2013): 113–35.

I would like to thank Elizabeth Lawton Kuriakose for preparing the bibliography and the table of contents. As always, I am indebted to the dedicated, efficient, and supportive editorial team at Eerdmans Publishing. In particular, I want to thank James Ernest, the Editor in Chief, for his support for this project, and Jenny Hoffman and Craig Noll, for the skill, professionalism, and patience that they brought to the task of preparing the manuscript for publication. Thanks, finally, to Jon Pott, now editor emeritus of Eerdmans, who has supported me in my research and writing for many years. It's an honor to have been associated with him, and I'm grateful for his friendship.

Finally, this book is dedicated to my husband, Joseph Blenkinsopp, whose love and support have been unflagging. I literally cannot say how much I owe him, but this book is dedicated to him with all my love.

CHAPTER 1

Justice as a Virtue

According to Aquinas, justice is a virtue, which he identifies, in terms taken from Justinian's *Digest*, as "a constant and perpetual will rendering to each that which is his right" (*Summa theologiae* II-II 58.1).[1] This is one of those points at which we are sharply reminded of the distance between Aquinas's intellectual world and our own. Aquinas's predecessors and interlocutors generally assume, as he does, that justice is a personal virtue of some kind. To most of our contemporaries, this way of thinking about justice is unhelpful at best. After all, what would the virtue of justice be, over and above a disposition to carry out just actions? Our conception of justice as a personal virtue would seem to presuppose some account of impersonal principles of justice—a theory of justice, in other words, such as we find in the magisterial work of John Rawls and his many students and critics.[2]

In one sense, Aquinas too has a theory of justice—that is, he offers a critical, integrated account of the ideals and precepts proper to this complex virtue. Nonetheless, he does not have a theory of justice in the contemporary sense, such as we find in Rawls and his interlocutors. Rawls begins *A Theory of Justice* with the claim that justice is the first virtue of social institutions, just as truth is the first virtue of systems of thought.[3] As he goes on to explain, "For us the primary subject of justice is the basic structure of society,

---

1. In order to minimize the number of notes, all references to the *Summa theologiae* have been incorporated into the text. Other references to Aquinas's works are included in the notes. Unless otherwise indicated, all translations from Aquinas's texts are my own.

2. John Rawls, *A Theory of Justice* (Cambridge, MA: Harvard University Press, 1971; rev. ed., 1999).

3. Rawls, *A Theory of Justice*, 3. Similarly, Ronald Dworkin remarks that "justice is an institution we interpret" (*Law's Empire* [Cambridge, MA: Harvard University Press, Belknap Press, 1986], 73).

or more exactly, the way in which the major social institutions distribute fundamental rights and duties and determine the division of advantages from social cooperation."[4] Thus, the ideal of justice is paradigmatically expressed through social systems that allocate communal benefits and burdens in an equitable way, while preserving the basic rights and freedoms of all. The key point here is that this way of thinking about justice focuses on institutions, understood as impersonal, self-sustaining systems of interlocking roles and functions that operate in such a way as to distribute opportunities, benefits, and burdens to the members of a society. A theory of justice, thus understood, proposes an account of the ways in which institutions ought to operate, which kinds of structural arrangements are acceptable, and which kinds of outcomes are acceptable, given basic criteria of fairness and respect.

So far as I have been able to determine, this line of analysis is very nearly absent from Aquinas's thought. He does comment on the legitimacy and desirability of different forms of governmental structures, but he does not evaluate these by reference to criteria of justice (I-II 105.1). Elsewhere, he addresses questions pertaining to the licitness and authority of laws and legal judgments, but in these contexts he has little to say about institutional arrangements as such (I-II 95–97; II-II 60). It is difficult to say whether he could have developed an institutionally oriented theory of justice along contemporary lines, given the conceptual resources available to him. The twelfth century was a remarkably creative and fruitful period for jurisprudence, and after the rediscovery of Aristotle's *Politics* in the thirteenth century, scholastic theologians and jurists began to reflect on the nature and scope of political authority, its purposes, and the conditions for its legitimate use.[5] As we would expect, they have robust notions of social roles, collective entities, and juridical personality, and the jurists in particular begin to work out the main lines of what we would describe as constitutional theory. However, their attention is focused on issues of legitimacy, authority, and power. They do not seem to think of institutions and social systems as playing a distributive role in the way that our own interlocutors do, and I am not aware of any examples of an institutionally oriented theory of distributive justice in this period. At any rate, Aquinas does not think of justice as a quality or an aim of institutional or social structures. He does devote a question to distributive

---

4. Rawls, *A Theory of Justice*, 7.

5. For an excellent introduction to the development of scholastic legal and political thought, focusing on its implications for constitutional theory, see Brian Tierney, *Religion, Law, and the Growth of Constitutional Thought, 1150–1650* (Cambridge: Cambridge University Press, 1982; repr. 2008), 30.

justice, but distributive justice as he understands it pertains to fairness with respect to allocations of commonly held benefits and burdens, public offices, and honors, in accordance with generally accepted criteria of fairness, suitability, or merit (II-II 61.1, 62.1, 63). It is a virtue of public officials acting on behalf of the community, not a quality of institutional systems of exchange, and Aquinas explicitly distinguishes it from general justice, which pertains directly to the common good (II-II 61.1 *ad* 4).[6]

Aquinas and his interlocutors, however, do have theories of virtue, and Aquinas's own theory stands out for its analytic clarity and comprehensive scope. This is the context within which we need to place his extended account of justice in order to understand it on its own terms and to appreciate its contemporary significance. According to Aquinas, justice is a virtue of the will (I-II 56.6; II-II 58.4). As we will see, this position implies that justice is a habit, that is to say, a kind of stable disposition that is grounded in an abstract, reasoned conception of the good as it pertains to human life and that is expressed through the agent's choices and actions. On both counts, the virtue of justice is central to the agent's moral personality. Through the virtue of general justice, she devotes herself to the common good of her community, especially as expressed through rational and appropriate laws (II-II 58.5–6). At the same time, through the virtue of particular justice, the

---

6. Of course, I would not deny that Aquinas's account of justice offers much that is relevant to our current debates over the justice of institutional arrangements, and we can legitimately draw on that extended account as a resource for constructive moral and political thought. My point is simply that Aquinas himself does not understand justice primarily, or perhaps at all, as a quality of institutional arrangements. For an excellent discussion of Aquinas's account of justice and its contemporary moral and political relevance, see Eleonore Stump, *Aquinas* (London: Routledge, 2003), 309–32. It is noteworthy, however, that, near the beginning of her remarks on justice, Stump notes, "I will not explain the way Aquinas situates justice in the broader context of the virtues, the opposed 'capital vices,' the 'gifts of the Holy Spirit,' the theological virtue of charity, the 'beatitudes,' or any of the other medieval lore in which Aquinas typically embeds his account of a virtue. Furthermore, I will also leave to one side Aquinas's considerable theoretical discussion of justice as a general and special virtue, as well as the 'parts' of justice, the virtues annexed to justice, and the natural law" (313). In other words, Stump's appropriation of Aquinas sets aside those aspects of his account of justice that, from Aquinas's own perspective, are central to that account. In order to fit Aquinas's account of justice into a contemporary context, she sets aside any consideration of justice as a virtue. In his *Politics for a Pilgrim Church: A Thomistic Theory of Civic Virtue* (Grand Rapids: Eerdmans, 2015), Thomas Bushlack approaches the question of Aquinas's relevance to contemporary social and civic life from another direction, proposing an account of civic virtue drawn from Aquinas's account of justice and the virtues annexed to it. Unfortunately, this book appeared too late for me to take account of it in this project.

agent is disposed to respect the claims of others, in accordance with normative ideals of due regard, fairness, and equity (II-II 58.7–8). Thus, justice in both of its forms directs the agent outward, so to speak, away from her own immediate interests and benefits, toward the more comprehensive good of the community and the distinct claims of other people. In this way, the virtue of justice operates in such a way as to integrate the agent's passions with her reasoned convictions and overall aims. For all these reasons, justice is the highest and most excellent of the moral virtues, although it is not the highest virtue overall. That place is reserved for the supernatural virtue of charity, which is also a virtue of the will (II-II 58.12; cf. II-II 23.6, 24.1).

Seen from this perspective, Aquinas's extended treatment of the virtue of justice is highly relevant to contemporary debates in moral theory. The debates in question, however, are not focused on theories of justice. They are taking place among proponents of Kantian, neo-Aristotelian, and Stoic theories of ethics, and they are focused on the meaning and significance of practical reason, motivation, character, and good disposition.[7] Aquinas's account of justice as a virtue provides the integrating key for a comprehensive account of moral value, seen as both grounded in, and yet qualitatively different from, the aims and values natural to us as living creatures of a certain kind. As such, this account offers an illuminating and cogent alternative to recent Kantian theories of morality, which emphasize the dichotomies between natural values and moral norms. At the same time, Aquinas does not simply equate moral and natural values, because for him the self-reflective judgments of intellect and will do introduce qualitatively new kinds of normative considerations. This line of argument distinguishes his theory of virtue from leading contemporary neo-Aristotelian approaches, which tend to identify natural and moral goodness or value.[8] For Aquinas, natural and moral goodness, while

---

7. For a good introduction to these debates, see the essays collected by Stephen Engstrom and Jennifer Whiting in *Aristotle, Kant, and the Stoics: Rethinking Happiness and Duty* (Cambridge: Cambridge University Press, 1996). Their introductory essay, "Introduction," 1–18, offers a helpful overview of the issues at stake. Candace Volger comments on the relevance of these debates to our understanding of Aquinas in "Aristotle, Aquinas, Anscombe, and the New Virtue Ethics," in *Aquinas and the Nicomachean Ethics*, ed. Tobias Hoffmann, Jörn Müller, and Matthias Perkams (Cambridge: Cambridge University Press, 2013), 239–57.

8. Christine Korsgaard offers what is perhaps the most thoroughgoing and influential contemporary appropriation of a Kantian ethic today. For an overview and defense of her overall approach, see Korsgaard, *The Sources of Normativity* (Cambridge: Cambridge University Press, 1996) and, more recently, *Self-Constitution: Agency, Identity, and Integrity* (Oxford: Oxford University Press, 2009). For influential defenses of neo-Aristotelian theories of value and moral goodness, see Philippa Foot, *Natural Goodness* (Oxford: Ox-

related, cannot simply be identified, because the latter presupposes distinctively human capacities for self-reflective judgment, choice, and action. This distinction is especially pertinent to the virtue of justice, which presupposes capacities to rationally grasp and freely respond to the claims of others.

At the same time, Aquinas's overall account of justice does share much in common with contemporary theories of justice. For both Aquinas and our own contemporaries, the idea of justice is bound up with ideals of equality, freedom, respect, and forbearance. It is preeminently an ideal of right relations, expressed through mutuality, restraint, and acknowledged obligations. Indeed, this general idea of justice can be traced to a much earlier period and has a good claim to be, in its general outlines at least, a cultural universal. Without attempting to offer a definitive statement of this ideal, we might characterize it as follows: A just individual is committed to fairness, equity, and respect for the legitimate claims of others. She is committed to ideals of impartiality and mutual accountability. She recognizes her dependence on and obligations to a community and is prepared to place the common good ahead of her own private interests, at least in some contexts. So when Aquinas claims that the virtue of justice is the highest connatural virtue, he implies that these specific values and precepts are in some way centrally important to morality itself.

My primary aim in this book is to offer an interpretation of Aquinas's account of the complex virtue of justice as set forth in the *Summa theologiae*, focusing on what I take to be the key to that account, namely, the claim that justice is a perfection of the will. This project is motivated by the conviction that Aquinas offers us a cogent and illuminating account of justice as a personal virtue that renders the agent and her actions good in some distinctive way. Not to put too fine a point on it, Aquinas gets justice right—which is not to say that his account is correct in every detail or fully developed at every point. As we have just noted, he does not raise, much less address, questions pertaining to social and institutional structures that are central to most contemporary theories of justice. His own theoretical presuppositions and aims lead to a very different approach. But when we consider his account of justice from the perspective of his own aims, we find that he offers a cogent, illuminating, and ultimately convincing account of justice as a personal virtue. In the process, he lays the foundations for a comprehensive theory of morality that has a commitment to right relations at its core.

---

ford University Press, 2001), and Rosalind Hursthouse, *On Virtue Ethics* (Oxford: Oxford University Press, 1999).

In order to defend these claims, it will be necessary at some points to go beyond what Aquinas explicitly says by drawing out the implications of his remarks, filling in connections that he leaves implicit, and attempting to resolve seemingly paradoxical elements of his overall theory. To some extent, this kind of expansive interpretation will inevitably play a role in any serious attempt to understand the theoretical writings of another, even a contemporary, let alone a premodern author. In order really to understand a medieval or classical thinker, as opposed to simply paraphrasing a text, it is necessary at some points to draw connections between the author's assumptions and claims and the corresponding views of one's own contemporaries. In the process, we will inevitably move at some points from interpretation to constructive theorizing. There is nothing problematic about this move, so long as we try to be clear about which task we are engaged in at any given point, even though admittedly it is not always easy to draw a line between expansive interpretation and constructive theorizing. In this instance, expansive interpretation is especially necessary, because Aquinas does not explain in any detail why he regards justice as a personal virtue, nor does he draw out the distinctive implications of this approach. It does not occur to him to do so, because, after all, everyone in this period thinks of justice in this way.

At some points in this project, I will offer a constructive expansion of Aquinas's views on justice, drawing on contemporary voices, as well as on some of Aquinas's own interlocutors. I hope to do so in such a way as to make it clear that I am developing Aquinas's theory in some way, rather than simply interpreting what he says. At the same time, at these points I will try to show that the constructive proposals in question illuminate some key aspects of Aquinas's views, resolve tensions in his thought, or revise his claims in some way that is consistent with his overarching principles. My overall aim in this project is to set out an account of justice as a personal virtue that is authentically Thomistic, in the sense that it is grounded in a convincing interpretation of Aquinas's own account and develops it in a consistent and illuminating way.

In this chapter I will set out, in a preliminary way, what it means to consider justice as a personal virtue. Our assumptions about the virtues and virtue ethics do not seem to fit well with a consideration of justice. Yet, as I will argue, the seeming incongruities stem from distinctive features of justice, having to do with its characteristic normative ideals or its status as a virtue of the will. The remainder of this chapter will be devoted to setting a framework and a set of reference points for what follows. Aquinas's account of justice as a personal virtue presupposes a distinctive theory of the virtues, and the second and third sections of this chapter will be taken up with a brief examination of the main lines of that theory, considered both as a kind of philosophical psychology and as a way of formulating and expressing normative claims. In the fourth section I will offer an overview of the main lines of Aquinas's treatment of justice. Finally, in the fifth section I will say something more about the approach taken in this project, specifically with reference to the theological character of Aquinas's theory of the virtues and his account of justice as a virtue.

Preliminary Considerations

I begin with a fundamental question. What does it mean to identify justice as a personal virtue—or at any rate, what would this understanding have meant for Aquinas and his immediate predecessors and interlocutors? By endorsing the traditional view that justice is a virtue, one of four cardinal virtues characteristic of the upright and admirable man or woman, Aquinas commits himself to the view that justice is a stable disposition oriented toward characteristic kinds of praiseworthy actions, thereby rendering both the agent and her actions good (I-II 55.1,3).[9] The disposition of justice renders its subject good because it is not merely a tendency to act in accordance with norms of justice but a stable disposition to care about and to pursue just relations, informed by some sense of the point or the worth of just actions and the kinds of relationships that they generate.[10] That is to say, the just individual not only does what is just, she does so knowingly, out of an informed desire to act justly.

9. For an exhaustive account of the development of scholastic views on the virtues, see Odon Lottin, "Les premières définitions et classifications des vertus au moyen âge" and "Les vertus cardinales et leurs ramifications chez les théologiens de 1230 à 1250," in *Psychologie et morale aux XIIe et XIIIe siècles*, vol. 3, pt. 2.1, pp. 100–150 and 154–93 (Louvain: Abbaye du Mont César, 1948).

10. As we will see, the distinction between a bare tendency to act justly and the virtuous disposition of justice depends, for Aquinas, on his theory of the will, although most theories of the virtues would draw a similar distinction. More generally, Aquinas holds that the moral virtues, which are dispositions of the appetites, presuppose the intellectual virtues of understanding and prudence, through which the agent grasps the first principles of practical reasoning and discerns how to attain the ideals of the particular virtues through rational deliberation (I-II 58.4). It is worth adding that prudence is, strictly speaking, a virtue of the intellect, although it is traditionally associated with the cardinal moral virtues of justice, courage, and temperance; see I-II 57.4–5.

Already, we can begin to see why a virtue-oriented approach might seem unpromising as a way of understanding justice. We are accustomed to think of justice in terms of abstract principles and the social and institutional arrangements expressing and safeguarding them—all of which are properly expressed in general, impersonal norms for conduct, which are accessible to all, at least within a given community, and which are correlatively binding on all.[11] This way of construing justice leaves little room for the kinds of appeals to personal sensibility, discerning individual choice, and integrity of character that we associate with the virtues. At best, justice as a personal virtue might be regarded as a disposition to carry out just acts, knowingly and with appreciation of their worth. Thus understood, a focus on justice as a virtue would suggest fruitful ways of addressing concerns, raised by Rawls and others, regarding the stability of institutions and practices of justice.[12] But of course justice as a virtue, thus understood, is dependent, conceptually and practically, on a substantive account of ideals or norms of justice, of a kind supplied by Rawls's theory of justice.

It is tempting to regard these reservations as distinctively modern in origin and inspiration, but that would be a mistake. Even in Aquinas's own time, and indeed for some time previously, the virtue of justice was regarded as more or less anomalous, seen in comparison to the other traditional moral virtues.[13] This was especially true for those working within the parameters of Aristotelian moral philosophy, including Aquinas himself.[14] Aristotle's analysis of the norm of justice in terms of equality of exchange in accordance with an arithmetic or geometric proportion is notoriously obscure. More fundamentally, justice fits badly with Aristotle's overarching analysis of the virtues in terms of a mean, an ideal of appropriateness falling between

11. For a discussion of the supposed differences between ideals of virtue and norms of justice, see Onora O'Neill, *Towards Justice and Virtue: A Constructive Account of Practical Reasoning* (Cambridge: Cambridge University Press, 1996). Similarly, Hursthouse, in *On Virtue Ethics*, 5, observes that virtue ethics today has some major gaps, and she goes on to say that "an obvious gap is the topic of justice, both as a personal virtue and as the central topic in political philosophy, and I should say straight out that this book makes no attempt at all to fill that gap."

12. For a discussion of these issues, see Rawls, *A Theory of Justice*, 453–512.

13. For further details, see Julia Annas, *The Morality of Happiness* (Oxford: Oxford University Press, 1993), 291–321.

14. For an excellent overview of Aristotle's account of justice seen in the context of his overall theory of virtue, see Robert C. Bartlett and Susan D. Collins, "Interpretative Essay," in *Aristotle's Nicomachean Ethics*, trans. Bartlett and Collins, 237–302 (Chicago: University of Chicago Press, 2011). Aristotle's discussion of justice appears in the fifth book of the *Nicomachean Ethics*, 90–114, in the Bartlett/Collins translation.

vicious extremes. This line of analysis seems to fit the characteristic virtues of the passions, courage and temperance, fairly well, although even in these contexts Aristotle's conception of the mean is not as clear as we might wish. But in any case it fits justice rather badly, or so we might think. Aristotle's analysis implies that each virtue is correlated with specific vices, characteristic deformities of passion or judgment, so that, for example, courage is contrasted with cowardice or recklessness, and moderation stands over against both licentiousness and insensibility. The difficulty here is that justice is not clearly correlated with specific vices of this kind. A cruel or greedy individual is likely to behave unjustly, but it is by no means the case that those who are characteristically unjust typically reflect these, or any other specific set of vices. On the contrary, someone can be led into injustice through admirable motives and traits of character—we all know men and women who are too empathetic or kindhearted to be consistently fair and equitable. Conversely, it is all too possible to behave justly out of vicious motives, for example, pride or cold self-interest. The only vice that seems to be directly opposed to justice is injustice, which is not a particularly helpful correlation.

At this point, we begin to get a clearer sense of why it is so difficult to characterize justice as a personal virtue. I suggest that the difficulties in question, as they emerge in classical, medieval, and contemporary contexts, reflect a sense of the incongruity between our assumptions about what a virtue is, on the one hand, and our assumptions about justice as a norm or standard, on the other. Most fundamentally, we assume that a virtue is intrinsically connected to the agent's disposition, her motives for acting, and a kind of quality that is manifest in the agent's choices and actions but cannot be reduced to these.[15] Otherwise, we could not appeal to our conceptions of virtues and vices in order to draw the kinds of distinctions that motivate an appeal to virtue theory in the first place—between acting out of one's character, commitments, or ideals, on the one hand, and, on the other, acting out of extraneous motives or out of habit or from conformity. Without some such distinction, it would be difficult, at best, to account for the value we place on a certain kind of character and disposition, apart from positive assessments of the agent's actions, or to explain how one's sensibilities might contribute to moral discernment and the development of moral norms.

So far, there would seem to be nothing incongruous in describing jus-

---

15. For a good overview of the relevant arguments, see Hursthouse, *On Virtue Ethics*, 108–40.

JUSTICE AS A VIRTUE

tice as a virtue in this generally accepted sense. Almost no one would deny the morally important differences between someone who is wholeheartedly committed to justice and another who does the right thing out of habit or expediency. However, virtue ethics is sometimes associated with the stronger claim that the moral character of a given act depends in some way on the agent's inner motivations or disposition.[16] It is more difficult to construe justice as a virtue in this sense because we typically associate justice with objective standards of fairness or due regard. Not every unjust act is vicious in the commonly accepted sense—on the contrary, men and women can subject others to unfair treatment out of admirable and worthy motives. Their actions are nonetheless unjust, in virtue of the fact that they transgress the claims of another in some way.

Alternatively, an emphasis on the contextual and open-ended character of ideals of virtues may be correlated with a de-emphasis on the objective character of moral norms, their status as demands of reason, and their binding force. These correlations are spelled out in different ways, with greater or lesser emphasis on the dichotomy between ideals of virtue and obligations of duty. According to Onora O'Neill, a commitment to justice is compatible with recognizing the place of the virtues in the moral life, but she appears to regard these as two distinct approaches to morality, which need to be harmonized for just that reason.[17] For others, the ideals and attitudes properly attached to the virtues are antithetical to the stringent rules that we associate with justice, although rules may provide helpful guidelines for those who, for one reason or another, are not capable of full practical rationality.[18]

Why would we assume that ideals of virtue are incompatible, or at least in tension, with the kinds of determinate rules that we associate with norms of duty and obligation? In part, because the ideals of virtue are just that, ide-

---

16. For a carefully qualified defense of this view, see Michael Slote, "Agent-Based Virtue Ethics," in *Virtue Ethics*, ed. Roger Crisp and Michael Slote (Oxford: Oxford University Press, 1997), 239–62.

17. For an overview of her argument, see O'Neill, *Towards Justice and Virtue*, 1–8. Similarly, Hursthouse claims that a theory of virtue can provide normative standards for right action, although she does not defend precepts of justice as such; see *On Virtue Ethics*, 25–42.

18. For example, Martha Nussbaum remarks that rules can serve a pedagogical function, and they can also serve as guidelines when we are not confident in our own judgment. But, she continues, "Aristotle's point in all these cases is that the rule or algorithm represents a falling off from full practical rationality, not its flourishing or completion" (in her *Love's Knowledge: Essays on Philosophy and Literature* [Oxford: Oxford University Press, 1990], 68). The context clearly indicates that Nussbaum agrees with Aristotle (as she reads him) on this point.

alized templates of praiseworthy or admirable behavior.[19] These ideals may be associated with exemplary examples of good individuals and narratives of worthy lives, or they may be expressed in terms of a general formulation of some aim or standard. In either case, ideals of virtue are hard to specify, and for many advocates of virtue ethics, that is part of the point. The moral life is complex, and the ideals we try to realize can be difficult to formulate, much less to express in concrete forms of action. Given these circumstances of our lives, the relative indeterminacy of the virtues is both realistic and salutary, because it allows ample scope for situational and contextual application of moral principles.

Virtues can be said to be ideals in another way, which is even more directly relevant to the perceived tensions between ideals of virtue and norms of justice. That is, ideals of virtue have historically been regarded as admirable or desirable.[20] From this perspective, the virtuous individual is admirable in two senses—morally praiseworthy, worthy of emulation, but also admirable in somewhat the same way that a physically attractive man or woman is admirable. Similarly, a virtuous life has historically been regarded as intrinsically desirable, in such a way as to link virtue ethics to a kind of eudaimonism. Classical and Hellenistic philosophers presupposed that there is some intrinsic link between virtue and an enjoyable, desirable life, that is to say, a happy life. While they developed this idea in a number of ways, including some that appear to offer counterintuitive accounts of happiness, they generally tried to show that a virtuous life is generally or normally a satisfying, desirable life. A number of contemporary virtue theorists similarly argue that the virtues and the happy life are linked in some way.[21] These two aspects of virtue—its attractiveness and its desirability—are brought together under the general category of the good, understood as the properly human good, whatever it is that exemplifies the excellence and promotes the well-being of this kind of creature.

On any plausible account of justice, it would seem that justice is anti-

---

19. For a recent defense of this view, see Julia Annas, *Intelligent Virtue* (Oxford: Oxford University Press, 2011), 16–51. Hursthouse, in contrast, argues that the ideals associated with the virtues do generate rules, which function in the same way as the rules associated with deontological systems of morality; see *On Virtue Ethics*, 25–42.

20. For an illuminating overview of virtue and happiness in classical philosophy, see Annas, *The Morality of Happiness*, 27–46. Annas defends her own version of eudaimonism in *Intelligent Virtue*, 66–82.

21. In addition to Annas, see, for example, Hursthouse, *On Virtue Ethics*, 163–91, and Foot, *Natural Goodness*, 81–98.

thetical to virtue at every point. We commonly associate justice with objective standards of equity, fairness, or respect.[22] Of course, almost everyone would recognize that, in some circumstances, it might be difficult to say what justice requires, but ideals of justice are not normally specified by the agent's dispositions or by contextual considerations in the way that ideals of virtue are thought to be. Furthermore, justice is correlated with relatively precise precepts that express or safeguard these objective standards in some way. Thus, justice would seem to fall squarely on the "rule" side of the "virtue ethic versus rule ethic" dichotomy. These precepts are generally regarded as strictly binding, in a way that the ideals of virtue are not. Someone might plausibly claim that he is trying to live by virtuous ideals, even though so far, he can only approximate them—but the precepts of justice cannot be approximated in the same way. They set standards and limits for acceptable conduct that we either observe or culpably violate. Finally, justice is commonly linked with standards of right, rather than some conception of the good. Indeed, most contemporary philosophers, including Rawls, would agree that the priority of the right to the good is foundational to any adequate analysis of justice.[23] If we were to reverse the normative order at this point, we would risk compromising fairness and equity by imposing an ideal on those who do not share it, or risk conferring benefits and imposing burdens on what should be irrelevant grounds.

Given that Aquinas identifies justice as a virtue, we might assume that he has a different understanding of justice and its demands. But when we turn to his extended account of justice, we see that he agrees with these general points. He claims that the standards proper to justice are objective and not situational, he associates these standards with relatively determinate precepts, and he claims that these precepts are stringently binding (see, respectively, [1] I-II 64.2; [2] I-II 100.3 *ad* 3; II-II 56.1 *ad* 1, 122.1; [3] II-II 80).

---

22. While these remarks are necessarily brief, I take them to summarize the overall conception of justice as fairness set out by Rawls in *A Theory of Justice*, 3–25. Ronald Dworkin offers a similar account in *Sovereign Virtue: The Theory and Practice of Equality* (Cambridge, MA: Harvard University Press, 2000), 1–10, 184–210.

23. Rawls, *A Theory of Justice*, 24, 31–32; for a similar argument, developed in terms of a contrast between human rights and eudaimonism, see Nicholas Wolterstorff, *Justice: Rights and Wrongs* (Princeton: Princeton University Press, 2008), 149–79. Not every contemporary philosopher shares this view, however; for example, Barbara Hermann, in *The Practice of Moral Judgment* (Cambridge, MA: Harvard University Press, 1993), remarks that "it is simply implausible to suppose that a moral theory could persuasively do its work without a grounding concept of value" (209; more generally, see 208–10).

Aquinas's account of justice does presuppose the priority of the good, insofar as he holds that the intrinsic goodness of human existence is foundational for the structures of equity, reciprocity, and right that structure our lives. Yet by the same token, we cannot flourish, as individuals or communities, unless these structures are reflectively grasped and respected. To put the point in modern terms, the right and the good cannot be defined independently of one another. In key part, if not entirely, right relations are constitutive of human goodness, and for that reason, claims of right can override otherwise legitimate appeals to the common good, and they set boundaries on what individuals can do in pursuit of even the highest aims.

How can Aquinas reconcile this account of justice with his overall theory of virtue? Briefly, Aquinas understands virtue itself differently from most of our contemporaries. To be more exact, he shares many of our assumptions about virtue, but he qualifies them in critical ways. On his view, the hallmarks of virtue, including its association with general ideals and its sensitivity to individual contexts, are characteristic of virtues of a certain kind, namely, the virtues associated with the passions. The virtue of justice does not reflect these hallmarks, or does so only in restricted ways, because justice is a virtue of the will (II-II 56.4). This point matters, because the will is naturally oriented toward actions *ad extra*, through which the agent enters into relations with the world around her and, most important, with other agents (I-II 56.6, 60.2).[24] As such, it contrasts with the virtues of the passions, for example, temperance or courage, which are naturally oriented toward the agent's own overall good. Correlatively, the normative standards associated with the virtues of the will are intrinsically tied to the claims of others in a way that the ideals proper to the virtues of the passions are not (I-II 56.6, 60.2–3; II-II 56.2,10). As we will see, Aquinas would regard our distinctions between rules and ideals as overly simplistic, but to the extent that he does imply such a distinction, he would characterize it as a distinction between two kinds of virtue, not a contrast between virtue ethics and some other kind of ethics.

---

24. Acts *ad extra* should be distinguished from exterior acts, which are actions brought about immediately (that is to say, elicited) by some faculty other than the will, although under the command of the will—they are thus "exterior" to the principle in virtue of which they are human actions, that is to say, the will itself. Acts *ad extra*, in contrast, comprise what we usually think of as actions, that is to say, performances carried out through bodily movement, with (actual or intended) effects on the outside world. All acts *ad extra* will also be exterior acts, but the converse is not true; for example, a purely mental act of deliberation would be an exterior act because it would be elicited by the intellect, although under the command of the will. For further details, see Stephen L. Brock, *Action and Conduct* (Edinburgh: T. & T. Clark, 1998), 173.

In one respect, Aquinas's claim that justice is a virtue of the will seems to sharpen the problems raised by the claim that justice is a virtue, rather than resolving them. On his account, the will is, among other things, a capacity for choice that is characteristically expressed through one's exterior actions (I 83.1). The will chooses and indirectly commands good actions in a distinctively human way, that is to say, as the result of judgments formed through processes of rational deliberation (I-II 13.1, 17.1). The processes of deliberation leading to a final judgment are complex, as Aquinas makes clear, but it would seem that the corresponding motion of the will is quite simple—being presented with some judgment regarding the good, it chooses accordingly. How can we characterize this kind of choice in terms of a mode of activity? One simply chooses, and that would seem to be all there is to say—unless, indeed, we want to argue that choice is illusory, because the will is compelled by whatever the intellect discloses as its supreme good. As Bonnie Kent has shown in her excellent study of late medieval ethics, these kinds of considerations played a key role in the eventual turn from virtue ethics, in both theological and philosophical contexts, and they would seem to rule out any kind of robust account of justice as a virtue of the will, even today.[25]

Yet this line of analysis presupposes an overly simplistic conception of the will that is not true to Aquinas's own view.[26] Certainly, the will *is* a faculty for choice, most immediately exercised through the acts that it elicits or commands, but its activities cannot be reduced to these discrete operations alone. Rather, the will characteristically elicits and commands actions in view of some overall stance toward the good, in accordance with some reasoned, general conception of goodness (I-II 8.3, 9.1,3, 10.1). This overall stance determines the mode of the agent's choice, which presupposes a reasoned judgment that this course of activity reflects an overall commitment to live in accordance with one's reflectively formed, deeply held desires for whatever is praiseworthy, satisfying, admirable, or in some other way worthy of pursuit. Seen in this context, the virtue of justice cannot be

---

25. See Bonnie Kent, *Virtues of the Will: The Transformation of Ethics in the Late Thirteenth Century* (Washington, DC: Catholic University of America Press, 1995), 94–149.

26. In the next chapter we will turn to an extended analysis of the will and its activities. For an excellent overview of Aquinas's account of the will as set out in the *prima pars* of the *Summa theologiae*, see Robert Pasnau, *Thomas Aquinas on Human Nature: A Philosophical Study of "Summa Theologiae" Ia 75–89* (Cambridge: Cambridge University Press, 2002), 209–64. In addition, Daniel Westberg offers a lucid analysis of what he calls the "metaphysics of agency," including the significance of the will's orientation toward the good, in *Right Practical Reason: Aristotle, Action, and Prudence in Aquinas* (Oxford: Clarendon, 1994), 43–61.

reduced to a sheer tendency to choose actions of a distinctively praisewor-thy kind, although it is of course expressed through such choices. Rather, the virtue in question is a disposition to choose certain kinds of actions, namely, those which embody ideals of fairness, equity, or reciprocity, out of a stable and reflective commitment to structure one's life in accordance with these ideals.

At the same time, the disposition of justice is shaped by specific pre-cepts to a greater extent than is the case for the other moral virtues. Aquinas does not claim that these precepts can be derived from a general theory of virtue or an abstract ideal of justice. Nonetheless, his overall theory of the virtues and his general account of justice do have important implications for our overall understanding of justice, as I hope to show in what follows. His claim that justice is a virtuous disposition implies normative criteria for assessing our received, prereflective ideals and sensibilities with regard to justice and the right, enabling us to distinguish the virtue of justice from its similitudes while drawing out and giving systematic form to the norma-tive standards proper to true virtue. The key point here, I will argue, is that Aquinas analyzes the virtues as perfections, that is to say, as integral and complete actualizations, of the capacities they inform, and by implication, of the men and women who act through those capacities.[27] Aquinas was by no means the only scholastic to take these views. In fact, they were anticipated in Peripatetic moral philosophy and transmitted to the medieval world by Cicero, among others. The distinctiveness of Aquinas's theory lies rather in the specifics of his complex conception of perfection and the way in which he thoroughly integrates his theory of the virtues into his overall metaphys-ical and theological framework. For him, the virtues enable the individual to act in accordance with the proper principles and norms of human action, characteristic of us as individuals of a particular kind of living creature.

Therefore, like every other virtue, justice is grounded in and presup-poses an account of the good. For Aquinas, the intrinsic goodness of hu-man existence is foundational for the structures of equity, reciprocity, and right, which structure our lives as social animals. Yet by the same token, we cannot flourish, as individuals or communities, unless these structures are reflectively grasped and respected. To put the point in modern terms, the

---

27. For an overview of Peripatetic theories of virtue, see Annas, *The Morality of Happiness*, 180–87. Very few contemporary scholars have taken account of Aquinas's claim that the virtues are perfections, and more specifically, perfecting habits of the cognitive and desiring capacities of the soul; for one recent exception, see David Decosimo, *Ethics as a Work of Charity: Thomas Aquinas and Pagan Virtue* (Stanford: Stanford University Press, 2014), 72–105.

right and the good cannot be defined independently of one another. Right relations among individuals and between the individual and the community are integral to the attainment of humanly good ways of life, at the individual and the social levels, and these relations imply claims of right as well as more general norms of nonmaleficence and due respect.

It is instructive in this context to consider Nicholas Wolterstorff's important recent work on justice, rights claims, and Christian love.[28] According to Wolterstorff, justice is grounded in objective rights, correlated with precepts calling for certain kinds of forbearance and respect, and especially, placing nonnegotiable boundaries on the kinds of harms that can be inflicted on anyone. These claims are justified by the worth of individual men and women, in such a way that the worth of individuals always trumps what Wolterstorff calls balance of life-good considerations.[29] In order to justify the kinds of unconditional rights claims that we associate with justice, this property of worth must be unique to human beings, it must be possessed by each individual, and it must be noninstrumental in character.[30] Wolterstorff goes on to argue that this kind of worth cannot rest on any kind of natural property or capacity that individuals possess or exercise by virtue of their humanity or their created excellence. It can be conferred only by God's free act of valuing individuals, through which he confers what Wolterstorff calls bestowed worth on each individual.[31] The upshot is that individual claims to forbearance and respect, and the moral order itself, rest on a divine conferral of value having no intrinsic relation to natural and rational characteristics of human life.

For Aquinas, in contrast, justice as a normative ideal need not, and indeed cannot, rest on external and contingent foundations in this way. Rather, the ideals of justice stem from the normative values intrinsic to a distinctively human life, understood in broadly Aristotelian terms as the natural life of a

---

28. Wolterstorff, *Justice: Rights and Wrongs*. The main lines of the argument summarized here are developed at 285–361.

29. Wolterstorff explicitly correlates this line of analysis with Kant: "In short, Kant's famous principle—act always in such a way as to treat human beings as ends and never merely as means—comes to the same as the principle I have been defending: Always act in such a way as to allow respect for the worth of human beings to trump balance of life-good considerations" (*Justice: Rights and Wrongs*, 310).

30. For a summary of this part of the argument, see Wolterstorff, *Justice: Rights and Wrongs*, 321.

31. For the overall argument, see Wolterstorff, *Justice: Rights and Wrongs*, 342–57; the idea of bestowed worth is developed at 352–60.

kind of living creature. Seen from this perspective, the goodness of human existence is normatively prior to claims of right, in the sense that claims of right are grounded in values intrinsic to a distinctively human form of existence. But precisely for that reason, these claims impose strict obligations of respect and forbearance that cannot be overridden, even in the name of some supposed ideal of human or divine good. So far from being antithetical, the goodness proper to human life and claims of right are mutually dependent, as the ground and the proper expression, respectively, of the normative structures of human existence. Aquinas does not formulate these issues in terms of a supposed dichotomy between the right and the good. On his view, right is the proper object of the virtue of justice—that is to say, the distinctive form of human goodness exemplified by the virtue of justice is characteristically expressed through a regard for the right as instantiated in particular human interactions. We will return to this claim in subsequent chapters. At this point, I hope I have said enough to indicate that Aquinas's understanding of justice as a virtue is at least plausible, both as an account of justice and as an analysis of a distinctive kind of virtue. In order to move forward at this point, we need to be familiar with at least the main lines of Aquinas's overall theory of the virtues, considered both as normative principles and as paradigmatic moral ideals. This will be the topic of the next two sections.

The Theoretical Framework

Aquinas's *Summa theologiae* is divided into three parts, the second of which is devoted to an analysis of human action, considered as the means through which we attain (or deviate from) our final end of happiness through union with God (I-II 6 intro.). The *secunda pars* is further divided into two sections, the first proposing an analysis of the human act as such, its normative structure and its constitutive principles, and the second, analyzing the specific normative ideals governing human life generally, as well as those that pertain to particular roles and states of life. In each of these subparts, the concept of virtue serves as a central organizing principle. In the *prima secundae*, virtue considered as a kind of stable disposition, that is to say, a habit (*habitus*), is identified as one of the intrinsic principles of human action generally considered (I-II 49 intro.).[32] As such, it is considered together with the cognitive capacities and

---

32. The translation of *habitus* as "habit," while common, is misleading, because the English word implies mindless or stereotypical behavior, whereas for Aquinas a true virtue is precisely

appetites and is contrasted with (but not opposed to) the extrinsic principles of human acts, namely Satan and God, the former of whom tempts us toward sin, and the latter of whom "both instructs us through law and aids us through grace" (I-II 90 intro.). In the *secunda secundae*, Aquinas organizes his material by reference to the virtues considered as normative ideals, in terms of which diverse elements of Christian moral reflection can be perspicuously analyzed and brought together in a coherent way (*secunda secundae* prologue). In these two sections, we will follow Aquinas's own division, considering virtue first as a general principle of human activity, and then as a normative ideal, or rather, as an integrated array of distinctive ideals, proper to the distinct spheres of human life.

In developing his theory of virtue, Aquinas draws on concepts that can be traced to Aristotle's *Nicomachean Ethics*, and that had by now been developed through intensive analysis and debate among the scholastics for more than a century.[33] He begins his analysis of virtue with Peter Lombard's well-known definition, drawn from elements of Augustine's writings: "Virtue is a good quality of the mind, by which we live righteously, of which no one can make bad use, which God brings about in us, without us" (I-II 55.4, quoting II *Sentences* 27.5). He immediately qualifies Lombard's definition in one critical respect, adding that the last clause applies only to the infused virtues, which God bestows on us without action on our part, in contrast to the acquired virtues, which, as the name suggests, can be attained through human effort without grace. Aquinas thus makes a point of including both categories of virtue, those presupposing divine grace and those that do not, under the general rubric of the formal definition of virtue. On closer examination, it is apparent that Aquinas draws extensively on both the concept of virtue as a mean and the scholastic analysis of virtue as a stable disposition, or habit. We will look more closely at Aquinas's interpretation of the

---

not mindless—on the contrary, it is a disposition formed through, and continually informed by, rational reflection. However, "disposition" is not a fully satisfactory translation either; as Aquinas notes, *habitus* is a disposition understood in one sense but not another (I-II 49.2 *ad* 3). I have chosen to translate *habitus* in the traditional way as "habit," in the hope that it will be clear, as we proceed, that Aquinas is not talking about habits in our sense.

33. As Cary Nederman points out, key ideas from Aristotelian ethics were in general circulation for at least 150 years before the full text of the *Nicomachean Ethics* became available in Latin; see "Aristotelianism and the Origins of 'Political Science' in the Twelfth Century," *Journal of the History of Ideas* 52 (1991): 179–94, esp. 180–81. For further background on scholastic theories of the virtues, see, in addition to the articles by Lottin cited above, István P. Bejczy, "The Problem of Natural Virtue," in *Virtue and Ethics in the Twelfth Century*, ed. István P. Bejczy and Richard G. Newhauser (Leiden: Brill, 2005), 133–54.

doctrine of the mean when we consider his analysis of the virtues as moral ideals. At this point, we turn to Aquinas's account of the virtues as stable dispositions of our capacities for desire and, with qualifications, our intellectual and rational capacities.

Aquinas's account of the virtues as habits, taken together with the analysis of habits that precedes it, is central to his overall theory of the virtues—indeed, it would hardly be an exaggeration to say that this analysis *is* his theory of virtue.[34] On Aquinas's account, a habit can best be understood as a stable orientation of the intellect, will, or passions toward one distinctive kind of action and away from other kinds (I-II 55.1). Without these habits, the relevant capacities of the soul cannot operate properly, and the agent cannot function as a rational agent, except in rudimentary ways. For example, the child's innate capacities for speech must be developed through the habit of a particular language before the child can actually talk (I-II 49.4). As this example indicates, habits of the intellect are virtues, albeit only in a qualified sense. These are of course morally neutral, although they are good in the sense of perfecting the agent in some respect (I-II 56.3, 57.1, 58.3). However, the virtues that shape the passions and the will, and also the intellect, insofar as it is oriented to action, are necessarily morally significant, because they incline toward actions of a kind that are good without qualification (I-II 58.1).

This line of analysis is important because it prepares the ground for Aquinas's analysis of the virtues as perfections—singly, perfections of the passions and the will through appropriate particular virtues, and taken together, a perfection of the human agent. (On virtues as perfections of the capacities, see for example I-II 55.3 *ad* 1–2, 56.1; on virtue as a perfection of the agent, see I-II 3.2, 4.7). In this way, he integrates his analysis of virtue into the comprehensive metaphysical and theological system, set out in the *prima pars* and further developed in the *tertia pars*. Within that structure, the idea of perfection serves to integrate the accounts of intelligibility, goodness, and causality in a perspicuous way.[35] According to Aquinas, actuality is the

---

34. The significance of the concept of habit for Aquinas's overall theory of virtue is frequently overlooked. Again, Decosimo's recent work is an exception to this generalization; see *Ethics as a Work of Charity*, 72–105.

35. For further details, including further textual references, see Robert Pasnau's illuminating discussion of the metaphysics of actuality in *Thomas Aquinas on Human Nature*, 143–51; in addition, see Decosimo, *Ethics as a Work of Charity*, 72–105, and Porter, *Nature as Reason: A Thomistic Theory of the Natural Law* (Grand Rapids: Eerdmans, 2005), 158–63. George Weiland points out that this general conception of happiness was widely shared by Aquinas's immediate predecessors and contemporaries; see "Happiness: The Perfection of Man," in *The Cambridge*

fundamental characteristic of any kind of existence—every actually existing thing is in act and can be said to be perfect insofar as it is fully in act (I 5.1,3; cf. I 4.1–2). Perfection is understood, correlatively, as the comprehensive development and expression of the creature's dispositions and capacities, in accordance with the form that is proper to the specific kind of thing that it is (I 5.1). It is important to note that Aquinas does not identify perfection with an unqualified ideal of superlative goodness. Rather, for him an ideal of perfection is always tied to some specific standard of well-being, integrity, or functional value, intrinsic to the kind of existence or activity that is under consideration (I 5.5). The complexity of the human creature implies that we, unlike other animals, can attain perfection in diverse ways and at disparate levels, including some that go beyond our natural capacities. But no matter how human perfection is understood, it will necessarily involve some kind of complete development of the capacities distinctive to us as creatures of a specific kind.

The ideal of complete development, in turn, is associated with acting or being actualized in such a way as to develop, express, and communicate the distinctive potentialities that are proper to a specific form (I-II 49.3). The habits are perfections because they represent a kind of intermediate actualization of a potential capacity and enable the agent to actualize the capacity fully on demand, as it were (I-II 49.3 ad 1). The human capacity to communicate through language is a sheer potency in the newborn infant, and unlike its potential for growth and physical development, its linguistic capacity cannot develop properly without some kind of formation, apart from the child's spontaneous development. Typically, this formation takes the form of the acquisition of a native language, through immersion in the linguistic activities going on around him. The child's command of a language is in itself a kind of perfection, insofar as it develops and completes what had previously been the sheer, unformed potential for linguistic communication. Given this intermediate perfection, the child can utilize his capacities as a linguistic being by speaking or reading or writing, all of which fully actualize, or in other words perfect, these capacities. The habit reflected in someone's command of a language can thus be said to perfect him in two distinct yet interrelated ways. In itself, it represents an actualization, an appropriate de-velopment, of innate capacities; and by the same token, the habit enables

History of Later Medieval Philosophy from the Rediscovery of Aristotle to the Disintegration of Scholasticism, 1100–1600, ed. Norman Kretzman, Anthony Kenny, and Jan Pinborg (Cambridge: Cambridge University Press, 1982), 673–86.

him to fully realize these capacities by actually speaking, thus playing an integral part in his development and activity as a human creature, naturally disposed to communicate through language.

We are not accustomed to think of our appetites as capacities that need to be formed or developed in order to function properly. Yet for Aquinas, the appetites, including both the passions and the will, are capacities of the soul that enable the individual to respond and act. Properly speaking, these capacities act through inclinations, that is to say, motions of desire toward some perceived good (I 80.1). More specifically, the appetites of the sensual part of the soul enable the agent to respond with desire, aversion, or some more complex motion of pursuit or resistance to perceptions or images of pleasant or noxious objects (I 80, 81.1–2). These appetites, which Aquinas identifies as the passions, are divided into two kinds, associated with concupiscence and irascibility (I 81.2). The characteristic appetite of the intellectual part of the soul is the will, which is the distinctively human capacity to respond with desire toward objects that are apprehended rationally as good, in accordance with some abstract conception of goodness (I 80, 82.1,3). Each of these appetites is naturally oriented toward some general kind of good, that is to say, the pleasant, the arduous, or the rationally comprehensible. However, the natural inclinations of the appetites cannot operate until these generic goods are specified in such a way as to correlate the inclinations of the appetites with determinate objects (I-II 50.5 *ad* 1).

The habits of the appetite might best be understood as dispositions to desire distinct kinds of activities and objects, specified within the indefinitely wide range of options provided by the natural orientation of the appetite in question. The capacities for sensual desire associated with concupiscence are naturally oriented toward pleasures associated with food, drink, and sex, but in themselves these pleasures do not offer suitable objects for desire and choice—or rather, they offer too much, in the form of diffuse and inconsistent desires that cannot be grasped as possibilities for action. The habits of the appetites, operating in tandem with rational instruction and reflection, bring order to these diverse possibilities by disposing the agent to desire and pursue distinctive kinds of objects through appropriate forms of action. We might think of the formation of habits as a process of sentimental education through which the agent develops a distinctive set of preferences, tastes, likes and dislikes, settled aversions and desires, all more or less integrated into a stable personality.

Correlatively, even though the habits of the appetites are not simply natural, in the sense of being innate qualities, they are natural in two other interrelated ways (I-II 51.1). First, and most fundamentally, they represent developments of key components of our natural life, namely, the appetites. The habits are thus natural to the human person insofar as they represent the proper and appropriate development of the potentialities of human nature. The key word here is "development." The habits do not suspend or supersede the expression of the appetites, but on the contrary, they bring them to a point at which they can function in a focused, stable way. By implication, the habits are natural in the sense that they facilitate the overall well-being and activities of the human person. They represent perfections of human nature as instantiated in this individual, precisely because they perfect her natural capacities to function in a distinctively human way.

This line of analysis is central to Aquinas's overall account of morality, because it provides a starting point for developing normative criteria by which to evaluate the habits and, by implication, the kinds of actions that they characteristically generate. Any habit is a kind of perfection insofar as it represents the development and actualization of a natural capacity for desire oriented toward action. At the same time, such developments can be partial or distorted, in such a way that the agent finds it difficult to act or acts in characteristically problematic ways (I-II 54.3, 71.1–2). This line of analysis implies that these varieties of inadequate development and distortion can be recognized as such because we know, sufficiently for practical purposes anyway, what it would mean to develop and express human capacities in accordance with natural principles, in such a way as to promote the overall well-being and activity of the human creature (cf. I-II 94.3 *ad* 2).

We can readily see how this line of analysis would apply to a habit such as linguistic competency. No one can speak at all until she learns a specific language, but the processes through which children learn languages can go wrong in all sorts of ways. A child might grow up with only a limited vocabulary, or she might never be taught the difference between correct and incorrect uses of certain parts of speech. Someone who has unfortunately received a poor formation in her native language can communicate linguistically, but not very well. Her habit of linguistic mastery is a perfection in a qualified sense, and yet it is also a distortion. But how far can we carry this line of analysis with respect to the habits that really count, that is to say, the moral virtues and vices? Is it really plausible to analyze the moral virtues, understood as habit of the passions and the will, as perfections of the natural structures and the overall operations of our fundamental human desires?

Aquinas believes that we can, but only in a carefully qualified way. The passions and the will are appetites of a living creature, and as such they are oriented toward naturally exigent and desirable activities and satisfactions. These components of human desire can be said to be normative, generating criteria for successful action, in the same way that the desires of any living creature can be said to be normative for that creature. They represent necessary conditions for, or intrinsic aspects of, life and well-being, and as such, they imply basic criteria for evaluating human habits and activities. Correlatively, we would expect that genuinely virtuous habits of the appetites will develop these in such a way as to promote, or at the very least not undermine, the agent's well-being as an organic creature. Aquinas apparently believes that criteria of these kinds set limits to what can count as an act of virtue. For example, he observes that, while fasting as a spiritual practice is generally a virtuous act, this practice becomes vicious if someone refuses to take enough food to meet his minimal needs (II-II 147.1 *ad* 2). The question is, can we account for the normative force of the virtues in these terms alone? Are the virtues, which by definition are fully perfecting habits, desirable and praiseworthy because they tend to promote our overall well-being, with perhaps a greater or lesser degree of success? Or to approach this issue in another way, what might it mean to say that a habit is a virtue in a moral sense, instead of, or in addition to, saying that it is a tendency to act in ways that tend to promote the agent's overall well-being? Aquinas's implied answer to these questions is complex, and it might be helpful to approach it by situating his thought within the context of recent debates over the status of normative claims.

The motif of normativity has received considerable attention over the past several years, and by this point, debates over normativity extend beyond moral philosophy to the philosophy of language and meaning, philosophy of science, and even the social sciences.[36] The expansiveness of the idea of normativity helps to indicate why this general idea has proven to be so fruitful. Normative claims are fundamentally claims about what ought to be the case, and these are by no means limited to moral claims. We naturally say that someone ought to do something in order to attain any kind of goal—this would be the hypothetical ought, in Kantian terms—or we might say that something ought to happen, given a set of conditions, or we ought to interpret a cryptic remark in this way, given our knowledge of the speaker and

36. Ralph Wedgewood offers a useful introduction to the issues involved in speaking of normativity in this wider sense in *The Nature of Normativity* (Oxford: Oxford University Press, 2007). For an overview of recent debates over normativity in the natural and social sciences, see the essays collected in *Naturalism and Normativity*, ed. Mario de Caro and David MacArthur (New York: Columbia University Press, 2010).

context. In all of these contexts, the normative claim expresses a judgment formulated by reference to some general standard of utility, correctness, causal connection, or interpretative plausibility. These are diverse considerations, but they are similar in one critical respect—that is, they cannot plausibly be reformulated in terms of statements about what is the case, without any reference whatever to some kind of evaluative judgment. This observation would be controversial, but if it is accepted, it raises interesting and potentially fruitful questions. What, if anything, do diverse kinds of normative considerations share in common, either at the level of meanings and practices or at more fundamental levels of causal or explanatory principles? More specifically, is there any connection between nonmoral and moral kinds of normative claims? To rephrase this question in terms of Aquinas's theory of virtue, are the normative claims of virtue essentially similar to the kinds of normative considerations that apply to other kinds of living creatures?

A number of contemporary moral philosophers, working within broadly neo-Aristotelian traditions of the virtues, would answer this question affirmatively. To take the most notable recent example, Philippa Foot claims,

> I believe that evaluations of human will and action share a conceptual structure with evaluations of characteristics and operations of other living things, and can only be understood in these terms. I want to show moral evil as "a kind of natural defect." *Life* will be at the centre of my discussion, and the fact that a human action or habit is good of its kind will be taken to be simply a fact about a given feature of a certain kind of living thing.[37]

Similarly, Rosalind Hursthouse argues that the virtues are praiseworthy and desirable because they represent our best overall strategy for attaining happiness, whether as individuals or collectively. They are therefore instrumental goods, desirable for men and women in much the same way as a horse's abilities to run swiftly while keeping its balance are good for the horse.[38]

This kind of ethical naturalism is attractive for at least two reasons. It underscores the undeniable continuities between ourselves and the rest of the living world, and it makes the task of analyzing and justifying specific moral claims much easier than it otherwise would be. Nonetheless, these advantages come at the price of a drastic and finally unrealistic simplification

37. Foot, *Natural Goodness*, 5; emphasis in the original.
38. Hursthouse, *On Virtue Ethics*; in particular, see 178–87.

of moral concepts, seen in relation to other kinds of normative concepts. If moral goodness is essentially the same in kind as the goodness exemplified by a flourishing parakeet, then how can we distinguish between someone's good character and his good health? What should we say about the many cases in which well-being and moral character come apart, as it were? If well-being and moral goodness are really equivalent, then it would make no sense to say that someone who suffers from a chronic illness is a good person, even though he is someone of good character, whose life is filled with praiseworthy activities. Nor could we say that someone is a bad person if she is healthy and prosperous, as the bad so often are. Of course, both of these alternatives would be deeply contrary to our moral intuitions. The normative criteria for organic well-being and human excellence in the fullest sense can and do come apart, and neither can simply be reduced to the other. Aquinas is well aware of all this. He acknowledges that a virtuous life presupposes some level of organic well-being, sufficient to maintain one's life and one's capacities for action (I-II 4.6–7). However, he clearly does not believe that human happiness, even considered at the level of what is naturally possible without divine grace, can be equated with this kind of well-being (I-II 55.3 *ad* 3). Rather, a humanly happy life for him consists in the practice of the virtues, which, as perfections of the agent, are intrinsically good and cannot be reduced to means toward, or conditions for, happiness (I-II 5.5; cf. I-II 2.4, 55.3 *ad* 3).[39] More fundamentally, the human person is said to be good without qualification by virtue of having a good will (I 5.4 *ad* 3). The key point is that the virtues represent a level of perfection that presupposes, but also goes beyond, the kinds of goodness that we share with all creatures: "Just as natural cognition is always true, so natural dilection is always right, since natural love is nothing other than an inclination of nature instilled by the author of nature. To say therefore that a natural inclination is not right, is to disparage the author of nature. However, the rectitude of the natural dilection is one thing, and the rectitude of charity or virtue is another, because one rectitude is perfective of the other" (I 60.1 *ad* 3).

The neo-Kantian philosopher Christine Korsgaard offers an alternative analysis of normativity and moral obligation that is, perhaps surprisingly, closer to Aquinas's views in some key respects than these neo-Aristotelian accounts. Korsgaard's analysis of normativity takes its starting point from the widely held sense that moral claims are in some way compelling. They are felt to impose a kind of necessity, and yet they are not coercive in any ob-

---

39. I argue for this interpretation of Aquinas in more detail in *Nature as Reason*, 163–77.

vious way. A man who encounters an injured and crying child may well feel that he has to stop and help. He cannot do anything else, and yet, nothing forces him to do so, nor is he compelled by threats of injury or loss. According to Korsgaard, these kinds of experiences of necessitation stem from the normativity proper to a moral demand, which she identifies as "the grounds of its authority and the psychological mechanisms of its enforcement."[40] Moral claims or laws are experienced as authoritative, which implies that they are grounded in considerations that cannot be reduced to the agent's well-being or to more general considerations of utility or expediency. In fact, they may require setting aside such considerations. This is a critically important point, and as we will see in more detail further on, Aquinas would fully accept it.

At the same time, Korsgaard approaches the problem of normativity within a teleological framework, which she explicitly attributes to Aristotle in general inspiration, if not in details. Her thesis is that "normative principles are in general principles of the unification of manifolds, multiplicities, or, in Aristotle's wonderful phrase, *mere heaps*, into objects of particular kinds."[41] She goes on to explain that "to be an object, to be unified, and to be teleologically organized, are one and the same thing. . . . At the same time, it is the teleological organization or form of the object that supports normative judgments about it."[42] Korsgaard initially illustrates this point with examples of artifacts, such as houses. We can identify this assembly of bricks and lumber as a house because we are aware of what a house is meant to be, and by the same token, we can judge whether this particular house is a good house or in some way defective. However, the logic of her argument takes her beyond a consideration of artifacts into the world of living creatures and especially rational men and women. She claims that the forms of life and activities of living creatures are "defined by certain standards that are both constitutive of it and normative for it," the key point being that operations and actions, like structures, are evaluated teleologically, by reference to their overall place in a way of life.[43]

It will be clear to anyone familiar with Aquinas's overall theory of the virtues that he and Korsgaard have a great deal in common. Both frame

40. Korsgaard, *Self-Constitution*, 2; she sets up the problem in 1–4.

41. Korsgaard, *Self-Constitution*, 27, italics in the original. Note that although she relies primarily on Aristotle's *Metaphysics* to develop a framework for teleological analysis, she remarks that this general thesis is shared by Plato and Kant, as well as Aristotle.

42. Korsgaard, *Self-Constitution*, 28; the remainder of the argument is developed in 28–41.

43. Korsgaard, *Self-Constitution*, 32.

their overall account of morality in terms of a teleological analysis drawn from Aristotle in order to make the point that moral norms are in some way grounded in the way of life natural to us as creatures of a specific kind. In order to do so, both begin by spelling out the normative force of moral claims in terms of a teleological analysis that applies, up to a point, to all substantial entities. At the same time, each wants to show that the normative force of moral claims is distinctive, in a way that can best be expressed by saying that moral claims necessitate action; they are authoritative and not merely normative. In order to do so, each theorist needs to spell out just how it is that the normative force of moral considerations is distinctive, while at the same time accounting for the continuities between these kinds of normative considerations and the nonmoral norms that apply in other spheres of existence. The normative criteria proper to morality cannot be separated from broader normative considerations stemming from what is natural to us as living creatures of a certain kind, nor can it be reduced to these considerations.

At this point, a Thomistic account of justice as a virtue parts company with Korsgaard. On Korsgaard's view, the normativity of reason is grounded in the exigencies of rational consistency and personal integrity as they apply to the agent. She goes on to argue that these exigencies generate norms of respect for others as rational agents, but the normative force of other-regarding norms is derivative. For Aquinas, in contrast, the norms of justice are grounded in the normative values and claims intrinsic to human existence, which each individual bears simply in virtue of his or her humanity. Correlatively, justice perfects the will by relating the agent directly to a value external to the agent himself (II-II 58.1–2,11, 79.1). This line of analysis raises further questions about the sense in which justice perfects the will, to which we will return in subsequent chapters. At this point, we should simply note that, for Aquinas, the will is perfected through right relations to others, rather than through rational self-consistency.

We return now to Aquinas's account of the virtues as perfections, seen in relation to the overall framework of teleological analysis that he consistently employs. We have already observed that, on Aquinas's view, habits of the intellectual capacities and appetites are perfections of a kind, and the moral virtues are perfections in an unrestricted sense. The criteria for qualified and unqualified perfections of the habits are derived from a broader conception of the perfection of the individual, seen as the full development and expression of the agent's capacities as a living creature of a specific kind. The same can be said, *mutatis mutandis*, of everything, so long as the entity in question is a unified individual substance and not a mere heap of stuff.

Every substance can be understood in terms of some ideal of existence and full operation, which implies some kind of normative criteria informing the operations of the creature (the main lines of this analysis are set out at I 5.5 and developed throughout the *summa*; see, for example, I-II 6.1, 8.1, 91.2). An inanimate creature is engaged in causal operations, through which it sustains a characteristic kind of existence. These operations take place spontaneously, and yet they can be said to be normative in a weak sense, captured for example by the remark that, if this ring is really gold, it should be relatively easy to scratch or bend. There is nothing especially desirable about being soft and flexible, but the point is that these indicate characteristic qualities that the creature is naturally inclined to display until it ceases to exist. Living creatures, including both plants and animals, sustain their existence through more active forms of engagement with their environment, through which they draw sustenance from the surrounding environment and integrate it into their own living forms, repel threats, and extend themselves, as it were, through some form of procreation. Plants do so through nonconscious but relatively independent and coordinated organic processes, whereas animals characteristically do so through some kind of more or less conscious inter-action with the world around them, through which they pursue or avoid whatever promotes or threatens them. Correlatively, plants live without moving from place to place, except perhaps passively, whereas the higher animals, at least, move around in response to the prompting of conscious desires and aversions.

What does all this have to do with human life, and more specifically human morality? Aquinas holds that human beings share in the same final end as every other kind of creature, in the sense that we too are oriented toward perfection, understood as the full and active development and expression of the capacities innate to us as creatures of a specific kind (I-II 1.8; cf. I-II 109.3). At the same time, we pursue and attain this final end in a distinctive way, in accordance with the kind of activity proper to us as human agents. This is the point at which the distinctively human capacities for rationality, freedom, and self-determination, so central to the work of contemporary Kantians, play a key role in Aquinas's account. These are characteristically human capacities through which we pursue and attain our perfection as men and women in a distinctively human way. More specifically, we do so through free, self-directed activities that correspond to the exigencies of a rational, well-formed sense of our own good, and a sound, free respect for the claims of others (I-II 91.2).

Aquinas's overall analysis of existence and operation in terms of actuality and perfection provides the necessary context within which to understand the distinctively normative character of moral considerations. The key point is that, for him, every kind of existence expresses normative principles, which can be ranked in accordance with increasing levels of comprehensiveness and complexity. Substantial existence at every level is characterized by dynamic principles of existence and causal operation that are intrinsically goal-oriented, if only in the minimal sense of expressing and sustaining a particular kind of existence. In this sense, existence and causality are normative all the way down, just as causal operations can be analyzed at every level as oriented toward a specific kind of perfection. At the same time, as we move from lower to higher forms of existence, we find more expansive and active forms of causality, corresponding to fuller kinds of perfection. Plants exist through a dynamic engagement with the environment and move through stages of development in an orderly way, in accordance with the active processes intrinsic to living creatures. Animals do the same, but their activities as living creatures are carried out through conscious perceptions and desires, leading to activities originating from within the animal itself, so to speak. Men and women likewise act out of conscious perceptions and desires, but these are shaped and directed by a self-reflective sense of what it means to be human, to live a properly human life and to relate rightly to others.

Correlatively, each level corresponds to a qualitatively new kind of normative consideration. In order to approximate a perfected existence, inanimate creatures do not need to do much of anything beyond continuing in existence through causal interactions with a characteristic kind of environment. Living creatures enjoy a more expansive kind of existence, but by the same token, the normative bar is higher for them. At a minimum, their activities are evaluated by criteria of growth, reproduction, and decay. For animals, these criteria are formulated in light of the animal's conscious involvement with these processes, governed by normative criteria of the pleasant and the painful. Similarly, at the level of human existence, we find a qualitatively new kind of goodness and perfection and, correspondingly, a distinctively new kind of normative consideration. Men and women live through processes of self-reflective activity, through which they knowingly and freely relate themselves to their own final good and to the good of others. These capacities give rise to normative criteria of accountability, responsibility, and justification, which reflect the ways in which men and women rely on reasoned judgments in their actions and their interactions with one another.

So far, we have had several occasions to observe that Aquinas believes that the virtues are connatural to the human person, in the sense that they are oriented toward a connatural kind of happiness and, correlatively, can be attained through the exercise of natural human capacities (I-II 5.5, 61.1,3). Those who are familiar with Aquinas's overall moral theology will realize that this account is incomplete. Aquinas holds that the human person is in fact called to a higher form of perfection, that is, the friendship and union with God initiated in this life through charity, and fulfilled in the direct vision of God after death (in addition to the texts just cited, see I-II 62.1, 110.1). This kind of perfection is literally supernatural, that is to say, it goes beyond the intrinsic capabilities of human nature. We can attain this perfection only through grace, which God freely bestows on the human individual. At the same time, grace is a principle of activity, analogous to nature, that is expressed through virtuous dispositions and the actions they generate (I-II 110.2–3). Aquinas describes these as infused virtues because they depend on God's bestowal of grace, and they include both the theological virtues of faith, hope, and charity and the infused counterparts to the acquired cardinal virtues (I-II 63.3–4).

Aquinas's distinctions between nature and grace, and between the acquired and infused virtues, play a key role in his overall theology. For our own purposes, however, we can bracket the distinction between acquired and infused justice in most contexts. The infused cardinal virtues and their acquired counterparts are specifically different in that they are oriented to two distinct ends, that is, supernatural union with God and connatural happiness (I-II 63.4). Yet they operate within the same spheres of activity and take account of the same relevant considerations, which are reoriented but not set aside through grace. As Aquinas frequently remarks, grace perfects nature, it does not pervert it (see, for example, I 60.5). He also remarks, in the context of a discussion of the obligations of charity, that the operations of grace are not less reasonable than the operations of nature (II-II 26.2; cf. II-II 31.3). Most notably, Aquinas argues that the obligations of justice expressed in our relations to family members and other close associates inform the obligations of charity (II-II 26.6–13).

In the next chapter, I will argue that an analysis of virtues as habits or stable dispositions presupposes some kind of developmental process. It might seem that, on Aquinas's terms, this line of analysis could not be extended to the infused virtues, which are bestowed directly by God. I do not believe that this is the case. Grace is a principle of activity for Aquinas, and like any other such principle, it can be actualized only through actions (I-II 110.2; cf. I-II 51.4 *ad* 3). I thus see no reason in principle why the operative principle of grace should not unfold and develop through processes of activity, leading to the formation of dispositions. These are not acquired through unaided human activities, since the activities of formation themselves are dependent on grace at every point. Nonetheless, on this view the infused virtues can be said to develop over time, through processes analogous to those through which we acquire the connatural virtues.[44]

The Virtues as Normative Ideals

At the beginning of the previous section, I noted that Aquinas offers both a constructive theory of the virtues as habits and an extended account of the virtues as substantive normative ideals. Taken in this latter way, as substantive ideals, the seven traditional virtues provide him with an organizing principle for the extended moral analysis of the *secunda secundae*. As he explains,

> If we were to determine the virtues, gifts, vices, and precepts separately, it would be necessary to speak of many things at once. For he who wishes to sufficiently deal with the precept "do not commit adultery" would find it necessary to inquire about adultery, which is a particular sin, the knowledge of which depends on the knowledge of the opposite virtue. He will therefore proceed by a more concise and expedient way if he proceeds by considering together under the same heading the virtues and the corresponding gifts, the vices, and the affirmative or negative precepts. (II-II prologue)

These remarks presuppose an extended, rich history of reflection on the virtues as normative ideals, sustained through popular wisdom, literature, and paraenetic discourses, as well as philosophical reflection.

---

44. It is therefore not necessary to postulate the existence of acquired and infused cardinal virtues in the same subject. I agree with William Mathison that Aquinas does not—and, in the terms of his overall theory, cannot—allow for this possibility. He offers a careful, textually grounded analysis of the infused cardinal virtues, seen in relation to their acquired counterparts, in "Can Christians Possess the Acquired Virtues?" *Theological Studies* 72 (2011): 558–85. Among much else, he argues that the infused virtues can be said in some sense to develop over time. A similar point is made by Luis Vera, "Tablets of Flesh: Memory, Media, and the Perfection of the Image in Digital Societies" (PhD diss., University of Notre Dame, 2015).

Our own contemporaries have given considerable attention to the place of our initial moral beliefs and intuitions in moral reflection. Many would agree with Rawls that these provide the moral philosopher with both necessary starting points and criteria for the adequacy and plausibility of her theories, although the theory will also imply some revision of these starting points.[45] Similarly, in Aquinas's time the popular, literary, and theological ideals of the virtues provided starting points and touchstones for normative reflection.[46] For Aquinas himself, these ideals provide the starting points and initial criteria for the theoretical analysis of the *prima secundae*, and correlatively, this analysis enables him to integrate diverse normative considerations into the formidable synthesis of the *secunda secundae*.

More specifically, the theoretical analysis of the *prima secundae* and the detailed ethical analysis of the *secunda secundae* come together in Aquinas's account of the object of a virtue, which he identifies as the characteristic kind of action correlated with the virtuous habit in question (I-II 54.2, 60.1; II-II 27.1). Each virtue is defined by reference to its object, which is formulated in such a way as to bring out the rational considerations that are proper to the virtue. Generally, these definitions are themselves traditional formulae, which Aquinas selects and interprets in the light of his overall schema of the virtues as habits oriented toward specific kinds of praiseworthy actions. Through this process of analytic redaction, Aquinas transforms traditional formulae into formal definitions of the virtues in terms of the object of the virtue, that is to say, the characteristic kind of action through which the virtue is expressed.

Seen from a theoretical perspective, the link between virtues and their characteristic objects follows from Aquinas's general analysis of the habits as dispositions of the capacities of the rational creature, especially those oriented toward action. As we recall, these habits are perfections, in the sense that they form or orient a capacity in such a way as to enable it to operate. Thus, the habits themselves can be said to be principles of action, and they are associated, conceptually and causally, with the kinds of actions that they characteristically produce (I-II 54.2). The habits are further distinguished in normative terms, in accordance with whether or not they dispose the ratio-

---

45. Rawls, *A Theory of Justice*, 46–53.

46. Siegfried Wenzel offers a very helpful introduction to popular and homiletic images of the virtues in his "Introduction," in *Summa virtutum de remediis animae*, ed. Wenzel (Athens: University of Georgia Press, 1984), 2–12.

nal creature to act approximately in accordance with her natural principles of activity (I-II 54.3). As we would expect, Aquinas interprets naturalness in this context comprehensively to include a full range of what we would describe as moral considerations, and the upshot of his analysis is that virtuous habits are specifically different from vices, even if these represent two alternative dispositions of the same capacity (I-II 54.3).

Aquinas's definitions of the particular virtues in terms of their formal objects are thus framed in such a way as to bring out the distinctively rational and moral aspects of the kind of act in question. As we would expect, these definitions tend to be abstract and highly general, and they can appear to be remote from actual experience. In a way, Aquinas's formal definitions of the virtues do stand at a distance from our experiences, but they do so as abstractions drawn from those experiences, not as ideals imposed from without. He does not develop his theory of the virtues out of formal definitions of the virtues and vices, any more than Rawls develops his theory of justice out of the two principles of justice. Like our own contemporaries, Aquinas takes the starting points for normative analysis from the moral traditions, shared intuitions, and commonly held beliefs that constitute the common morality of his society. In particular, he draws freely on the paradigms of virtuous and vicious actions contained within his society's stock images of good or bad behavior, exemplifying what it means to be just or fair or greedy or lustful, for example.[47] These paradigms are not equivalent to the object of the act, formally defined as such. Nonetheless, the paradigmatic kinds of actions associated with a habit are connected to the object of an act stemming from that habit, insofar as they represent typical or noteworthy instances of kinds of actions exemplifying the proper object of the habit. In other words, our paradigms for kinds of actions offer concrete examples and images, in terms of which we are able to formulate reflective concepts of the kind of action, that is to say the object, corresponding to a particular virtuous or vicious habit. Thus, the identification of the object of a given virtue presupposes that we are familiar with the concrete kinds of actions that provide the paradigms for virtuous and vicious kinds of actions. This aspect of Aquinas's analysis draws on the full range of moral beliefs, intuitions, and debates that find their way into the *secunda secundae*, and correlatively, this line of thought

47. I take the idea of paradigmatic examples of a practice or an ideal from Ronald Dworkin, *Law's Empire*, 72. Although he does not speak in terms of paradigmatic examples, Julius Kovesi offers an illuminating analysis of the relationship between particulars and general moral concepts; see *Moral Notions* (London: Routledge, 1967), 37–65. Annas offers a similar interpretation of ideals of virtues in particular; see *Intelligent Virtue*, 16–57.

provides him with the critical perspective needed to sort through these diverse considerations.

Admittedly, Aquinas does not describe his moral methodology in these terms, but this line of analysis fits with what he says about concept-formation more generally. On his view, we form general concepts through a process of abstraction from particular images, through which we apprehend individuals as instantiations of some general kind. Furthermore, our ongoing processes of understanding and knowledge are never detached from these particulars, because, for us, understanding implies not only a grasp of formal principles but an ongoing ability to see how these principles are expressed in and through particulars (I 84.6–7, 85.1).[48] I may be able to grasp and reproduce the formal definition of "cat," but I cannot be said to understand what it means to be a cat unless I know one when I see it. Moreover, as I reflect on feline existence with the aim of understanding cats better, I will continually reflect on images of particular cats, seen as exemplifying, perhaps in different ways or with instructive qualifications, what it means to instantiate this specific kind of existence.

Similarly, I cannot be said to grasp what it means to be brave or chaste or just, simply because I can give a good formal definition of these virtues in terms of their proper objects. I need to be able to identify examples of these virtues in action when I see them and to offer some explanation for why I understand these particular actions in terms of these formal categories. This presupposes both some experience and some reflection on paradigms of good (and bad) behavior in terms of formal categories, which themselves emerge and develop through this very process. Again, Aquinas does not describe his procedures in exactly these terms, but he does observe at one point that practical reason operates through a discriminating abstraction from the phantasms generated by our desires and fears, as mediated through reasoned judgments.[49] At any rate, this overall program fits his actual way of proceeding in moral argumentation throughout the *secunda pars*.

Since we will be examining paradigms of just and unjust behavior in some detail, it may be helpful initially to begin with an example taken from another virtue. The example of courage or fortitude is especially illuminating, precisely because we have so many paradigms of courageous behavior,

48. For an excellent summary of Aquinas's account of intellectual cognition and its relation to images and to the rational grasp of particulars as exemplifications of form, see Robert Pasnau, *Thomas Aquinas on Human Nature*, 278–302.

49. *In De anima* III.16, 840–42; he explicitly extends the process of abstracting general forms from particulars to the operations of practical reason at para. 842.

which cannot readily be harmonized into a single account. Does fortitude pertain only to the dangers of death, or can someone show courage by facing lesser, but still serious, dangers (II-II 123.4)? Is fortitude properly so called limited to the battlefield, or can it be exhibited by facing death in other contexts, including martyrdom (II-II 123.5)? Is it especially relevant to situations of sudden or unexpected danger (II-II 123.9)?

In order to address these questions, Aquinas draws on his general theory of the virtues, as well as his views on courage, in order to explain why these are paradigms of fortitude that exhibit some aspect of courage as a virtue in an exemplary way. He argues that fortitude is most fully exemplified in response to the danger of death, because "it pertains to the virtue of fortitude to guard the will of the human person lest it draw back from the good of reason on account of the fear of some bodily evil. . . . And therefore we must say that fortitude of the soul is that which securely holds the will of the person to the good of reason over against the greatest evils, because he who stands firm against great things can consequently stand firm over against lesser things, but not conversely" (II-II 123.4). Thus, only someone who displays this kind of courage can be said to possess fortitude simply as such: "A person is not considered to be brave without qualification from bearing any adverse things whatever, but only from this, that he well endures even the greatest evils. From bearing other things, however, someone is said to be brave in some respect" (II-II 123.4 *ad* 1). As the latter comment implies, however, those who are willing to risk lesser goods can legitimately be said to be brave in a qualified sense. In this way, he accounts for the intuition that someone who risks, say, her place within her community for the sake of some ideal is genuinely courageous, although perhaps not courageous in the exemplary way of a soldier or a martyr. Similarly, fortitude is paradigmatically linked to bravery on the battlefield: "Fortitude strengthens the soul of the human person against the greatest dangers, which are dangers of death. But because fortitude is a virtue, which as such always moves to good, it follows that the human person does not flee death on account of pursuing some good" (II-II 123.5). This aspect of fortitude is exemplified by the bravery of soldiers fighting for the common good, but it can also be exercised in other ways, for example, when a judge is threatened with death if he renders a just verdict. In these kinds of situations, Aquinas adds, the dangers in question are commonly referred to as a kind of war. And martyrs exhibit courage in this sense because they face death in pursuit of the highest good of all, union with God (II-II 123.5 *ad* 1). Finally, fortitude is especially associated with someone's response to sudden dangers, because a prompt, courageous response to sudden dangers indicates that her bravery is rooted in a well-established habit, that is to say, a true virtue (II-II 123.9).

Stepping back, we see here an example of a general principle. Aquinas typically argues that the ideals informing particular virtues are exemplified in a particularly clear and normatively significant way in situations of special difficulty or importance. Just as the ideal of fortitude is especially evident in face of the dangers of death, so the general ideal of temperance is especially evident with respect to the intense pleasures connected to the processes sustaining human life, that is, food, drink, and sex (II-II 123.2 *ad* 2, 123.4, 141.4). This line of analysis enables Aquinas to identify the formal features that define the object of a virtue in terms of what we might describe as the point of the virtue. Thus, the virtues traditionally associated with fortitude are identified as such by reference to those kinds of dangers and risks that are most likely to deflect someone from her commitments to an overall good; similarly, the virtues traditionally associated with temperance are identified by reference to those natural satisfactions that readily take on an excessive or distorted place in individual lives. Reflection at this level necessarily proceeds by reference to general paradigms for praiseworthy or admirable behavior, which take account of our shared sense of common human vulnerabilities, needs, and capacities. At the same time, the test of this kind of moral reflection comes when it is applied to particular acts and individual character. These ideals will inevitably look somewhat different in individual cases, because individuals have different temperaments and face unique moral challenges and opportunities.

This overall line of thought is developed in another way through Aquinas's interpretation of the Aristotelian claim that virtuous acts characteristically observe a mean between excess and deficiency. By Aquinas's time, this claim was already something of a truism, and yet it can be difficult to know how to interpret it in a way that is both plausible and applicable to the virtues generally speaking. It makes intuitive sense to claim that someone who is temperate with respect to eating, for example, exhibits neither the immoderate desires of the glutton nor the positive distaste for eating of the anorexic. She has a nice appetite, but it is moderate and easily satisfied—a mild, undemanding desire. But can we legitimately understand marital chastity in the same way? Whatever we take to be the extremes of excess and deficiency with respect to this virtue, surely it is not a sign of good character or a good marriage for someone to feel only a moderate, easily gratified sexual desire for his wife, all the time, throughout their lives together. Sometimes, a passionate response, in the popular sense of the term, does reflect a virtuous habit of the passions.

For Aristotle, the mean of a virtue is a relative ideal, identified by reference to characteristic ways of going wrong. For example, courage represents a kind of midpoint between cringing cowardice and reckless abandon, and temperance with respect to food and drink represents a midpoint between heedless gluttony and drunkenness, and a fastidious, unhealthy indifference to the joys of the table.[50] Thus understood, the doctrine of the mean, so called, is not so much an attempt to identify a moral criterion as another strategy for moving reflectively from paradigms—in this case paradigms of bad behavior—toward the formulation of an ideal that at least avoids certain characteristic ways of falling short of a standard or of exceeding it. This can be a very fruitful way of proceeding, but it can also lead to an identification of the mean with facile ideals of moderation or emotional equipoise, as if tepid feelings were in themselves the marks of excellence of character.

Aquinas's interpretation of the doctrine of the mean reflects, once again, his theory of the virtues as perfections. The ideal of the mean is identified with a standard of appropriateness in accordance with rational criteria for what is proper, exigent, or required in a given situation (I-II 64.1, esp. 64.1 *ad* 2).[51] Thus understood, the ideal standard corresponding to the mean of a virtue generally presupposes paradigms for vicious behavior, which set the outer limits on what can count as virtuous behavior in a given field of action. Gorging oneself to the point of nausea or, alternatively, refusing to eat anything at all cannot plausibly count as temperate acts under any imaginable circumstances.[52] However, what would count as temperance cannot be determined by simply splitting the difference between extremes. On Aquinas's view, the mean observed by temperance is set by the overall human good, which our appetites and activities of nourishment are meant to promote and not to subvert. Seen from this perspective, both binging and anorexia

50. Aristotle's account of the mean may be found in the *Nicomachean Ethics* 2.6–9, pp. 33–41, in the Bartlett/Collins edition. For a helpful summary of the virtues and their correlative vices, as Aristotle presents them, see 303–4.

51. My interpretation of the mean of a virtue as Aquinas understands it is indebted to J. O. Urmson's insightful interpretation of the Aristotelean doctrine of the mean; see "Aristotle's Doctrine of the Mean," in *Essays in Aristotle's Ethics*, ed. Amélie Rorty (Berkeley: University of California Press, 1980), 157–70.

52. It does not follow that these and similar kinds of actions are always necessarily vicious, any more than actions that fit the paradigms for temperate behavior are necessarily virtuous. The actions in question may not be fully voluntary, or in the latter case, we may find that a good act is being performed for bad reasons. My point is simply that, whatever we may make of examples of gorging or self-starvation, these cannot count as temperate acts—we could not make sense of such a claim.

are bad because they subvert the agent's overall well-being in drastic ways, but there are many more subtle ways of going wrong with respect to food and drink, not all of which can be mapped onto a spectrum of excess and deficiency (cf. II-II 147.1 *ad* 2). Similarly, the mean of temperance will reflect the many ways in which the appetites for food and drink can be pursued and satisfied appropriately, in accordance with the agent's overall needs and capacities as a living organism, a social being, and a spiritual entity.

Each of the moral virtues can be said to observe a mean, but not in the same way. On Aquinas's account, the virtues associated with the passions, that is to say, fortitude and temperance and the virtues related to these, are all said to observe a rational mean. That is, they reflect standards of appropriateness that are inextricably tied to individual needs and capacities. The virtue of justice, in contrast, observes a real mean, a standard of appropriateness determined by objective standards of obligation, equity, and fairness (I-II 64.1-2; II-II 58.10). Again, Aquinas takes this distinction from Aristotle, but he accounts for it in terms of his overall conception of the virtues as perfecting habits.[53] The virtues of the passions observe a rational mean, he explains, because they direct the agent's inclinations toward particular satisfactions in such a way as to promote her overall good; they thus observe standards that are irreducibly bound up with the individual's own needs and circumstances. We need these virtues because our passions are naturally oriented toward particular goods, without any necessary reference to the agent's overall well-being and moral perfection. In contrast, the will is naturally oriented toward the agent's overall good and has no need for virtuous dispositions in order to incline toward the comprehensive good. However, the will is also the principle of external acts that draw us into relations with others, and in this respect, it does stand in need of habits to operate appropriately and well (in addition to the texts just cited, see I-II 50.5, 56.6). The criteria for justice are therefore set by interpersonal, objective criteria that can be formulated without reference to the specifics of individual temperament, circumstances, and the like. Thus, justice is said to observe a real mean determined by objective standards of equity and appropriateness, as these are instantiated in the agent's relationships with other agents and collective entities (II-II 58.10).

This brings us to another issue, namely, the relation between ideals of virtue and moral precepts. To many of our contemporaries, this relationship is problematic, because we tend to assume that ideals of virtue and moral

---

53. See the *Nicomachean Ethics*, 5.3-5, 95-103, in Bartlett/Collins.

laws represent two disparate and perhaps incompatible ways of expressing normative claims. This whole line of thought would be foreign to Aquinas and his interlocutors. The scholastics were the heirs of many traditions of normative reflection, including specifically scriptural and theological motifs such as the gifts of the Holy Spirit and the Beatitudes, as well as fundamental normative concepts of virtues and precepts. These were regarded as diverse normative standards and ideals that needed to be harmonized, but the scholastics do not generally express the sense that they are prima facie incompatible, much less inherently at odds.

In order to see how Aquinas integrates the ideals of the virtues and the precepts of natural law, we need to turn to his analysis of the object of an action. As we have seen, Aquinas claims that the habits of the passions and the will, both virtues and vices, are defined by reference to the object of their characteristic act. At the same time, those who are familiar with Aquinas's overall theory of action as set forth in the *prima secundae* will recall that he first introduces this term in the context of the overall normative analysis of human action outlined in I-II 18–21, specifically at I-II 18.2. There we read that the goodness or evil of human actions is determined by the object of the act, which in turn is defined by reference to its appropriateness. And so, for example, the act of using what is one's own is said to be generically good, whereas the act of taking what is another's against her will is generically bad. Correlatively, actions that are similar in kind, seen from one perspective, may be different in kind, seen from a moral standpoint. Making use of one's own car and taking someone else's car are similar, insofar as they are both acts of appropriation and use of a material object. Yet considered from a moral standpoint, they are specifically different. The first is an instance of the act of using what is one's own, whereas the second is an instance of theft, and this moral distinction implies a fundamental, specific difference in kind. Aquinas would say that these two actions differ with respect to the object of the act, that is to say, the kind of action, described from a moral standpoint, that each represents (I-II 1.3 *ad* 3).

Aquinas's analysis of the object of the act yields a normative system that looks a great deal like a deontological, rule-based morality. I have argued elsewhere that Aquinas's analysis of the object of the act, seen in relation to other normative considerations, is in fact an account of moral rules; furthermore, it is an attractive and persuasive account.[54] The object of the act,

54. See Porter, *Moral Action and Christian Ethics* (Cambridge: Cambridge University Press, 1995), 125–66, and *Nature as Reason*, 177–203.

on this analysis, is a concept of a kind of action, appropriately expressed through a formal definition bringing out the morally salient considerations that separate this kind of action from other, superficially similar kinds of actions. Compare this to our concept of a moral rule. We generally formulate rules in terms of imperatives, usually negative in force, such as, "Do not commit murder." But we cannot understand, much less apply, these and similar imperatives unless we have some idea of which kinds of actions count as murder or other prohibited kinds of actions, and which similar kinds of actions do not. Our concepts of morally salient kinds of actions are thus more basic than our grasp of moral rules, which express the normative significance of certain kinds of actions in imperative form.

By now, it will be apparent that the dichotomy between ideals of virtue and moral rules is not so sharp as many have supposed. Moral rules are correlated with generic kinds of actions that constitute the object of the relevant acts, in such a way that we cannot grasp the rules without some concrete comprehension of the kinds of actions in question. Similarly, a habit, which is a disposition oriented toward activity, is defined by reference to the kind of action that it characteristically generates, which Aquinas identifies as its object (I-II 54.2). Moreover, just as the object of an act—that is to say, the specific kind of action that it represents—is determined by moral criteria, so the species of the habits are determined by moral criteria (I-II 18.2, 54.3). Thus, any given virtue and its opposing vices are specifically different, even though they are habits of the same faculty, exercised within the same field of operation. Chastity is specifically different from a stable disposition to play around, although each is a stable disposition pertaining to the exercise of one's sexual faculties. The key point here is that this distinction is correlated with the moral distinction between the two kinds of sexual act that form the object of the virtuous and vicious habit, respectively. Aquinas's point is that human actions, and the habits of desire correlated with those actions, are formally distinguished by reference to the most comprehensive normative standards, good and evil seen in moral terms.

For this reason Aquinas uses the traditional schema of the cardinal and the theological virtues as the organizing principle for the detailed discussion of normative ideals and precepts in the *secunda pars*. The diverse elements of the Christian moral tradition, including not only normative ideals and precepts of law but the traditional schema of the Beatitudes and the gifts of the Holy Spirit, can all be related to the virtues in some way. Traditional paradigms of virtue and vice are analyzed in terms of an overall theory of virtue in such a way as to yield formal definitions of the virtues in terms of the object of their characteristic kind of action. The object of the virtue, in turn, is correlated with precepts enjoining the practice of this kind of action or the avoidance of what is contrary to it. The gifts of the Holy Spirit and the Beatitudes are analyzed, respectively, as distinct habits through which the human spirit is made responsive to the Holy Spirit in the application of the virtues to specific acts, or as the immediate effects of the virtues and the gifts in the life of grace (I-II 68.1–3, 69.1). None of this implies that the precepts of law, or much less the Beatitudes and the gifts, are inessential to the Christian moral life—quite the contrary! But this approach does reflect Aquinas's overall approach, signaled at the beginning of the *prima secundae,* of analyzing human activity in terms of its internal principles, that is to say, the capacities and dispositions that lead to action, and the external principles, which determine the normative criteria by which these operations are evaluated (see the prologue to the *prima secundae* and, for more detail, I-II 6 intro.).

Seen from this perspective, the distinction between a virtue-based and a rules-based ethic appears to be overly simplistic, at least in many of its formulations. What might appear to us to be differences between virtue-oriented and rule-oriented evaluations can better be understood as differences among the virtues themselves, and among the different contexts and purposes within which we engage in normative evaluation. Our ideals of restraint, sexual purity, bravery, and the like cannot generally be captured by sharply formulated, strict rules of conduct. We apply them contextually, taking a general sense of appropriateness as a benchmark and taking account of both the situation at hand and the individual's own overall temperament and needs (I-II 64.2, II-II 58.10). The virtue of justice, in contrast, is correlated with relatively well-formulated precepts that set strict, objectively verifiable standards for acceptable conduct (II-II 57.1, 80). These contrasts do not reflect a general division between virtue-based and rule-based morality; rather, they track the fundamental division between the virtues of the passions, which observe a rational mean only, and justice, which observes a real mean. As we have seen, this distinction itself reflects the salient differences between the passions and the will, implying differences in what it means for each of these faculties to develop and operate in appropriate and well-directed ways.

Furthermore, on reflection, these differences are not so stark as we might at first assume. Certainly, our ideals of self-restraint, chastity, courage, and the like are relatively general and open-ended, but the same cannot always be said with respect to the corresponding paradigms of viciousness. There is no plausible way to regard eating until one vomits to be an expression of self-restraint, nor can we consider someone brave who runs at the first sight of the enemy. We may not regard these kinds of actions as culpable, especially if we have reason to question whether they are fully voluntary, but the point is that they set outer boundaries for what can plausibly count as restrained or brave conduct. Correlatively, the norms of fairness and non-maleficence correlated with justice are relatively fixed, but they also tend to be formulated in such a way as to take account of the complex normative claims that arise in any community. For example, the norm against murder is not an absolute prohibition against killing, as we sometimes assume. Rather, it comprises a set of distinctions among permissible and forbidden kinds of killing, reflecting a long history of judgments regarding the value of human life, the scope of one's right to immunity from harm, and a range of other normative considerations. (The details are set out over the eight articles of II-II 64.) Furthermore, general concepts such as "murder," "adultery," or "theft" cannot always be applied with certainty to particular acts, as Aquinas notes (I-II 100.8 *ad* 3). These kinds of concepts will always be to some extent indeterminate, allowing for more than one defensible application in unusual, difficult, or unanticipated cases. Just as the norms associated with temperance and courage do imply some boundaries, so the norms associated with justice leave room for interpretative judgment at the point of application.

We turn now, finally, to one other aspect of Aquinas's analysis of the virtues as normative ideals and organizing principles. In his analysis and ex-position of the virtues as normative ideals, Aquinas appropriates the schema of four cardinal and three theological virtues, which was by this time well established among theologians as the preferred classification of the virtues. (For Aquinas's own defense of this schema, see I-II 61–62.) This schema has many advantages. It identifies certain general virtues that are central to the moral life on almost any showing, and it does not leave out any major field of human concern. Furthermore, it offers the advantage from Aquinas's standpoint of lending itself to a correlation between the cardinal virtues and the appetites, in such a way as to lend credence to the view that the virtues are perfections of the capacities they inform. At the same time, the formal precision of the schema as Aquinas develops it generates difficulties. On Aquinas's own terms, there are many virtues, including some that are central to human life, which do not fit within the framework of his formal definitions of the virtues. With respect to justice, these include a set of virtues identified by Cicero as the key components of justice, including religion, piety, due re-spect, and obedience, each of which presupposes some kind of asymmetrical relationship of dependence or indebtedness (I-II 60.3; II-II 80). Aquinas certainly does not want to deny that these are virtues, and yet on his analysis, they cannot be identified with particular justice in the strict sense, since justice aims at equality.

Aquinas accordingly expands the schema of the seven virtues in accordance with an analysis of the parts of a virtue, namely, the good qualities and secondary virtues related in diverse ways to a central ideal (II-II 48; cf. II-II 80). He begins by saying that we refer to the parts of some whole in at least three senses. In one sense, we refer to the integral, that is to say, the constitutive parts of something, without which it would be badly damaged or would cease to exist—for example, the roof and walls of a house. In a second sense, we divide a general concept into the specific parts, that is to say, the distinct kinds or species, each of which exemplifies the general kind—for example, "lion" and "ox" represent two distinct exemplifications of "animal." Aquinas refers to these as the subjective parts of something. Finally, we refer to the potential parts of something, meaning its parts in the sense of its potencies, for example, the nutritive and sensitive parts of the soul.

Aquinas goes on to apply these distinctions to the virtues as follows (we are continuing with II-II 48). The integral parts of a virtue refer to those qualities or components of a virtuous habit that must necessarily work together in order to give rise to the perfect—that is to say, integral and complete—act of the virtue. The virtue of prudence, which provides the immediate context for this analysis, has eight integral parts, including such qualities as memory, understanding, and providence. The subjective parts of a virtue refer to its species, those distinct virtues each of which fully expresses the formal ideal of the virtue. In the case of prudence, these include the virtue of being prudent in one's own affairs and the different ways of being prudent with respect to others, including military prudence, political prudence, and the like. Finally, the potential parts of a virtue refer to those virtues that fit the core ideal of the central virtue in some ways but not others—for example, those qualities of sensitivity and discrimination that enable someone to exercise sound judgment in private or judicial contexts. These are not themselves species of prudence, since they are directly related to deliberative reflection rather than the final prescription of an act, which is the object of prudence. We are nonetheless justified in classifying them as potential parts of prudence because they pertain to spheres of activity that overlap with the field within which prudence operates, that is to say, reflective deliberation leading to the determinations of a course of action.

It may appear that, at this point, Aquinas goes into more analytic detail than is really necessary for his overall theory. But as we track the way in which he makes use of these distinctions throughout the *secunda secundae*, we see that these or some similar distinctions are necessary in order to preserve the flexibility that he needs to accommodate diverse kinds of ideals and considerations into one overarching moral system, without sacrificing analytic precision and the integrating power that precision brings. Throughout his analysis of the specific virtues, Aquinas builds up a system of distinct virtues and related ideals, each of which is placed in relation to the ideals of the central virtues, which are in turn connected through the architectonic virtues of justice and charity (II-II 23.8, 58.5–6). As a result, he offers a persuasive defense of the rational connection of the virtues that demonstrates the integral connections among diverse normative considerations, without reducing them to one unitary value or first principle (I-II 65.1).

An Overview of the Virtue of Justice

In this section of the chapter, I present an overview of Aquinas's account of the virtue of justice. By doing so, I hope to indicate, in a preliminary way, how his overall theory of the virtues, and especially his formal schema of the virtues as normative ideals, is applied to this central and complex virtue. At the same time, this overview is meant to serve a more basic purpose. Not everyone will be familiar with the details of Aquinas's account of justice, and it will be useful to have a summary of that account at hand as we consider what it means, on his terms, to consider justice as a perfection of the will.

Aquinas devotes sixty-five questions in the *secunda secundae* to justice, more than twice the number allotted to any other virtue. Length of treatment is not necessarily a sign of importance, but in this case Aquinas's extensive analysis of justice and the virtues connected with it at least indicates the complexity of justice as Aquinas understands it, as well as the wide range of normative considerations that are relevant to it.

As we have just observed, every virtue is defined by reference to its object, understood as a characteristic kind of action. In the case of justice, uniquely among the moral virtues, Aquinas discusses the proper object of justice first, before turning to an examination of the virtue of justice as such (II-II 57.1). Like the other scholastic theologians, he identifies the object of justice as the *jus*, the right, which can be understood in terms of what is rendered or in terms of the act itself, rendering to another that which is his right or his own (II-II 57.2). Yet Aquinas understands the right in a distinctive way. In contrast to many of his interlocutors, he does not identify it with the claims and duties arising between unequals, for example, between parent and child, or servant and master. On the contrary, justice is paradigmatically exercised through activities involving exchanges of all kinds in accordance with a norm of equality determined by some relevant criterion. Someone renders to another that which is her right through an exchange that preserves some kind of equality between them (II-II 57.1). It is not always easy to see what an equality of exchange means practically, and we will examine this ideal in more detail in due course. At this point, we should simply observe that Aquinas introduces categories drawn from contemporary theories of natural right or natural law to develop the general idea of right. Most fundamentally, he observes that the criteria for one's right, one's claim on another, can be established either through nature or through human law—in other words, through natural right or positive right. Both are binding, although as Aquinas will later observe, human law cannot override the claims of natural right (II-II 57.2, 66.7).

Turning to the virtue of justice itself, we see that Aquinas begins his exposition by defending Justinian's definition, reformulating it in the process into a proper formal definition: "Justice is a habit in accordance with which someone, through a constant and perpetual will, renders his right to each one" (II-II 58.1). Aquinas goes on to lay out the salient features of the virtue of justice along what are by now familiar lines. Because the proper object of justice, the right, implies a relation between two agents, justice is always directed toward another, and it takes shape and operates in and through the agent's actions *ad extra* (II-II 58.2). As such, it is a distinct virtue, a disposition of a specific capacity, the will (II-II 58.4). General or legal justice, which is oriented toward the common good, can be said to be a general virtue insofar as it directs the operations of the other virtues toward its own proper end, the common good of the agent's political community (II-II 58.5–6). For this reason, general justice is said to be preeminent among the moral virtues. Nonetheless, general justice is a particular virtue with its own distinctive object, and Aquinas explicitly denies that it can be identified with virtuousness in a generic sense (II-II 58.6). As for particular justice, which disposes the agent rightly toward other individuals, this is still more clearly a discrete virtue with its own limited field of operation (II-II 58.7–8). As a virtue of the will expressed through the agent's relational actions, justice does not presuppose or direct the passions, except perhaps indirectly, and correlatively, it observes a real, and not only a rational, mean (II-II 58.9–10). The object of the act of justice, in terms of which the virtue is defined, is the act of rendering to another that which is her right (II-II 58.11).

Aquinas turns next to the vice of injustice, about which he has surprisingly little to say (II-II 59). His primary concern here seems to be, again, to assert the distinctiveness of injustice as a particular kind of bad behavior, or viciousness. Thus, he begins by identifying two kinds of sins against justice, namely, illegality and the infliction of unfair loss or harm on another (II-II 59.1). While illegality, which implies contempt for the common good, can lead on to every other kind of sin, in itself this is a particular sin with its own distinctive object, and the same is even more clearly true of injustice against individuals. The habit of injustice is identified by Aquinas as a stable disposition to appropriate more to oneself by way of benefits or privileges, or less to oneself by way of burdens and suffering, than one properly should (II-II 59.2). However, it is possible to act unjustly without being vicious in this way—for example, someone under the grip of acquisitive passion might make off with someone else's car, even though he endorses, and generally observes, the principle that one should not appropriate another's property without her permission.

In the next article, Aquinas turns to a consideration of judgment, considered as an act of justice. We quickly see that he refers here to judgment in judicial contexts, and more specifically, to the action of a judge. Formally speaking, forensic judgment is not the object of the virtue of justice, but Aquinas does seem to regard it as, in our terms, a paradigmatic act:

> The judge is said, as it were, to be saying the right [*jus dicens*]. Now, the right is the object of justice, as was said above. And so judgment implies, according to the primary meaning of the term, the definition or determination of the just, or the right. Now, the fact that someone determines something well in virtuous operations characteristically results from the habit of the virtue, just as chastity rightly determines those things that pertain to chastity. And therefore judgment, which implies right determination of that which is just, characteristically pertains to justice. (II-II 60.1)

Aquinas goes on to discuss the conditions for legitimacy and the proper exercise of judicial authority in some detail, with a clear eye to offering practical guidance to those involved in adjudication and their advisers (II-II 60.2–6). We might take this approach for granted, but Aquinas is distinctive, if not unique, among the theologians of his time with respect to the attention that he gives to judicial proceedings and what we might call ideals of proper legality. As we will see, this approach is a characteristic and significant element of his overall account of justice.

In the next question, Aquinas takes up Aristotle's distinction between distributive and commutative justice, which he analyzes as two species of particular justice (II-II 61.1).[55] Particular justice, as we know, is characteristically directed toward individuals, not toward the common good, but distributive justice does presuppose some relation with the community, since it pertains to the fair allocation of honors, rewards, shared benefits, punishments, burdens, and the like. Nonetheless, Aquinas explicitly says that distributive justice pertains directly to relations with individuals, that is to say, the recipients of whatever is being distributed; as such, it is a species of particular rather than general justice (II-II 61.1 *ad* 4). Commutative justice pertains to individuals' relations to one another as individuals, not as representatives or as members of a community. It is paradigmatically identified with buying and selling, but Aquinas extends it to include every kind of interaction between individuals through an expansive interpretation of exchange. Aquinas attempts to spell out the norms of equality proper to distributive and commutative justice by way of Aristotle's torturous distinction between geometric and arithmetic proportion (II-II 61.2). This line of analysis can go only so far, and Aquinas soon drops it. We can see the full significance of distributive and commutative justice for his overall account only when we turn to his identification of the proper acts of these virtues, and especially, the contrary sins.

Aquinas identifies restitution as the paradigmatic act of commutative justice, taking restitution in such a way as to include both the return of what has been voluntarily handed over and compensation for unjust appropriations of all kinds (II-II 62). As for distributive justice, he does not focus on any one paradigmatic act but devotes considerable attention to the characteristic sin against distributive justice, namely, the reception of persons, defined as the conferral of some benefit or burden for extraneous reasons (II-II 63). Both of these questions reflect exigent practical and pastoral problems, which Aquinas examines in some detail. Yet by focusing on these in this way, he also provides us with further paradigms for justice, directly or by way of comparison to a characteristic sin against justice. As such, these offer an entrée into understanding how Aquinas and his interlocutors would have understood justice as a practical ideal, embedded in the practices of his society.

---

55. For Aristotle's distinctions, see the *Nicomachean Ethics*, 5.3–5, 95–103, in Bartlett/Collins. Aquinas departs from Aristotle's treatment of the modes of equality in significant ways, but it is not clear whether he does so intentionally. For details, see Jeffrey Hause, "Aquinas on Aristotelian Justice: Defender, Destroyer, Subverter, or Surveyor?" in *Aquinas and the Nicomachean Ethics*, 146–64.

However, the most telling aspect of Aquinas's treatment of the sins against commutative justice is yet to come. Aquinas includes within this category every kind of exchange between individuals that in itself—that is to say, as part of the defining structure of the act—involves the infliction of some kind of unjustified harm or loss (II-II 64 intro.). Thus, the sins against commutative justice include murder, theft, adultery, and other kinds of transgressions against someone else's person, property, or familial ties. These also include unjustified harms through speech, in both judicial and extrajudicial contexts, and unfairness in voluntary transactions, including various forms of fraud, cheating, and usury. It is not immediately obvious why these should all count as unfair, in the sense of depriving someone of that which is hers or taking for oneself something that is not one's own. This description does seem to apply to such sins as theft or fraud, but it is by no means so clear that it applies to direct injuries to the person or to the act of damaging another's reputation through gossip or the like. It seems that we are stretching a point to describe these kinds of actions as transactions; while the victim clearly loses something, it is not always clear that the perpetrator gains at the victim's expense. Nonetheless, as we will see, Aquinas interprets this claim in such a way as to tie central norms of maleficence to an expansive ideal of equality, understood as a kind of natural equality of status. This interpretation helps to explain why Aquinas regards sins of maleficence as variants of unfair exchange—over and above any harm or loss that the victim may suffer, she also suffers a loss of status, being placed at the mercy of another in some way, while the perpetrator aggrandizes himself at her expense.

Aquinas's extended discussion of the sins against commutative justice concludes his treatment of the species of justice. Before moving on, it is worth noting that throughout these sections, he focuses almost exclusively on particular justice, that is to say, justice as it pertains to interactions with individuals. He says very little in these questions about the demands of general or legal justice, and while distributive justice clearly presupposes a social context, this virtue is most directly concerned with the claims that the individual can make on the community, and especially, on those acting as agents on its behalf. Aquinas says very little about the individual's specific obligations to the community in this context, although he does address this question briefly at other points in the *secunda secundae*. Given the importance that Aquinas gives to general justice and his insistence that this too is a particular virtue with its own proper object, we would expect him to say a great deal more about it. We cannot follow up this point now, but we will return to it in a subsequent chapter.

Aquinas turns next to the integral parts of justice, those qualities or actions that are jointly necessary to the full expression of the virtue (II-II 79.1). These he identifies as to do good and avoid evil. This summary presents us with another puzzle, because this is nothing other than the first principle of practical reason, which serves as the fundamental principle for all virtue. Yet, as Aquinas himself points out, general and particular justice are both specific virtues, implying an orientation toward delimited kinds of goods and an aversion from definite kinds of evils.

In fact, that is just what "do good and avoid evil" does imply in this context. After noting that this principle, generally understood, does apply to all virtue, Aquinas goes on to explain that it is qualified with respect to justice. Particular justice aims at the good, formally understood as that which is due to another, and avoids evil, understood as injury to another; and general justice aims at the obligatory good in relation to the common good and avoids the contrary (II-II 79.1). Thus, Aquinas appears to regard the integral parts of justice as a specification of the first principle of practical reason—more limited in scope, and yet perhaps similarly foundational to the processes of practical reason. This point, too, will call for further examination.

Aquinas turns finally to the potential parts of justice, the virtues that, as he says, fall short of the perfect expression of the ideal of justice in some way (II-II 80). As he himself notes, this language can be misleading—the virtues associated with justice are no less important or praiseworthy than justice itself, and indeed one of them, the virtue of religion, is said to be a higher virtue than justice. The deficiency in question is a logical, rather than a normative, lack—that is, these virtues do not fit the full definition of justice in some way or another. Either they do not aim at equality in exchanges, or they do not imply a relation of strict obligation to another. They are nonetheless associated with justice because they too are immediately concerned with our relations to one another.

The virtues of deference, obedience, and due respect, which Aquinas's interlocutors take to be central to justice as such, appear now in his account of justice as virtues annexed to justice. These virtues, as Aquinas explains, share the same field of operation as strict justice—that is to say, they dispose the agent well with respect to some aspect of her relations to others. However, they fall short of what he calls perfect justice in one of two ways. Either they do not aim at an equality of exchange, because the relation is such as to render equality impossible or inappropriate, or else they do not presuppose strict obligations. Aquinas follows Cicero in identifying those social virtues that do not aim at equality, namely, religion, piety, gratitude,

due respect, and obedience. The virtues that do not presuppose strict obligation are drawn partly from Cicero, partly from Macrobius and others,
and include amiability, truthfulness, vindication, and liberality. Again, we
will examine some of these more closely in due course. At this point, we
should simply again note how the ideal of equality has shaped Aquinas's
reading of his sources. Together with his interlocutors, he acknowledges
that such qualities as a disposition toward religious observance and piety
toward one's elders are genuine virtues, without which human life would
be diminished or rendered impossible. The virtue of religion can be said to
be preeminent among the moral virtues, since it is oriented toward honoring God (II-II 81.6).[56] Nonetheless, all these virtues fall short of the ideal of
justice, insofar as they do not aim at establishing equality between those
involved in transactions with one another. Some of them may represent
higher ideals than justice itself, but it is justice—or more exactly legal and
particular justice working in tandem—that determines the overall shape of
morality as Aquinas understands it.

Aquinas concludes the treatise on justice by correlating the virtue of justice with two elements of his overall normative framework that do presuppose Christian revelation and the life of grace, in accordance with the plan
set forth in the prologue to the *secunda secundae*. Like almost every other
theological or cardinal virtue, justice is correlated with one of the seven gifts
of the Holy Spirit, and with a set of precepts taken from divine, that is to
say, scriptural, law. The gift correlated with justice is piety, which, Aquinas
explains, is not the virtue of piety annexed to justice but a distinctive quality
of readiness to acknowledge God as one's father (II-II 121.1). As we might
expect, the scriptural precepts that Aquinas identifies as most closely correlated with justice are the precepts of the Decalogue, which he represents
elsewhere as paradigmatically linked to justice, even though they pertain in
some way to all the virtues (II-II 122). It is tempting to dismiss these texts as
arcana, but they reflect a carefully thought out element of Aquinas's overall
synthetic program. We cannot fully understand justice as Aquinas saw it,
as a contextualized ideal expressed in terms of actual beliefs and practices,
unless we take account of this theological context.

---

56. However, religion is not the highest virtue absolutely considered, because it is not
oriented directly toward union with God—its proper object is the act of paying homage to
God as the creator and governor of the universe (II-II 81.3). It is thus distinguished from the
theological virtues, faith, hope and love, which unite the human person directly to the triune
God (II-II 81.5).

Reason, Revelation, and Justice

This brings us to one final point that needs to be addressed before we turn to Aquinas's account of justice, seen as a perfection of the will. So far, I have focused on the fundamental rational structure and the philosophical implications of Aquinas's theory of the virtues. But of course Aquinas did not write a *summa philosophiae* but rather a *summa theologiae*. Given this focus, can we legitimately consider Aquinas's theory of virtue, or any other aspect of his complex theory, from a philosophical standpoint? To what extent does his moral theory presuppose or depend upon specific Christian beliefs, rather than on considerations and forms of argument open, in principle at least, to all?

Until recently, most interpreters of Aquinas would have agreed that his fundamental theory of virtue rests on general rational considerations and does not depend on specifically theological claims for its justification or its persuasive power. According to one influential line of interpretation, associated with Ralph McInerny among others, Aquinas's theory of virtue is essentially dependent on Aristotle's theory. According to the alternative, widely influential interpretation defended by Germain Grisez and John Finnis, Aquinas holds that moral norms are dependent on basic goods and modes of responsibility that are rationally apprehended through the operations of practical reason. On this view, morality does not depend on either theological or metaphysical presuppositions. More recently, and partially in response to these lines of interpretation, a number of scholars have defended the claim that Aquinas's account of the virtues, or some other aspect of morality as he understands it, is derived from specifically theological claims, or at least presupposes a theological context in some substantive way.[57]

---

57. These controversies have generated a considerable literature, and what follows is only a sampling. For a good example of Ralph McInerny's approach, see *Ethica Thomistica: The Moral Philosophy of Thomas Aquinas*, rev. ed. (Washington, DC: Catholic University of America Press, 1997; originally, 1982), 12–34. Kevin Flannery takes a similar view, qualified by elements of the theory of practical reasoning developed by Germain Grisez, John Finnis, and their associates; see *Acts amid Precepts* (Washington, DC: Catholic University of America Press, 2001). John Finnis offers an extended exposition and defense of his reading of Aquinas's moral and legal theory in *Aquinas* (Oxford: Oxford University Press, 1998); see esp. 56–102. For a recent, widely influential interpretation of Aquinas that reads him as purely theological, at least in his late works, see Eugene Rogers, *Thomas Aquinas and Karl Barth: Sacred Doctrine and the Natural Knowledge of God* (Notre Dame: University of Notre Dame Press, 1995). Finally, Paul O'Grady offers a very helpful discussion of this and other recent attempts to argue that Aquinas's mature arguments are purely theological in character, in "Philosophical Theology

These theological critiques of earlier, more philosophically focused interpretations of Aquinas offer a salutary corrective to earlier attempts to draw a sharp line between Aquinas's supposedly pure philosophy and his theological aims and convictions. Aquinas, like everyone else, presupposes a world and a way of life in his critical reflections. For him, the central doctrines of Christianity express the deepest realities, and any fully adequate philosophical theory, on any subject whatever, will inevitably reflect those realities in some way. At the same time, however, he also distinguishes between reason and revelation as two disparate starting points for intellectual reflection, and similarly, he distinguishes between nature and grace as two disparate principles of virtue and action (I 1.1–2; I-II 109.1–2, 4). These distinctions imply a chastened view of reason and nature, which at their best are limited, lesser principles, in comparison to revelation and grace. At the same time, however, Aquinas develops these distinctions in such a way as to safeguard the relative integrity and independence of reason and nature, and to affirm their value as aspects of created existence. Only in this way can we do full justice to the integrity and goodness of God's creation or take account of the ways in which the transformative principle of grace presupposes and preserves the natural principles of virtue inherent in human nature.[58]

Aquinas's overall theological commitments are reflected in his use of sources and his critical orientation toward these sources. As we would expect, he regards Scripture as the supremely authoritative and inerrant word of God, which as such provides the final touchstone for the interpretation of every other text (I 1.8). At the same time, he also regards a wide range of other authors, from pre-Christian antiquity to early Christianity, as being in some respects authoritative. Scripture provides the final interpretative key for understanding these texts, but by the same token, the interpretation of Scripture is shaped by assumptions about the ultimate consistency between scriptural teachings and our best traditional and philosophical judgments.[59]

---

and Analytical Philosophy in Aquinas," in *The Theology of Thomas Aquinas*, ed. Rik van Nieuwenhove and Joseph Wawrykow (Notre Dame: University of Notre Dame Press, 2005), 416–43.

58. I defend these claims in more detail in *Nature as Reason*, 378–400. O'Grady similarly argues, with considerable textual support, that Aquinas defends the possibility of a limited but genuine natural knowledge of God, apart from revelation, throughout his work; see "Philosophical Theology and Analytic Philosophy in Aquinas," 423–29.

59. M. D. Chenu provides an invaluable overview of Aquinas's thought, seen in the context of scholastic presuppositions and methods of working, in *Toward Understanding St. Thomas*, trans. Albert M. Landry and Dominic Hughes (Chicago: Henry Regnery, 1964), see esp. 126–202. My reading of Aquinas's presuppositions and his use of sources has also been

Given his overall orientation, we should not be surprised to find that Aquinas draws extensively on pre-Christian authors, including Cicero and the Roman jurists, as well as Aristotle, in developing his account of justice. He clearly takes these authors seriously as perceptive commentators on justice and right, and Aristotle in particular provides him with the broad outlines of his analysis of justice as a virtue. He interprets and engages them on their own terms as reliable authorities, within limits and with qualifications, for moral analysis.

In his irenic stance toward his authorities, Aquinas is very much a man of his time, that is to say, a scholastic engaged in intensive, collaborative, and textually oriented forms of inquiry, aimed toward bringing order and practical expression to the wisdom that a generous God has offered to all humanity. At the same time, his approach is also consonant with the substantive account of justice that he develops. On his account, the ideals of justice and the tenets of natural right are articulated and confirmed both scripturally and in classical texts, but they do not fundamentally depend on either revelation or classical traditions. As we have seen, he argues that the precepts of justice are grounded in the first principle of practical reason, as it operates in matters pertaining to the agent's relations to others. Correlatively, he draws on the tools of philosophical analysis in order to identify the claims that individuals have on one another and on the community, and to spell out the practical implications of these claims. He does not derive the claims of justice from distinctively Christian doctrines, nor does he say that only Christians are capable of grasping and carrying out what justice demands. Given his overall theological commitments to the integrity of creation and the value of diverse traditions, we would not expect him to do so. Moreover, a distinctively theological analysis of this kind would be especially inappropriate in this context. Justice is the highest and most comprehensive connatural virtue pertaining to individuals' relationships with one another and with their community. It presupposes that all men and women stand in a relation of fundamental equality, each exercising, and responding to, claims of natural right. Understood in these terms, the claims intrinsic to justice cannot depend on special knowledge or insight, accessible only to some members of the community, nor can they be restricted in scope to believers or to some other delimited group of people. The obligations of charity or religion do not supersede the demands of natural right, and Christians are bound by natural right in their dealings with non-Christians (II-II 10.10,12, 104.6).

---

shaped by R. W. Southern, *Scholastic Humanism and the Unification of Europe*, vol. 1 (Oxford: Blackwell, 1995), 15–133.

Not only do the claims of justice apply impartially to believers and nonbelievers, they also apply within the Christian community itself. Grace perfects nature, as Aquinas frequently reminds us, and the higher demands of charity do not set aside the obligations of justice. He makes this point very clearly in the context of discussing the order of love in charity, that is to say, the possibility that charity in itself might demand a greater love for some than for others (II-II 26.6–13). In discussing this question, he refers to Augustine's claim that charity calls for a love for neighbor that is in principle equal, even though we will necessarily express this love more directly and fully toward those who are closest to us. Aquinas sets this claim aside through a pointed reinterpretation of Augustine's text. He argues, to the contrary, that we are obliged by charity to love some more than others, in accordance with the differential obligations of honor, gratitude, and care that we owe to those who are bound to us by familial or personal ties. As he explains, "The disposition of charity, which is an inclination of grace, is no less ordered than natural appetite, which is an inclination of nature, for each inclination proceeds from divine wisdom" (II-II 26.6). Charity expands and transforms the claims of natural right, but it does not set them aside, much less lead to their transgression.

At the same time, it is undeniably true that Aquinas thinks of justice in distinctively scriptural and theological terms. We have just observed that he identifies the basic precepts of justice with the Decalogue, and as we will see, he formulates the first principle of practical reason as it operates in relation to others in terms of the twofold commandment to love God and neighbor. His paradigms for just and equitable relations are drawn in part from scriptural ideals of restraint and mutual deference. He asserts that the demands of justice are also demands of charity, with the implication that someone who acts unjustly toward another is guilty of mortal sin (II-II 59.4). This line of argument presupposes that justice sets parameters on charity, but it also implies that Aquinas's overarching convictions about charity have shaped his overall account of natural right and justice. At the very least, he cannot interpret the claims of right in such a way as to render these inconsistent with the imperatives of charity, which include but go beyond the claims of justice.

Furthermore, Aquinas's presuppositions about charity and its relation to justice reflect a wider conception of human nature, its capacities and its normative claims, that has clearly been shaped by his theology, even though it is not derived exclusively from that theology. On Aquinas's account, charity is most fundamentally a kind of friendship with God, implying a mutual, personal intimacy (II-II 23.1). This mutuality goes beyond the capacities of human nature and can come about only through the transformation of divine grace, through which the rational creature is given the capacity to know and love God directly, in God's inmost personal reality (II-II 23.3; cf. I 12.13; I-II 109.1,3). God's bestowal of grace, as Aquinas understands it, is not equivalent to the conferral of worth on each individual that Wolterstorff postulates, if only because God does not extend saving grace to everyone (I 23.1). Nonetheless, Aquinas's doctrine of grace and his account of charity are relevant to his overall conception of morality, because taken together, they imply that each man and woman is potentially capable of the highest and best kind of created existence. This potential can be actualized only through God's initiative, but the claim that it exists at all implies a strong sense of the intrinsic dignity and value of each individual.[60]

At the same time, Aquinas does not say that we can establish or know about the value of individual men and women only through reflection on charity, which on his terms would presuppose revelation. On the contrary, he claims that the fundamental precepts of justice are grounded in an innate knowledge of the value and the normative claims of individual human existence, as we will see. He formulates the first principle and the precepts of justice in scriptural terms, but he does not derive these from scriptural claims, nor does he say that the demands of justice can be grasped only through revelation. Men and women are capable of grasping the fundamental normative claims of human nature, no matter what their theological or other presuppositions may be. Revelation confirms the value of the individual, it gives salience to the claims of others, and it provides a language for formulating basic moral principles in such a way as to underscore the link between justice and charity. For precisely these reasons, Aquinas's theological construal of human nature offers a way of thinking about and valuing human existence that makes sense of a wide range of commonly held moral intuitions in a persuasive way.

Aquinas would therefore expect wide agreement with respect to the starting points for moral reflection, and we have some reason to think that he is right about this expectation. To a really remarkable extent, contemporary

60. Although it would go beyond the scope of this project to pursue the point, the same observation would apply to Aquinas's doctrine of the incarnation. For a good introduction to this doctrine, seen in relation to Aquinas's conception of human nature, see Joseph Wawrykow, "Hypostatic Union," and Paul Gondreau, "The Humanity of Christ, the Incarnate Word," in *The Theology of Thomas Aquinas*, 192–221 and 222–51, respectively. For an excellent overview of Aquinas's teachings on grace, see Joseph Wawrykow, *God's Grace and Human Action: "Merit" in the Theology of Thomas Aquinas* (Notre Dame: University of Notre Dame Press, 1995), 60–259.

moral and political philosophers agree on the fundamental and irreducible value of the human individual, which is tied in complex ways to human capacities for moral discernment and autonomous, self-determining activity. Ronald Dworkin captures the main points of this consensus in spelling out two principles of ethical individualism: "The first is the principle of equal importance: it is important, from an objective point of view, that human lives be successful rather than wasted, and this is equally important, from that objective point of view, for each human life. The second is the principle of special responsibility: Though we must all recognize the equal objective importance of the success of a human life, one person has a special and final responsibility for that success—the person whose life it is."[61] Elsewhere, he refers to the sacredness of human life, a sense of irreducible value that, as such, cannot be defended discursively. Similarly, near the beginning of *Self-Constitution*, Christine Korsgaard claims that the distinctively human form of life is "the life of rational activity. Rational activity, as I have already suggested, is essentially a form of self-conscious activity, and it is this that leads to the construction of personal activity." In other words, "We constitute our own identities in the course of action"; as she goes on to argue, this process of self-constitution is the basis for normative judgments.[62] For a third example, consider Martha Nussbaum's interpretation of the capabilities approach to understanding human well-being: "The core idea is that of the human being as a dignified free being who shapes his or her own life in cooperation and reciprocity with others, rather than being passively shaped or pushed around by the world in the manner of a 'flock' or 'herd' animal. A life that is really human is one that is shaped throughout by these human powers of practical reason and sociability."[63] Furthermore, "this must be understood as a *freestanding moral idea*, not one that relies on a particular metaphysical or teleological view."[64]

I have quoted these examples at some length in order to make the point that Aquinas's central commitments to the value of individual lives and the normative significance of rational freedom and self-determining action are by no means distinctive to him, nor do they represent any obvious sectarian bias. When Dworkin speaks of the sacredness of human life or Nussbaum refers to a freestanding moral intuition, Aquinas would readily agree, even

61. Dworkin, *Sovereign Virtue*, 5.
62. Both quotations are taken from Korsgaard, *Self-Constitution*, 42.
63. Martha C. Nussbaum, *Women and Human Development: The Capabilities Approach* (Cambridge: Cambridge University Press, 2000), 71–72.
64. Nussbaum, *Women and Human Development*, 83, emphasis in the original.

though he would express the core intuition in another way. He would say that the philosophers just cited, together with many others, are offering sophisticated articulations of a fundamental truth that each man and woman is valuable in a way comparable to the agent's own value, worthy of a love that is comparable to the agent's own self-love. We will return in chapter 3 to a further examination of these claims. For now, the critical point is that Aquinas does not say that the fundamental principles of justice or morality depend on any kind of Christian revelation. These principles can be interpreted in theological terms as reflecting the wisdom and goodness of God's creation, and they are centrally relevant to theology because they are appropriated, as it were, by the virtue of charity. Yet Aquinas also recognizes that they can be grasped and respected by others, men and women of any religion or none, and as such, they can provide a framework for common moral reflection and a shared way of life.

We may still wonder whether Aquinas and our own contemporaries are right to say that we intuitively grasp fundamental moral principles in the way indicated. Might it not be the case that these supposedly intuitive principles reflect a distinctively Western rationalism and individualism? Or more immediately, that they reflect allegiance to shared sources, including especially Aristotle and, for our own contemporaries, Kant? Or it may be that this moral vision is actually theological after all, reflecting a long-standing and now-obscured tradition of the sacredness of the individual, understood in its full theological sense. These are difficult questions, and fortunately we do not need to resolve them definitively in order to move forward. I will later defend Aquinas's claim that the first principle of justice is foundational in the way that he claims. But even if that is not the case, at the very least it is clear that Aquinas and our own contemporaries share a great deal, enough to allow for fruitful comparisons.

To those who would object to the project of trying to develop Aquinas's insights in terms of generally persuasive arguments, I would say only that this is what Aquinas himself does. My aims in doing so are essentially the same as Aquinas's own aims in his scholarly and discursive work, namely, to understand a key thinker more fully and to draw out the implications of his moral theory for our own reflections on the moral life.

CHAPTER 2

Virtues and Vices of the Will

According to Aquinas, justice is a virtue of the will. Given his overall theory of virtue, this claim implies that justice is a habit of the will, through which the agent is disposed to respect the due claims of others and to choose and act accordingly. By implication, justice is a perfection, that is to say, a full and appropriate development of the capacity of the will. The habit of justice perfects the will itself by orienting it toward one characteristic set of desires out of many other options, and it perfects the agent by disposing her to choose and act in accordance with the claims of right.

All this being said, we would expect Aquinas's analysis of the will to tell us something about the virtue of justice. After all, if justice is a perfection of the will, then we should be able to trace some kind of connection between the will in its undeveloped or immature state and the will as it is informed by the virtue of justice. This hypothesis initially motivated this project, and one of the aims of this book is to see just how far, and in what ways, an analysis of the will contributes to our understanding of justice as a virtue and a moral ideal. At the same time, the claim that justice is a perfection of the will must be carefully qualified if we are to avoid misrepresenting Aquinas's thought. Aquinas is neither the first nor the last to claim that justice is a kind of perfection of the soul or the capacity for rational autonomy, and it is important at the outset to distinguish his approach from other common construals of this claim.

For Plato and his followers, justice as a personal virtue consists of a right ordering of the capacities of the soul, through which desires are brought under the control of reason.[1] Augustine holds that the capacities of the soul are

1. Although Plato's conception of justice as a personal and social virtue has been much debated, it seems clear that, for him, justice is essentially characterized by harmony among

perfected through charity, which directs all the desires and activities of the agent toward the ultimate end of union with God. Justice, like every other virtue, is nothing other than charity, expressed in this case through obedience to God and right rule over those things subject to human agency. To take a contemporary example, Christine Korsgaard appropriates Plato's ideal of the soul as a well-ordered city as a starting point for what she describes as the constitutional model of agency. On this account, the agent attains unity through processes of rational deliberation and self-governance, in which justice serves to regulate and harmonize particular drives in accordance with the deliberations of reason.[2] In each instance, justice or a comparable virtue can be said to perfect the soul or the agent's rational powers in a straightforward way, by bringing order to the diverse elements of the agent's psychic constitution or safeguarding his integrity as a rational agent.

Aquinas, in contrast, claims that justice perfects the soul by bringing it into right relation with other agents, who are external to the agent's own soul. The point of justice, so to speak, is not to promote the agent's own inner harmony or personal integrity but, rather, to dispose her to act rightly toward others. Aquinas makes this point in the course of explaining why justice and other similar virtues are necessary to the will.

> Since the object of the will is the good of reason proportionate to the will (as has been said), the will does not need to be perfected by virtue with respect to this object. But if a good confronts the individual who is exercising the will which goes beyond what is proportionate to the one willing, either with respect to the whole of humankind, such as divine good, which transcends the limits of human nature, or with respect to the individual, as the good of the neighbor, at that point, the will needs virtue. And therefore those sorts of virtues that orient the desire of the human person to God or to the neighbor are in the will as their subject, such as charity, justice, and other virtues of this kind. (I-II 56.6)

---

the disparate elements of the soul and the commonwealth. For helpful accounts of his view, seen in relation to that of other classical philosophers, see Michael Slote, "Justice as a Virtue," in *The Stanford Encyclopedia of Philosophy*, ed. Edward N. Zalta, July 22, 2014, http://plato .stanford.edu/archives/fall2014/entries/justice-virtue, and Julia Annas, *Platonic Ethics, Old and New* (Ithaca, NY: Cornell University Press, 1999), 72–95. For Augustine's remarks on justice and charity, see John Rist, *Augustine: Ancient Thought Baptized* (Cambridge: Cambridge University Press, 1994), 160–61.

2. Christine M. Korsgaard, *Self-Constitution: Agency, Identity, and Integrity* (Oxford: Oxford University Press, 2009), 133–58.

The critical point here is that justice perfects the will by placing it in right relation to something or someone distinct from, and in that sense external to, both the will itself and the agent whose will it is. We might be tempted to think that the right relations established through justice are in some way necessary for the proper functioning or integrity or full rational freedom of the will, but Aquinas does not make any of these claims. As Candace Vogler rightly notes, Aquinas understands the operations of practical reason at the level of particular choices in instrumental terms, and immoral choices are not necessarily irrational in these terms.[3] By the same token, the will can be subject to vicious habits as well as virtues, and these vices of the will function in such a way as to bring order and force to the agent's inclinations, thus enabling her to act promptly and effectively in pursuit of her preferred ends. Thus, the vices of the will do not undermine the rational integrity and freedom of the agent, although they dispose her to wicked desires and choices.

Vogler concludes that, since immoral acts and dispositions do not necessarily violate the canons of practical rationality or undermine the agent's rational freedom, therefore these kinds of acts and dispositions can be condemned only on theological grounds.[4] But as we noted in the previous chapter, this is not what Aquinas intends to say. Ideals and norms of justice are grounded in the objective normative claims of others, and the virtue of justice perfects the soul by disposing it to respect these claims, thus bringing it into right relations with others. Of course, a disposition toward right relations with others is good by definition, and a right relationship can plausibly be construed as good for those involved. If this is the way in which Aquinas understands perfection, it may be hard to disagree with his claim that justice perfects the will, but by the same token, we may well wonder whether his account of justice offers anything of contemporary interest. However, when we place Aquinas's remarks in the context of his overall theory of the virtues and his account of the will, they imply a more complex and interesting set of claims.

The key point to keep in mind is that justice, like every other virtue, represents a development of natural capacities that are intrinsically oriented toward the immediate well-being or the overall good of the agent (I-II 52.1, 63.1). While Aquinas does not claim that rational agency requires justice, he is committed to the claim that justice represents an appropriate and salutary development of the agent's capacities for volition and choice, in such a

---

3. See Candace Vogler, *Reasonably Vicious* (Cambridge, MA: Harvard University Press, 2002), 34–41 and 66–73.

4. Vogler, *Reasonably Vicious*, 34–41.

way as to enhance rather than undermine the agent's freedom. By the same token, if justice is a perfection of a natural capacity, then we would expect that, at a minimum, men and women would be spontaneously attracted to justice as something naturally admirable and desirable. A plausible account of justice developed along these lines would therefore need to bring out the attractiveness of the virtue in order to show that its goodness is not simply stipulative but something that is confirmed by experience and intuition.

More generally, the claim that justice is a perfection of the will implies that, to some extent at least, the distinctive features of the virtue of justice can be explained by reference to some aspect of the structures and functions of the will. This line of inquiry need not imply that an account of the will can explain every aspect of justice, but it does imply that such an account will illuminate key aspects of justice in significant ways. By the same token, we should not expect to derive a full theory of justice from a theory of the will. As we observed in the last chapter, Aquinas's treatment of the virtues as normative ideals takes its starting point from paradigmatic instances of the virtue and general moral intuitions, which are then developed and placed into systematic order through critical, theoretically informed analysis. He follows this approach with justice, as with every other virtue. To a very considerable extent, his overall account of justice draws on his contemporaries' views, as well as his sources. But on closer examination, it is apparent that he interprets these starting points within the framework set by his theory of the will, and at critical points, his interpretation of justice is determined by that theory.

These claims can be substantiated only through a closer examination of Aquinas's account of justice as a normative ideal, considered in the light of his theory of the will. In the next two chapters, we will look more closely at what Aquinas identifies as the hallmarks of justice, properly so called, namely, its connection with equality and its association with stringent precepts. Each of these characteristics is drawn from Aquinas's contemporaries or his sources, and yet each, in complex and distinctive ways, has been interpreted in such a way as to take account of some aspect of the will. In order to pursue this line of thought, it will be necessary first to present Aquinas's theory of the will, which is the purpose of this chapter.

Over the course of the *Summa theologiae*, Aquinas considers the will from two interrelated yet distinct perspectives: as a kind of natural appetite, and as the principle of the voluntary character of human actions.[5] In the first

---

5. As we will see further on, the will is a natural appetite in one sense but not in another. Generally, Aquinas identifies natural appetite with the inclinations of nonsentient creatures,

section of this chapter, we will accordingly consider the will as an appetite, and in the second, we will focus on the will as the originating principle of human actions, considered as voluntary. This latter consideration will bring us to the much-debated question of the freedom of the will, seen in relation to the intellect and to our capacities for choice and action. Aquinas's final position on the freedom of the will implies a more complex account of the relation between volition and choice than he explicitly develops. This more complex account, in turn, provides a starting point for explaining how the will can be said to develop virtuous and vicious habits, which will be the focus of the third section. Aquinas's somewhat terse remarks suggest that the habits of the will emerge out of a process that integrates the general stance of the will with particular choices, in such a way as to preserve both the freedom and the rationality of the will. Finally, in the last section we will take a first look at what it might mean to construe justice as a perfection of the will, keeping in mind that for Aquinas, a disposition toward justice is a necessary component, but by no means the only component, of a well-disposed will.

The Will as a Causal Principle

Human actions are appropriately subject to admiration or reproach, praise or blame, reward or punishment. They place the agent in relation to others and to her community, as one who merits the respect due to an upright individual, or as someone who is guilty, deserving reproach. These kinds of normative evaluations presuppose that human acts are voluntary, reflecting the agent's own free judgment in some distinctive way. These at any rate are the generally accepted starting points for the extensive discussions of voluntariness, freedom, and choice that emerged in the late eleventh century and continued well beyond Aquinas's lifetime.[6] Initially, these discussions were not framed in terms of the freedom of the will. The early scholastics focused on the scriptural and Augustinian motif of *liberum arbitrium*, free

---

which operate without any kind of awareness at all. However, in another sense the will is a natural appetite—that is to say, it is an appetite of a creature of a certain kind, structured in accordance with the needs and desires natural to that kind of creature. These distinctions are set out in I-II 10.1 *ad* 1.

6. Odon Lottin offers an exhaustive account of the development of scholastic theories of free judgment, freedom, and the will in "Libre arbitre et liberté depuis saint Anselme jusqu'à la fin du XIIIe siècle," in *Psychologie et morale aux XIIe et XIIIe siècles*, vol. 1 (Louvain: Abbaye du Mont César, 1942), 11–389. For our purposes, the most relevant sections are 11–280 and 382–89.

judgment, understood as a capacity for independent judgment leading to free choice, as the most appropriate way to understand voluntariness. In the early thirteenth century, theologians began to associate the quality of voluntariness with *voluntas*, the will, understood as a general capacity for freedom correlated with free judgment. Nonetheless, scholastic analysis remained focused on free judgment, which is regarded as the proximate principle of the voluntary quality of human actions. The will was generally discussed briefly, as a kind of afterthought.

Aquinas is well aware of the importance of normative evaluations, and he agrees with his interlocutors that these presuppose that human actions are voluntary (I 83.1; I-II 6.1). He considers the will to be the ultimate principle of voluntariness, and he devotes considerable attention to the moral significance of its operations. At the same time, he also considers the will from another perspective, placing it in the wider context set by his overall analysis of causality, desire, and goal-directed operation. Fundamentally, the will is an appetite, that is to say, a capacity for desire, which operates through inclinations toward suitable objects (I 80.1). It is a distinctive kind of appetite, unique to rational and intellectual creatures, and it enables the agent to act with an unparalleled degree of independence and self-determination. Nonetheless, it represents one example of what for Aquinas is a general category, exemplified at every level of created existence.

In order to see what Aquinas is getting at here, we need to return to his overall account of existence, form, goodness, and perfection. As we saw in the first chapter, for Aquinas these are mutually implicating ways of analyzing what it means to exist and to operate as a creature of a specific kind. As is well known, Aquinas holds that existence itself is the most fundamental metaphysical category (I 3.4, 5.2). As Aquinas understands it, the created world is made up of individuals interacting with one another in such a way as to sustain an orderly cosmos of causal interactions. Aquinas, like Aristotle before him, does not believe that the forms of existence exemplified by these individuals have any kind of independent reality, nor do such general qualities as goodness and perfection (I 15.1, 44.3). At the same time, individuals are not bare particulars, either. They exist over time and move through a trajectory of development, full expression or maturity, and decay, while remaining the same individual. We naturally think of them as entities with potentials that have not yet been actualized, or as lacking abilities and characteristics that they once had. While all the entities we know through experience are material, we cannot know them as sheer inert lumps; rather, they exist in and through dynamic operations, which unfold over time in intelligible ways.

Aquinas expresses the diachronic and dynamic features of existence through traditional metaphysical conceptions of form, causality, goodness, and perfection. Understood in these terms, every individual substance is a particular instantiation of a general kind of existence, and as such it exists in accordance with dynamic principles of development and operation characteristic of the specific kind of thing that it is. These principles are identified in Aristotelian terms as its form, corresponding to the ideal type identified with its formal cause (I 5.1; cf. I-II 85.4). The form is thus not an independently existing element within something's make-up, but the intelligible principles expressed in and through its operations, through which this thing can be understood to be something of this or that kind. Correlatively, because these characteristic operations are directed to sustaining a form of existence, they are goal-directed and appropriately analyzed in teleological terms. Appealing to Aristotle's dictum that "the good is that which all desire," Aquinas argues that, since everything can be said to seek or desire its own existence, therefore the fundamental categories of existence and goodness are mutually implicating (I 5.1–2). Existence is good in itself, and goodness is correlated with full existence, or actuality. Goodness in the fullest and most unqualified sense is identified with perfection, which in turn implies the full actualization of something's specific form:

> Each thing is said to be good insofar as it is perfect, for this is desirable, as was said above. Now perfection is said of that to which nothing is lacking, in accordance with the mode of its perfection. And since each thing is that which it is through its form, and the form presupposes certain things, and certain things necessarily follow from it, thus, in order for something to be perfect and good, it is necessary that it have form, and those things that are preconditions to it, and those things that follow from it. (I 5.5)

Aquinas goes on to say, "An inclination to the end proceeds from the form, either to action, or to something of this kind, for everything, insofar as it is in act, acts and moves to that which is appropriate to it in accordance with its form" (I 5.5). Thus, the formal cause of the substance, that is to say, the intelligible principles of existence that characterize it, can also be construed as its final cause, the purpose toward which its operations are directed (cf. I 44.4). The creature's goal-directed operations are elicited through inclinations, which prompt some kind of movement toward whatever can be regarded as sustaining or completing the creature in accordance with the potential of its form of existence. An appetite is nothing other than a capacity for inclinations of this kind, and understood as such, appetites are constitutive components of every kind of substantial existence (I 80.1).

We may seem to be a long way away from the substantive and practical questions that initially motivated scholastic discussions of free judgment, choice, and voluntary action. Yet Aquinas's metaphysics plays an important role in his overall account of freedom, choice, and the will. By framing his general analysis of substance and causality in terms of appetite and inclination, Aquinas places the operations of human desire and action within a wider metaphysical framework. In this way, he sets up a context for analyzing voluntary human action in terms of what it most fundamentally is, that is to say, the operation of general principles of causality, as these are expressed in creatures of our specific kind. The critical category in this context is the category of appetite, which Aquinas identifies with the inclination to sustain one's form of existence (I 80.1). As Robert Pasnau says, "One might suppose that this ascription of appetite to all of nature is some kind of crude anthropomorphism. In fact, Aquinas's project is precisely the opposite. He is not trying to bring psychology to bear on the rest of nature, but rather to use his general theory of the natural order to understand human beings."[7]

The key to understanding Aquinas's strategy lies in tracing the analogous ways in which inanimate, living, and sentient creatures can be said to act out of appetite, corresponding to the goal-directed inclinations proper to their specific form of existence (again, the key text is I 80.1; in addition, see I-II 6.2, 13.2). Those creatures that lack any kind of sentience operate in such a way as to develop and interact causally in fixed ways, through what Aquinas describes as inclinations stemming from a natural appetite. Plants and the lower forms of animal life operate in accordance with internal principles, through active processes of taking nourishment, avoiding dangers, and the like. Nonetheless, in Aquinas's view these kinds of living creatures cannot be said to be active agents in their own processes of life and growth. They spontaneously grow and flourish in a predetermined way but cannot be said to move themselves reflexively through these processes. Thus, they too can be said to act out of natural appetite, through which they pursue fixed aims in accordance with a relatively simple and determinate form of existence.

In contrast, the characteristic inclinations of the higher animals are mediated through the animal's consciousness, in such a way that it can be said to take an active part in its own continued existence, growth, and reproduction.

---

7. Robert Pasnau, *Thomas Aquinas on Human Nature* (Cambridge: Cambridge University Press, 2002), 201.

Aquinas, following Aristotle, holds that animals interact with their environment through the mediation of sensate images, to which they respond with spontaneous desire, aversion, or fear, leading to activities of pursuit or avoidance (I 81.3).[8] Aquinas identifies these characteristically animal forms of appetite with the passions. The passions resemble the natural appetites of nonsentient creatures, insofar as they are correlated with inclinations stemming from the creature's specific form of existence. However, the inclinations of the passions differ from those generated by natural appetite in one critical respect. They are elicited by objects within the consciousness of the creature, in the form of some perceived, remembered, or desirable target of desire or avoidance. These inclinations are intentional in our sense of the term, that is to say, they are modes of consciousness determined by an object, in this case an object of desire. They are not affective states or moods, detached from any kind of cognition. At the same time, these inclinations depend on conscious apprehensions or cognitions of some kind, but they are not themselves cognitions but motions of desire or aversion.[9]

8. In the following discussion, I bracket Aquinas's distinction between the passions proper to concupiscence, or simple desire, and the irascible faculty, which generates complex inclinations of desire and aggression, such as anger; see I 81.2; I-II 23.1 for details. In the case of the irascible passions, the animal is moved by a complex image, eliciting both aversion and some kind of aggressive resistance, which is experienced as a kind of desire. Nonetheless, these passions, like every other appetite, operate through intentional inclinations in such a way as to generate operations of some kind.

It should also be noted that the images generated by sensate perception, imagination, and memory are not simple perceptions of qualia but, rather, schemata, which represent the world in coherent ways. In nonhuman animals, sense perceptions and images are organized in such a way as to represent reality in terms relevant to the creature's survival and well-being. Such organizations are probably true to some extent for us as well, but Aquinas emphasizes the relatively unformed character of our sensory perceptions and the need for some kind of rational formation in order for them to function properly. Recently, studies of nonhuman behavior, especially among the great apes, suggest that some kinds of animals perceive the world in terms of physical and causal relations, in such a way as to enable a kind of instrumental rationality. For Aquinas's own analysis of human and animal sense perception, see I 78.4. For an overview of Aquinas's account of the passions and their relation to sensate cognition, see Robert Miner, *Thomas Aquinas and the Passions* (Cambridge: Cambridge University Press, 2009), 11–108; Miner discusses the complexity of sensate cognition and particular reason at 69–82. In addition, Diana Cates offers a lucid account of the passions seen in relation to the sensory powers of the soul, in *Aquinas on the Emotions: A Religious-Ethical Inquiry* (Washington, DC: Georgetown University Press, 2009), 103–63. For further details on the perceptual and cognitive capacities of the great apes, see Michael Tomasello, *A Natural History of Human Thinking* (Cambridge, MA: Harvard University Press, 2014), 15–25.

9. I am belaboring this point in order to make it clear that Aquinas does not believe that

Strictly speaking, the proper act of a passion is an intentional inclination of this kind. At the same time, these inclinations elicit further activity on the part of the living creature, through which it pursues, avoids, or resists whatever the inclination targets (again, see I 81.3).[10] In this way, the higher animals, unlike lower forms of life and inanimate creatures, can be said to move themselves to act—that is to say, they initiate activities in response to their own internal perceptions and desires in such a way as to actively engage their environment, sometimes with considerable spontaneity. Thus, the passions play a necessary role in the life of a sentient creature. Without these capacities for targeted desire, the animal could not respond to its environment in appropriate ways, nor would it move itself to carry out the operations necessary to sustain life. Through the inclinations of the passions, animals take an active role in the expression and dissemination of a specific form of existence, as instantiated in themselves, and perhaps also in their offspring.

Correlatively, as we observed in the first chapter, the activities of animals introduce a new level of normative judgments. Even nonsentient creatures have appetites, which are expressed through inclinations toward expressing and maintaining a specific form of existence. But of course there is no question here of any sort of yearning toward the good or any kind of displeasure at failure. We may appropriately regret the destruction of a beautiful crystal, but the crystal itself does not. Animals, in contrast, are consciously drawn toward attractive objects and are moved to flee or resist what they perceive to be noxious or harmful. They act in accordance with normative standards determined by the pleasant and the unpleasant, and clearly they have a stake in attaining the one and avoiding the other. Furthermore, their operations can be evaluated—by us, not them—in terms of promoting the overall well-being of the organism, which itself is a more complicated standard than the integral existence of nonliving creatures.

We can now begin to see how human freedom is both similar to and distinct from a nonrational animal's capacities for self-motion. Because the higher animals, unlike other kinds of nonrational creatures, move themselves to act on the basis of internal perceptions, they can be said to act on the basis of *arbitrium*, judgment. But unlike rational animals, they do not act

---

the inclinations of the passions, which we can reasonably identify with the emotions, are simply cognitive states or normative judgments. For a good discussion of this approach and its critics, see Ronald de Sousa, "Emotion," in *The Stanford Encyclopedia of Philosophy*, ed. Edward N. Zalta, January 21, 2013, http://plato.stanford.edu/archives/spr2014/entries/emotion.

10. Aquinas's fullest explanation of this point is found in the commentary on Aristotle's *On the Soul*; see *In De anima* III.6, 655-70.

in accordance with *liberum arbitrium*, free judgment, because they do not exercise deliberation and choice (I 83.1; I-II 6.2, 13.6). They do not need to do so. They perceive their world in terms set by their own natural needs and vulnerabilities, and these perceptions generate more or less fixed desires, aversions, and activities (I 81.3). Usually these processes, coordinated by a kind of estimative sense, work together in such a way as to promote the animal's successful operations within its environment (I 78.4). This is just what we would expect, because living creatures of a given kind are naturally suited to a particular kind of environment.[11] The animal's engagement with its environment is thus determined by its overall desires and aversions, in such a way that it experiences the world in terms of what is good or bad for an animal of its kind. At the same time, these perceptions and desires are generally veridical, that is to say, the objects that the animal perceives as suitable for food, an appropriate mate, potential danger, and the like really are such, seen in reference to the kind of animal that is in question. The animal's perceptions are narrowly focused, but they are sound and adequate for its purposes—normally so, at any rate.

Like the other higher animals, human beings are tethered to their immediate environment through sensory perceptions, leading to spontaneous inclinations of desire or aversion, grounded in the passions. Because they are grounded in sensory perceptions, including imagined or remembered, as well as immediately perceived images, these kinds of inclinations presuppose some kind of bodily change, and they are directed toward particular objects (I 80.2, 81.1; I-II 22.1–2). In both respects, human passions are essentially similar to their counterparts in nonhuman animals, and Aquinas accordingly identifies the inclinations of the passions as actions of a kind that we share with the other animals (I-II 6 intro.; cf. I-II 50.5 *ad* 1). Yet, seen in comparison to the passions of nonrational animals, human passions are relatively unformed, and they do not track the creature's actual good in the way that the passions of nonhuman animals tend to do. This indeterminacy is by no means a defect in itself. Because our perceptions and feelings are indeterminate in this way, they can be shaped through reflection and direction in such a way as to reflect rational judgments (I 81.3). At the same time, these

11. Modern evolutionary theorists are by no means the first to analyze the operations of living creatures in terms of suitability to a particular environment—Aquinas, like Aristotle before him, was well aware of the ways in which living creatures are shaped by their accustomed environment. Tomasello offers an excellent overview of the most recent research, documenting the ways in which animal perceptions and desires are shaped by their characteristic needs and vulnerabilities; see *A Natural History of Human Thinking*, 7–31.

unfocused desires and aversions cannot, in themselves, move the rational creature to act. Thus, Aquinas argues that the passions of the rational creature must be shaped and developed through habits, which bring specificity and coherence to naturally indeterminate desires and aversions (I-II 49.4). If these habits are well-formed, in such a way that the person's desires and aversions spontaneously track her overall good, they are virtues, but even vices will serve to facilitate action in accordance with focused desires and aversions of some kind or other.

Aquinas identifies the will as the characteristic appetite of the rational and intellectual part of the soul. As such, it has no direct counterpart in the capacities of nonrational animals, but it does have a kind of functional counterpart in the ensemble of animal passions, which operate together in such a way as to elicit appropriate operations. The passions of nonrational animals are innately oriented toward appropriate objects, but in addition, they also spontaneously operate in tandem, in accordance with an estimative sense, which prompts an overall response to a complex set of perceptions and desires (again, see I 81.3). In this way, the animal's perceptions and inclinations lead directly to appropriate, coordinated activities, naturally oriented toward its full development and operation as a creature of a certain kind. In contrast, the passions of the human creature do not spontaneously operate in such a way as to lead her to act in accordance with her overall good. This would seem to be true, even assuming that the agent's passions are formed through virtuous habits, in such a way as to be oriented toward appropriate objects of desire and aversion. The passions and their characteristic virtues respond to the kinds of particular goods that we perceive through the senses, and in themselves, they cannot generate principles that would enable them to integrate diverse satisfactions and aversions in the necessary way (I 81.3; I-II 56.6). For this reason, the human creature, uniquely among material beings, needs an appetite directed toward her overall good, which integrates diverse inclinations toward particular goods into a higher-order inclination toward the good as such.

This appetite is the will, which is innately oriented toward the agent's overall existence and perfection as a creature of a certain kind. In contrast to the passions, which incline toward particular objects as perceived through sensory perception, memory, or imagination, the will inclines toward something judged to be good in accordance with a general, abstract conception of goodness (in addition to the texts just cited, see I 80.2; I-II 8.1, 22.3). This line of analysis implies that the will is a distinctively human kind of appetite because it depends for its operations on the distinctively human capacity of reason. Of course, this is just what Aquinas does say, but in order to appreciate the full significance of this point, we need to place it within the context of his comparative analysis of appetite and inclination as these are manifest at every level of existence. The distinctively rational character of the will corresponds to its distinctive function within the operations that sustain human life. The will is the capacity to desire and pursue one's own overall existence and full development in accordance with some reasoned conception of what it means to live an appropriate or desirable or ideal human life (I-II 8.2, 9.1,3, 10.1). Other kinds of animals neither have nor need this kind of capacity, because their passions naturally operate in such a way as to generate appropriate, salutary behavior. Our passions cannot play a similar part in our own lives, even after they are informed by habits, because they are not sufficiently integrated to work together in a coordinated way to promote the agent's overall good. Over and above the specific desires generated by the passions, the human person needs an overarching desire to exist and to live and flourish in an appropriate way—which is to say, she stands in need of the appetite of the will, which provides the impetus for action throughout her life.

We can now begin to see how Aquinas situates the will within the context of his overall metaphysical account of existence, operation, and perfection. The inclinations of the will are naturally oriented toward goods that are in some way constitutive of, or a means toward, or an expression and extension of, the creature's full actuality—in other words, its perfection (I-II 10.1). Understood in these terms, the will is essentially similar to any other appetite, including the appetites of nonliving creatures. More specifically, the will is an appetite of a living, sentient creature, that is to say, an animal. As such, its operations depend on some kind of conscious awareness of a desirable object, which calls forth an inclination of desire, thus moving the creature to action. Understood as a distinctive kind of appetite, the will— the rational appetite that characterizes human existence—is an appetite that depends for its operations on a reasoned, abstract conception of one's good, eliciting inclinations toward those objects that the agent judges to be necessary to, or appropriately suited to, the attainment and enjoyment of that good. In the initial questions of the *prima secundae*, Aquinas adds that every rational agent necessarily desires its perfection and directs all his or her activities toward the attainment or enjoyment of that end (I-II 1.4,6–8). And since, as we are elsewhere told, the perfection of a rational creature is equivalent to its beatitude or happiness, this is equivalent to saying that everyone necessarily desires happiness and directs all actions, in some way or other, toward that end (I 62.1; cf. I-II 1.6–7).

71

We observed earlier that, when we move from the operations of natural appetite to the inclinations and operations of the higher animals, we encounter a distinctively new kind of activity, corresponding to a new level of normativity. Similarly, the operations of rational creatures introduce a new level of activity and, correspondingly, a new level of normative considerations. The other higher animals can be said to move themselves to act, insofar as they act out of inclinations elicited by objects held within their own consciousness. The rational creature, in contrast, acts out of a reasoned, self-reflective conception of her overall good, comprehensively considered. Aquinas makes this point in the context of comparing the diverse ways in which various kinds of creatures are subject to divine providence. As he explains, all creatures are subject to God's providence, which unfolds through the dynamic operations of the specific forms of existence in which each is created—thus, creatures can be said to desire and seek God, simply in virtue of the operations of their natural or sensual appetites for their own perfection. The same may be said of the rational creature, but Aquinas adds an important qualification: "Among the rest, however, the rational creature is subject to divine providence in a more excellent way, insofar as he becomes a participant in providence, being provident for himself and others" (I-II 91.2; cf. I 22.2 *ad* 4). In contrast to other kinds of animals, the human person is capable of thinking about herself as the subject of a kind of life, reflecting on what it would mean to live well, and reflectively desiring and choosing activities in accordance with her overall aims. Indeed, without some degree of reflection on her aims and activities, the human person cannot live an independent, properly human life at all.

The distinctively human capacity for self-reflective activity opens up possibilities for self-evaluation and appraisals of others' conduct, in accordance with objective, mutually acknowledged standards. As we noted above, nonhuman animals act in accordance with normative standards of the pleasant and the unpleasant, and the criteria for their overall success are determined by natural tendencies to live and reproduce. Rational agents act in accordance with normative standards of the reasonable and the unreasonable, or what is contrary to reason (I-II 94.2 *ad* 2, 94.3). These standards open up possibilities for qualitatively new kinds of normative practices, grounded in practices of giving reasons for one's actions, offering rational objections to the actions of another, demanding something on the basis of a reasonable claim, and the like. These practices, in turn, are correlated with fundamental moral concepts such as responsibility, accountability, and authority, each of which implies some kind of demand or justification for conduct framed in terms of one's reasons for acting.

The Will as the Principle of Voluntary Actions

These considerations bring us to Aquinas's second way of approaching the will—namely, as the principle of the voluntary, in virtue of which men and women are responsible agents, held accountable for their acts, and subject to praise and blame, merit and guilt, reward and punishment (I 83.1). Aquinas discusses the will and, more specifically, free judgment as the principle of voluntariness in the *prima pars*, and he develops this aspect of his overall theory more fully in the early questions of the *prima secundae*. In this part of the *summa*, Aquinas moves from a consideration of fundamental theological and metaphysical principles to a more focused examination of human existence and activity, seen in relation to its overall end.

The *secunda pars* is devoted to an extended consideration of human action, seen from the standpoint of general analytic and normative principles in the *prima secundae*, and seen in relation to the specific ideals or counterideals of particular virtues and vices in the *secunda secundae*. This complex account is grounded in Aquinas's metaphysical analysis of causality, perfection, and action, and its coherence depends in key part on the claim that acts are directed toward an end and can be understood only in terms of that end. He accordingly begins the *prima secundae* with the claim that all men and women have the same end, formally speaking, that is to say, their perfection, and all their actions are directed in one way or another to this end (I-II 1.7). Taken by itself, this statement would scarcely be informative. However, as we noted in the first chapter, Aquinas also identifies the perfection of a rational or intellectual agent with happiness, and on this basis he turns to an extended discussion of classical and theological traditions concerning happiness and the good life. The overarching identification of happiness with perfection enables him to offer a unified account of the distinct levels and kinds of happiness that may legitimately be pursued, including both supernatural and connatural forms, each of which can be seen as a kind of perfection attained and expressed through activities (I-II 4.8, 5.5).[12] The upshot is that supernatural happiness in its fullest sense consists of the vision of God, whereas connatural happiness consists in the practice of the virtues. In any case, perfection and happiness at every level are intrinsically linked to the agent's actions, which can be

12. I defend this claim in more detail, and with a consideration of a wider range of texts, in *Nature as Reason: A Thomistic Theory of the Natural Law* (Grand Rapids: Eerdmans, 2005), 141–63.

considered in one sense as a means, and in another sense as the exemplification, of the agent's happiness.

Having set out an overview of perfection and happiness, Aquinas introduces the central subject of the *prima secundae*, observing that "since it is necessary to come to happiness through some actions, in consequence it is necessary to consider human acts, that we might know by which acts one comes to happiness, or through which the way to happiness is impeded" (I-II 6 intro.). More specifically, he sets out to consider questions pertaining first to human actions generally considered, and second, the principles of human actions. These latter include the internal and external origins of human actions, including the habits, virtues and vices, and law and grace. As we noted above, Aquinas includes inclinations of the appetites, including the passions, as well as the will, among our actions. Nonetheless, the agent's ultimate perfection as an agent depends on his distinctively human acts, namely, the inclinations of the will and the external acts commanded by the will. Aquinas accordingly begins his consideration of human actions with an analysis of the concept of the voluntary, seen as the defining characteristic of human actions properly so called. He then turns to an analysis of the will, considered in itself and as a principle of voluntary choices and actions.

Aquinas's initial analysis of the voluntary takes its starting point from the account of the different levels of appetite and inclination set forth in the *prima pars*. Once again, he observes that inanimate substances move toward their end without awareness, and animate creatures move toward an end without grasping it as such. He then goes on to say, "Those things that have a conception of an end are said to move themselves, because the principle through which they not only act, but act on account of an end, is within them. And since both of these—that they act, and that they act on account of an end—proceed from one intrinsic principle, therefore their motions and acts are said to be voluntary, because the term 'voluntary' implies that a motion and act are from one's own inclination" (I-II 6.1). Aquinas is clearly speaking metaphorically when he says that sentient creatures act on a principle that is within them. We can readily see what he means, however. For both sentient and rational creatures, an appetite elicits motion through some conscious apprehension of a desirable object, although the mode of apprehension is different in each case. In either case, the mental events of apprehension and desire are themselves causal forces, but they cannot plausibly be said to operate on the creature, as if they were distinct entities. On the contrary, they are themselves operations of the creature, and as mental events, they are operations of a distinctive kind. They are within the creature in the sense that they are directly accessible only to the creature itself, and also in the sense that they stem from principles of activity that are proper to it as a living entity of a specific kind.

In order to count as a voluntary action, the behavior in question must stem from the creature's appetites, since only these can be said to be internal to it in the requisite way. This is a necessary condition for voluntariness, but is it sufficient? Aquinas addresses this issue in the course of considering whether nonrational animals can be said to act voluntarily (I-II 6.2). He begins by observing that the formal notion of the will implies that a voluntary act stems from something within the creature, namely, a conscious apprehension of the end to be attained. He goes on to say that the end can be grasped either perfectly or imperfectly. "Perfect" in this context implies that the comprehension of the end includes not only an apprehension of something to be pursued but the awareness of the desideratum as an appropriate object for pursuit, or to put it another way, as one within a general category of desirable objects. Aquinas adds that the perfect grasp of the end also implies some understanding of the way in which one might pursue and attain the end through activity. It is thus self-reflective, insofar as it presupposes some grasp of oneself as a desiring and acting agent, potentially standing in some kind of causal relation to an object outside the self. Understood in this way, the perfect grasp of the end clearly presupposes categorical thinking, and therefore rationality. We might say that a perfectly voluntary act proceeds from within the agent, in the sense that not only the object itself but the object considered as a target for activity, and also oneself as acting to attain the object, are all present to the agent's consciousness. Nonrational animals, in contrast, are capable only of imperfectly voluntary activities, because they are conscious only of the end for which they act. They do not consider it as an end, nor do they reflect on the relation between their activities and the attainment of their desires.[13] Aquinas goes on to say,

> The voluntary in accordance with its perfect sense follows a perfect cognition of the end, insofar as someone, grasping the end and deliberating on the end and those things oriented toward the end, is able to move himself toward the end, or not to do so. However, the voluntary in an

13. In fact, recent research indicates that at least some kinds of animals are aware of their capacities and limitations in specific situations, and they appear to adjust their operations accordingly; see Tomasello, *A Natural History of Human Thinking*, 24–31. Nonetheless, there is no evidence that they think of themselves as agents who have specific powers that can be related to goals in various ways—in other words, they are self-aware but not self-conscious.

imperfect sense follows an imperfect cognition of the end, as indeed apprehending the end; it does not deliberate but is moved immediately toward the end. Hence, the voluntary, considered as perfect, pertains only to the rational nature, but considered imperfectly, it also pertains to brute animals. (I-II 6.2)

In this text, Aquinas sets out the conditions that must be met in order to develop an adequate analysis of voluntary acts and their underlying principles. An action that is voluntary in a broad sense can be said to come from within the agent in the sense that it is causally dependent on a conscious inclination of desire, directed toward some desirable or noxious object. An action that is voluntary in the strict sense depends on an intentional inclination directed toward an end that is understood as such, that is to say, understood as falling in some way within the category of the good, that which is worth pursuing. In either case, the inclination of the appetite is intentional in our sense; that to say, it is directed toward a specific object in such a way that the object defines the mental state. At the same time, the voluntary strictly so called presupposes that the agent's action is contingent. In contrast to nonrational animals, which are immediately moved to desire or aversion through the apprehension of an object, the rational agent may or may not move toward any particular object of desire.[14] The relative freedom of the rational agent is dependent on deliberation, which implies that it is in some way dependent on the intellect, as indeed the initial grasp of some object as potentially desirable depends on a kind of rational cognition (I 81.3). Aquinas's initial analysis of the voluntary thus brings together the two elements traditionally associated with claims of responsibility and accountability, namely, rationality (we hold ourselves and others to account on the basis of justifying or explanatory reasons) and contingency (we are responsible for what we do, what we bring about on our own initiative, and not for what was bound to happen anyway). Correlatively, the appetite that generates voluntary acts must be understood in such a way as to account for both the reasonableness and the contingency of voluntary acts. We need to be able to explain how the appetite in question is responsive to or dependent on reasons, while at the same time accounting for the contingency of its motion with respect to reasons.

After a question devoted to the moral and theological significance of

14. Although he does not make the point here, the relative contingency of human desires operates even at the level of the passions themselves—that is, we do not necessarily desire or turn from naturally desirable or noxious objects, as he explains at I 81.3.

the circumstances of human actions, Aquinas turns to a consideration of the will seen as the principle of human actions. He begins with the fundamental point that the will is an appetite, and as such, it is necessarily oriented toward the good, or the seeming good (I-II 8.1; cf. I 80.2, 82). More specifically, the will as rational appetite is oriented toward the good as apprehended through reason (I-II 8.1). He goes on to say that the will, considered as a capacity, is oriented toward both the end of one's actions and the means by which these actions are secured (I-II 8.2). Strictly speaking, the proper act of the will, in terms of which the capacity is defined, is the volition of the end. Through its inclination toward some end, the will extends itself, so to speak, to those intermediate goals that can be regarded as means toward, or partial realizations of, the end. However, these inclinations are dependent on the volition of the end, in much the same way that reasoning is dependent on the grasp of the first principles of the intellect. Correlatively, the inclination of the will toward some end is distinct, logically and sometimes temporally, from its inclinations toward intermediate means toward or realizations of the end (I-II 8.3).

What is the point of these finely grained distinctions? In the first place, by reminding us that the will is an appetite, Aquinas underscores the point that the will is a principle of motion through which the creature is naturally inclined to operate in such a way as to preserve itself and to act in such a way as to express and develop its capacities. As such, it is the fundamental driving force within our lives, an active tendency toward our own existence, without which we would not be moved to do anything at all.[15] The will thus plays a part in human life analogous to the natural appetite of inanimate creatures or the coordinated appetites and desires of the higher animals, providing the continued impetus necessary for sustained operations. At the same time, the will is a principle of self-motion in the fullest sense, because it is dependent on the agent's rational apprehension that something is good and worthy of pursuit, in accordance with some general notion of goodness. Finally Aquinas also calls attention to the structural complexity of the will, which extends its operations to the means, as well as to the end. This point is significant because it implies that the will moves itself, insofar as its inclination toward some end leads to inclinations toward intermediate goals (I-II 9.3). Sensual appetites,

---

15. As Matthias Perkams says, "One cannot decide to strive for the end qua end: one simply does so." See Perkams, "Aquinas on Choice, Will, and Voluntary Action," in *Aquinas and the Nicomachean Ethics*, ed. Tobias Hoffmann, Jörn Müller, and Matthias Perkams (Cambridge: Cambridge University Press, 2013), 84.

in both nonhuman and human animals, operate in such a way as to move the creature to act, but they are themselves moved, necessarily or contingently, by the objects toward which they are directed. The will is moved by its object in a certain sense, as every appetite is, but it also moves itself through active processes of deliberation and choice, through which the general orientation toward the good is specified in such a way as to elicit action (again, see I-II 9.3). In virtue of this capacity, the human agent can be said, not only to be moved from within, but to move herself through will and free judgment.

Recall that for Aquinas, voluntary action, properly so called, is marked by two features. First, it stems from principles that are internal to the agent, insofar as they operate through the agent's conscious perceptions and inclinations, and second, it is contingent, that is to say, not necessitated by the desired object. It is clear that the actions of the will meet the first of these two criteria. The inclinations of the will, including both the volition of the end and free judgment leading to choice, are grounded in the agent's consciousness in such a way that the agent is aware of the desirable object as such and aware of himself as one who has both a motivation to pursue this object and the ability to do so. At the same time, the will can operate in this way only because it is in some way dependent on the agent's reasoned judgments, through which he grasps that some potential object is worth pursuing and considers that he might attain this object through his actions. This understanding raises a question about the second of Aquinas's two criteria for voluntariness, namely, contingency with respect to the object of the voluntary act. If the will is a capacity for inclinations directed toward the good as presented by the intellect, then it would seem that its motions would be determined by the agent's rational perceptions and judgments. We might still argue that the inclinations of the will are contingent, in the sense that they depend on judgments of practical reason that, for various reasons, are themselves contingent. Someone might have desired a different object or chosen a different state of affairs than she did in fact pursue if her intellect had presented her, so to speak, with a different option. Nonetheless, this is at best a limited kind of freedom. It is consistent with the view that the inclination of the will is determined by the good as it is actually presented by the intellect at any given point. Given a specific judgment of the intellect, the inclination of the will is not contingent, relative to the deliverance of the intellect; rather, the will necessarily inclines toward the good that the intellect presents to it. Or so the argument goes.

In his earlier writings, Aquinas apparently does believe that the freedom of the will, judgment, and choice can be explained adequately as a consequence of the indeterminacy of reason. Further reflection on the concept of voluntariness perhaps led him to reconsider this line of analysis, but in any case, by the time of the *prima secundae*, he has apparently concluded that it is inadequate.[16] In its place, he sets out an extended analysis of the operations of the will, in the course of which he defends the view that its inclinations are contingent, even with respect to the objects presented to it by reason.[17] At the same time, he does so in such a way as to avoid the suggestion that the will operates in an arbitrary way, or in such a way as to be independent of intellect in any way whatever. His strategy depends on developing a finely grained analysis of the motions of the will, over the course of which he draws out its structural complexity and its innate naturalness. The will is not simply an undifferentiated capacity for sheer desire; rather, it is the central organizing appetite of a certain kind of living creature, with its own proper tendencies toward certain kinds of aims, which reason must, as it were, respect.

16. The development of Aquinas's perspective on the will is not limited to the *prima secundae*. It is also apparent in the *De malo* VI, which, according to Jean-Pierre Torrell, should probably be dated to about 1270, just prior to the composition of the questions pertaining to the will in the *prima secundae*; see Torrell, *Saint Thomas Aquinas: The Person and His Work*, vol. 1, trans. Robert Royal (Washington, DC: Catholic University of America Press, 2005), 201–5. While I emphasize the connections between Aquinas's conception of the voluntary and the development of his account of the freedom of the will, there is no doubt that other factors came into play, including his reactions to ongoing scholastic debates on the topic. See Lottia, "Libre arbitre et liberté," 382–86, for further details.

17. In contemporary terms, Aquinas therefore holds a libertarian, as opposed to a compatibilist, theory of the freedom of the will. That is, he holds that the motions of the will are not determined by anything outside the will itself, in contrast to the view that the freedom of the will is compatible with some such determination, so long as the operations of the will are in some way tied to something internal to, or natural or proper to, the agent. This way of reading Aquinas is of course controversial, and it would go well beyond the scope of this chapter to sort out the details of this debate in any detail. Pasnau offers a powerful defense of a compatibilist reading of Aquinas in *Thomas Aquinas on Human Nature*, 221–33. Kevin Flannery argues, contrary to Lottin (see note 18), that Aquinas's conception of the will and rational freedom is fundamentally Aristotelian throughout his career, implying, if I understand him correctly, a compatibilist reading similar to Pasnau's, though not expressed in those terms; see *Acts amid Precepts: The Aristotelian Logical Structure of Thomas Aquinas's Moral Theory* (Washington, DC: Catholic University of America Press, 2001), 111–43. Those who defend a libertarian reading include Perkams, "Aquinas on Choice, Will, and Voluntary Action"; Bonnie Kent, "Losable Virtue: Aquinas on Character and Will," in *Aquinas and the Nicomachean Ethics*, 91–109; Scott MacDonald, "Aquinas's Libertarian Account of Free Choice," *Revue internationale de philosophie* 52 (1998): 309–28; and Stephen L. Brock, "Causality and Necessity in Thomas Aquinas," *Quaestio* 2.1 (2002): 217–40. My own views are closest to those of Perkams and Brock.

Aquinas begins to develop this line of analysis in the next question, which deals with the motion of the will. In the first article, he takes up the fundamental question whether the will is moved by the intellect (I-II 9.1). Given that he defines the will as appetite of the rational part of the soul in the *prima pars*, we would expect him to answer this question in the affirmative (cf. I 80.2). At this point, however, he offers a more carefully qualified response. Because it is a rational appetite, the will is oriented toward the good as such. In virtue of this general orientation, the will is both mover and moved, in distinct ways. Because it is oriented toward the comprehensive good of the human creature, it moves the other capacities, including the passions and the intellect, to their proper operations (I-II 9.1, 12.1). Once again, we see that the will provides the driving force sustaining the operations of human life, in such a way as to allow the agent to take the initiative in her own continued existence and her engagement with the world. At the same time, this innate orientation toward the comprehensive good cannot itself elicit the inclinations of the will, because goodness in the abstract neither engenders desire nor moves anything to action. The innate orientation of the will needs to be specified by some conception of what it would mean to pursue and attain the good, in order to lead to actual desires. We recall that for Aquinas, the inclinations of any kind of appetite are always intentional, in the sense that they are specified by the object toward which they are directed. In the case of the will, the objects that define its inclinations as inclinations of this or that kind are specifications of the general category of goodness, which presuppose rational judgments of some kind. In this way, reason can be said to move the will by specifying the general conception of the good, in such a way as to provide determinate objects for desire and pursuit. The will can thus be regarded as the efficient cause of the activities of the other capacities of the soul, whereas reason is the formal cause of the motions of the will (again, see I-II 9.1; this point is developed further at I-II 13.1).[18]

---

18. Lottin underscores the significance of the claim that reason functions as the formal, rather than the final, cause of the will; see "Libre arbitre et liberté," 386. Reason does not determine the end toward which the will inclines; this is set by the necessary object of the will, that is to say, goodness as perfection, together with those operations that are integral to continued human existence. Reason shapes the forms under which these objects are pursued, through its rational judgments regarding the agent's perfection, the appropriate and salutary ways in which to pursue the natural aims of a human life, and the like. It therefore informs the way in which the will pursues its objects, but these would not be the objects of the will if the will were not an appetite of a specific kind, with its own proper orientation toward its natural objects.

Aquinas returns to the relation between intellect and will in the next question, which considers the way in which the will is moved. He begins by asking whether the will is naturally moved toward anything. He replies by comparing the intellect and the will. Just as the intellect depends for its functioning on first principles, which are naturally known, so the motions of the will depend on something that is naturally willed. This includes both the proper object of the will and all those things that can be said to be naturally willed in a more general sense, as he explains:

> This, however, is the good in general, to which the will naturally tends, just as any other capacity does with respect to its object. And this is also itself the ultimate end, which stands in relation to what is desired, as the first principles of demonstration stand to what is understood. And more generally, these include all those things that are appropriate to be willed in accordance with its nature. For we do not desire through the will only those things that pertain to the capacity of the will, but also those that pertain to the particular capacities, and to the whole human person. Hence, the human person naturally wills not only the object of the will but also all those things that are appropriate to the other capacities, as for example the cognition of the truth, which is appropriate to the intellect, and to be and to live, and others of this sort, which provide for natural existence, all of which are included under the object of the will, as certain particular goods. (I-II 10.1)

Aquinas's point is that the will is a kind of natural appetite, and its operations cannot be understood in purely abstract terms. His terminology at this point is potentially confusing, as he himself admits, since he usually identifies natural appetite with the inclinations of nonsentient creatures. Nonetheless, he acknowledges that the will can be understood as a natural appetite in another sense—that is, it is grounded in some nature and shares in the motions proper to that nature (I-II 10.1 *ad* 1). Understood in this sense, the will is not simply a principle of causation, nor is it a pure desire for an undifferentiated universal good. Rather, it is the characteristic appetite of a certain kind of living creature, playing a necessary role within the ensemble of organic and rational functions that sustain a natural kind of life. Thus, prior to any specification by the intellect, the will is already naturally inclined toward certain kinds of objects. These tendencies cannot be expressed until the intellect provides them with something to work with, in the form of mental representations of natural desiderata. Nonetheless, the natural tendencies of the will shape its responses to these representations, if only by giving a particular salience to those most immediately connected to our natural needs and desires. At the same time, Aquinas carefully notes that, just because the will is naturally oriented toward certain kinds of objects, it does not mean that it necessarily inclines toward any particular object falling within the relevant categories (I-II 10.1 *ad* 3).

Finally, in the next article, Aquinas considers whether the will is necessarily moved by its object; since the object of the will is presented to it by the intellect, this is tantamount to asking whether the will is necessarily moved by the intellect (I-II 10.2). In order to address this question, he begins by drawing a distinction between two senses in which the will can be said to be moved, namely, through the exercise of its act and through the specification of its act. He deals crisply with the first alternative: "In the first way, the will is not moved from necessity by any object, because someone is able not to think about any object whatever, and consequently, not to actively will it." The second alternative calls for a more complex response. The will is an appetite for the good as disclosed by reason. If it were presented with an object that is good without qualification, lacking nothing and satisfying every desire, then it would necessarily incline toward that object. But none of the potential objects of desire that we encounter in this life will meet this criterion.[19] Any such object, however attractive, will be deficient in some way, and seen from that perspective, it is not regarded as good. We can make sense of the claim that someone simply is not attracted to a potential object, however desirable it might be, because there will always be some respects in which a given object is not desirable.

If this is the right way to understand the relation between the will and its potential objects, then how do we account for its actual inclinations? How can we explain the fact that the will inclines toward this particular object, as opposed to some other alternative? On this view, we cannot do so. This demand reflects a misunderstanding of the will and the voluntary character of human actions.[20] Recall that Aquinas identifies the voluntary in its full

---

19. God would do so, but in this life we cannot apprehend God fully or completely, although Aquinas believes that the blessed dead do enjoy the direct vision of God that fully satisfies their will for goodness (I-II 2.8, 3.8).

20. The worry here is that the contingency of the inclinations of the will implies that they are arbitrary, leading to what MacDonald describes as virulent libertarianism; see "Aquinas's Libertarian Account of Free Choice," 315; and compare Pasnau's remark that "Aquinas explains human freedom without any recourse to an uncaused, undetermined act of will or intellect—as if only an uncaused decision could count as a free decision," in *Thomas Aquinas on Human*

and perfect sense with control over one's acts, in contrast to imperfectly voluntary operations, which are directed toward determinate outcomes. Voluntariness implies that the inclinations of the will are contingent, even with respect to the alternatives presented by the intellect, since otherwise the will would not be the ultimate determinant of its own act. As Stephen Brock puts it, "Under the very conditions in which a person chooses in favor of something, he can also choose against it (or even choose to abstain). No 'relevant further difference' is needed in order for him to choose otherwise."[21] Yet this contingency does not imply that the will can operate without the intellect. Recall that for Aquinas, the intellect relates to the will as a formal cause, that is to say, it provides the rational specification necessary to inform the intentions of the will. Without the informing operations of the intellect, the will could not operate at all, any more than the intellect could function without some rational apprehension or proposition to consider, accept, or reject. But the formal cause does not bring something about in the way that an efficient cause does. The intellectual consideration of desirable objects does not, in itself, give rise to desire, any more than simply entertaining a proposition will engender belief (I-II 10.2 *ad* 2,3).[22]

At this point, it will be helpful to return to the contrast that Aquinas draws between the imperfectly voluntary operations of nonrational animals and the perfectly voluntary actions of mature men and women. Both nonrational and rational creatures can be said to act out of internal principles, in the sense that they are moved to act through some apprehension of a desir-

---

Nature, 221. But as Brock observes, there is a difference between saying that the inclinations of the will are caused and claiming that they are necessitated by their causes. As he remarks, "The indeterminacy of choice does not require that a given choice have no cause or causes at all. It only requires that the presence of the causes not make the choice necessary. They must not preclude the possibility of an opposite choice or preempt the person's own self-determination" ("Causality and Necessity in Thomas Aquinas," 237).

21. Brock, "Causality and Necessity in Thomas Aquinas," 237.

22. It is important to keep in mind that the intellectual part of the soul, including presumably the will, does not operate in time, even though the operations that it commands are temporal. For this reason, we cannot account for the volitions of the will in terms of a chronological sequence, as if it inclined toward whichever desirable object occurs to it first. The processes of deliberation and choice are of course temporal, and for that reason they can be shaped by the happenstance of what the agent considers and when he considers it. Even at this level, however, the will itself remains sufficiently outside these processes to command further reflection and deliberation. That is one reason why, for Aquinas, a mistaken judgment of conscience does not excuse—the agent is never completely limited by his immediate perceptions and desires in such a way that the will could not intervene from outside the processes of deliberation, as it were. See I-II 53.3 *ad* 3; cf. I-II 19.6.

able or noxious object (again, see I-II 6.2, 12.5). However, the nonrational creature is only moved to act, whereas the rational creature moves itself to act, "being provident for itself and others" (I-II 91.2). Aquinas's point is that human desire and action depend on rational judgments, through which particular objects of pursuit are grasped as instances of a more general category of that which is worth pursuing—the good, in other words—and the agent's potential or actual operations are understood to be feasible or appropriate ways of pursuing the object in question. A nonrational animal is moved by something internal to it, but it does not move itself through active, self-determining capacities for desiring this or that. It is drawn to suitable objects through instinct, which Aquinas attributes ultimately to God's creative activity (again, see I-II 91.2). The rational creature, in contrast, does move itself through self-reflective processes of volition, deliberation, and choice. Not only does it act in response to what is desirable, it chooses to act because it understands that something is worth pursuing and can be attained through its act. It pursues the end as such, as a reasonable target for activity, and furthermore, it does so through an act of volition and choice that lies within its own power, since its will and choice might have inclined in another way.

For Aquinas, the inclinations of the will toward or away from some object, grasped through the intellect as good or bad, are the acts of the will properly so called (I-II 9.1, 12.1 *ad* 4, 12.2). These are the immediate expressions of the capacity for rational desire, and it is critically important for Aquinas that they are within the power of the will itself.[23] At the same time, these inner acts of the will are paradigmatically bound up with the external acts that, as we say, manifest the agent's will. A human action, understood as an external act, is a unified causal event in which the agent's self-reflective judgment and choice bring about some external operation, relating the agent to something outside herself through the exercise of her causal powers. Human acts may be more or less successful, because the external performance and its effects are not entirely within the agent's power. Nonetheless, the agent's inner act of choice cannot logically be separated from the causal operation that he chooses. The agent does not just choose this or that desideratum in the abstract; she chooses to pursue this desirable aim through that causal operation. By the same token, we cannot fully understand the will unless we consider it in relation to the capacity for choice and action.

Aquinas, together with nearly all his interlocutors, identifies the human

---

23. Both Perkams and Kent emphasize this point; see respectively "Aquinas on Choice, Will, and Voluntary Action," 81–85, and "Losable Virtue," 99–102.

capacity for deliberation and choice most directly with a capacity for *liberum arbitrium*, that is to say, free judgment, which is in some way distinct from the will as such (I 83, esp. 83.4). Nonetheless, the will and free judgment are intrinsically linked in accordance with the fundamental ends/means structure of deliberation and choice. The will is the appetite of the human person for her comprehensive good, and as such, it is the ultimate originating principle for all the agent's choices and actions. Free judgment is a capacity for choice, directed toward particular acts and objects that the agent judges to be good in the light of her overall grasp of her comprehensive good, and as such it is rationally but not really distinct from the will itself (I-II 13.1,3). The will moves itself to act through the exercise of free judgment, through which its general volition is directed toward some specific object, connected to the general aim of the will instrumentally or in some other way. Normally, by moving itself to act in this way, the will also moves the agent to act in pursuit of his overall good, as instantiated in some way in this particular object.

On Aquinas's view, the will is a complex faculty of desire, naturally oriented toward the well-being and the natural activities of the human creature, as these are reasonably judged to be good. The freedom of the will is a concomitant of its complexity as a natural and rational appetite, which is always informed by some consciously held reasonable aim, but not in such a way as to be necessitated in its operations. At the same time, the complexity of the will implies that it cannot function properly without some kind of formation through which it is oriented toward specific kinds of objects, although even prior to this point, it is still capable of those fundamental inclinations that are bound up with the natural life of the human creature. Through this process of formation, the will is disposed to incline toward and choose certain kinds of actions, and to turn from and reject others, in terms of general, reasoned categories of the desirable or permissible, and the undesirable or forbidden. These dispositions are nothing other than the habits of the will, and we now turn to closer consideration of the formation and functioning of these habits.

Habits of the Will

Near the beginning of the *prima secundae*, Aquinas identifies what he describes as the internal principles of human action, which work together in such a way as to generate distinctively human operations (I-II 6 intro.). These include the intellect, which, as he says, is discussed in the *prima pars*, the will, the passions, and the habits. It is noteworthy that Aquinas mentions the appetites and the habits together as originating principles of human action, implying that each plays a necessary role in human activity. Later in the *prima secundae*, at the beginning of his extended treatment of habits, he explicitly asks whether habits are necessary, replying that they are (I-II 49.4). This claim is by no means obvious. What does Aquinas mean by it, and to what extent is it plausible?

We began to address this question in the first section of this chapter, where we observed that the cognitive capacities and appetites of the rational creature are relatively indeterminate, seen in comparison to analogous capacities in nonrational animals. This indeterminacy allows these capacities to be shaped through processes of reflection and formation in such a way that the agent comes to perceive the world in consistent ways and to desire some kinds of satisfactions and not others. Thus, the relative indeterminacy of human capacities accounts for the possibility of habits, but at the same time, it also renders habits necessary. This claim applies in somewhat different ways to both the cognitive capacities and the appetites; in what follows, I focus on the latter.

Recall that for Aquinas, an appetite is a principle of motion through which something acts in such a way as to develop or sustain its existence as a substance of a certain kind. Nonliving and nonsentient creatures can be said to have appetites in this general sense because they spontaneously operate in such a way as to express and sustain their existence as this kind of mineral or that kind of plant. The appetites of sentient creatures, in contrast, are consciously experienced as desires and aversions, which move the animal to pursue some kinds of objects and to avoid others. The critical point is that, while the appetites of a sentient creature elicit operations through its own consciousness, the operations in question are nonetheless more or less determined, in accordance with the overall dynamic of activities that characterizes its form of life.[24] A chimpanzee naturally desires the kinds of

24. More or less, because the appetites and the proper operations of many kinds of animals do allow for some degree of variation and modification, and even rudimentary forms of distinctive cultures. Nonetheless, at the level of essential operations and patterns of interrelationships, there is basically one way of being a chimpanzee or an African elephant or a dog. Furthermore, the variations in ways of living that we find among such animals appear to arise spontaneously, without self-reflective deliberation on the part of the creatures themselves. The appetites of these kinds of creatures are determinate enough to move them to act in ways that express and sustain their characteristic existence, without the necessity for reflection or formation. For a good overview of recent research on the cultural lifestyles of nonhuman animals seen in comparison to human cultures, see Michael Tomasello, *The Cultural Origins of Human*

things that are good for it and is adverse to the things that are bad for it, if not infallibly, at least with enough reliability to live and to function through the impetus of its desires and aversions.

We can also identify characteristically human ways of acting, which are intelligible in light of the fundamental needs and desires of a distinctive kind of social animal. But any accurate description of the natural form of human life will necessarily be highly general, in order to allow for the tremendous diversity of ways of living that we find among human populations. Human life is too complex to be explained in terms of natural templates of desires that spontaneously elicit appropriate kinds of operations. There are many ways of being human; furthermore, the differences among these cannot be explained as the effects of random variation. The various forms of human life reflect a range of self-reflective determinations of value, commitments, and collective judgments of all kinds, leading to diverse, richly textured cultures. Correlatively, the appetites of a rational creature are oriented toward general objects, identified with broad categories of simple sensual desire or aversion, complex sensual states of arousal, and a rational desire for the good as such. These appetites must be shaped in accordance with some specific construal of what it means to be human, in such a way that the agent is consistently led by her desires and aversions to pursue a characteristically human way of life, specified in such a way as to be practically attainable.

The point that should be underscored here is that, without some such formation, the appetites of the rational creature cannot function in the way that the appetites need to function if the agent is to be moved to act in necessary or salutary ways. Unformed appetites would generate inclinations of desire, but these desires would not reliably correspond to the agent's actual needs, and they would not reflect the orderly patterns of a characteristically human life. Thus, these appetites would be ill-suited, at best, to do what the appetites need to do, namely, to move the creature to appropriate, salutary, and life-sustaining operations. Aquinas explicitly extends this line of analysis to the will, as well as the sensual appetites:

> Just as there is in the intellect some species that is the similitude of an object, so it is necessary that there should be something in the will, and in every appetitive power, through which it is inclined to its object, because

Cognition (Cambridge, MA: Harvard University Press, 1999), 1–55; note that Tomasello goes on to revise his theoretical account of the origins of distinctively human cultures in *A Natural History*, for reasons summarized at 1–6.

the act of an appetitive power is nothing other than a certain inclination. . . . Because it is necessary to the end of human life that an appetitive
power should be inclined toward something determinate, to which it is
not inclined from the nature of the power, which can be directed to many
and diverse things, therefore it is necessary that there should be certain
inclining qualities, which are called habits, in the will and the other appetitive powers. (I-II 50.5 *ad* 1)

Even though Aquinas clearly regards habits as necessary to the functioning of the will, scholars have given very little attention to this aspect of his
theory.[25] This oversight extends to treatments of justice and other virtues of
the will, which are seldom analyzed in these terms. To some extent, Aquinas
himself contributes to the relative neglect of this aspect of his thought. While
he offers an extended analysis of habits, he does not focus on habits of the
will in such a way as to address the distinctive questions that arise when
we consider the habits of a rational appetite. But more fundamentally, our
own assumptions about reason and will have made it difficult to understand
how the will could be said to have its own stable dispositions, apart from
the ensemble of rational judgments that inform its volitions and choices. In
order to interrogate these assumptions, we will need to return to questions
pertaining to the freedom of the will, although we will formulate the relevant issues in a somewhat different way, in order to clarify the connection
between the freedom of the will and the necessity for habits of the will.

The text just cited offers a good starting point. In this text, Aquinas
explicitly extends a general analysis of appetites and habits to include both
the sensual appetites and the will. Yet we might wonder whether he has
overstated the similarity between these two kinds of appetite. As he says
at another point, the passions are innately responsive to reason, but only
in certain respects and imperfectly. Insofar as they stem from instincts of
nature, they operate in determinate ways that do not leave any scope for
the formation of habits (I-II 50.3, esp. *ad* 3). This seems to explain why even

25. There are some noteworthy exceptions to this generalization, including Bonnie Kent,
who in "Losable Virtue" discusses the significance of Aquinas's concept of *habitus*, with special
attention to his reading of Averroes; see 106–9. However, she focuses here on Aquinas's claim
that the will can freely choose to exercise a *habitus*, or not, rather than considering his claim
that habits are necessary to the will itself. It is worth adding that, although these two claims
sound incongruous, they are not inconsistent. Habits are necessary in order to orient the will
in such a way as to pursue its final end in a consistent, well-ordered, and appropriate way, but
this general orientation need not compel choice in every instance in order to be effective.

virtuously disposed passions retain natural motions of their own that some-times oppose reason (I-II 56.4 *ad* 3). Because they are responsive to reason without being directly dependent on it, the inclinations of the passions can be directed in more than one way, for good or evil, and they need rational di-rection in order to operate in a coherent way over time. The will, in contrast, is naturally oriented toward the good as grasped through reason. In contrast to the passions, which operate through inclinations toward particular goods that are responsive to reason, the will is naturally oriented toward univer-sal good, the good as such, and its inclinations are immediately elicited by goods that are rationally apprehended as means to, or instantiations of, the universal good. We might say that the will is not just responsive to reason but directly oriented to rational apprehensions, in a way that the passions are not.

Why are these considerations relevant to our inquiry into habits of the will? Taken in one way, they might imply that the will has no need of habits to function, because its innate orientation toward the good, comprehen-sively considered, provides it with a sufficient object for its operations. Al-ternatively, we might acknowledge that the will's orientation toward the good stands in need of some further, substantive development in order to incline toward a determinate object. But this need does not require the for-mation of habits of the will itself, except in a rudimentary sense, because the determinate good that is the object of the will is adequately specified by the intellect. In either case, the inclinations of the will would not seem to be in-determinate, in such a way as to need, or to allow for, habits of the will itself.

Let us consider the first alternative. We might say that the will as such does not need to be perfected through habits, because it is innately oriented toward a sufficient object, namely, the comprehensive good as disclosed by reason. Aquinas makes short work of this objection: "The will from the very nature of the capacity is inclined toward the good of reason. But because this good can be turned in many directions, it is necessary that the will be inclined toward some determinate good of reason through some habit, in order that operation might follow more readily" (I-II 50.5 *ad* 3). The will as a capacity is naturally directed toward what is good, rationally apprehended as falling within an abstract category of goodness, but this does not mean that abstract goodness is itself the natural object of the will. This is so, be-cause good in the abstract cannot provide sufficient starting points for the processes of practical reasoning, leading to the exercise of free judgment through choice. Practical reason always implies some kind of intelligible relation between general goals, ideals, or norms, on the one hand, and the particular objects or actions that promote or instantiate them, on the other (I-II 13.2–3). Thus, it requires a conception of the good sufficiently determinate to serve as the end in an ends-mean relationship or a general ideal in relation to a particular instantiation or the like.

In order to move forward at this point, we need to look more closely at the way in which Aquinas understands the rational good, toward which the will is innately oriented. As we saw in the previous section, the will is innately oriented toward the agent's own good, its perfection in accordance with the ideals of existence proper to it as a natural creature of a certain kind (I-II 7,8; cf. I 5.1). This orientation is significant because, while "goodness as perfection, in accordance with a given kind of existence," is an abstract conception, it is not purely formal. As we saw in the previous section, the orientation of the will toward the agent's perfection naturally extends to those goods that play a central role in human life. Of course, most people do not think in these metaphysical terms, but we are spontaneously drawn to satisfactions and activities that sustain and express our existence as existing, living, and rational creatures (I-II 10.1, 94.2). These tendencies themselves constitute a kind of subjective orientation toward the perfection of the creature in accordance with its natural form of life, whether they are regarded in that light by the agent or not. At the same time, the prerational operations and activities of the human agent are not, in themselves, sufficient to sustain rational action, grounded in some self-reflective sense of what one is doing, and why. These kinds of operations are targeted on particular objects, and if they are to be integrated into the inclinations of the rational appetite, the will, they need to be placed in relation to one another through some general conception of what it means to live a good life, within which these diverse satisfactions have an appropriate place.[26] Otherwise, the agent would have no basis for choice among disparate goods, and no way to deal with conflicts among incommensurable aims in an intelligent, consistent way. The innate orientation of the will provides starting points for developing a conception

26. Aquinas was aware of this difficulty, as we see from his commentary on the *De anima*; see *In de anima* III.16, 840–42. Elijah Millgram argues that the relevant kinds of judgment can be developed only through processes of practical induction, through which the agent learns by experience how to prioritize and balance diverse kinds of goods in a way that he finds appropriate and satisfying; see *Practical Induction* (Cambridge, MA: Harvard University Press, 1997), 67–85. By implication, the kinds of judgments in question require the formation of habits of the will through processes of practical induction, in the way described below. In addition, see Vogler's remarks on so-called incommensurable goods in scholastic thought, in *Reasonably Vicious*, 62–65.

of the rational good, but they must be integrated in some way if the agent is to be capable of rational, fully voluntary action.

We can now see more clearly why Aquinas claims that the will needs habits in order to be rightly disposed toward its object. The will is innately oriented toward the agent's perfection or happiness. In order for this innate orientation to sustain action, however, it must be specified through some determinate conception of perfection or happiness, not necessarily couched in those terms, but framed in terms general enough to be comprehensive, yet specific enough to provide a basis for practical deliberation leading to choice (I-II 1.7–8, 62.4). The agent's perfection or happiness, thus understood, constitutes the determinate object of the will. The will is innately oriented toward the rational good, which Aquinas identifies with the agent's perfection. But it is not innately oriented toward any one determinate conception of the agent's perfection—it needs to be directed in some way toward some plausible ideal of human existence in order to operate properly.

We come now to the second alternative suggested above. That is, let us grant that the will needs habits in order to specify its object, namely, the perfection of the agent, comprehensively considered. It might still seem that these habits of the will play only a secondary or derivative role in shaping its operations. As we observed above, the inclinations of the will are always specified by the intellect, which stands in relation to the will as a kind of formal cause. In the previous section, I argued that this does not mean that the will is necessarily drawn to whatever good objects the intellect may present. If the will is drawn to anything, it will be drawn to some rationally discerned good, but that does not mean that the consciousness of some good will necessarily elicit an inclination of the will. Nonetheless, even if this argument is generally sound, we may still ask whether it applies in the case of the agent's intellectual grasp of her overall good, whatever it is that would constitute her perfection and happiness. Although it is certainly true that no particular object is necessarily desired by the will, Aquinas does say that the will is necessarily drawn to its comprehensive perfection, so long as the agent is thinking about it (I-II 10.2). Given that someone has an adequate conception of what it means for her to attain her overall perfection and is attentive to that conception, it would seem that this conception in itself should be enough to elicit the inclination of the will toward its proper end. The resultant dispositions of the will directed toward the practice of justice, hope, and charity might still count technically as habits of the will, but they would not stem from the activities of the will itself, except in a very limited way.

Yet Aquinas apparently does not believe that even a sound grasp of the agent's comprehensive good necessarily compels the will, either at the level of inclinations toward particular choices or at the level of the agent's volition toward her final end. In other words, he believes that someone might have a sound idea of the kind of life that would be objectively appropriate and satisfying for her, while nonetheless preferring a different, objectively limited or distorted way of life. Without a habitual volition toward one's best way of life, one's sound intellectual ideals of human life will have little or no practical effect. This point comes out most clearly in his analysis of the sin of definite malice (*certa malitia*), which, as he explains, is associated with (although not limited to) bad actions stemming from a vicious disposition toward one's overall good (I-II 78.2–3). Sins of definite malice are thus contrasted with sins of inconsistent choice, which stem from a misjudgment of a particular seeming good under the influence of a badly integrated passion (I-II 77.3; II-II 156.1–2). It is all too possible to be sincerely committed to a sound ideal of self-restraint with respect to eating, while at the same time failing in a particular instance to apply that ideal in an effective way under the influence of passion, which focuses the mind on the immediately desirable aspects of this chocolate cream pie or that double cheeseburger. The inconsistent individual knows better, as we say, and soon comes to regret the inconsistent choice.

In contrast, someone who sins out of definite malice acts with the explicit knowledge that what he is doing is contrary to the demands of moral reason and divine law (II-II 156.3).[27] This kind of sin may not stem from a vicious habit, but in some cases it does. In such a case, the individual's overall aim in life is constituted by a way of life that is objectively corrupt and disordered but that the agent nonetheless regards as the kind of life he wants to live. We might be tempted to think that someone who sins in this way is simply mistaken about the overall aims and the value of human life, in such a way that, if he could be reasoned out of his false beliefs, his dispositions and behavior would change accordingly. But this is clearly not what Aquinas is saying. According to him, the sin of definite malice presupposes that someone knows that he is acting contrary to the demands of reason and divine law, to the detriment of his overall perfection and ultimate salvation (I-II 78.1; II-II 156.3). Thus, someone who sins from definite malice is not weak or inconsistent, nor is he just mistaken about the real character of

---

27. As Vogler argues, deliberate wrongdoing and vice do not violate the canons of practical reasoning as such, nor do they imply any kind of inconsistency, nor do they undermine the agent's free self-determination; see *Reasonably Vicious*, 53–73, esp. 66–73.

his comprehensive good. It is entirely possible for someone to have a correct theoretical understanding of one's final end and yet to incline toward a distorted or incomplete version of human perfection as one's own end (as Aquinas elsewhere says; I-II 72.5). In one sense, a sin of definite malice does presuppose ignorance of the true good, since the agent believes that her sinful choice is more satisfying or better suited to her or in some other respect preferable to a choice consistent with the unqualified good—but this kind of ignorance would appear to follow from the disorder of the will, rather than causing it, and at any rate it does not obviate the agent's theoretical grasp of what the comprehensive good is (I-II 78.1 *ad* 1; cf. II-II 156.3 *ad* 1). In such a case, the distorted disposition of the will presupposes some kind of intellectual conception of the good, along the lines that this is the way of life that suits me or the way of life that I really admire or that I find rewarding here and now (I-II 78.3). But someone can hold this kind of belief while also grasping that one's true end, comprehensively or rightly considered, is inconsistent with the final end that one's will actually has.

It seems clear that an intellectual judgment concerning one's overall perfection cannot compel the will, even when the agent is actively considering it. In order for the agent to incline toward those activities that promote her true perfection in some way, she needs something more than a sound grasp of what it would mean to attain this end. She also needs to desire her true end, not only from time to time, but consistently and effectively. In other words, she needs habits of the will, which dispose her to pursue certain kinds of activities and relationships and to turn from others, out of her stable desire to live in a certain way. These habits of the will presuppose intellectual judgments of all kinds, but they cannot be reduced to sheer tendencies to desire and choose in accordance with the good as disclosed through the intellect. They are stable dispositions of an appetite, grounded in and expressed through characteristic desires and aversions, even though these will be rational, rather than sensual, in character.

We began this section by noting the differences between the passions and the will, and it will be helpful at this point to remind ourselves of their essential similarity, considered as human appetites. The passions, as appetites of the sensual part of the soul, operate in response to images of desirable or noxious objects, as conveyed through sense perception, memory, and imagination. In the rational creature, these images do not emerge spontaneously but arise out of ongoing processes of experience and reflection (I 78.4). Even so, these reflective processes, through which we learn to perceive, are not in themselves sufficient to form the passions in the needed ways. We also need to learn to feel, and for this reason acquired habits can be formed only through repeated actions (I-II 51.2–3). The passions are capacities for desires and aversions of certain kinds, in response to appropriate objects, and therefore they can be developed only through a kind of sentimental education, through which someone's desires and aversions are elicited and encouraged in some circumstances, discouraged in others, and continually interpreted for the agent in such a way that she comes to appreciate the significance of what she is feeling and to direct her own inclinations in a self-reflective way.

Similarly, the will, as the appetite of the intellectual part of the soul, emerges in response to some reasoned judgment regarding its proper object. But just as right perceptions of the world do not necessarily elicit appropriate inclinations of desire and aversion, so a correct understanding of one's true good cannot guarantee that the will has a right disposition toward the final end. The will, as an appetite, needs to be oriented toward the good disclosed by reason through processes of inclining toward that good. Once we take account of this point, we can more easily see how someone could develop settled dispositions toward vice, even though she also has an adequate conception of what her comprehensive good, rightly considered, would look like. There is a difference between knowing abstractly that this or that way of life would be appropriate and salutary for me as a human being, and inclining toward that way of life as my final end. It may be that my will is actually drawn by some other alternative that my intellect presents, in such a way that I come to desire and pursue this as my end, that is to say, *my own* ultimate end, in contrast to the abstract good for someone like me. While the will presupposes some intellectual judgment about the agent's overall good, we cannot account for the orientation of the will in terms of this or that intellectual judgment alone. The volition of the will remains contingent, and its consistency depends on habits of the will, that is to say, stable dispositions to desire and choose in consistent ways.

Understood in this way, a habit of the will is a stable disposition to desire and choose in certain ways, informed by a rational apprehension of some lovable object or some desirable way of life. This kind of stable disposition cannot be reduced to specific desires and choices, but neither can it be formulated and expressed without reference to these. A habit of the will emerges out of, and expresses itself through, a range of choices and acts, through the agent's characteristic motivations and ways of perceiving the world, and very often also by the motivations, feelings, and sensibilities elicited by the object of the habit. We see many such examples of these kinds of habits—in the commitment sustaining a marriage, in someone's devotion to

his profession, or in a lifetime of efforts on behalf of some cause or some social ideal. In all these instances, the disposition of the agent's will is expressed
through ongoing, coherent patterns of choice and action, sustained through
a structure of motives, feelings, and perceptions, and comprehensible to the
agent and to others as reflections of the agent's active commitment.

How can we account for the formation of these stable dispositions of
the will? We can see readily enough how the passions, which take shape
through inclinations toward particular goods, can be exercised and shaped
in the needed ways. But initially, it is hard to see how habits of the will could
develop through any comparable process. After all, the processes through
which the passions are formed are carried out under the direction of the will,
which shapes the passions through the actions that it commands (I-II 51.3; cf.
I 81.3). In order to account for the formation of the will in similar terms, we
need to show that the will can act on itself in such a way as to habituate itself.
Aquinas does not address this issue directly. Yet he does offer the starting
points for such an account, and these, taken together with contemporary
work on practical reason, point the way toward a cogent analysis of the way
in which habits of the will take shape, in such a way as to dispose the will
toward one particular construal of the agent's comprehensive good.

In order to develop this account, we need to reexamine Aquinas's remarks about the relationship between the will's volition of the final end and
the choice of a particular good through free judgment. We will see that Aquinas's analysis of volition and choice implies a more intimate and reciprocal
relation between the two than we might expect. Dispositions of the will toward some ultimate end do not just precede deliberation and choice. Rather,
these dispositions emerge and take shape in and through processes of choice,
as the maturing agent develops her capacities for fully voluntary action. The
will cannot direct itself from without as it directs the passions, but it does
move itself to act through the exercise of free judgment, and this capacity
enables it to shape its own development in a way analogous to, although not
identical with, the processes through which it shapes the other appetites.
This, at any rate, will be the argument of the remainder of this section.[28]

Habits of the will, in whatever way they come about, are stable dispositions directed toward goods that are in some way external to, or greater or

---

28. Both Pasnau and MacDonald claim that the will plays some part in its own formation,
which MacDonald identifies with the will's volition of second-order aims. See, respectively,
Thomas Aquinas on Human Nature, 221–33, and "Aquinas's Libertarian Account of Free Choice,"
322–28. However, neither associates this aspect of the will's activity with the formation of
habits, as I will do in what follows.

more comprehensive than, the agent herself (cf. I-II 56.6). These habits are all oriented, directly or indirectly, toward the agent's own subjective perfection, which is equivalent to happiness. In order to move forward at this point, we therefore need to return to Aquinas's conception of the good as happiness. Recall that Aquinas defines happiness as perfection, that is to say, the appropriate and full development of the natural capacities of the rational or intellectual creature (I 62.1; cf. I-II 1.5). Thus understood, every rational or intellectual creature necessarily desires its own happiness, although not necessarily understood in those terms, and directs all its activities toward that end in some way or other (I-II 1.6–7; cf. I-II 5.8). Given the mode of activity proper to the rational creature, happiness can be willed and pursued only under some description or other, which need not be couched in metaphysical terms but which will capture some idea of what it would mean to attain an ideal proper to the kind of thing I take myself to be (I-II 1.7).

After an initial consideration of traditional and theological views concerning the true purpose and fulfillment of human life in I-II 2, Aquinas turns to the question of what happiness is. He begins this question by distinguishing between the objective states of affairs or objects that men and women pursue, and the activities through which these are attained and enjoyed (I-II 3.1). This distinction is critical to his overall argument, because the identification of subjective happiness with activity allows him to identify happiness, formally considered, with the perfection of the rational creature (I-II 3.2–3). As we recall, perfection is always linked to activity in accordance with some normative ideal, determined by the form of a specific kind of existence. By implication, the perfection of the rational agent, the happy life, will necessarily be an active life of some kind, through which the agent's capacities are expressed in a full and appropriate way. Seen from one perspective, the happy life can be described in many different terms, reflecting the many objects and states of affairs that men and women pursue in their search for happiness. But seen from the perspective of happiness as the perfection of the agent, the happy life can be understood only in terms of sustained, goal-directed, and appropriate activities, through which individuals enjoy whatever it is that makes them happy. The disposition of the will toward its final end, thus understood, is a disposition to desire, pursue, and hold onto a way of life, expressed through actions corresponding to the kind of life that the agent wants to live. Similarly, human activities of any kind can be said to perfect the agent in some respect, insofar as they represent the actualization of human capacities for action. Furthermore, the indefinite variety of human ideals, possibilities, and experiences offers many ways of construing one's overall perfection, or happiness, many different ways to envision a life that is fulfilling or praiseworthy or admirable or suitable, or whatever terms one uses to describe the kind of life one seeks. The agent's overall perfection can credibly be understood in more than one way, involving distinct and even incompatible ways of realizing the open-ended possibilities of human nature.

In the opening questions of the *prima secundae*, Aquinas gives the impression that the agent's conception of his final perfection, the inclinations of his will toward that final state, and his corresponding actions form a stable and harmonious unity of understanding, desire, and activity (see esp. I-II 1.4–7). While he certainly acknowledges that men and women can understand their perfection in more than one way, he also holds that the individual arrives at a determinate conception of his or her final end at an early stage of life, and he seems to regard this conception as relatively fixed, although not, of course, immutable (I-II 89.6). Elsewhere, however, we see reasons to believe that his overall views on the agent's conception of her final end, and its relation to her habitual disposition to desire that end, are more complex than we might initially assume. To recapitulate: Aquinas claims that each person necessarily desires happiness, understood as one's own perfection, and directs every action toward attaining that final end (I-II 5.8). Furthermore, he claims that the rational agent necessarily pursues his final end under some description or other, in accordance with a reasoned conception of the good (I-II 1.6–7, 10.2). Yet he also explicitly says that there are some kinds of voluntary, rational acts that are inconsistent with the agent's overall conception of the good, namely, actions of inconsistent choice and also venial sins (I-II 72.5; II-II 156.1–2). How is this possible, if the agent directs all his actions toward his final end?

For Aquinas, the ideal of rationality is set by a mature, self-reflective agent who has a well-developed and sound conception of her final end, and who governs her deliberations and choices by reference to this end (cf. I-II 91.2). This is pretty clearly an ideal, and yet it is not so far outside the bounds of possibility as to be unrealistic or unpersuasive. We know what it would mean to live a life of integrity, consistency, and conscious purpose, and without trying to argue the point, I would suggest that, even at the subjective level, this is the most satisfying way that a person can live. Most of us are not going to live up to this ideal, but we can approximate it sufficiently to develop a taste for this kind of autonomy and self-command. In contrast, we have the ideal, if that is the word, of the inconsistent person, whose general idea of the good is sound but who fails to follow through on his best insights. The point is that even someone who chooses inconsistently can nonetheless be said to pursue his final end of perfection in a qualified sense. More specifically, through inconsistent choice, the agent pursues his final end subjectively understood as perfection through appropriately fulfilling activity. Unfortunately, he does so in terms of whatever strikes him as fulfilling here and now, under a rational description that is tweaked to reflect his immediate desires. At the same time, however, someone who chooses badly in this way, under a distorted conception of the good, is not wholly mistaken or irrational. In one sense, at least, the activity that he chooses is indeed a component of his overall subjective happiness, understood as the realization of his capacities for judgment, choice, and action.

We are now in a position to see how a rational yet inconsistent choice is possible. Someone who chooses inconsistently does so because her overall conception of the ideal life, which she normally finds attractive and compelling, does not in this instance attract her (II-II 156.1–2; cf. I-II 10.3). Her will is not exercised in the right way at the critical moment, because, for whatever reason, it is engaged by some alternative possibility for satisfying activity (I-II 78.3). This kind of inconsistency is possible only because the attractive alternative does offer a kind of happiness, in the qualified sense of an activity that fulfills some human potentiality. As such, it implies an alternative to the agent's own (by hypothesis, sound) ideal of life, an alternative that would allow for the pursuit of many more such satisfactions.

The case of inconsistent choice thus prompts us to look more closely at the relation between the volition of the will toward a final end and the exercise of free judgment through which this volition is pursued and realized. The point I want to make is that both the agent's comprehensive good and the concrete possibilities for pursuing that good here and now can be understood in multiple ways by the same person at any given point, not simply as abstract possibilities, but as practical alternatives emerging out of the processes of deliberation, choice, and action. The agent's conception of her final good, the state of perfection or happiness or fulfillment at which she aims, is always at least potentially open to expansion and revision, and her affective dispositions toward different ways of life are similarly open to development and redirection, in accordance with her experiences. Because the agent's conceptions of her final good and her desires for this or that way of life are mutable in these ways, she is always at least potentially capable of changing her fundamental orientation toward her final good—that is to say, she is always potentially open to desiring and pursuing a way of life that is different, perhaps radically different, from the way of life to which she is committed at any given point. Furthermore, she is capable of taking an active role in the processes through which her understanding of, and her stable disposition toward, her happiness or fulfillment take shape and undergo revision.

It might seem that Aquinas could not allow that the agent's overall volition of her end could develop through experience and reflection. He seems to presuppose the unqualified priority of the volition of the will over the exercise of free judgment, the latter being in every way dependent on the former. We read that the proper act of the will, that is, the operation in terms of which it is defined, is the volition of the final end (I-II 8.2). Of course, the inclinations of the will extend to those things desired as means to, or instantiations or components of, the end that is willed, which can themselves serve as intermediate ends (I-II 8.3, 12.2). Correlatively, the act of choice is always directed to something that is a means or an instantiation of some end (I-II 13.3). It seems that the processes of volition and choice can run in only one direction. The processes of practical reason seem to presuppose that the will already is disposed, well or badly, toward its object, the final end as understood intellectually. For this reason, when Aquinas says that the will moves itself to act through choice, he does not seem to leave any space for the kind of self-reflective processes of formation that we would associate with habits.

Yet this conclusion would be premature. It is clear that for Aquinas, practical rationality implies that any particular choice or action can always be understood in relational terms. The agent chooses this determinate act for the sake of that wider aim, in terms of which the particular choice is rationally justified (I-II 13.3). But this structure need not imply that the wider aim is clearly formulated in advance. On the contrary, we can, and we often do, discover what our overall aims really mean in and through processes of choice. Once again, we need to bear in mind that every choice involves an inclination toward activity, which is in some way perfecting (I-II 13.4). For that very reason, every act can be construed as a means to, or a component of, a wider ideal of life. At the same time, most of our choices are framed by natural and social contexts in such a way as to open up further possibilities for fulfilling activity, together with unexpected deprivations and sacrifices. These, too, are experienced as in some way fulfilling, or not, and these inclinations prompt further reflection on the kind of life that they imply. My point is that, through this process, the inclinations of the will begin to take on a patterned shape, characterized by the tendency of the will to engage itself with respect to these kinds of activities, to turn actively from other, inconsistent or damaging activities, and not to engage others. The will thus disposes itself to its act in and through processes of inclining toward certain kinds of subjective perfections and rejecting, or simply failing to advert to, others.

I therefore want to claim that, in many cases, at least, the agent arrives at some sense of her own desires, aims, and commitments in and through the processes of choice. Recently, the philosopher Elijah Millgram has offered a persuasive way of thinking about these processes, in terms of what he describes as practical induction.[29] Millgram's theory is meant to challenge the widespread assumption that practical reason in itself is always limited to means-end reasoning, which takes its starting points from predetermined ends. On the contrary, he argues, our choices themselves provide the starting points for genuine reasoning about the aims for which we act. Through experience and reflection, we build up an extensive sense of the kinds of activities that we find rewarding, and we also get a sense of which out of a range of incommensurable values are most important to us. This extended practical sense provides the basis for practical induction, through which we form conclusions about the overall ends that have prompted our choices, and in terms of which they can be rationally justified.

I believe that Aquinas could accept this way of construing practical reason, at least in its main lines. It fits well with his overall account of the way in which the intellect moves from apprehension of particulars to a grasp of specific forms, seen as exemplified in these particulars, an account that he explicitly extends to practical reasoning (again, see I 80.2 *ad* 3).[30] He would add that the processes that Millgram describes also involve the operations of free choice and will, operating in tandem with practical and speculative reasoning (I-II 13.1). Millgram emphasizes that the agent learns what she really wants in and through induction from her specific choices. Aquinas would add that this works only because the agent really wants something— that is to say, her free choice and will are engaged through her inclinations toward some kinds of choices, as well as her aversion or distress at others, inclinations that themselves provide the starting points for the processes of practical induction that Millgram describes. The agent's natural desire for happiness sets the processes of activity in motion and informs her activities and reflections at every point. We act, most fundamentally, because we naturally desire life and effective operation in accordance with the structuring principles of our existence. Through our experiences of our actions, we come

29. For an overview and defense of Millgram's theory of practical induction, see *Practical Induction*, 43–66.

30. In addition, see *In De anima* III.16, 842.

to regard certain kinds of activities as appropriately fulfilling and others as not worth our pursuit or even downright noxious.

At the same time, practical induction cannot be limited to the level of reflection on diverse courses of action, considered seriatim.[31] At many points we will face choices among diverse aims and values that are incommensurable with one another and at least potentially incompatible. If we are to sustain a course of activity over time with any degree of reasoned self-determination and consistency, we need to be able to arrive at some comparative judgments regarding priorities. Which courses of activity should be privileged, which are to be rejected, and how do we deal with the indeterminate middle range of options? Aquinas offers both a way of thinking about this problem and an indication of how we address it. On this view, what we are thinking about as we reflect on options and priorities is nothing other than the true meaning of happiness, given what we understand ourselves to be and how we reflectively experience ourselves in our active engagement with the world. This line of reflection will necessarily move in the direction of comprehensive integration of our desires, values, and ideals, because only in this way can we arrive at the needed sense of the overall meaning and purpose of our lives—needed, if we are to take possession of ourselves, determining the course of our lives autonomously through the exercise of reasoned judgments. By the same token, this orientation toward happiness sets general parameters for the kinds of reflections that Millgram envisions. As we reflect on which activities are satisfying or not, we also place these experiences in wider contexts, testing our options for consistency and placing them in a wider framework of meaning and purpose.

It is worth emphasizing that, at every point in this process, the operations of the will play an independent role in shaping the agent's conception of, and his active desire for, his comprehensive good.[32] It is true that the

31. Throughout his analysis of practical induction, Millgram argues cogently that unity of agency presupposes ongoing processes of deliberation through which one's choices and desires are related coherently to one's past dispositions and are associated, in some suitable way, with a future trajectory: "Unity of the self in the practical domain will in like manner be exhibited in one's ability to—and in the likelihood that one actually *will*—bring to bear, in the course of practical deliberation, one's practical judgments . . . as they become relevant to the question one is considering" (*Practical Induction*, 53). Although I cannot defend the point here, I would add that Aquinas's theory of the metaphysical unity of the self, expressed through natural inclinations toward one's final end of perfection, provides the formal structure of desire and deliberation needed to account for the possibility and rationality of Millgram's practical induction.

32. As Daniel Westberg has shown in some detail, will and reason operate in tandem at every stage in the complex processes of deliberation leading to choice and action; see his *Right*

operations of the will, which are intentional inclinations toward some object, presuppose some intellectual judgment to the effect that this or that is in some way good, worthy of pursuit. Yet, as we have already noted, nothing that the intellect can offer in this life by way of an apprehension of the good can compel the exercise of the will. Even though the agent grasps that one alternative is rationally more compelling or more fulfilling than other possibilities, he may not desire that alternative, because he prefers another option that he also grasps to be good in some way. These volitions and the choices they inform will in turn shape the agent's further reflections, in such a way as to incline him progressively to construe his life and his choices in terms of what he actually loves, in contrast to other, perhaps objectively better, objects of love. Prompted by some idea that this or that is in some way good, the will inclines toward the object and moves the agent to act accordingly, and experience subsequently either confirms or calls into question the soundness of the initial apprehension. The agent's experiences thus inform his sense of what the true good is, while his ongoing inclinations toward the good, thus understood, dispose him toward activities that promote that overall good or at least do not undermine it. The key point is that these processes of practical induction do not just shape the agent's intellectual judgments regarding what he finds satisfying or worthwhile—they also shape, and are then directed by, dispositions of the will, which come to be directed toward some kinds of satisfactions rather than others. The will moves itself to act through processes of choosing specific acts, each of which is in itself an actualization, a perfection of the agent's active powers, and each of which is regarded in some more specific way as a means to, or an element of, the agent's overall happiness as he understands it.

Ultimately, these processes of practical induction dispose the will toward its proper object, namely, the agent's perfection or happiness, now given relatively determinate shape by the intellect and desired as such by the will. The determinacy of the agent's conception of his final end should also be underscored. The agent's conception of his final good and his habitual volition of that end take shape through an extended process of desire, action, and reflection, through which the agent's initial ideals and commitments are applied, challenged, and extended or rejected in the particular

Practical Reason: Aristotle, Action, and Prudence in Aquinas (Oxford: Clarendon, 1994), 119–83. Similarly, Perkams argues that every stage in the processes of deliberation can be interpreted as involving a kind of free choice, which is informed but not necessitated by some reasoned judgment; see "Aquinas on Choice, Will, and Voluntary Action," 84–85.

circumstances of his actual life. In this way, his ideals and aims gradually take a concrete shape, in the form of a life that he can imagine living and regards as the right way for him to live. This concrete sense of self does not replace the agent's overall conception of his final good. Rather, that conception is formed and grasped in and through his growing capacity to understand how his overall ideal is exemplified by particular actions, or perhaps undermined or contradicted by his acts. To borrow a term that Aquinas uses in another context, the agent can now grasp the quiddity of particular actions—that is, he understands his particular actions as particular instantiations of universal ideas, in this case, ideas of the human good and its contraries (I 85.8).

So far in this analysis of habits of the will, we have focused on the agent's stable desire for her final, comprehensive good. On Aquinas's terms, this stable desire is itself a habit of the will, which may be well-formed or vicious, as in the case of definite malice. In the case of a well-formed disposition, he identifies the habit with rectitude of the will, which, as he explains, is necessary to the attainment of happiness:

> The rectitude of the will is required for happiness both antecedently and concomitantly. Antecedently, because the rectitude of the will comes about through a requisite ordering to the ultimate end. Now the end is compared to that which is ordained to the end as form to matter. Hence, just as matter cannot attain form unless it is disposed to it in the requisite way, so nothing can attain an end without the requisite ordering to it. And so no one can attain happiness unless he has rectitude of the will. (I-II 4.4)[33]

From his remarks in this article and elsewhere, we see that the formal quality of the rectitude of the will is identified with the supernatural virtue of charity. Since Aquinas also holds that we are capable of attaining a connatural form of happiness through the practice of the virtues, presumably we are capable of a connatural rectitude, which disposes the will toward happiness, understood as a morally upright life pursued through the practice of the virtues.[34] In either case, this habitual desire for one's final end

---

33. Aquinas goes on to say that rectitude of the will is concomitantly necessary to happiness because ultimate happiness consists in the direct vision of God, which necessarily elicits the agent's love (I-II 4.4). Since Aquinas elsewhere identifies connatural happiness with the practice of the virtues, which by definition are expressed through rightly ordered desires of the passions and will, presumably he would also say that rectitude of the will is concomitantly necessary to connatural happiness (cf. I-II 5.5).

34. Should connatural rectitude be considered to be a virtue? In many respects, it fits

plays an architectonic role with respect to the other virtues, coordinating their operations and directing them to the attainment of the final end of the human person. It might seem that this architectonic habit would be the only habit necessary for the complete development of the will, but Aquinas clearly does not think so. The architectonic habit of charity coexists with other infused virtues of the will, namely hope and infused justice, and connatural rectitude of the will presumably coexists with acquired justice (I-II 54.1, 65.3,5). He also refers to vices of the will, and while he does not say so, I think we can reasonably consider stable commitments of all kinds as habits of the will. Considered as stable dispositions, these habits can be explained and understood in the terms just set out, as stable dispositions to ideals or aims that are grasped and pursued in terms of a specific set of relationships, practices, or ways of living.

Justice as a Perfection of the Will

I now turn to a preliminary consideration of the central question motivating this project. What does it mean on Aquinas's terms to say that justice is a perfection of the will, and what might this account tell us about the substantive ideal of justice? At this point, it will be helpful to review what we have established so far. According to Aquinas, the will is the characteristic appetite of the rational creature, innately oriented toward the agent's overall perfection, understood as sustained activity that in some way develops and expresses natural principles. Through the activities of the will, as informed by some intellectual construal of one's comprehensive good, the agent moves himself to act out of what are, in the most comprehensive way possible, his own inner principles of activity—beliefs, desires, and commitments with which he can identify, and out of which he freely acts. Seen from this perspective,

---

Aquinas's definition of a virtue as set out in I-II 49—that is, it is a stable disposition of an appetite, which orients the capacity itself and the agent whose capacity it is toward something good, in this case, the attainment of a genuinely happy, perfecting life. The difficulty is, it is hard to identify a characteristic act correlated with rectitude, corresponding to the characteristic act of its supernatural correlate, charity, which is oriented toward a distinctive form of the love of God. Apart from charity, rectitude of the will would seem to be expressed through a wide range of actions that shape and display the overarching disposition toward rectitude without being formally correlated with it. We perhaps may need to expand Aquinas's overall framework of virtues and vices in order to accommodate dispositions of this kind, but that is a task for another day.

the will is the ultimate principle of substantial unity, analogous to the natural and sensate appetites of nonsentient and sentient creatures.

So long as we focus on Aquinas's claim that the will is a rational appetite, we may be tempted to think of it as a simple capacity for volition in accordance with the deliverances of reason. As we have seen, the will is actually a complex faculty that can be oriented toward its object in more than one way, some better than others. For this reason habits of the will are both possible and necessary, and also for this reason these habits can be well-formed or vicious (I-II 49.4). Vices of the will are expressed through distortions of natural human ways of acting and living; similarly, the virtues of the will dispose the agent toward naturally salutary activities (I-II 71.2). The overarching dispositions of rectitude and charity dispose the agent in such a way as to desire and pursue happiness in the truest sense, which Aquinas identifies with a life of virtue or friendship with God. At the same time, he also holds that this overarching disposition is not sufficient for human perfection or right living. The will and the other appetites must also be disposed in appropriate and salutary ways toward a whole range of other activities and satisfactions, which are distinguished by their specific fields of operation and integrated through the agent's overarching disposition toward her final good.

These observations suggest two criteria for a satisfactory account of justice as a virtue, that is to say, a perfection of the will. First, this way of thinking about justice implies that justice can be seen as an expansive development rather than a contraction or a distortion of natural human capacities. By implication, we should be able to offer an account of justice that presents it as one component of a humanly desirable and admirable way of life. In saying this, I do not mean to imply that the life of the just man or woman will always be comfortable or safe. Justice on Aquinas's view cannot be regarded as an instrumental means to security or general well-being. Rather, justice, like every other virtue, is an intrinsic part of the rational agent's overall perfection. Nonetheless, this line of analysis implies that men and women are naturally attracted to justice, just as we are naturally attracted to human excellences of all kinds. By the same token, we should be able to offer an account of justice that presents it as an attractive ideal, an integral component of a way of life that we would consider to be both desirable and admirable. We should be able on this basis to see how justice relates to the other virtues, and we should come away with a clearer sense of what the ideal of justice implies for individual and social practice. At the very least, we should be able to show that justice is genuinely a perfection of the will, and not a perversion of its innate structures.

The second criterion is closely related to the first. Justice, on Aquinas's account, is one perfection of the will, but it is not the only, nor even the fullest possible, perfection of the will. Aquinas confirms this understanding through his emphatic insistence that both forms of justice, general as well as particular, are distinctive virtues with their own proper field of operation (II-II 58.6,8). In that case, we should be able to show that the ideals and actions associated with justice are distinct from, and yet compatible with, the comprehensive perfection of a truly happy life. This general criterion would apply to all the virtues, but it is especially relevant to justice because justice, in contrast to the other connatural virtues, is an other-regarding virtue. Thus, we will need to explain how the other-regarding dispositions proper to justice can be integrated into the agent's overall virtuous life, in such a way as to maintain the integrity of justice while also safeguarding the overall harmony and value of a life that includes other concerns and pursuits.

At this point, we need to consider a potential objection to the overall consistency of Aquinas's account of justice, seen in the context of his overall theory of virtue. That theory is generally regarded as a version of eudaimonism, a view according to which, in Nicholas Wolterstorff's words, "the ultimate and comprehensive goal of each of us is that we live our lives as well as possible, the well-lived life being, by definition, the happy life, the *eudaimon* life."[35] As he goes on to explain, eudaimonism is not to be equated with hedonism or ethical egoism:

> It is important to understand what sort of goal happiness is. "Happiness" is not the name of experiences of a certain sort. "Pleasure" names experiences of a certain sort; "happiness" does not. The eudaimonist is not saying that one's sole end in itself is or should be bringing about experiences of a certain sort, everything else being a means. Happiness does not belong to the content of the good life; it *characterizes* the content. The good life is constituted of activities; and what characterizes those activities is that together they make one's life a well-lived life.[36]

Although he is not speaking specifically of Aquinas here, Wolterstorff's remarks capture two important aspects of the ideal of perfection or happiness as Aquinas understands it, namely, its integral connection with activity and,

---

35. Nicholas Wolterstorff, *Justice: Rights and Wrongs* (Princeton: Princeton University Press, 2008), 150.

36. Wolterstorff, *Justice: Rights and Wrongs*, 151, emphasis in the original.

by implication, its independence from subjective feelings of pleasure or satisfaction. The latter point should be underscored. Whatever Aquinas means by saying that all men and women necessarily desire happiness, he is not advocating a life devoted to pleasures and satisfactions.

However, Wolterstorff goes on to identify a deeper problem with eudaimonism, at least seen from the standpoint of an ideal of justice: "Thus one's own happiness is one's ultimate goal in the sense, and only in the sense, that it is one's ultimate reason for selecting as one does from among all the good things one could do, whether as ends or as means. To aim at happiness is to aim at bringing it about that the entirety of one's activities possesses the character of being a well-lived life."[37] On his view, this aim is inconsistent with the acknowledgment that others have rights, grounded in their independent worth. Wolterstorff acknowledges that some theorists, including perhaps Aquinas, try to reconcile eudaimonism with a respect for the rights or worth of others, but he goes on to say, "I reply that to add the idea is to give up eudaimonism."[38]

I have quoted Wolterstorff at some length because he offers an especially clear and cogent formulation of long-standing worries about eudaimonistic theories of morality. While he does not direct his critiques to Aquinas in particular, except in passing, clearly he would regard Aquinas's theory as falling within their scope. Furthermore, Wolterstorff's critique of eudaimonism identifies a paradoxical tension within Aquinas's own thought. That is, even though Aquinas claims that each individual necessarily wills happiness and directs all actions toward that end, he also says, in different contexts, that the will ought to be oriented toward something other than the agent's own perfection or happiness. We have already observed that, on his view, the will is naturally oriented toward the agent's own good, and for that reason it needs virtuous habits in order to be properly disposed toward those goods that are greater than, or simply other than, the self (I-II 56.6). This implies that the

---

37. Wolterstorff, *Justice: Rights and Wrongs*, 151.

38. Wolterstorff, *Justice: Rights and Wrongs*, 179. I do not attempt to address every aspect of Wolterstorff's critique of eudaimonism, which is closely tied to his distinctive theory of rights, life-goods, and worth. The most critical aspect of that critique, from our standpoint, is his claim that eudaimonism is essentially incompatible with a genuine, nonderivative regard for another. For a more extended statement of his critique, see 176–79. He also remarks in passing that, although Aquinas thinks of justice as rendering to each his or her due, he nowhere gives an account of what is due another; see 179 n. 46. As we will see, Aquinas offers an extended, closely reasoned, and detailed account of that which constitutes a person's due, or better, right, in the questions devoted to particular justice.

will is in some way naturally disposed to love something or someone other than the agent's own good, independently of the value of that other for the agent, since otherwise the other-regarding virtues would be perversions of the will. Elsewhere, Aquinas explicitly says that we are to love other people for their own sake, and not for the sake of whatever they may provide us (cf. I-II 26.4). Furthermore, he claims that the rational agent not only can, but necessarily does, love greater goods more than itself, as does every other creature, in accordance with the natural, sensate, or intellectual appetite directed toward placing oneself in a cosmic order (I-II 109.3).

The key to resolving this tension lies in the now-familiar distinction between what we might describe as the objective and the subjective components of an agent's happiness or perfection. Considered subjectively, the agent's happiness necessarily consists in activities that together make up a well-lived life, as Wolterstorff says. The identification of happiness with activity, seen from this perspective, follows from Aquinas's metaphysical account of perfection. Perfection at every level of existence is constituted through operations through which the creature develops and expresses its natural potential, in accordance with its kind. For rational agents, happiness is necessarily understood in terms of perfecting activities, because these are the only terms in which an agent can conceive of his final end in a practically efficacious way. No matter how the agent envisions the life that would be ideal or praiseworthy or satisfying or, in short, perfecting for him, he must understand it, in key part if not entirely, in terms of the activities through which such a life would be pursued and lived out. For this reason, any conception of final perfection or happiness will necessarily be self-regarding, in the sense that it will be tethered to notions of the kinds of actions that are exigent or appropriate for the agent, given this overall conception of the good.

It does not follow, however, that the agent necessarily evaluates the objective entities or states of affairs that she pursues in terms of their value for her or, more generally, that her happiness provides her with the ultimate criterion for choosing to pursue some goods and not others. Aquinas believes that each mature, fully rational individual governs his or her life on the basis of some conception of what it would mean to live well, but that does not mean that the agent's conception of her perfection and her desire to live accordingly provide the immediate starting points and motivations for everything that she does. Indeed, this way of understanding the agent's volition of an end would seem to reverse the way that we actually do form our basic volitions. Men and women devote themselves to ideals, aims, and other persons because they apprehend these as good in themselves, worthy of some kind of reverence or rational love. Because they value these objects of devotion, they shape their conceptions of an appropriate or worthwhile life around the corresponding commitments. To turn to the issue at hand, the just individual does not respect someone's right because doing so would in some way promote his own perfection. Rather, he conceives of his perfection in such a way as to include actions such as this, because he is committed to honoring the value and the due claims of another, out of a sense of the other's independent normative value.

Over the course of a series of important essays on Kant's theory of practical reason, Barbara Hermann proposes a way of dealing with a similar problem in Kant's theory that illuminates Aquinas's approach.[39] Hermann's argument goes as follows. Kant seems to say that our actions are morally good only if they are done out of respect for the moral law—implying that morally good actions cannot be motivated directly by any kind of concern for other persons, communities, and the like. But as Hermann reads him, Kant's overall position is more subtle and persuasive. That is, he holds that the good will is informed by a commitment to morality, in such a way that the agent cares about certain kinds of things and not others, commits herself to acting in some ways rather than others, and rules out certain kinds of behavior, or at the very least regards them as problematic. Thus, the overall ensemble of reasons governing the actions of a morally good person will be determined by norms of rational consistency and equal regard implied by the categorical imperative, in such a way that the reasons governing her choice in any specific instance will stem from this overall ensemble in some way. But that does not mean that the person of good will necessarily acts in order to respect the moral law—that is to say, this stance does not imply that the morally good person always acts for the reason that her act fulfills the requirements of morality. The commitment to duty enters in at an earlier level, so to speak, structuring the agent's motives in accordance with an overarching commitment to live in accordance with the requirements of morality. In her day-to-day actions, the moral agent will act for a diverse range of reasons, but the particular reasons for which she acts, the way she acts, and the constraints she observes will all reflect an overarching commitment to the moral law.

39. Barbara Hermann, *The Practice of Moral Judgment* (Cambridge, MA: Harvard University Press, 1993). In what follows, I rely especially on "Integrity and Impartiality," 23–44, but my thinking on these issues is indebted to her other essays as well.

I suggest that something similar can be said about the agent's orientation toward her perfection, seen in relation to her other-regarding dispositions and acts. Aquinas is committed to the view that the rational agent necessarily desires her perfection in accordance with some conception of the good, and seeks that aim in whatever she does. But as we have seen, this is tantamount to saying that a rational agent necessarily acts in accordance with some general idea of the kinds of activities that are exigent or appropriate, given her overall ideals, commitments, and desires. In other words, she acts out of a reasoned apprehension that her act fits within a coherent way of life to which she is committed. However, the agent's conception of the kind of life that is appropriate for her, as well as her habitual commitment to act in accordance with this way of life, need not be derived from considerations stemming from a self-referential desire for her own perfection. She may well have shaped her conceptions and commitments toward a way of life in accordance with a sense of objective duty or devotion to some artistic ideal or a rational love of other people. If this is the case, then her desire for her own perfection, understood in terms of a desire for a perfecting activity, will be grounded in and will promote her habitual disposition to respect and serve something or someone outside herself.

Aquinas's analysis of intention, considered as an act of the will, provides us with a way of understanding the rational structure of the agent's motivations in such a case. According to this analysis, the agent's intention is always directed toward some end that moves her to action (I-II 12.1; cf. I-II 72.1). At the same time, however, intention is not limited to the agent's ultimate end, in which the will could rest (I-II 12.2). The will can also be said to intend an intermediate end that moves the agent to act and provides a kind of stopping point, insofar as it satisfies the immediate inclination of the will. In such instances, we would say that the agent is immediately and directly motivated to act by the considerations that elicit her intention. At the same time, she is moved by these considerations because they are consonant with the way of life that she is trying to live—and she has arrived at this commitment because these kinds of considerations have moved her to commit herself to live in this way. Someone who respects the claims of another may well do so out of a rational love that moves him to care about her claims for her sake. At the same time, he cares about her and wants to respect her claims, not just for her sake but also because he is committed to a way of life in which regard for the rights of others plays a central role. And finally, he is committed to this way of life because he was initially drawn, through early experiences and personal leaning, to value and to care for others in this way. The same rational love of others that initially formed the habitual dispositions of his will in one way rather than another continues to move him as he acts justly in this or that particular instance.

I want now to begin to make a case that the virtue of justice, in both its forms, can plausibly be regarded as a perfection of the will, that is to say, a salutary and appropriate development of a natural human capacity. The key to doing so lies in placing justice within the context of the wider ensemble of goods and activities that constitute a complete human life.[40] The object of the will, understood in this wider context, is constituted by the ensemble of ideals, causes, interpersonal relations, activities, and satisfactions to which the agent is in some way committed, held together through some overall sense of an appropriate or desirable way of life through which these diverse aims can be pursued in appropriate ways. It will include some rough sense of priorities and comparative values and will also take account of boundaries and parameters, both normative and practical. Furthermore, it will be tethered in some way to the natural forms of life proper to us as living creatures and rational beings. This does not mean that everyone must or should commit herself to one particular natural way of life, and no one can build a life around the project of successful organic functioning. Nonetheless, there are only so many ways in which we can live lives that are recognizably human at all. Furthermore, most of us find the pursuit of distinctively human forms of association to be deeply satisfying. We are typically drawn to intimacy and family life, meaningful work, and active participation in our communities, and on Aquinas's showing, these desires are entirely natural and good in themselves. If this is so, then in at least most instances, we would expect to find that whatever rational agents grasp and desire as their comprehensive good, this good will usually take the concrete form of an ordinary human life, lived through the pursuit and enjoyment of the satisfactions of human existence.

We are now in a better position to say what it means on Aquinas's terms to say that the virtue of justice disposes the will in an appropriate way toward its proper object, understood as the agent's comprehensive good. This claim does not imply that someone who is just cares about justice alone, as if her life included no other values, ideals, or satisfactions. Someone may be genuinely just, while still pursuing all kinds of other satisfactions and ideals, in ways that do not directly raise issues of justice at all. Nonetheless, the dis-

---

40. In the remainder of this section, I am drawing on an account of happiness and the virtues developed at greater length, and with a fuller treatment of the relevant texts, in *Nature as Reason*, 141–230.

position of justice as Aquinas understands it does qualify the orientation of the will toward its object in fundamental ways. On his view, general justice is an architectonic virtue—that is to say, it brings a certain ordering to the acts of the other virtues, directing their more limited activities toward its own immediate object, that is, the common good (II-II 56.5). This does not mean that justice in this sense is equivalent to the rectitude of the will, because the common good of the political community is not equivalent to the comprehensive goodness toward which the upright will is oriented. Nonetheless, general justice is the highest of the moral virtues because it orients the agent toward a collective good of great value (I-II 66.4; II-II 56.6). Particular justice, which orients the individual rightly toward other agents, is not similarly architectonic, but it qualifies the orientation of the will in another way. That is, it sets boundaries on the ways in which the individual interacts with others, including strict prohibitions that may rule out otherwise admirable or expedient activities (II-II 58.7).

Aquinas clearly believes that the demands of justice are immediately grounded in the claims that the community places on its members, and that individual men and women place on one another, for certain kinds of respect, forbearance, and assistance. They do not depend for their normative force on considerations internal to the individual agent or on the exigencies of human happiness generally considered. He would not say that someone who prefers, for example, scientific inquiry to justice is either irrational or unfree. He would not even need to deny that the single-minded pursuit of truth is admirable in its way. He would nonetheless claim that someone who sets other aims or obligations over the demands of justice in this way is badly disposed, and insofar as she acts out of this disposition, she acts wrongly. Furthermore, just acts are praiseworthy, and their contraries are blameworthy, in key part because the virtuous disposition of justice is contingent on the inclinations of the will itself. Someone loves justice or she does not, and while she ought to do so, she may freely and consistently adopt and pursue some other comprehensive ideal instead.

Yet this possibility does not mean that the inclination of the will toward justice is arbitrary. The agent's initial inclinations toward fair and respectful behavior and his mature commitment to an ideal of justice as a way of life reflect an accurate sense of the intrinsic value and standing of other people, together with a good sense of one's own standing in relation to others. They presuppose a sense of the claims of one's community and its value as a way of sustaining a way of life. Most fundamentally, one's orientation toward justice reflects a sense of the value of a distinctively human form of life, which provides the matrix for societies and cooperative relationships of all kinds. These are the values fundamental to human life itself, and, as such, they are naturally attractive to human agents. These values are not so attractive as to compel the will. Someone might very well feel the value of human society and the interpersonal relations that it opens up, while still freely loving some other set of values more, committing himself to a way of life that is objectively unjust. Nonetheless, someone who acts justly out of a settled commitment to justice can be regarded as behaving reasonably, in accordance with inclinations that most people will naturally regard as at least credible.

Of course, a disposition to justice and its corresponding choices are not only reasonable, on Aquinas's terms. They are morally praiseworthy because they represent an adequate response to the real values and claims intrinsic to human life. For this reason Aquinas regards justice as a perfection of the will in an unqualified sense. Nonetheless, given his overall analysis of the will, we would expect that, if justice really does perfect the will in this unqualified way, this perfection should somehow be reflected in the structures and the functioning of the will itself. If justice is a perfection in an unrestricted sense, then we might expect it to strengthen or extend the capacities of the will itself in some way, or to open up possibilities for further perfections that would otherwise be foreclosed. The moral value of justice does not depend on salutary effects such as these, but they do confirm the view that the dispositions and practices of justice play a central role in human life. At the very least, this line of analysis implies that authentic justice cannot pervert the will, in the sense of rendering the agent less free, more isolated from her fellows, or less capable of keeping one's priorities in good order. These considerations will prove to be especially important in the context of general justice, which pertains to the individual's relations to the political community.

At this point, we are taking Aquinas's analysis further than he explicitly does himself, but I believe that he offers ample grounds for extending his thought in this direction. That is what I hope to do over the next three chapters, following along the lines set by Aquinas's detailed analysis of particular justice, and his briefer but highly suggestive remarks on general justice. In each context, I will try to show that Aquinas's analysis of particular and general justice, seen in relation to their proper objects and to the other virtues, has been shaped by an overall sense of justice as a perfection of the will. He is of course working with traditional sources, but his overall theories of the will and the virtues have shaped his interpretations of these sources at key points, leading to him to the highly original theory of justice outlined in the first chapter.

CHAPTER 3

Justice as a Moral Ideal

In this chapter, we turn to Aquinas's extended account of the specific precepts and ideals associated with the virtue of justice. If the analysis of the previous chapter is sound, this account should reflect Aquinas's overall conception of justice as a perfection of the will, at least in some key respects. In this chapter and the next, I hope to show that this is indeed the case by tracing the ways in which his overall conception of justice as a perfection of the will has shaped his interpretation of traditional perspectives on justice and right relations generally. Our inquiry will follow the line set out in the opening questions of his treatment of justice in the *secunda secundae*. In these questions, Aquinas identifies the object of the virtue of justice, the rationale for distinguishing different species or kinds of justice, and the characteristic ways in which justice orients the will toward other individuals and the common good.

Like every other virtue, justice is defined by its formal object, which Aquinas identifies as the act of rendering to another that which is his or her right, or alternatively, as the right to be brought about in a particular act (II-II 57.1). Further on, he adds that the right considered as the object of justice has two characteristics, which together define the virtue of justice properly so called—that is, the right aims at equality in every kind of exchange between two persons, and it generates strict and binding obligations (II-II 80). In chapter 4 we will look more closely at what Aquinas means by saying that the precepts of justice are distinctively stringent. In this chapter we begin by examining the ideal of equality as Aquinas understands it, taking account of the classical and theological sources for this ideal, as well as of the intellectual and social context that shaped his interpretation of these sources. As we will see, Aquinas's general ideal of equality is associated with an account of the right as a rationale for a claim that provides the basis for a defense of active, self-determining freedom. Even more fundamentally, Aquinas's analysis of the right as the object of justice is integrally linked to what we would describe as his fundamental theory of morality.

In this chapter and the next, we will focus primarily, although not exclusively, on Aquinas's account of particular justice, considered both as a normative ideal and as a set of precepts. This way of proceeding has the advantage of following Aquinas's lead by directing attention to those aspects of justice that he himself emphasizes. While Aquinas refers to general justice as an architectonic virtue, preeminent among the connatural virtues, he does not devote a single question to general justice as such or to its proper object, the common good. In contrast, he devotes sixty questions to particular justice and the virtues annexed to it.[1] Length of treatment does not always reflect the overall importance of a given topic for Aquinas, but at the very least, he clearly believes that particular justice offers more in the way of substantive content than does general justice. Furthermore, Aquinas's analysis of particular justice turns out to be foundational for his overall account of justice as a perfection of the will, considered in both its other-regarding operations and in its overall orientation toward the comprehensive good. While general justice plays an architectonic role with respect to the other virtues, particular justice included, it is particular justice that provides the framework and, as it were, the normative grammar necessary for any morally acceptable way of life. General and particular justice work together in such a way as to direct the agent rightly toward the human good—nothing more, since any higher good would be the province of charity, but also nothing less, and nothing else. Justice perfects men and women by humanizing them, in the fullest sense, orienting them rightly toward one another and the human world they share.

Justice, Equality, and Right

Aquinas begins his analysis of *jus*, the right, by asking, "Whether the right is the object of justice?" In his response, he begins by observing that justice implies a kind of equality:

> It is proper to justice, in comparison to the other virtues, that it directs the human person with respect to those things pertaining to others. For

1. I am including here II-II 60–120, excluding II-II 79, concerning the potential parts of justice.

it brings about a certain equality, as the name itself shows, for those things that are equalized are commonly said to be justified. . . . The rectitude of an operation of justice, even apart from any comparison to the agent, is constituted through comparison to another, for that is said to be just in our work that responds to another in accordance with some equality, as for example, the payment of due wages for a service rendered. (II-II 57.1)

Aquinas thus identifies the *jus*, the object of justice, with some kind of equality. This identification would not have been obvious to his interlocutors. Justinian's definition of justice as a constant and perpetual will rendering to each his or her right was widely, although not universally, preferred among thirteenth-century scholastics. However, throughout the early and middle decades of this century, theologians generally interpreted the right by reference to Cicero's treatise *De inventione*, which analyzes the claims of justice in terms of the relations of obligation between unequals, for example, between the deity and humanity, or parents and children, or political rulers and subjects. Understood in this way, particular justice is paradigmatically linked to hierarchical relations, and the right is identified with the claims of superiors to respect, consideration, or obedience.[2] It would be a mistake to assume that these theologians have no commitment to some kind of normative equality. On the contrary, they clearly regard all human persons as fundamentally equal, at least from a moral standpoint.[3] They simply do not associate ideals of equality with particular justice. Rather, for them particular justice, while important in its own sphere, is limited in scope to one set of human relations among many.

Aristotle's *Nicomachean Ethics*, which became available to Western scholars in the latter part of the thirteenth century, offered an alternative account of justice and the right that transformed scholastic thinking about

2. For further details, see Odon Lottin, "Le concept de justice chez les théologiens du moyen âge avant l'introduction d'Aristote," *Revue Thomiste* 44 (1938): 511–21. The relevant text is Cicero, *De inventione* I.2 c.53; for Aquinas's own treatment of this key classical text, see II-II 80. For more extensive treatments of early and middle scholastic definitions of justice, see Stephan Kuttner, "A Forgotten Definition of Justice," *Mélanges G. Fransen, Studia Gratiana* (Rome) 20 (1976): 75–109; and István P. Bejezy, "Law and Ethics: Twelfth-Century Jurists on the Virtue of Justice," *Viator* 2.3 (2005): 197–216.

3. For further details, including a discussion of relevant texts, see Jean Porter, *Natural and Divine Law: Reclaiming the Tradition for Christian Ethics* (Grand Rapids: Eerdmans, 1999), 259–67.

justice.[4] In particular, Aristotle identifies justice paradigmatically with an ideal of equality, exemplified by fair exchanges in financial transactions.[5] Aquinas transforms the meaning of the right by interpreting it in Aristotelian terms as a normative standard of equality, rather than construing it as a claim arising between unequals. Yet it is not clear how far this transformation extends. Clearly, the right as Aquinas presents it is conceptually linked to equality of some kind, but it is not immediately obvious that the right implies any kind of commitment to the actual or normative equality of all persons.

Among our own contemporaries, equality is generally understood in just this expansive way.[6] A number of contemporary philosophers claim that all human beings are in fact equal, at least in some respect, while others argue that we ought normatively to regard all men and women as equals, even if we cannot say that this is in fact the case. On either alternative, each individual ought to be treated in the same way in some key respects, usually spelled out by reference to norms of nonmaleficence and respect for autonomy. This normative ideal, often referred to as equal regard, is usually formulated in such a way as to allow for some kinds of differential treatment and unequal relations, so long as these are rationally defensible and limited in scope. Nonetheless, differential treatment and social inequalities cannot simply be taken for granted—they call for special justification, argued in such a way as to leave intact a general commitment to normative equality.

Does Aquinas think of equality in similar terms, or does he interpret equality in a narrow or restricted way? An Aristotelian ideal of equality of exchanges implies that those involved in the relevant transactions are at least similar in status and capacities, sufficiently so to provide a context within which to make judgments of fairness and reciprocity. But in itself, these presuppositions do not necessarily imply any kind of commitment to a general

4. Again, see Lottin, "Le concept de justice," for further comment.

5. For Aristotle's own identification of justice with what is equal, see the *Nicomachean Ethics*, 5.3, 1131a 10–14, in *Aristotle's Nicomachean Ethics*, trans. Robert Bartlett and Susan Collins (Chicago: University of Chicago Press, 2011), 95.

6. It is difficult to think of any major moral or political philosopher who does not endorse some version of normative equality—the debates, as we would expect, have to do with the meaning and justification of this centrally important ideal. For a comprehensive review and defense of the claim that all human beings are in fact equal by nature, see John E. Coons and Patrick M. Brennan, *By Nature Equal: The Anatomy of a Western Insight* (Princeton: Princeton University Press, 1999), 3–90. Among contemporary political philosophers, Ronald Dworkin stands out for his defense of a normative equality as the "sovereign virtue" of political systems; for an overview of the argument, see *Sovereign Virtue: The Theory and Practice of Equality* (Cambridge, MA: Harvard University Press, 2000), 1–10.

principle of normative equality. We might argue that not everyone is capable of entering into mutual exchanges of the relevant kind, and in that case, the virtue of justice would be limited in scope, important though it might be within its proper context. Aristotle himself famously does not believe that all persons are fundamentally equal, as moral agents or otherwise, and he believes that relations of domination and subordination are natural, necessary, and potentially salutary for subordinates as well as superiors. Strict justice between superiors and subordinates is thus impossible. Aristotle does allow that justice of a kind is possible between unequals, but he clearly regards this kind of justice as derivative, justice by a kind of concession—somewhat in the way that the courage of a woman is intrinsically a lesser kind of courage.[7]

At the same time, we cannot assume that Aquinas's interpretation of equality and the right is simply derived from Aristotle's views. His account of justice in the *Summa theologiae* is profoundly indebted to Aristotle, but he also draws on a wide range of other sources, which he integrates in terms of his overall theory of the virtues. Given his synthetic and constructive approach to his sources, we would expect Aquinas to transform Aristotle's conception of justice, even though it is not always clear to what extent he does so deliberately. In particular, we would expect his interpretation of equality to be shaped by his overall account of justice as a perfection of the will. Aristotle himself does not appear to have any conception of the will as a distinct capacity, and he does not analyze the virtues as perfections, although arguably both claims develop elements of his thought.[8] This being so, we would expect that Aquinas's distinctive analysis of justice as a perfection of the will might lead him beyond Aristotle's own account of justice.

Aquinas's initial remarks on the right as the object of justice suggest that this is indeed the case. His opening remarks in the text cited above remind us

7. The relevant texts are the *Nicomachean Ethics*, 5.6, 103–4 in the Bartlett-Collins edition, and the *Politics*, 1.4–5 and 1.12–13, in *Aristotle's Politics*, 2nd ed., trans. Carnes Lord (Chicago: University of Chicago Press, 2013, originally, 1984), 6–9, 21–24.

8. While this point has been debated in the past, it seems fairly clear that Aristotle does not have a conception of the will as a capacity distinct from the passions and the capacity for rational choice, which depends on reasoned deliberation; see Michael Frede, *A Free Will: Origins of the Notion in Ancient Thought* (Berkeley: University of California Press, 2011), 19–30. Bonnie Kent comments on the significance of this difference for Aquinas's interpretation of the Aristotelian theory of the virtues, in "Losable Virtue: Aquinas on Character and Will," in *Aquinas and the Nicomachean Ethics*, ed. Tobias Hoffmann, Jörn Müller, and Matthias Perkams (Cambridge: Cambridge University Press, 2013), 91–109. For a discussion of Antiochus of Ascalon, who played a key role in transmitting Peripatetic views on virtue ethics, see Julia Annas, *The Morality of Happiness* (Oxford: Oxford University Press, 1993), 180–87.

that justice is distinguished by its orientation toward others, rather than to the agent's own well-being (again, see II-II 57.1). This is so, because justice is the connatural virtue perfecting the will, which is the principle of human actions *ad extra* (I-II 56.6; cf. II-II 58.4). He goes on to say that justice can be a virtue only of the will, because it presupposes rational judgments about the claims of others (II-II 58.4). At each point, the perfecting qualities of justice are connected to constitutive elements of the capacity of the will. This approach implies that, however we may understand justice, we cannot regard it as limited in scope. It would seem that its field of operation is as comprehensive as the operations of the will itself. Admittedly, so far Aquinas's remarks are not strictly inconsistent with a limited ideal of equality, restricted to certain kinds of exchanges. The scope of the virtue of justice need not be understood in such a way as to correspond to the scope of the operations of the will. Nonetheless, the trajectory of Aquinas's thought is clearly moving in this direction. He speaks as if justice disposes the will in such a way as to pursue what is truly good and appropriate in all the agent's external actions, and by implication, in all her relations to other persons or collective entities (cf. I-II 60.2–3). The claim that justice is a perfection of the will suggests, even if it does not entail, that the ideals proper to justice have some bearing on every aspect of the agent's interactions with others. Seen within this context, equality is transformed from an important but limited ideal to a standard that directly or indirectly touches on every aspect of our lives.

This trajectory of thought is reinforced by the very considerable differences between the social and intellectual contexts shaping the work of these two authors. Of course, Aquinas lives in a Christian world and Aristotle does not, but the salient differences do not stop there. Aristotle's ideal of equality of exchange emerges within a social context in which the mutual exchanges proper to the market or to a legal forum would by no means have been the norm for every kind of interaction.[9] Athenian society was at this point structured along fairly clear divisions, above all between men and women, and also among freeborn citizens, slaves, and resident aliens. Within this context, a normative ideal of equality of exchange will necessarily be limited in scope, because individuals in such a society would have relatively few occasions to enter into straightforward exchanges with others of different status.

9. For a good overview of Athenian legal practices seen in relation to the wider society, see S. C. Todd, "The Language of Law in Classical Athens," in *The Moral World of the Law*, ed. Peter Coss (Cambridge: Cambridge University Press, 2000), 17–36.

Aquinas's thought was shaped by a strikingly different set of intellectual and social conditions. Intellectually, his thought is informed by what we might call two traditions of equality, namely, the classical tradition of natural law and natural right, which takes equality of status to be one of the touchstones of the pristine law of nature, and a Christian scriptural tradition, which insists on the fundamental equality of all men and women as bearers of the divine image and, at least potentially, participants in a shared friendship with God. These two traditions came together at a relatively early point, and in the late eleventh century, theological construals of right and natural law began to play a central role in jurisprudence and political thought.[10] Aristotle, Aquinas's interlocutors, and Aquinas himself agree that relations of dominion and subordination rule out the kind of equality of exchange proper to strict justice, at least in some respects. Nonetheless, for Aquinas and his interlocutors, these relations of inequality never go all the way down, so to speak—that is, they are almost always conventional rather than natural, and always presuppose that the parties involved stand as equals to one another simply by virtue of shared humanity. This line of thought was reinforced by those strains of Christian thought that identify distinctively human capacities for rational thought and freedom with the image of God, which is indelibly stamped on every human being, simply in virtue of his or her rational nature.

Socially, the institutions and practices of Aquinas's time reflected newly established, hard-won, and fragile arrangements aimed toward promoting and safeguarding equality and freedom, as far as the conditions of the time permitted.[11] Western European society in the twelfth and thirteenth centuries was structured by hierarchical relations of all kinds—between husband and

---

10. Again, see Porter, *Natural and Divine Law*, 34–62 and 129–63, for further details.

11. The social, economic, and cultural developments in western European society between the end of the eleventh and the beginning of the fourteenth century have been extensively studied. I do not believe that the main lines of the following account would be controversial, although of course a closer study of this period would raise many questions that would be. For a good overview of the social conditions of the time, see R. W. Southern, *Scholastic Humanism and the Unification of Europe*, vol. 1: *Foundations* (Oxford: Blackwell, 1995); see esp. 134–62. Giles Constable offers an illuminating discussion of the interplay between theological ideals and social conditions in *The Reformation of the Twelfth Century* (Cambridge: Cambridge University Press, 1996); see esp. 296–328. Finally, for a powerful account of the resurgence of relations of dominion and servility in the twelfth century, leading to the formulation and implementation of new forms of political authority, see Thomas N. Bisson, *The Crisis of the Twelfth Century: Power, Lordship, and the Origins of European Government* (Princeton: Princeton University Press, 2009).

wife, between those of free and servile status, between the man or woman of substance and the pauper—yet these hierarchies were both limited in scope and to some extent permeable. No one was defined by his or her place in any one of these hierarchies to such an extent that he or she had no social identity and no scope for action except as a man or a woman, a free or servile individual, a priest or a layman or laywoman. As these relations were structured, challenged, and restructured, indirectly or through intentional reforms, the men and women of these societies moved in and out of them, negotiating their status and their relations with others as they went. The ideals and practices of the church at this time generally supported an individual's claims to a high degree of self-determination. Canon law acknowledged an almost unqualified right to marry or to refrain from marriage, and it also acknowledged a right to change religious orders in order to pursue a more strict way of life.[12] More generally, canon law aspired to upholding an ideal of equality before the law, and even though the jurists often fell short of this ideal, it is worth noting that they tried to keep it at all.[13]

In this context, a social theory developed along Aristotelian lines, presupposing fundamental disparities and fixed social hierarchies, would have been unhelpful, not to say flatly inconsistent with experience. At the same time, Aristotle's references to justice and equality, as read by thirteenth-century readers, might well imply a more comprehensive ideal of equality than Aristotle himself had in mind. At any rate, it would appear that Aquinas reads Aristotle in just this expansive way. Aquinas is firmly committed, on both philosophical and theological grounds, to the view that all human beings are equal in virtue of sharing in a common human nature. He reads Aristotle in the context of this wider commitment, in such a way as to transform the Aristotelian notion of equality of exchange into a robust ideal of normative equality.

In order to appreciate what Aquinas means by equality considered as

12. On the right of those in a state of servitude to marry, see Antonia Bocarius Sahaydachny, "The Marriage of Unfree Persons: Twelfth Century Decretals and Letters," in *De iure canonico medii aevi: Festschrift für Rudolf Weigand*, ed. Peter Landau, Studia Gratiana 27 (Rome: Libreria Ateneo Salesiano, 1996), 483–506. Charles Reid offers a more comprehensive account of the rights pertaining to marriage and sexual functions; see Charles J. Reid Jr., *Power over the Body, Equality in the Family: Rights and Domestic Relations in Medieval Canon Law* (Grand Rapids: Eerdmans, 2004), 25–68. On the right to change one's monastic community in pursuit of a higher spiritual ideal, see Constable, *The Reformation of the Twelfth Century*, 262–63.
13. James A. Brundage, *Medieval Canon Law* (London: Longman, 1995), 3.

normative ideal, we need first of all to look more closely at his remarks on the natural equality of all human persons. Aquinas is of course well aware that human beings are unequal in many ways, for example, in bodily or mental capacities, and these kinds of disparities would have existed even if our first parents had not sinned (I 96.3). Nonetheless, he holds that all human persons are equal in the critical respect that each is an individual of the same specific natural kind, namely, humanity. This view implies for him that each human individual, without exception, is potentially capable of intellectual understanding and discursive reasoning, which he identifies with the image of God borne by every human being (I 93.1,4). Not every human being is capable of developing and exercising her rational faculties, but they are intrinsic to human existence, structurally built into the substance of each individual, and fundamental to our sense of what we owe to one another. Aquinas's remarks on the divine image in the *prima pars* emphasize rationality and intellectual capacity, but in the introduction to the *prima secundae*, he quotes a well-known remark of John of Damascus, identifying the divine image with human capacities for self-governance and dominion over one's own actions. The upshot is that all human beings are equal, in that each possesses at least the innate capacities for intellectual understanding, discursive reasoning, and free, self-determining action. Furthermore, the natural equality of all men and women implies that the hierarchical structures of society, legitimate and necessary though they may be, are almost always conventional rather than natural, and always presuppose that the parties involved stand as equals to one another, simply by virtue of shared humanity.[14] Aquinas makes this point crisply, in order to contrast rule among angelic agencies with human rule: "The demons are not equal with respect to nature, and so there is among them a natural prelate. This is not the case among human beings, who by nature are equal [*pares*]" (I 109.2 *ad* 3).

Seen within this context, Aquinas's claim that justice aims at bringing about an equality of exchange appears as central to his overall account of justice. For him, the ideal of equality of exchanges is paradigmatic, because in every encounter or relationship, we are engaged with someone who is in some fundamental way an equal, if only by virtue of our shared humanity. This does not mean, of course, that the paradigmatic ideal of justice will be attainable or desirable in every encounter with another—in many contexts,

---

14. Almost always, because family relations are partially natural—but Aquinas nonetheless insists on the fundamental equality of men and women, and on the political character of the marriage relationship. And children, of course, grow out of their dependence on parents.

an equal return for benefits or losses would be impossible or inappropriate. Nonetheless, we can readily see why equality of exchange is paradigmatic for him, if only because many everyday encounters in such a community will involve exchanges of the relevant kind. Aquinas's conception of justice thus gives a central place to ideals of equality of exchange, equity, and fairness, because these are always potentially relevant and will often be directly relevant in a society of those who are equal in some fundamental ways.

Correlatively, we can now see why Aquinas identifies judicial judgment as a paradigm of just action, and why he gives so much attention to judicial procedures and to what we would call norms of due process. Legal procedures play a central role in Aquinas's overall theory of justice because they represent one of the most important institutional contexts within which men and women are held accountable and take responsibility, in accordance with mutually acknowledged reasons for action. Moreover, as we have already observed, legal procedures in Aquinas's time reflected a commitment to an ideal of equality before the law, even though this ideal was not always respected. By focusing on the prudent and well-disposed judge as a paradigm of justice, Aquinas thus connects the virtue of justice to institutionalized practices of equality (II-II 60.1; the rationale for identifying the judge as a paradigm of justice is spelled out at II-II 57.1 *ad* 1). He goes on to devote five further articles to the theoretical and practical questions that emerge within legal contexts, including the fundamental question of the legitimacy of judicial judgment, the norms governing judicial deliberation, the importance of judging in accordance with written law, and the legitimacy, or otherwise, of judgment without due authority (II-II 60.2–6). Over the course of working through these questions, Aquinas develops widely held ideals of political rule, equality before the law, and what we would describe as norms of due process and proper legality. Such discussion suggests an ideal of equality that extends well beyond judicial contexts. Negatively, equality implies that no one can be subject to the private judgments or wishes of another. Positively, the claims that individuals exercise on one another must be rationally justifiable in terms of cogent, impartial standards of reasonableness or fittingness.

This emphasis on equality construed as impartiality continues through Aquinas's analysis of distributive and commutative justice, which, as we have seen, are the two fundamental forms of particular justice. As such, each is defined by reference to an ideal of equality. Distributive justice aims at rectitude or equity in the distribution of communal benefits and burdens, while commutative justice pertains to relations between private individuals (II-II 61.2; see esp. II-II 61.2 *ad* 2).

The first point to be noted is that distributive justice is a kind of particular justice, not to be identified with general or legal justice. This point is sometimes overlooked, because distributive justice presupposes a set of communally shared standards for merit and excellence that govern its operations. Nonetheless, even though distributive justice operates within social contexts, it is immediately concerned with individual claims of right, and as Aquinas explicitly says, it is a kind of particular justice (II-II 61.1 *ad* 4). In a way that is reminiscent of Cicero's interpretation of justice, distributive justice operates within a context of asymmetrical relations, in this case, between those who are responsible for distributing benefits, burdens, offices, and distinctions of all kinds, and the potential recipients of these distributions (II-II 61.1 *ad* 3). In the case of distributive justice, however, the criteria for appropriate and right exchanges are not determined by reference to personal relations of affinity and beneficence. Rather, they are set by the impersonal criteria determined by the rationale governing the distribution (II-II 61.2, 63.1). Just distributions are proportionate in some way to the objective claims and liabilities, or the abilities and qualifications, of the recipients. Aquinas is thinking in particular of the distribution of public offices and honors, which can and indeed should take account of candidates' differing abilities or merits, as these are relevant to the office or honor to be awarded (II-II 63.1). To take another kind of example, the citizens of a commonwealth, as such, have an equal claim on the material and cultural benefits of the community, and equal responsibilities for bearing its burdens. It would be unjust to set up one's financial system in such a way as to consistently benefit one social class to the detriment of others, or to place the burdens of economic hardship on one region of the community rather than another.[15] The key idea here is that distributive justice preserves equal respect for all parties by operating in accordance with rational criteria, derived from the purposes served by a particular set of social arrangements, a role or office, and the like. Because men and women are rational agents, they can grasp, and ideally endorse, distributions governed by these kinds of criteria, even when they work to someone's disadvantage. When the norms of distributive justice are observed, no one is placed at an advantage, or a disadvantage, based solely on the arbitrary whim of another.

15. This is not Aquinas's example, and it is admittedly not clear that he would regard the operations of social structures and institutions as falling within the scope of distributive justice. At any rate, he does say that a law that imposes burdens on some more than others without justification is unjust, even though it is otherwise legitimately aimed at the common good; see I-II 96.4.

Relations between individuals are generally governed by the norms of commutative justice, which aims at some kind of parity in exchanges of all kinds (II-II 61.4). The paradigmatic act of commutative justice is thus restitution, the restoration of some equitable balance of burdens and benefits among individuals (II-II 62.1). Aquinas's remarks on restitution appear to reflect the sacramental and legal practices of his time. Nonetheless, these practices clearly presuppose social bonds of accountability and responsibility, and Aquinas's analysis offers another opportunity to develop the ideal of natural equality as he understands it.

Restitution is the characteristic act of commutative justice, but the significance of this virtue becomes clearer when Aquinas turns to the kinds of actions that would call for restitution, that is to say, the characteristic sins against commutative justice (on restitution, see II-II 62). The action calling for restitution comprises the generally recognized norms of nonmaleficence, identified as more or less immediate implications of the precepts of the Decalogue, including prohibitions against murder, theft, fraud, and the like (II-II 64 intro.; see II-II 64–78). In developing this point, Aquinas once again takes his starting points from Aristotle, but it is worth noting that Aristotle does not explicitly say that these kinds of actions violate a norm of equality, although arguably he implies as much.[16] Aquinas does not say so either, but he does say that these kinds of actions are forms of dishonor that fail to give due acknowledgment to a kind of excellence. This point occurs in the context of a discussion of offenses committed verbally, including invective, detraction, and the like. These kinds of offenses imply a kind of disrespect, as he observes. He compares this disrespect with that shown by actions directed against the person, the associates, or the possessions of another. The critical point is that in each case, Aquinas associates the disrespect in question with a kind of dishonor:

> Contumely implies dishonor to someone. This can happen in two ways. For since honor follows from some excellence, someone can dishonor another by depriving him of an excellence on account of which he had honor. This comes about through sins of deeds, which we treated above. In another way, this comes about when someone brings that which is contrary to the honor of another to his attention and that of others. And this properly pertains to contumely. (II-II 72.1)

16. See the *Nicomachean Ethics*, 5.2, 1130b 30–1131a 9, and 5.4, 1132a 1–19, for the relevant texts.

In order to appreciate the full significance of these remarks, we need to keep in mind that the sins of deed to which Aquinas refers include assaults on the person, the associates, or the property of another, for example, murder, adultery, or theft (II-II 64–71). These kinds of actions are strictly prohibited, no matter what the status or circumstances of the intended victim might be. Thus, when Aquinas characterizes these as deprivations of excellence, what he has in mind can be only some natural excellence, on account of which every man and woman should be honored. In this way, Aquinas draws on the language of personal fealty and differential status as a way of articulating a very different set of ideals, according to which human individuals relate as equals on the shared ground of mutual respect and common commitments.

By now, it will be apparent that, although the Aristotelian ideal of equality in exchanges provides Aquinas with a starting point, his overall account of equality and justice draws on non-Aristotelian sources as well. The language of honor and excellence reflects his own social and legal context, and it looks back to the Roman jurisprudential tradition that shaped that context. We will look more closely at these strands of his thought in the next section. Before doing so, however, we need to consider one further aspect of his general approach to justice as equality, namely, his treatment of the virtues annexed to justice (II-II 80). These are the virtues that Cicero identifies as key components of justice, namely, religion, piety, gratitude, vindication, observance, and truthfulness.

As we observed at the beginning of this section, for Aquinas's immediate predecessors, these virtues are not annexed to justice, but rather, taken together, they constitute the normative ideal that is central to the virtue. Given his commitment to an ideal of equality, we might be surprised to find that Aquinas identifies these ideals of inequality with justice in any sense at all. However, he has strong reasons for doing so. Cicero's taxonomy of virtues is too deeply embedded in scholastic thought to be disregarded, and even more important, it reflects aspects of general experience and intuitions that Aquinas needs on his own terms to address. We all participate in particular relationships, including hierarchical relations both of authority and of subordination, as well as interpersonal ties of blood, friendship, and beneficence. These relations are not only legitimate but necessary for existence and well-being at both the individual and the social levels. Aquinas certainly recognizes the value of these kinds of relations, and Cicero's virtues provide him with a framework for subjecting them to moral analysis. In order to do so, he first establishes that these virtues are legitimately associated with justice, even though they deviate in some way from the ideal of justice strictly so called. Each aims at a qualified form of right, appropriate to contexts in which an equal exchange or strict obligation would be impossible or inappropriate. It is apparent that Aquinas here qualifies his commitment to an ideal of equality. What is less apparent is that he also affirms and extends his commitment to the core ideal through a careful analysis of the ways in which our equality as participants in a shared nature qualifies and constrains the obligations we have as occupants of particular roles. Even in these contexts, the paradigmatic ideal of equality associated with strict justice enters into Aquinas's analysis.

We see this element most clearly in the terms within which Aquinas analyzes the paradigms for right associated with the virtues of religion, piety, and observance. He argues that these should all be considered to be variant forms of justice, on the grounds that they aim at an analogous kind of equality, that is, an adequation between claims and benefits, on the one hand, and one's capacities for a fitting response, on the other (II-II 57.1 *ad* 3, 102.1 *ad* 3). More fundamentally, Aquinas presupposes that all of these relations, with the partial exception of our relationship to divinity, are limited in scope and qualified by a range of other claims.[17] Even in these contexts, Aquinas presupposes a social world in which individuals, equal with respect to their shared nature, stand in all kinds of relations to one another, moving in and out of these and sorting out their competing claims against a baseline ideal of equality, broadly understood.

For example, someone can never make an adequate return to his mother for all that she has done for him, and she can legitimately ask certain things of him and expect certain kinds of respect and deference, simply because she is his mother. His relations to his mother as such fall within the scope of piety, due deference to one's parents, rather than justice strictly so called (II-II 101.2). Yet this relationship, fundamental and inescapable though it may be, does not define either her life or her child's life. Their lives unfold in an ever-changing matrix of multiple relations, including different kinds of relations to one another as well as complex relations to others. These relations generate claims that qualify the claims that they can appropriately

17. This is apparent when we work through the detailed casuistry of the questions on piety (II-II 101), observance (II-II 102), and the component parts of observance, namely, veneration (II-II 103) and obedience (II-II 104), on which more below. In addition, Aquinas sorts out the different obligations that we owe to parents, spouses, children, and others in his question on the order of charity, which he clearly regards as grounded in reason and not in divine grace alone (II-II 26.6–12).

make on one another as parent and child. Aquinas will not say that the demands of one virtue can contradict that of another, but what counts as, for example, piety in a given situation will take account of other kinds of claims in an appropriate way. To continue with this example, someone may wish to enter religious life, even though his mother does not want him to do so. He may be obliged to respect her wishes on other grounds, if, for example, she depends on him for her support, but he is not otherwise obliged to defer to his mother's wishes on such a fundamental decision (II-II 101.4).

In a similar way, Aquinas's commitment to equality as both a human reality and a normative ideal qualifies what he has to say about relations of authority and subordination, which fall under the scope of observance, veneration, and obedience (II-II 102–4) He does acknowledge that, under the actual conditions of our lives, which reflect the effects of sin, as well as natural discrepancies of ability and rectitude, it is inevitable that we will stand in relations of dominance and subordination to one another, including some that are harsh and onerous, and others that are honorable and not excessively burdensome (I 94.6). Nonetheless, he insists that all these relations, including the most onerous forms of servitude, operate within parameters set by the demands of shared humanity. As we have seen, he rules out the possibility of natural hierarchies among human beings because we all share equally in a fundamental human nature. Elsewhere, he identifies this commonality more specifically with our status as rational agents, capable of free judgment and voluntary, responsible action (II-II 47.12). In effect, he denies Aristotle's claim that some are natural slaves, because they lack the use of reason in critical respects, by reinterpreting Aristotle's remarks in such a way as to limit what he says to the proper functions of a slave, considered as such. Considered as a human being, he adds, the slave is capable of reasoned, free judgment, just as anyone else is, and therefore capable of acquiring and exercising the virtue of practical wisdom (again, see II-II 47.12).

Aquinas's remarks on obedience are especially relevant to his overall account of justice as equality, because they offer a good indication of the way in which he moves from an ideal of equality to practical judgments. Aquinas begins his discussion of obedience by considering the claim that relations of authority and subordination are themselves illegitimate, on the (partial) grounds that God created the human person free and wills that the individual should be governed only by his or her own judgment (this is the first of three objections offered at II-II 104.1, "Whether one person is bound to obey another?"). He replies that, just as lower creatures are moved by higher creatures in the order of natural causality, so in the realm of human action, the will of a subordinate is appropriately moved by the command of a superior authority. This does not imply, however, that a subordinate surrenders his or her own judgment and will:

> God leaves the human person in the hand of his own counsel, not because it is licit for him to do everything he wishes, but because he is not bound to that which is to be done by a necessity of nature, as irrational creatures are, but by free choice proceeding from his own counsel. And just as other things that are to be done ought to proceed from his own counsel, so this also, that he obeys his superiors. (II-II 104.1 *ad* 1)

This qualification suggests that Aquinas wants to resist any suggestion that the obligations of obedience are absolute and unconditional. When we come to II-II 104.5, "Whether subordinates are bound to obey their superiors in all things?," we find that this is indeed the case. First, no one is bound to obey another if doing so would contravene God's law—on the contrary, one is positively obliged not to obey in such a case. This response is what we would expect. However, Aquinas goes on to qualify the obligation of obedience in another way. "No inferior is held to obey a superior if he commands something in which [the inferior] is not subordinated" (II-II 104.5). This comment implies, first of all, that no one is obliged to obey another human being with respect to those things that pertain to the inner motions of the will. The scope of human obedience extends only to those things that are done externally through the body. Second, even with respect to external actions, the scope of human authority and the obligations of obedience are further limited in particular contexts by the rationale for the authority in question. For example, a soldier is required to obey his commander in military matters, but not in other spheres of life. Finally, just as the obligation to obedience is grounded in nature, so nature sets limits on the extent of this obligation:

> With respect to those things that pertain to the nature of the body, a human person is not obliged to obey another human person, but only God, because human persons are equal by nature, for example, in those things that pertain to the sustaining of the body and the generation of children. Hence, those in a state of servitude are not obliged to obey their lord, nor are children obliged to obey their parents, with respect to contracting matrimony or preserving virginity or anything else of this sort. (II-II 104.5)

Here we see Aquinas asserting a general claim to freedom in certain fundamental aspects of human life, including most centrally those having to do with marriage and celibacy. We are all equal, insofar as we share in a common human nature, and for Aquinas this natural equality places strict limits on the scope of human authority. Aquinas's argument indicates clearly that, for him, justice is tied to an ideal of equality that is closely linked, conceptually and practically, to the fundamental conception of the human person as a voluntary agent, capable of determining the course of her own life and entitled to do so, at least within limits. The disposition of justice, which is a perfection of the will, presupposes a social world of free, responsible, and accountable men and women, and it consists in key part, although not entirely, in a disposition to respect the freedom and the justified claims of others. As we will see, this line of analysis reflects a second strand of Aquinas's account of equality and justice.

At this point, it will be helpful to take stock of what we have seen so far. Aquinas takes his starting point for analyzing the concept of right from Aristotle's analysis of the right in terms of equality of exchange. By choosing to take this, rather than Cicero's virtue of unequal obligation, as his starting point, Aquinas effectively makes the point that equality of some kind, rather than sheer obligation, is central to the ideal of justice. Equality of exchange in itself does not imply that persons are in fact equal or should be treated as such. However, Aquinas is in fact committed to actual and normative equality on other grounds, and for him, the ideal of equality of exchange is always at least potentially relevant, and usually actually relevant in any interaction between two people. He accordingly extends Aristotle's paradigms of equal exchange, taken from economic transactions, to include exchanges of such intangibles as honor, forbearance, and benefit. As he reflects on these and similar considerations, he draws on a second set of sources, taken from jurisprudential traditions and the social and legal practices of his own day. We now turn to a consideration of this strand of his thought.

Equality, Right, and Obligation

So far, we have focused on the ways in which Aquinas appropriates and transforms Aristotle's claim that particular justice aims at establishing a kind of equality in transactions between individuals. Nonetheless, the definition of justice that Aquinas sets forth is drawn from the tradition of Roman jurisprudence, which identifies justice with right, and more specifically, with someone's own right. These two ways of thinking about justice, drawn from two distinct philosophical and social traditions, are not obviously compatible. Aristotle's analysis of justice focuses on exchanges, especially but not only financial transactions, which are to be understood in terms of relations of commensuration and ideals of fairness and equity. Within a broad range of cases, the actual substance of the exchanges is relatively unimportant; what matters, rather, is the overall fairness of the transaction. The Roman juridical perspective, in contrast, focuses on the right, considered as a kind of claim that one person has on another. It does not take account of exchanges or transactions, except insofar as the act of rendering someone's right is itself a kind of transaction, and by the same token, it does not aim at equalizing exchanges or agents. It does, however, direct attention to what we might call the substance of the interaction. The just individual renders another his or her right by honoring some claim that the other has on the former, typically a fairly specific claim to some kind of performance or to respect for some immunity or liberty.

Aquinas's attempts to integrate these two perspectives lead him at some points to awkward or unpersuasive formulations. Nonetheless, he clearly has a stake in holding on to both perspectives on justice, and not only because each has a venerable tradition behind it. The relation between ideals of equality and claims of right is one of the central issues within contemporary theories of justice, and we can readily see why this would be so. Each ideal captures some key elements of our intuitions about justice, and we would expect a satisfactory account of justice to integrate these ideals, preferably in such a way as to set out the interconnections between them. Yet this has proven to be a surprisingly difficult program. Most of those writing on justice and related topics have argued that standards of equal regard and rights claims are interrelated in some way, but there is considerable disagreement over the proper relation, and especially the proper order of priority, between the two.[18] And not everyone agrees that ideals of equality and right should be integrated into a comprehensive theory of justice, at least not in such a way

18. According to John Rawls, claims of right set constraints on what can be done in pursuit of equality, whereas Dworkin argues that equality is the more fundamental principle, sufficient to generate claims of right; see, respectively, John Rawls, *A Theory of Justice* (Cambridge, MA: Harvard University Press, 1971), 54–117, and Dworkin, *Sovereign Virtue*, 120–83. For an example of an attempt to analyze the idea of a right in utilitarian terms, see Richard B. Brandt, *Morality, Utilitarianism, and Rights* (Cambridge: Cambridge University Press, 1992), 179–214. Finally, for the main lines of Robert Nozick's argument for the overriding force of rights claims, see *Anarchy, State, and Utopia* (New York: Basic Books, 1974), 26–53.

as to preserve the distinctiveness of these two ideals. A number of political theorists argue that justice should be understood in terms of equality, usually interpreted in a utilitarian fashion, while there are a few, most notably Robert Nozick, who associate justice with overriding claims of right, interpreted in terms of entitlement grounded in the productive activities of persons.

Aquinas does not discuss equality and right as abstract principles, and it would therefore be misleading to say that he sets out to integrate these in the way that so many of our contemporaries do. Nonetheless, he clearly holds that particular justice implies commitments to both standards of equality and claims of right, and he seems to present these as two distinct yet mutually interpreting ideals. We have already seen some indications of his overall approach in his discussion of the legitimacy and the limits of obedience. While he affirms the legitimacy and necessity of obedience in human affairs, he also places strict constraints on the kinds of demands that can be placed on anyone, appealing to our equality with respect to fundamental aspects of our shared human nature. Claims of right are therefore grounded in natural equality and represent perhaps the most important practical implication of our equal status.

On this reading, Aquinas's conception of right comes very close to a contemporary notion of a subjective natural or human right. This line of interpretation would be rejected out of hand by many contemporary scholars, who read Aquinas's conception of the right in very different terms. On this reading, the right identified as the object of justice simply refers to whatever is due to another, in accordance with legal or contractual obligations or the demands of objective morality. Furthermore, until recently, most historians and political theorists assumed that the idea of individual subjective rights is a distinctively modern phenomenon, dating at the earliest to the fourteenth century, but coming into prominence only in the late sixteenth century.[19] Given this general view, the question of whether Aquinas might have entertained a theory of natural rights in the contemporary sense did not arise, because on this view, no one at his time could have done so.

More recently, Brian Tierney and Charles Reid have conclusively shown that the general historical view just sketched is wrong.[20] Beginning in the

19. Brian Tierney offers a good overview of this view in *The Idea of Natural Rights: Studies on Natural Rights, Natural Law, and Church Law, 1150–1625* (Atlanta: Scholars Press, 1997), 13–42. For a good example, see Richard Tuck, *Natural Rights Theories: Their Origin and Development* (Cambridge: Cambridge University Press, 1979).

20. Tierney, *The Idea of Natural Rights*, 43–77; Charles J. Reid Jr., "The Canonistic Contribution to the Western Rights Tradition: An Historical Inquiry," *Boston College Law Review* 33.1 (1991): 37–92, and in greater detail, *Power over the Body, Equality in the Family*.

mid-thirteenth century, some canon lawyers were already defending individ-ual claims to some performance or some forbearance, in terms that clearly indicate that they understood these as subjective natural rights. Further-more, individuals could claim their rights in a number of tribunals, in the reasonable hope of a fair hearing and the possibility of vindication. Rights claims were central to the theory and practice of marriage law, and they also emerged in many other contexts. Admittedly, the jurists do not develop sys-tematic theories of natural rights, nor do they extend rights claims to every domain of moral thought or legal practice. Nonetheless, it seems clear that by Aquinas's time, some scholastic jurists are already defending subjective natural rights, in at least some contexts.

Almost no one, however, including Tierney himself, is prepared to say that Aquinas recognizes subjective natural rights, even implicitly. On the contrary, Tierney regards Aquinas as an eminent representative of what was already an old-fashioned tradition:

> Habermas and De Lagarde both drew a contrast between the modern doctrine of natural rights and the thought of Thomas Aquinas, in whose work the older tradition of natural law found classical expression. *This observation, a commonplace in much recent writing on natural law theories, is true enough so far as it goes*; but it has led to a radical error of periodiza-tion in most modern writing on the history of natural rights. . . . It may be that a juristic, distinctively non-Aristotelian theory of natural rights had grown up before Aquinas, that Aquinas did not choose to assimilate such ideas into his Christian-Aristotelian synthesis, but that they did enter the mainstream of Western political thought through other channels.[21]

On this interpretation, Aquinas's account of justice is more or less deter-mined by one source, namely Aristotle. But we have already seen reason to question Aquinas's sole reliance on Aristotle, and at the very least, we cannot presume it here. Certainly, Aquinas does identify the right with an objective standard or claim to be realized in a relation between two (or more) parties, and in this sense he identifies right with an objective state of affairs. But this line of analysis does not commit him to any particular construal of what con-stitutes a just relation. In particular, it does not rule out the possibility that in some situations the right, understood as an objectively equitable relation, presupposes that someone's claim of a right or a claim by right is duly ac-

---

21. Tierney, *The Idea of Natural Rights*, 45, emphasis mine.

knowledged. When we examine the relevant texts, we find that Aquinas very often does say that individuals can claim certain liberties and immunities on the basis of some natural right, in terms that make it clear that these claims lie within the discretion of the individual. His overall conception of natural law and natural right implies that individuals can legitimately make certain claims by right, claims that emerge within some contexts and not others. He does not have a theory of rights, but neither do the scholastic jurists of the time, and his appeals to what someone can claim by right are reminiscent of their views. If they can be said to have a notion of subjective natural rights, the same can be said of Aquinas himself.

The question of what Aquinas or any other medieval author would have meant by right or a right or the right is complicated by the fact that we ourselves are by no means clear about this important and controversial concept. For many scholars and activists, rights talk offers a vivid, rhetorically effective way of expressing moral claims that could just as well be formulated in other terms. Nonetheless, as Tierney observes, modern and contemporary theories of human or natural rights characteristically make stronger claims, to the effect that rights are subjective moral powers inhering in individuals and exercised at their discretion.[22] Although this division is by no means exhaustive, subjective rights characteristically take one of two forms. On the one hand, a right may be regarded as a claim that imposes a duty on another. Alternatively, a right may be regarded as an immunity from some kind of coercion or harm, implying that someone else has no right to coerce or harm another in some specific way. A subjective right would accordingly be interpreted as a moral power of the individual through which she can authoritatively claim something from another at her discretion or claim immunity from some kind of coercion or harm.

What does it mean to say that at least some of the scholastic jurists have a conception of natural subjective rights? They do not develop theories of rights, as we have noted. Rather, their conception of natural rights is reflected in their practices, insofar as they defend substantive claims to

22. I draw on Tierney and Reid for the following account of what is distinctive about modern and contemporary theories of subjective natural rights; see Tierney, *The Idea of Natural Rights*, 43–56; Reid, "The Canonistic Contribution," 59–65. While no summary could do justice to the complexities of contemporary theories of rights, I believe that Tierney and Reid offer insightful analyses of what is at stake in the defense of subjective rights, which would be generally accepted as such. For an independent summary of recent theories, covering many of the same authors and issues as Tierney and Reid, see Kieran Cronin, *Rights and Christian Ethics* (Cambridge: Cambridge University Press, 1992), 26–56.

natural rights that reflect the normative logic just outlined. That is to say, they regard at least some appeals to right as discretionary claims through which one individual obliges another to perform some duty, or demands immunity from coercion in some specific respect. The clearest indications of the scholastic jurists' views on rights claims can be found, unsurprisingly, in the legal practices that they defend and the innovations that they support. While they do not offer theories of natural rights, they justify individuals' claims to their rights, which are theirs by nature. These claims, as well as the jurists' reflections on them, emerge within the context of juridical practice and reflect processes of reflection on, and official recognition of, preconventional bases for claims upon others.

As Tierney has observed, Europe in the twelfth and thirteenth centuries was a litigious society, within which traditional and novel claims of right played a central role in the expansion and reform of judicial procedures.[23] Men and women of every condition laid claim to rights of all kinds, on whatever basis, in whichever courts would give them a hearing. Initially, these claims were justified by appeals to prior agreements or historical grants of privilege or immunity or some enactment of human or divine law. However, scholastic jurisprudence, especially among canon lawyers, drew on an alternative tradition of right, according to which there is a natural right, or natural law, that precedes and in some way supersedes human agreements and enactments. In its earlier philosophical and juridical forms, this natural right was not identified with rights in anything like our sense; rather, it was associated with immutable legal or moral principles, which are known through one's natural powers of reasoned judgment but which are in no way under the individual's control. For the scholastic jurists and theologians, in contrast, natural right is associated most fundamentally with the individual's capacities for moral discernment or with the foundational first principles that provide the starting points for such discernment. Natural right thus understood is a kind of individual capacity or power, integrally connected to the human person's freedom and her standing as a responsible moral agent. This conception of natural right does not necessarily imply any kind of belief in rights as subjective moral powers, but within the scholastics' context, it would readily suggest such a view. As Tierney remarks:

23. Tierney, *The Idea of Natural Rights*, 54–58; for more general accounts of the expansion and development of legal activities and fora in this period, see Southern, *Scholastic Humanism*, 134–62, 237–82, and James A. Brundage, *The Medieval Origins of the Legal Profession: Canonists, Civilians, and Courts* (Chicago: University of Chicago Press, 2008), 75–125.

Once the term *jus naturale* was clearly defined in this subjective sense the argument could easily move in either direction, to specify natural laws that had to be obeyed or natural rights that could licitly be exercised; and canonistic arguments soon did move in both directions. Stoic authors, when they wrote of *jus naturale*, were thinking mainly in terms of cosmic determinism; the canonists were thinking more in terms of human free choice. When the concept of *jus naturale* was associated in the canonists' glosses with words like "power" "faculty," "free will," it was moving in a different semantic field of force, so to speak, and took on new meanings. Stoic reflection on *jus naturale* never led to a doctrine of natural rights; canonistic reflection did so, and quickly.[24]

Natural rights, thus understood, are claims to some kind of performance or some immunity that is grounded in natural (that is to say, preconventional) aspects of human life. These kinds of claims might have been construed in such a way as to yield a system of objective, impersonal duties that all are bound to observe without reference to any one individual's claims. Tierney's point, however, is that the close association between the concept of right and notions of freedom, faculty, and power led the canon lawyers of the time to construe these claims in terms of individual freedoms or powers, stemming in some way from the agent's natural capacities and needs. Thus understood, someone who claims his right to some benefit or forbearance exercises a discretionary claim that goes beyond general obligations by specifying that these are to be performed in some specified way, for the benefit of the one exercising the claim. Thus, the recognition of natural rights added two things to the accepted framework of mutual obligations, namely, the recognition that individuals enjoy a discretionary power to enjoin or forbid certain kinds of actions in their regard, and second, by implication, that individuals have the power to specify general obligations in such a way as to render them concrete and exigent.

Seen from one perspective, rights claims thus represent a reasonable, if not inevitable, development of long-standing philosophical and doctrinal commitments. Seen from another perspective, these claims reflect a logical extension of practices already in place, in both civil and ecclesiastical contexts, for safeguarding individual freedom. Tierney cites the example of the thirteenth-century canon lawyer Laurentius, who reformulates the obligation of the rich to supply the necessities of the poor in terms of a *jus*,

---

24. Tierney, *The Idea of Natural Rights*, 65–66; more generally, see 58–69.

a claim possessed by the poor individual himself: according to Laurentius, when the poor person takes from another under press of necessity, it is "as if he used his own right and his own thing." Furthermore, this right came to be regarded as a claim having juridical effect, insofar as it could be asserted and secured through a public process of adjudication. Of course, such a process would require some kind of legal structure, but for that very reason, it is incumbent on society to put the necessary procedures in place. And indeed, as Tierney goes on to observe, scholastic canon lawyers did set up legal fora through which the right to surplus wealth could be publically defended and enforced.[25]

Where does Aquinas fit within this overall trajectory? We can readily see why Tierney and other scholars might conclude that Aquinas does not have a conception of subjective rights. He does not offer a theory of natural or human rights, nor does he generally refer to a right in possessive terms, that is to say, as someone's own right. Neither did the jurists themselves develop theories of rights, but as we have seen, at least some of them refer to rights in possessive terms, implying discretionary moral powers inhering in individuals. Aquinas clearly does believe that natural law and natural right are morally significant, but he appears to treat these as considerations justifying or ruling out some line of conduct, without reference to individual claims and immunities.

When we examine the relevant texts more closely, however, the distinction between his view and that of the jurists turns out to be less sharp than we might have thought. It is true that Aquinas does identify the right in its most general sense with an objectively just state of affairs, or with the normative considerations that determine what counts as right relations among individuals. But as Tierney himself points out, natural right can be understood in objective as well as subjective terms; these are not mutually exclusive options.[26] The jurists whom Tierney and Reid consider do recognize objective duties generated by natural right, but this recognition does not keep them from grounding subjective claims of right in natural right, comprehensively understood. By the same token, Aquinas's general construal of the right in terms of an objective state of affairs is consistent with identifying respect for individuals' subjective claims as among the relevant normative considerations. At any rate, any theory of rights is bound to include some objective normative considerations, in virtue of which someone is justified in claiming

25. For further details, see Tierney, *The Idea of Natural Rights*, 74.
26. Tierney, *The Idea of Natural Rights*, 65–66.

a right or in asserting this or that specific right. Subjective rights depend critically on individual discretion, but that does not mean that individuals can create rights claims out of sheer fiat. We cannot assume that, simply because he appeals to objective considerations of naturalness or right in a given context, Aquinas has no conception of subjective rights. These appeals should prompt us to ask how these moral considerations become salient in a particular case. Does this consideration apply in the same general way in every case, or does it depend for its force—in part, if not entirely—on someone's discretionary claim?

Aquinas's analysis of justice and right resembles that of the jurists in another, more specific way. As we have already observed, he takes judicial judgment as paradigmatic for the virtue of justice, and he discusses legal procedures in such a way as to reflect familiarity with legal norms and practices. This should not surprise us, because Aquinas shares the same social context as the canonists, and while he does not have a lawyer's familiarity with courtroom procedures, he is clearly aware of the kinds of claims and justifications informing the legal practices of his own time. More specifically, Aquinas is well aware that in certain contexts, the language of right is associated with the practices of making and justifying claims. Someone claims something by right, referring to the consideration that justifies him in claiming some immunity from interference, or some service or material object, from another. It is true that Aquinas does not generally refer to someone's right in possessive terms, as the canonists do, except at one point. But that point is critically important—that is, in citing Justinian, he says that the object of justice is to render *jus suum unicuique*, to each his or her own right.[27] He goes on to say that the right, generally speaking, includes both natural and positive right, a distinction that can be traced to Aristotle, but that was by now generally incorporated into legal theory (II-II 57.2).[28] For Aristotle himself, the categories of what is right by nature and what is right by convention are associated with generally applicable normative claims rather than individual powers. But by placing Aristotle's distinctions within the context of Justinian's definition, Aquinas at least leaves open the possibility

27. Some have argued that *jus* as understood in this formula refers to the complex of rights and duties attached to some particular object, for example, the advantages and liabilities attached to owning a particular tract of land. However, as Reid argues, by the thirteenth century "*jus* was transformed unequivocally into an individual power or claim; it signified an individual's legal advantage, not the advantages and disadvantages inhering in a tangible object" ("The Canonistic Contribution," 55).

28. The relevant text in Aristotle is found in the *Nicomachean Ethics*, 5.7, 1134b 18–24.

that the claims of right to which Aristotle refers ought to be understood as grounds for the claims of individuals, which remain to some extent within individual discretion.

This suggestion is further reinforced by the central place that Aquinas gives to the paradigmatic figure of the judge and to judicial procedures in his extended analysis of the virtue of justice. In Aquinas's day, a judge was characteristically one who adjudicated among the claims of individuals who petitioned the court to uphold their right or to grant them immunity or redress from the improper claims or acts of another. Aquinas's focus on judicial paradigms does not prove that he is thinking of the right in juridical terms, and indeed, he clearly does not limit claims of rights to what can be adjudicated. Nonetheless, at the very least we can say that his intuitions about justice have been shaped by judicial contexts, which opens up the possibility that he does have a conception of natural rights understood subjectively, as grounded in some way in the moral powers of individuals.

Yet even if Aquinas could have thought of claims of right in this way, do we have good, textually grounded reasons for thinking that he does understand the right in these terms? I believe that we do. Consider, first, Aquinas's comments on the widely discussed question of whether it is licit to take what is another's in order to sustain one's own life. As we have seen, some jurists resolve this question through an appeal to the right of the poor individual to the necessities of life. Aquinas shares the same moral convictions, but his analysis of the case would seem initially to fit squarely within the paradigm of an objective order of justice and right:

> Those things that depend on human right cannot restrict natural right or divine right. Now according to the natural order instituted by divine providence, lower things are directed to this end, that human necessities are to be supplied by them. And therefore, the division and appropriation of material things, which proceeds from human right, does not prevent human necessities from being supplied by things of this kind. [Aquinas adds that, ordinarily, human needs will be met through such practices as almsgiving.] Nevertheless, if the need be so urgent and evident that it is manifest that the immediate need must be relieved by whatever things occur, as when some danger to the person is imminent and cannot be relieved in another way, then someone may licitly relieve his necessity from another's things, whether taken openly or in secret. Nor does such an action have the rational character of theft or robbery. (II-II 66.7)

In other words, the primary purpose of material things, as determined by a providentially instituted natural order, sets limits to the claims that can be made on the basis of human right, grounded in legal enactments. Normally, the necessities of those without property of their own should be met through almsgiving. In some circumstances, however, someone can literally take matters into his own hands, taking what is another's in order to relieve his urgent need. Aquinas goes on to say that "the use of another's things taken secretly in the case of extreme necessity does not have the rational character of theft, properly speaking, because through such necessity, that which someone takes to sustain his own life is made his own" (II-II 66.7 *ad* 2). He adds that the same considerations apply when someone takes what is another's in order to meet the immediate needs of a third party (II-II 66.7 *ad* 3).

It will be clear by now that Aquinas's treatment of this case is closer to the jurists' views than we might have initially suspected. Clearly, the claims generated by human and natural rights to the appropriation and use of material things go beyond the imperatives of an objective order of mutual obligations. The critical point is that in these circumstances, the primary purpose of material things, which is a matter of natural right, is put into effect through someone's free choice and action. In the case of extreme and urgent necessity, someone can simply take what she needs from the property of another in order to sustain her life, and what she takes is regarded as her own. It was a commonplace that the goods of the rich should be regarded as belonging to the poor, generically considered, but for Aquinas, the specific goods taken by this particular desperate person belong to her. Thus, she cannot be said to be guilty of theft or robbery, and, by implication, she can claim immunity from punishment. Admittedly, Aquinas does not say that the rich individual has a duty to hand over his possessions to the poor individual. However, the category of subjective rights can plausibly be extended to include claims to immunity, as well as powers to impose duties, and given this line of interpretation, Aquinas can be said to defend the right of the desperate individual to claim what necessity renders her own, without fear of punishment.

Consider, second, Aquinas's response to the question of whether the children of Jews and other unbelievers can be baptized against the will of their parents (II-II 10.12). He begins by asserting, in the strongest terms, that this practice is contrary to the universal custom of the church, which has greater authority than any individual theologian, however eminent. He goes on to say that this custom is justified on two grounds, the second of which is relevant here. That is, it is repugnant to natural justice to baptize a child against the will of its parents, because before it attains the use of reason, a child is under the care of its parents by natural right (*de jure naturale*). On a first reading, it seems that Aquinas is asserting that it would be contrary to the objective duties set up by the order of justice and right to baptize a child against its parents' will. But this way of framing the case implies that something more is at stake here. After all, Aquinas says that it would be contrary to natural justice to baptize the child of unwilling parents, implying that these parents, as individuals, are asserting a claim to raise their child as they see fit. The general considerations that Aquinas sets out are salient only because these individuals are asserting a claim, as individuals, pertaining to the upbringing of this specific child. Once again, what Aquinas seems to have in mind is a claim to an immunity that is grounded in a general natural right but takes the form of a specific claim pertaining to one's freedom of action with respect to a particular object, in this case, this specific child.

In addition to these examples, we can identify other texts in which Aquinas defends immunities from coercion or punishment by appealing to some aspect of our shared human nature, without necessarily invoking natural right explicitly. For example, those who are accused of a crime are entitled to appropriate judicial procedures, and those who are convicted of crime retain immunities from harm from other private individuals, in virtue of the claims of humanity that they hold in common with the rest of us (II-II 64.3, esp. *ad* 2).[29] Someone can defend himself against attack, even by lethal force, because the natural inclination toward maintaining one's life justifies him in placing his own self-preservation ahead of the claims of his attacker (II-II 64.7). In the former case, Aquinas formulates the claims of judicial procedure, as we would describe them, in terms of the duties of public officials and private individuals toward those accused of crimes. Yet it is difficult to believe that, in this context, these particular duties would not be closely correlated with the claims of the accused—to be heard, to enjoy immunity from private vengeance, and the like. Aquinas's formulations suggest that he has some notion of rights as claims imposing duties, as well as rights understood as immunities. At any rate, in the latter example Aquinas clearly sees the individual's natural inclination to self-defense as a

---

29. Aquinas's brief remarks here should be seen in the context of his extended discussion of what we would describe as norms of due process and proper legality, which he regards as obligations of justice grounded in considerations of fairness, equity, and natural equality; see II-II 67–71.

basis for a claim to act in a certain way and to be vindicated in the confessional or in a court of law.

By now, it appears that Aquinas does have something like a conception of subjective rights, insofar as his moral analyses depend at critical points on individual claims, grounded in some consideration of natural right or nature. Generally, although not always, these claims are to some kind of immunity, implying that no one has a right to constrain the individual's freedom in specific ways. The predominance of immunity claims in Aquinas's analysis implies that he associates claims of right with the human capacity for free judgment and self-governance. Men and women can claim certain immunities because they are by nature free, and as we have already seen, the needs and desires intrinsic to our shared nature provide the field within which claims of natural right operate.

At this point, we can begin to see how Aquinas integrates an Aristotelian ideal of equality of exchanges with Roman-juridical ideals of right. In the previous section we noted that for Aquinas, someone who harms another in fundamental ways violates the excellence that each person has, simply in virtue of the excellence of human nature itself. By doing so, he indicates that his analysis of the norms of nonmaleficence takes place within a distinctive semantic field, as Tierney would say, shaped by considerations of status, honor, and respect. These considerations fit awkwardly within an Aristotelian discourse focused on equality of exchanges, but they fit naturally, as it were, within a juridical discourse shaped by claims of right.

We have already observed that Aquinas moves within the same social and intellectual world as the jurists, and he draws freely on the same traditions of natural right and natural law as they do. In order to move forward, we need at this point to consider one specific element of these traditions, namely, the place they give to free status, seen in contrast to servitude.[30] We usually associate freedom with someone's ability to act without constraint or to act effectively in such a way as to exercise her capacities or to attain her goals. Men and women in the thirteenth century recognized and prized these elements of freedom, but in addition, the general idea of freedom was associated with a complex of social and political ideas that would be largely absent today. In this society, freedom was a status, a social condition im-

---

30. Janet Coleman offers a good summary of the complex ideals of freedom and servitude, seen in relation to ownership and poverty, in "Property and Poverty," in *The Cambridge History of Medieval Political Thought, c. 350–c. 1450*, ed. J. H. Burns (Cambridge: Cambridge University Press, 1988), 607–48.

plying both some degree of independence and honorable estate. As such, it contrasted with servitude, which implies constraint, dependence, and a lack of social honor. Servitude was universally regarded as onerous, a condition to be avoided or escaped if at all possible. No one regarded it as a natural part of human existence, but rather, it was generally regarded as one of the regrettable results of the sin of our first parents. For the scholastic jurists, this complex of ideas provides a context within which to integrate ideals of freedom and equality.[31] Following the Roman jurists, they hold that all men and women are equal by natural right, insofar as each person is naturally free, and by natural right, material goods are held in common. Natural equality, seen from this perspective, is most fundamentally an equality of status, implying equality of honor, dignity, and respect, as well as a protected share in the common possessions of humanity. At the same time, it would seem that natural equality, liberty, and community of possessions are set aside by the law of nations, and scholastic jurists and theologians spend considerable efforts to explain how the supposedly unchanging natural right can be qualified in these ways.

We have already observed that Aquinas associates basic norms of non-maleficence with the ideal of equality proper to commutative justice, on the grounds that actions that violate these norms are acts of dishonor that violate the respect due to someone's excellence (II-II 72.1). Since he is referring here to acts that are generally prohibited, no matter what the social status or particular qualities of the victim may be, it is clear that the excellence in question can be only the excellence proper to human nature itself. This association of ideas may seem forced to a contemporary reader, but given the intellectual context just sketched, we can readily see what he has in mind. That is, together with his interlocutors, Aquinas regards human nature itself as conferring free status and, by implication, a natural equality of estate or condition, together with an equal claim to honor. Like the jurists, he acknowledges that this natural status is qualified, and to some extent compromised, through social arrangements that introduce division and dominion into human society. Nonetheless, natural right cannot be set aside by the right set up by human enactments, as he explicitly says at II-II 66.7. The claims of private ownership are to be set aside in favor of a claim based on the natural right to sustain one's life through the appropriation of material goods. The claims of dominion and the disabilities attached to servitude are

---

31. For a fuller account of scholastic views on equality, free status, and possessions, together with textual citations, see Porter, *Natural and Divine Law*, 245–93.

inextricably part of our fallen world, but they are also limited in scope by claims of natural right, including critically the right either to marry or to refrain from marriage. In short, for Aquinas natural right, natural equality, and the fundamentally honorable status of each man and woman are expressed and qualified, but not set aside, by the law of nations.

Seen from this perspective, natural equality and the capacity to claim certain things by right are inextricably tied together. Men and women have the authority to claim certain things by right, because in certain fundamental respects, we share equally in the same status, an honorable status attached to the human estate itself. More specifically, the fundamental equality enjoyed by all men and women is an equality of status as free, self-directed rational agents. For Aquinas this is not only a matter of status, having no practical implications for one's capacities for action. Rather, it implies that individuals ought to be free to act as they see fit in certain critical respects, and to claim certain immunities and certain kinds of sustenance for themselves. The ideal of equality as Aquinas understands it is not limited to an equality with respect to claims of right, since it also integrates broader considerations of equity and general claims of nonmaleficence. Nonetheless, natural equality is centrally connected to claims of right, and equal regard, as we would express the normative ideal, is bound up with respect for the honorable status of all men and women, who are equally free by nature.

Of course, individual authority is not unlimited, any more than political authority is. Individuals can be constrained for good reasons. But if the authority of the individual is not to be rendered nugatory, he must have some recourse, as it were, to claim certain immunities and freedoms over against those who would constrain him in unjustifiable ways. These claims are grounded in the same kinds of consideration that ground legislative activity. The general concept of *jus*, right, is a legal concept, and as such, it carries practical implications. Understood in its most general sense, *jus* refers to a principle of justice or a basis for a legitimate claim of some kind. As such, it is frequently contrasted with *lex*, written law, which is said to be an authoritative formulation of some principle of right or justice. The correlation between the right and legal enactments is critically important for the jurists in this period, but they never lose sight of the broader sense of rights, as conventional or natural grounds for some kind of claim.[32]

This latter way of construing the right is central to Aquinas's moral anal-

---

32. At this point, I am summarizing a line of interpretation I developed in *Ministers of the Law: A Natural Law Theory of Legal Authority* (Grand Rapids: Eerdmans, 2010), 70-82.

ysis. For him, the critical moral power inhering in individuals is an authority to pursue one's natural aims and overall beatitude independently, in accordance with one's own best judgments. This authority cannot be exercised without restraint, because without some framework of mutual obligations and constraints, no society could exist at all. At the same time, however, the individual has to have the authority to set certain limits on the constraints of others, since otherwise, our human capacities for judgment and self-determining freedom would be otiose. Aquinas assumes that individuals exercise their authority through claims, and these claims are grounded in considerations of natural right, which he believes to be generally accessible to all. Aquinas does not seem to think of rights as discrete moral powers, and in that respect, his approach would differ from that of many contemporary theories of natural or human rights. Nonetheless, he holds that the individual possesses the authority to determine the course of her own life in certain critical ways, and this authority implies moral powers to claim certain immunities and performances by right. The individual does not possess rights as discrete powers, but she does possess a general moral power for self-determining action, which she can exercise preemptively on the basis of some claim of right. At the same time, the claims inherent in natural right are not simply legal principles, under the sole domain of legislators and judges. They are also accessible to individuals, as the basis for claims over against others, and they play an especially important role in those situations in which legal enactments are inadequate or poorly differentiated.

Justice, Practical Reason, and First Principles

So far, we have been considering Aquinas's treatment of the concept of the right from two perspectives, drawn from an Aristotelean ideal of equality of exchanges and a Roman-juridical ideal of justified claims. In this section, we will continue with Aquinas's appropriation of the notions of natural law and natural right, starting now from the way in which he distinguishes between these terms. Why is this an important distinction? As we will see, Aquinas follows a general scholastic practice of distinguishing *jus* from *lex*, but the specific distinction that he draws is his own. As we trace the main lines of this distinction, we will uncover aspects of Aquinas's account of justice that would not otherwise be apparent. His interpretation of the notions of law and right turns out to be central to his overall theory of the virtues, the place of justice within that theory, and ultimately, the basis and justification of moral norms.

The exact meaning of *jus*, right, is disputed, but there is no question that in Aquinas's day this term had strong legal overtones, even though it was used in other contexts as well. As such, the term *jus* is often correlated with *lex*, law, and we find both terms being used, in different contexts and apparently with different connotations, by both Aquinas and his interlocutors. When we compare Aquinas and his predecessors and contemporaries on the use of these terms, we find that they nearly all draw an explicit distinction between *jus* and *lex*, associating the former with fundamental claims stemming from justice, nature, and reason, and the latter with conventions or enactments that codify the demands of justice in some way.[33] Of course they recognize that some rights claims are grounded in positive law, but the point is that they identify the *jus*, the right, taken in an unqualified sense, with the preconventional grounds of right judgment, however these are understood. Their general conception of right, therefore, implies both a preconventional origin and obligatory force. When they discuss what we would generally refer to as natural law, or the law of nature, they almost always speak in terms of *jus naturale*, that is, natural right.

In contrast, when Aquinas discusses the natural law in general terms, seen within the context of the fundamental forms of law identified in the *prima secundae*, he does refer to a *lex naturalis*, a natural law (I-II 91.2, 94). Yet he also carefully distinguishes between *lex* and *jus*, not in such a way as to mark a distinction between the preconventional grounds of normative claims and their formulations, but in order to distinguish between two kinds of preconventional principles, those stemming from the natural law generally and comprehensively understood, and the relatively determinate claims associated with natural right. He distinguishes these, but not in such a way as to disassociate them, because as we will see, the fundamental norm of natural right is itself a specification of the first precept of the natural law.

Aquinas's initial treatment of the natural law comes in the context of a general analysis of *lex*, which he elsewhere identifies with the objective normative principles by which our conduct is evaluated.[34] These include the

33. For further details, see Porter, *Ministers of the Law*, 78–80.
34. In the introduction to I-II 6, in which Aquinas sets out the plan for the *prima secundae*, he indicates that he will consider the internal and external principles of human action, the latter comprising God, who instructs us through law and aids us by grace, and Satan, who tempts us to sin. These appear to be traditional formulae, and in fact when Aquinas turns to the external principles of human action, he focuses on law, considered comprehensively as comprising objective principles of all kinds, including those that are intrinsically reasonable, as well as the mandates of divine law and human enactments.

highest preconventional normative standard of all, that is, the *lex aeterna*, the eternal law, identified as the wisdom through which God brings about and governs all that exists (I-II 91.1). He goes on to identify the *lex naturalis*, the natural law, with the rational creature's participation in the eternal law (I-II 91.2). As he explains,

> Since all things that are subject to divine providence are governed and given measure by the eternal law, as is plain from what has been said, it is clear that all things participate in some way in the eternal law, insofar as they receive from it inclinations toward their own acts and ends. Among others, however, the rational creature is subjected to divine providence in a more excellent manner, insofar as he himself is also made a participant in providence, being provident for himself and others. Hence, in the rational creature there is also a participation in eternal reason, through which he has a natural inclination toward a due act and end. And this participation of the eternal law in the rational creature is called the natural law. (I-II 91.2)

Clearly, Aquinas is here drawing on his general metaphysics of causality and agency. Every creature acts in accordance with inclinations toward the kind of existence that is natural and proper to it. The rational creature does so in a distinctive way, freely, through self-reflective awareness of what he is and what he is doing. Like every other creature, he is moved to act through inclinations toward suitable objects and activities, but unlike these others, his actions are guided by deliberative processes leading to free judgment and choice. These processes, in turn, presuppose, not only that the agent is aware of the ends for which he acts, but also that he is aware of them *as* ends, worth pursuing and appropriately to be enjoyed. Aquinas picks up on this line of analysis in the question devoted to the natural law, and more specifically, in the second article of that question, which asks whether there are many natural laws or only one (I-II 94.2).[35]

---

35. This text serves as the basis for a widely influential theory of the natural law developed by Germain Grisez, John Finnis, and their associates, generally called the "new theory of the natural law." At the risk of oversimplifying a complex and extensively debated set of arguments, this theory takes the desiderata disclosed by the inclinations as the criteria for fully reasonable action. These are grasped by the intellect as basic, noninstrumental goods, which cannot rationally be placed in preferential relations to one another. We are obliged to remain open to the fullest instantiation of each of the basic goods, and correlatively, it is always wrong to foreclose or act against the emergence or instantiation of one of these goods. The difficulty with this position, considered as a reading of Aquinas, is that it sets aside the

This may seem like an odd question, but it is important to Aquinas because he has a stake in maintaining the unity of the natural law. The natural law is the ultimate and most comprehensive rational standard by which all human activities are evaluated, and the unity and coherence of moral judgment thus depends on showing that there is ultimately only one natural law. Yet for Aquinas and his interlocutors, this position was by no means obvious. At that time, almost any preconventional principle of action could be described as a natural law or a natural right, and Aquinas's immediate predecessors frequently referred to natural laws or rights in the plural, without attempting to bring these into any kind of coherent framework. Others, not satisfied with this normative pluralism, attempted to analyze distinctive kinds of natural law or right in terms of some one key or primary meaning, most commonly reason.[36] Aquinas agrees that reason is in some sense the proximate norm for all human conduct and the formal ideal for every connatural virtue. But in order to defend this claim, it is necessary to say more about the way in which reason unifies the diverse normative considerations that can be associated with natural right or natural law. This is the task that Aquinas sets for himself in the text we are considering.

Aquinas begins by observing that practical reason, like speculative reason, can operate only on the basis of first principles (I-II 94.2; cf. I-II 51.1).

---

metaphysical analysis of goodness in relation to form and causality that he himself represents as central to his moral analysis. As a result, this approach gives the basic goods a normative weight that they cannot bear, considered either as an interpretation of Aquinas's views or as the starting points for a theory to be considered on its merits. The literature generated by the Grisez/Finnis debate is at this point very extensive. The key statements of the theory include John Finnis, *Natural Law and Natural Rights* (Oxford: Clarendon, 1980) and *Aquinas: Moral, Political, and Legal Theory* (Oxford: Oxford University Press, 1998); Germain Grisez, Joseph Boyle, and John Finnis, "Practical Principles, Moral Truth, and Ultimate Ends," *American Journal of Jurisprudence* 32 (1987): 99–151; and Germain Grisez, *The Way of the Lord Jesus*, vol. 1: *Christian Moral Principles*; vol. 2: *Living a Christian Life* (Chicago: Franciscan Herald Press, 1983–93). For a summary of my own response to this theory, see "Reason, Nature, and the End of Human Life: A Consideration of John Finnis' *Aquinas*," *Journal of Religion* 80.3 (July 2000): 476–84, and *Nature as Reason: A Thomistic Theory of the Natural Law* (Grand Rapids: Eerdmans, 2005), 127–31. Similar arguments are developed by Anthony J. Lisska, *Aquinas's Theory of the Natural Law: An Analytic Reconstruction* (Oxford: Clarendon, 1996), 139–65, and Ralph McInerny, *Aquinas on Human Action: A Theory of Practice* (Washington, DC: Catholic University of America Press, 1992), 184–92, and "Grisez and Thomism," in *The Revival of Natural Law: Philosophical, Theological, and Ethical Responses to the Finnis-Grisez School*, ed. Nigel Biggar and Rufus Black (Sydney: Ashgate, 2000), 53–72.

36. For further details, see Porter, *Natural and Divine Law*, 76–93, and Jean Porter, *Nature as Reason: A Thomistic Theory of the Natural Law* (Grand Rapids: Eerdmans, 2005), 68–82.

These cannot be demonstrated, since they provide the necessary starting points for reasoning in some sphere of inquiry. However, they can be formulated in propositions that are *per se nota*, that is to say, evidently true to anyone who grasps the meaning of the relevant terms. Aquinas adds that a proposition may be self-evidently true in itself and yet not be evident to everyone. The true meaning of the terms may not be apparent readily or at all, and the proposition might be evident only to "the wise," or perhaps only to God. In the case of practical reasoning, however, the first principle is not only self-evidently true in itself, it is manifestly true to everyone:

> Just as being is that which first falls under apprehension simply so called, so the good is that which first falls under the apprehension of practical reason, which is directed toward something that is done, for every agent acts on account of an end, which has the rational character of good. And therefore the first principle in the practical reason is that which is grounded in the rational character of good, that is, "good is that which all desire." This is therefore the first precept of law, that the good is to be done and pursued and evil is to be avoided. And on this are founded all the other precepts of natural law, insofar as all things to be done or avoided, which practical reason naturally apprehends to be human goods, belong to the precepts of the natural law. (I-II 94.2)

As we saw in the last chapter, Aquinas holds that the will is naturally, although not necessarily, moved by the proper objects of all the capacities natural to the human person, since these are either necessary to human existence or bound up in some way with human development and well-being (I-II 10.1). In this way, the operations of the will reflect general structures of existence and causality. We recall that each creature is oriented toward its perfection, understood as the full actualization of its form, and correlatively, each creature is naturally inclined toward whatever is presupposed as a condition for that actualization and whatever follows as an expression of its natural causal powers (I 5.5). The point is that the natural inclinations of any creature move it in such a way as to pursue, develop, and express the form of existence proper to its specific kind, and as such, they are structured in accordance with an intelligible form of existence. Having established that diverse moral precepts can be analyzed in terms of one common conception of goodness, he goes on to argue that the natural inclinations of the will, which reflect the intelligible form of human existence, provide a framework for integrating the diverse precepts of the natural law.

Although he does not develop it at this point, Aquinas's argument for the unity of the natural law implies an account of the way in which the natural inclinations of the human agent serve as starting points for good action and virtuous dispositions.[37] On this account, the agent is initially moved to action in accordance with fundamental inclinations toward the natural needs and satisfactions of human life, and then, through self-reflective judgment, she begins to pursue these as elements of an overall conception of the good, the kind of life that she values for herself. Given that her overall judgments are sound, and providing that she succeeds in directing her desires and activities accordingly, she can be said to act in accordance with the natural law rightly understood by pursuing the fundamental inclinations of her nature in an integrated way in accordance with right reason (I 60.3 *ad* 3; I-II 94.3). By the same token, she can be said to be virtuous, since every cardinal virtue aims at a rational mean, that is to say, a formal ideal of perfection as attained in some aspect of life (I-II 64.1). In this way, Aquinas integrates his theory of the virtues, understood as dispositions of the agent's interior principles of action, with the strongly juridical tradition of natural law thinking.

Yet Aquinas does so with qualifications. In the next article he asks whether all the acts of virtue belong to the natural law (I-II 94.3). He replies that they do, insofar as they are virtuous, since the order of virtue is equivalent to the order of reason. However, the same cannot be said of all virtuous acts, considered specifically as acts of this or that particular virtue. These actions may stem from conventions that are not in themselves directly natural, or they may call for contextual judgments that cannot be generalized in such a way as to yield universally valid moral precepts. Aquinas's comment on the latter possibility (raised in the third objection) is especially telling: "This argument proceeds from acts insofar as they are considered in themselves. For thus, on account of the diverse conditions of human persons, it happens that some acts are virtuous to some, insofar as they are proportionate and appropriate to them, which are however vicious to others, insofar as they are not proportionate to them" (I-II 94.3 *ad* 3). In other words, those actions that attain the rational mean of contextual appropriateness can be said to stem from the natural law formally understood, but not necessarily in any more specific way. And as we have seen, such actions are associated with

---

37. Elsewhere, Aquinas is more explicit about the importance of the natural inclinations as starting points and normative guidelines for the creature's return to God; see especially *De divinis nominibus* X 1.1, 857. For a fuller discussion of this text, see *Nature as Reason*, 175–77.

temperance, courage, and their associated virtues, which aim at a rational mean, but not the real mean set by objective standards of right relations.

In contrast, the virtue of justice aims at a real mean corresponding to an objective standard of equity between agents engaged in some kind of interaction (II-II 58.10). This implies that justice as an ideal standard is correlated more strongly with relatively specific, strictly binding precepts than the other cardinal virtues, and Aquinas confirms that this is so (II-II 80). More specifically, the precepts of justice are paradigmatically formulated through the Decalogue, which Aquinas identifies as revealed law, but which he also identifies as immediate implications of fundamental precepts of the natural law (I-II 100.1,3). The precepts of the Decalogue as they pertain to interpersonal relationships express "the very order of justice to be observed among human persons," and for that reason they do not allow for any dispensation, even by God (I-II 100.8). He goes on to say that justice is more closely linked to the natural law than the other virtues, because "the rational characteristic of the due, which is requisite to a precept, appears most clearly in justice, which is directed toward another" (II-II 122.1; cf. I-II 100.2 *ad* 2, 3 *ad* 3). In other words, the law-like quality of the natural law is most evident in justice. Of course, the other cardinal virtues are also correlated with some relatively specific obligatory precepts. But these precepts almost always pertain to situations involving relations to other people or to the commonwealth or to God, and as such, they are generally connected in some way to justice as well as to temperance or courage, as the case may be (see, for example, II-II 154.1). The key point is that for Aquinas, the virtue of justice is paradigmatically connected to binding precepts in a way that the other virtues are not, precisely because it is directly responsive to the claims of others. The language of *jus* captures both of these aspects of justice, which, I want to suggest, is why he reserves the language of natural right for justice, while associating the other virtues, or cardinal virtue generally considered, with natural law.

In the question devoted to the integral parts of justice, II-II 79, Aquinas draws on this distinction in such a way as to qualify his overall theory of morality in a decisive way. Recall that the integral parts of justice refer to those constitutive elements that are necessary in order for a given act to count as an act of justice. Aquinas identifies these as *declinare a malo et facere bonum,* to refrain from evil and to do good (II-II 79.1). This formulation looks suspiciously like the first principle of natural law, which pertains to all the virtues. Aquinas accepts this point, but he goes on to say that, within the context of interpersonal and communal relations, this general principle takes on a specific meaning, appropriately expressed in terms of the language of obligation and injury:

> If we speak of good and evil in general, to do the good and to avoid the evil pertain to all virtue. And in this sense, these cannot be placed among the parts of justice. . . . But justice, insofar as it is a particular virtue, aims at the good under the aspect of what is due to the neighbor. And according to this, it pertains to particular justice to do the good under the rational character of what is owed in relation to the neighbor, and to avoid evil to another, that is, that which injures the neighbor. It pertains to general justice to do the good that is due in relation to the community or to God, and to avoid the opposed evil. (II-II 79.1)

Aquinas clearly holds that the first principle of practical reason as it pertains to other-regarding action is a specification of the first principle of practical reason generally understood. This claim is plausible in itself, but considered within the context of the *Summa*, it raises a further question. This becomes apparent when we turn back to his treatment of law, and more specifically, his discussion of the Decalogue. Aquinas regards the Decalogue as divine, that is to say, revealed law, but he also believes that it recapitulates the judgments of practical reason operating within the sphere of other-regarding acts. In fact, he appeals to the rational structure of the Decalogue in order to account for the structure, as well as the omissions, of the biblical text. Having established that the Decalogue is a comprehensive outline of morality (I-II 100.2–3), Aquinas asks why the first and most fundamental principles, the evangelical commands enjoining love of God and neighbor, are left out. He replies that these precepts are not included, because they need no promulgation: "These two precepts are first and universal precepts of natural law, which are self-evident to human reason, either through nature or through faith. And therefore all the precepts of the Decalogue are referred to these, as conclusions to universal principles" (I-II 100.3 *ad* 1). He goes on to say that the neighbor-regarding precepts of the Decalogue follow immediately from these first principles with only a modicum of reflection (I-II 100.3,5).

It looks as if Aquinas offers not one but two first principles of practical reason, counting the two love commandments as one complex principle. But this seeming inconsistency is easily resolved if we take these to be two ways of formulating the same first principle of justice. Again, this is clearly what Aquinas means. In the course of analyzing the logical structure of the precepts of the Decalogue, which are all derived from the twofold love commandment, he observes that we act rightly toward the neighbor when we fulfill our obligations to those to whom we are indebted and refrain from injuring anyone—in other words, when we refrain from what is evil and do what is good (I-II 100.5). Similarly, in his remarks on the integral parts of justice, he says that "it pertains to particular justice to do the good under the rational character of what is owed in relation to the neighbor, and to avoid evil to another, that is, that which injures the neighbor" (II-II 79.1). Of course, he would not claim that these two formulations mean the same thing at the level of ordinary linguistic usage. The point is that both of these formulations express a foundational insight into the value of human existence, the normative claims that stem from that value, and the concepts of obligation and injury that form the necessary framework for expressing that claim. The specific formulations through which these foundational principles are expressed are secondary to the rational agent's innate grasp of the normative structures of human existence.

In order to appreciate this point, we need to look more closely at what Aquinas means by identifying these principles as self-evident. As we have seen, propositions are said to be self-verifying in this way when the meaning of the predicate is contained within the meaning of the subject. These meanings are not determined by linguistic usage, however. Self-evident propositions are self-evident only for those who know the true meaning of the terms, which are dependent on the realities to which they refer.[38] This referential realism helps to explain why Aquinas can allow for two linguistically distinct formulations of one first principle. Even more important, it suggests that these formulations are themselves expressions of a more fundamental insight or capacity.

When we return to Aquinas's earlier remarks on the natural law and moral knowledge, we see that this is indeed the case. These topics first arise in the context of his analytic taxonomy of the intellectual capacities of the soul developed in I 79. In the course of that question, he addresses the topic

---

38. In "MacIntyre and Aquinas," in *After MacIntyre: Critical Perspectives on the Work of Alasdair MacIntyre*, ed. John Horton and Susan Mendes (Notre Dame: University of Notre Dame Press, 1994), Janet Coleman observes that "for Aquinas there is a notion of actual existence that is more basic than logical existence. . . . For both Aristotle and Aquinas actual existence is intuited as a first principle that is indemonstrable" (69). Something similar should be said about the first principles of practical reason; that is, they reflect exigencies of operation stemming from the human person's character as a creature, an animal, and an animal of a specific kind. In other words, they stem from and reflect our rational awareness of the human form as the immediate impetus and structuring principle of all our activities.

of synderesis, which was traditionally identified with the natural law. According to Aquinas, synderesis is not itself the natural law but, rather, the innate, habitual knowledge of the first principle of natural law. As such, it plays the same role in practical reasoning that the innate understanding of first principles plays in speculative reasoning:

> Human reasoning, since it is a kind of motion, proceeds from the understanding of certain things that are naturally known without the inquiry of reason, as if from a certain fixed principle, and understanding also terminates at this point, insofar as we judge through naturally self-evident principles concerning those things that we discover from human reasoning. Now it is agreed that just as speculative reason deliberates concerning speculative matters, so practical reason deliberates concerning things to be done. We therefore need naturally innate principles of practical as well as speculative reasoning. (I 79.12)

Elsewhere, Aquinas explains how these innate dispositions work: "Indeed, by the very nature of the intellectual soul, it is appropriate to the human person that, on knowing what a whole is and what a part is, at once he knows that every whole is greater than its part, and similarly in other matters. But what a whole is and what a part is he cannot know, except through intelligible species taken from phantasms. And on this account, the Philosopher shows . . . that the knowledge of principles comes to us through the senses" (I-II 51.1). The habitual knowledge of first principles is not propositional in form, although we necessarily formulate these principles in this way. Rather, it is a disposition to grasp the meaning and the logical relations of fundamental concepts, as these present themselves through experience. Again, Aquinas's position presupposes a referential realism. The intellect is capable of spontaneously grasping that the whole is greater than its parts because its operations naturally track fundamental logical relations of this kind. In a similar way, the intellect spontaneously grasps that good is to be sought and done, and evil is to be avoided, because it is capable of grasping and formulating the general principle underlying the human creature's operations as a causal agent. Every creature necessarily pursues good and avoids evil in the way appropriate to it, but the rational creature does so knowingly, with understanding of the causal principles underlying its operations.

We noted above that Aquinas relates the first principle of justice to the first unrestricted principle of practical reason as a specification of a general principle. This line of analysis implies, and Aquinas elsewhere confirms, that the twofold precept to love God and neighbor is self-evident (I-II 100.3 *ad* 1). Immediately upon grasping what it means to be indebted or to injure another, the rational agent grasps that one's obligations should be honored and that one ought not to injure anyone. We cannot fully appreciate the significance of this claim without taking account of Aquinas's realism. We spontaneously grasp that the neighbor is to be loved in certain ways, because each man and woman naturally has a certain value, implying certain kinds of claims. The first principle of justice is thus grounded in an innate capacity to grasp and formulate the normative structure that informs human relations. Moreover, this principle is a specification of the unrestricted first principle of practical reason and not simply an application of that principle, because the concepts of obligation and injury are themselves foundational. In other words, the general concepts of good and evil in themselves cannot be extended to include the claims of the neighbor. Meeting one's obligations is one way of doing good, to be sure, and injuring one's neighbor is a way of doing evil, but these are distinctive and fundamental ways of doing good and evil, not specifications of general categories (II-II 79.1, especially *ad* 1).

In this way, the distinction between natural law, which is oriented toward the moral virtues generally considered, and natural right, which is oriented toward justice, introduces a distinction between two kinds of normative considerations. In the last chapter, we noted that the processes of deliberation are capable of dealing with incommensurable values, in such a way as to yield coherent judgments and choices among these. Aquinas's theory therefore has the resources to deal with this diversity. Nonetheless, given his emphasis on the unity of the natural law and the coherence of moral judgment, we may well wonder why he introduces a fundamental distinction between two kinds of normative considerations at this point.

I believe that he does so because only in this way can he account for the complexity of the operations of the will. As we have already seen, the will, like every other appetite, operates through inclinations, directed toward some consciously apprehended good. Furthermore, since the will is a rational appetite, it can operate only in response to something that fits some general conception of goodness, as the agent apprehends it. At the same time, the operations of reason do not emerge out of nowhere. Rather, the agent's incipient desires for the necessities and pleasures of life offer practical reason the starting points it needs for judging that this or that desideratum represents an instance of a general category, of something worthy of pursuit—that is to say, of something good. In this way, Aquinas can account for the operations of the will as an appetite in terms of the innate capacities of the human creature. The human agent has within himself the principles needed to generate volitional activity, namely, the incipient inclinations of the will toward natural desiderata, together with a general conception of the good, which enable the agent to grasp these desiderata as instances of goodness, comprehensively considered.

However, the general capacity to grasp that some things are worthy of pursuit and to act accordingly cannot by itself account for the kinds of rational apprehensions presupposed by justice and the other virtues of the will. As we saw in chapter 2, Aquinas claims that the virtues of the will orient the agent toward something or someone apart from the agent herself. In order for the will to operate in accordance with the demands of its proper virtues, the intellect must be capable of grasping the independent value of other agents. Yet it is not clear how this recognition would be possible, given the general template of practical reason just set out. The agent's incipient inclinations toward natural desiderata, her grasp of these as instances of a general category of goodness, and her rational desire and pursuit are all intrinsically self-referential. They stem from the agent's natural inclination toward her own perfection, and they develop in accordance with a conception of goodness understood as one's own true, comprehensive goodness.

The operations of practical reason, understood in these self-referential terms, could plausibly be extended toward other people, on the grounds that one's own integrity as a rational agent requires one to do so. This is essentially what Korsgaard attempts to do, by deriving moral norms from the agent's concern for her own self-constitution as an agent. We might assume that Aquinas moves from self-love to neighbor-love in a similar way, especially in light of his formulation for the basic precept of other-regard, to love one's neighbor as oneself. But for Aquinas, the agent's self-love stems from an immediate metaphysical necessity, whereas other people cannot be loved in the same way (II-II 25.4,6). The agent does not love herself by virtue of some general principle or value that she instantiates, in such a way that consistency would demand her to extend love to relevantly similar others. In general, for Aquinas the agent's self-love cannot fully account for the other-regarding character of justice and the other virtues of the will. His point is that these virtues introduce a distinctively new orientation, implying a normative standard that cannot be derived from the natural inclination of the agent toward its own perfection.

Justice perfects the will by orienting it in such a way as to place the agent in right relations to others. Thus, the criteria for perfection in this context are not derived from agent-referential considerations. Rather, they are bound up with the claims of right that confront the agent from without. At the same time, these claims would not exert any kind of normative force unless the agent were capable of grasping them through the operations of the intellect. In this sense, the demands of justice do depend on something within the individual—more specifically, on something that is immediately accessible to the intellect. We now see what that something is, namely, the self-evident, habitually known first principle of justice. This innate awareness of the value of other persons, together with a general sense of the claims that go with human existence, provides the necessary basis for rational other-directed inclinations of the will. If we were not naturally and immediately aware of the value of others and the moral claims that they place upon us, we would not be able to care about others, to respect their rights, or to seek their well-being, for their own sake.

At the same time, like every other finite good, the value and claims of the neighbor can attract the will, but they need not do so. The disposition of justice is possible on this basis, but no one is compelled, even by the most manifest claims of others, to be just. Nonetheless, the intrinsic value and the claims of others cannot simply be disregarded, even by those who do not choose to honor them. They play a central role in human activity at the individual and the social level, so much so that we cannot imagine a properly human existence in which these claims are altogether absent. In order to appreciate this point, we need to look again at the parallel that Aquinas draws between the unrestricted first principle of practical reason and the first principle of other-regarding practical reason. By identifying the principles of right relation to God and neighbor with the first principle of practical reason, Aquinas sets up a parallel between the central concepts of practical reason in an unrestricted sense, and the corresponding concepts as these emerge within the context of justice and charity. We have already observed that the basic concepts of good and evil, generally understood, are grounded in the structural principles of action itself, and indeed, of causal agency generally. Someone who acts, necessarily does so in pursuit of some perceived good—otherwise we could not make sense of the agent's operations as action, and more to the point, the agent would have no criterion of success or failure to guide his operations in any coherent way. This does not imply that men and women rely on some conscious conception of good and evil in order to act, but it does imply that, once these concepts are presented to them, they will immediately grasp their meaning in terms of their own self-reflective experiences of agency.

By the same token, the fundamental conceptions of obligation and injury are grounded in the structures of action and response through which men and women relate to one another in accordance with a distinctively human way of life. It is impossible to relate as a human being to other human beings without some working ideas of this sort—otherwise, one would be incapable of entering into fundamental human relations in any adequate way. This does not imply that our interactions with others presuppose explicit moral conceptions, but it does imply that, once these conceptions are for-mulated, men and women spontaneously see that these are presupposed in their interactions with one another. The basic moral concepts of obligation and injury are built into the structures of the practical intellect, and moral reflection cannot proceed at all, except within these terms.[39]

Aquinas's analysis of the claims of right in terms of evident principles of other-regard, obligation, and the avoidance of injury provides him with a necessary and sufficient basis for asserting the normative force of the pre-cepts of justice. Because the precepts of justice reflect objective claims, they can readily be formulated in forensic terms. We have already observed that, for Aquinas, judicial judgments are paradigmatic for the virtue of justice (II-II 60.1). The paradigmatic precepts of justice are formulated through legal enactments of a distinctive kind, that is to say, the precepts of the Dec-alogue, which as revealed can be considered to be enactments of divine law (I-II 100.1; II-II 122.1). We might conclude that, for Aquinas, the normative

---

39. At this point, someone is likely to object that there do seem to be some people, psy-chopaths or sociopaths, who simply do not grasp even the most fundamental moral principles. Not everyone is persuaded that there are true psychopaths, people who are incapable of any real sympathy, fellow-feeling, or a sense of duty toward others, but it seems overwhelmingly likely that some are deficient in this way. Nonetheless, I would question whether anyone who is capable of reasonable behavior at all can be completely lacking in moral concepts of any kind. I would suggest that psychopaths do think in terms of some moral categories, especially entitlement and injury; they just cannot apply them to anyone but themselves. Apparently, they think of themselves as entitled to pursue certain satisfactions, as justified by need or circumstances to act in a given way, or as victims of some injury or slight. They are simply incapable of applying these categories to other people, and the deficiencies in question stem from failures of the emotions, rather than failures of the intellect. Because they cannot feel in the normal ways, they do not experience the kind of sympathetic identification with others that appears to be necessary for both the formation of robust moral concepts and a disposition of the will that inclines the agent to respond appropriately to the needs, immunities, and claims of other people. For a good summary of recent research in this area, see Joseph P. Newman and Amanda R. Lorenz, "Response Modulation and Emotion Processing: Implications for Psychopathy and other Dysregulatory Psychopathology," in *The Handbook of Affective Sciences*, ed. Richard J. Davidson, Klaus R. Scherer, and H. Hill Goldsmith (Oxford: Oxford University Press, 2009), 904–29.

force of the precepts of justice rests on some kind of divine legislative authority. But as we have seen, he clearly rules out this line of interpretation. The authoritative force of the precepts of the Decalogue rests on the intrinsic demands of justice in our dealings with others, and for this reason they do not admit of dispensation, even by God himself (I-II 100.8). In contrast to Francisco Suárez, Aquinas neither needs nor has any place for a distinctive divine command to account for the obligatory force of these precepts.[40] Similarly, he does not need to account for the stringently binding character of these precepts by appealing to God's conferral of worth on the individual, as Nicholas Wolterstorff argues.[41] For Aquinas, God confers value on each man or woman by calling him or her into existence, just as he bestows goodness on every creature through its creation. The value thus conferred is not infinite or absolute, but as the intrinsic value of human existence, it is properly and sufficiently expressed through the binding precepts of justice.

This brings us to an objection. Aquinas claims that the precepts of love of God and neighbor are immediately evident to all, and he regards the categories of obligation and injury as structuring principles of practical reason as it pertains to the agent's relations to others. This looks suspiciously like a stipulative solution to fundamental problems of normativity. Rather than defending his account of justice as right relation, Aquinas claims that we are innately disposed to recognize that we ought to meet our obligations and to refrain from injuring others. If we cannot justify this claim, how can we place any weight on it?

But this objection is too quick. Self-evident claims and the fundamental categories of thought associated with them cannot be justified in terms of more basic principles, because they provide the necessary starting points and conceptual framework for reasoning within a given domain of thought. For this reason, we cannot mount a moral argument in defense of the first principle of justice, because this principle is foundational for any kind of moral reasoning, or at least, any kind of moral reasoning that pertains to our relations to others. At the same time, it is possible to defend the first principle indirectly, by introducing considerations that lend credibility to the claim that this principle does play the necessary and foundational role that Aquinas gives it. It is not difficult to do so, so long as we stay focused on

40. For an illuminating discussion of Suárez's theory of natural law and moral obligation, see J. B. Schneewind, *The Invention of Autonomy: A History of Modern Moral Philosophy* (Cambridge: Cambridge University Press, 1998), 58–65.

41. Nicholas Wolterstorff, *Justice: Rights and Wrongs* (Princeton: Princeton University Press, 2008), 285–310, 342–61.

the general injunction to respect one's obligations and to avoid injury. The notions of obligation and indebtedness do appear to be simple and foundational. They cannot be analyzed in a clear and persuasive way in terms of more basic concepts, and yet, we do grasp what they mean, and we are able to communicate with others on that basis. Indeed, it is difficult to imagine how we could reason morally without drawing on these basic concepts.

We will have occasion to return to this objection in the last chapter, and at that point we will have the resources to address it more fully. At this point, I would simply point out, once again, that Aquinas's account of the first principle of justice in its diverse formulations is grounded in an essential realism. The key point is that for Aquinas, the logic of self-evident propositions follows the metaphysical and natural structures of reality. The first precepts of other-regarding practical reason are true because God and the human person are lovable in the way presupposed by the virtue of justice. To limit ourselves to human existence, the immediately evident precept of neighbor-love reflects the conformity of the human intellect with a fundamental reality, namely, the objective value and the normative claims of each human individual. We may take issue with Aquinas's fundamental realism, but if his overall approach seems plausible, then in consistency we should apply it to what he says about the first principles of practical reason and justice as well. Human existence is intrinsically normative, and moreover, it is normative in a distinctive way, proper to creatures who are capable of acting for reasons, and for taking responsibility for themselves and one another—in other words, creatures whose lives are governed through the exercise of the will.

The Common Good, Political Rule, and the Ideal of Equality

Aquinas's account of justice and moral knowledge presupposes the real and objective value of other people, which is itself the direct foundation for each individual's obligations toward others. On this view, particular justice perfects the will, and by implication the agent, by relating it rightly to what is outside the agent herself, including other people and God. At the same time, the ideals of right relations with others presuppose some appropriate balance among competing interests, including the agent's own and those of other people. Aquinas does say that no one can suffer injustice unwillingly or inflict injustice on himself (II-II 59.3). Nonetheless, it is difficult to see how right relations can be established and sustained apart from some sound assessment of the diverse potential claims that are in play in any human relationship. If the agent disregards his own needs and interests in some inappropriate way, or fails to take account of the claims of third parties, it is difficult to see how his actions can sustain appropriate, genuinely perfecting relations with others. He may not act out of bad faith or malice, but he will be liable in such a case to undermine his own standing as a part of a social network and even to harm others, perhaps unknowingly, by placing them in distorted relations to himself and others.

On Aquinas's view, morality is informed by a diverse range of considerations, including self-regarding as well as other-regarding ideals and values, which must be integrated through the operations of prudence (II-II 47.7; cf. I-II 100.2,3, II-II 58.10). By implication, the perfection of the will is grounded in a disposition to act in accordance with well-formed judgments of this kind, which implies that the perfected will operates in such a way as to pursue a course of action in which the agent's own concerns and the claims of others are balanced in appropriate ways. This line of interpretation may appear to be inconsistent with Aquinas's claims that general justice plays an architectonic role among the cardinal virtues, and that its object, the common good, is the highest humanly attainable object. But in fact, Aquinas's account of the relation between general and particular justice, and correlatively, the relative priority of the common good to individual interests, is more complex than a first reading might suggest. The priority of the common good has to be seen in its proper context as a way of safeguarding the political character of public authority. Understood in this way, the ideal of the common good, so far from subordinating the individual to an undifferentiated whole, functions in such a way as to safeguard the equality and freedom of individuals, considered as equally sharing in the benefits and burdens of a political community. Thus, Aquinas's account of the common good serves to bring general justice under the scope of the ideal of equality that explicitly informs his account of particular justice. In what follows, I will defend these claims in more detail.

We have already observed that Aquinas says remarkably little about the common good, considered as the object of general justice. This is surprising, given his claim that general justice is an architectonic virtue that directs the operations of the other virtues to its final end (II-II 58.6). Surely this claim implies that the overall perfection of the will presupposes a sound grasp of the common good. If so, then Aquinas's sketchy remarks about the common good can only appear to be inadequate, especially seen in comparison to his detailed analysis of the right, the object of particular justice.

When we place Aquinas's account of general justice in the context of similar accounts offered by his immediate predecessors, we can begin to make sense of what seems at first to be an unbalanced treatment. The theologians in the generation prior to Aquinas, including Albert the Great in his earliest works, agree that general justice is equivalent to virtue, comprehensively considered, or in other words, justice generally understood is equivalent to morality.[42] Aquinas, in contrast, insists that general justice is a particular virtue with its own distinctive object, namely, the common good (II-II 58.6). This way of formulating the claim is potentially confusing, but Aquinas cannot express himself in any other way if he wants to engage his predecessors in the generally accepted terms of preceding discussions. He goes on to say that general or legal justice can be identified with virtue generally considered, as his predecessors claim, but only in a carefully qualified sense,

> insofar as it orders the acts of the other virtues to its end, that is, to move all the other virtues by command. Just as charity can be said to be a general virtue, insofar as it orders the acts of all the virtues to divine goodness, so also can legal justice, insofar as it orders the acts of all the virtues to the common good. Therefore, just as charity, which considers divine good as its proper object, is a certain specific virtue in accordance with its essence, so also legal virtue is a specific virtue in accordance with its essence, insofar as it considers the common good as its proper object. And so it is in the prince principally, and as it were architectonically, and in subjects secondarily and as it were ministratively. (II-II 58.6)

Aquinas thus compares general justice with charity, in order to explain how general justice can be identified with the virtues, comprehensively considered. In its own sphere, it directs the other virtues by orienting them to its own proper object, in somewhat the same way that charity directs every other virtue to its proper object, that is, union with God. At the same time, Aquinas's comparison implies a significant difference between general justice and charity. The theological virtue of charity is at least potentially proper to everyone, and it operates in and through all the inclinations and activities of the individual who possesses it. General justice, in contrast, is a virtue that is centrally important within its own field of operation, but restricted in scope. Properly speaking, the virtue of general justice pertains to the governance of a community, and as Aquinas goes on to explain, general justice

---

42. Again, see Lottin, "Le concept de justice," for details.

is an architectonic virtue because well-framed, just laws operate in such a way as to direct virtuous activities of all kinds to the common good. General justice is thus paradigmatically a virtue of political rulers and especially lawgivers (II-II 58.6). This is not to say that general justice has no place in the lives of private citizens, but that place is limited to a disposition to act in accordance with the laws and directives of the community's rulers, for the sake of the common good, in which all participate.

Nonetheless, even though general justice is limited in scope, it still plays a key part in the overall perfection of the will. Furthermore, general justice operates in such a way as to promote and safeguard the fundamental equality and the authoritative claims of individuals, in relation to one another and to the community, which compose the object of particular justice, the right. This is so, whether we consider general justice in its paradigmatic form as a virtue of lawgivers, or in its more generally diffused form as a virtue of well-disposed citizens. In order to draw out the significance of general justice, we will need to look more closely at Aquinas's account of the common good. Admittedly, he does not develop a systematic account of the common good. Rather, he appeals to this motif in a number of different contexts having to do with questions about legal authority, political rule, and, of course, general justice. Taken together, however, his remarks offer a distinctive perspective on social life and on the proper disposition of the virtuous agent toward her political community. Seen from our standpoint, these comments are particularly interesting for two reasons. First, Aquinas's accounts of the common good and legitimate political authority are developed by way of a contrast with servile dominion and private interest, in such a way as to underscore the connection between political authority and free status. The upshot, as we will see, is that the common good is tied to civic equality in such a way as to bring together what we might call the constitutive ideals of general and particular justice. Second, Aquinas's paradigms for appropriate regard for the common good appear to have been shaped by his overall account of justice as a perfection of the will. This shaping appears most clearly when we compare his early remarks on the relation of the individual to political society in the *prima pars* with his treatment of the common good and legal authority set forth later in the *prima pars* and further developed in the *prima secundae*. In this latter context, Aquinas qualifies earlier claims about the overriding authority and value of the common good, in such a way as to set limits on what the community can ask of the individual—boundaries that protect the individual's core identity as someone capable of, and responsible for, determining the course of his own life through his judgment and free will.

Given Aquinas's overall analysis of the will as a capacity for desire oriented toward the good generally considered, we might assume that general justice would perfect the will by directing it toward some comprehensive good that subsumes the good of the individual. Initially, Aquinas would appear to confirm that assumption. In the *prima pars*, Aquinas claims that a rational or intellectual creature naturally loves the common or divine good more than itself:

> We see that naturally a part exposes itself for the conservation of the whole, as the hand is exposed to be cut off without deliberation to conserve the whole body. And because reason imitates nature, we find such an inclination in the political virtues, for it pertains to civic virtue that one should expose himself to the danger of death to preserve the whole republic, and if the human person were naturally a part of a commonwealth, this inclination would be natural to him. (I 60.5)

The analogy of individual and community to a relation of part to whole reflects one obvious and well-established way of thinking about one's status as a member of a community. However, it is difficult to reconcile the image of the human person as a part of a communal whole with the motif of the person as image of God, irreducibly valuable and capable of governing both herself and other creatures. Aquinas himself seems to have been uneasy with the implications of this language. Even at this point, he will go only so far as to say that the relation of the human person to the community is like the relation of part to whole, and if one were naturally part of a polity, then he would naturally sacrifice himself for the community. He thus qualifies classical paradigms of self-sacrifice in such a way as to preserve some sense of the independent value and autonomy of the human person.

When Aquinas turns his attention specifically to the common good, we find that he drops the analogy of part-whole relations altogether, starting instead from the very different conception of political, as opposed to servile, authority. He first raises this issue in the context of the conditions of human life as it would have unfolded in paradise, if our first parents had not sinned. In order to address this question, he begins by distinguishing between two kinds of dominion. The first of these, servile dominion, is directed toward the master's own private interests, in such a way that the subordinate's activities are put in service of another's will. Aquinas agrees with his interlocutors, and indeed with the whole classical and Christian natural law tradition, that this kind of dominion would not have existed apart from some kind of sinfulness or moral corruption—which is not to say that servile dominion presupposes any distinctive sinfulness or failing on the part of the subordinate herself.

However, there is another kind of dominion and subordination that stems directly from the exigencies of human nature, and that therefore would have existed even apart from the effects of sin:

> Someone exercises dominion over another as a free person when he directs him to the proper good of the one being directed or to the common good. And such dominion of a human person would have existed in a state of innocence, for two reasons. The first, because the human person is naturally a social animal; hence, human persons in a state of innocence would have lived in society. But the social life of a multitude is not possible unless someone is in charge who aims at the common good, because a multitude as such aims at many things, whereas one aims at one thing. Hence the Philosopher says that whenever many are ordained to one thing, there is always found one as the principle and director.... Second, because if one person should be preeminent over another with respect to knowledge and justice, this would be inappropriate unless it were directed toward the well-being of the other. (I 96.4)

We see here the central elements of Aquinas's understanding of the common good. Most fundamentally, the common good is understood by contrast with one's private good, or with the good of an individual. As such, it provides the rationale for political authority. By the same token, it provides a rationale for laws, and it serves to justify the ruler in some courses of action that would be closed to private citizens. Finally, political authority does not compromise the free status of its subjects, because it does not place one individual at the service of the private volitions and whims of another. Men and women are subject to political rule and legal authority for the sake of a greater good, for which they are jointly responsible and from which they all benefit (II-II 47.10). Aquinas does not say, but his remarks imply, that the benefits of community include not only the material and social advantages of a shared life but, even more, the structures necessary to enable and safeguard the equality and freedom of each individual within a community.

At the same time, we should also take note of what Aquinas does not say. He does not defend the naturalness of political rule by appealing to the claim that individuals are parts of a larger whole, nor does he draw on the kind of organic metaphors of society as one body that he uses in the earlier text. He acknowledges the reality and naturalness of inequalities among persons, but as we saw in the first section of this chapter, he regards these as differences of degree along a continuum of shared capacities, and he does not identify superior abilities with any particular class of individuals. There is no suggestion here that we can identify a natural ruling class, or much less a naturally given social hierarchy of a fixed kind. Rather, Aquinas simply reminds us of the exigencies of social life, which at its best draws on the outstanding talents of some, offers special protections to the weak, and encourages mutual cooperation among all. So far from undermining human equality and freedom, this way of life is meant to safeguard these ideals by enabling each individual to participate freely in communal activities and to share equitably in communal benefits and burdens.

Aquinas's subsequent remarks on the common good occur mostly in the closely related contexts of legal authority and the role-specific privileges and responsibilities of political rulers and their agents (see, for example, I-II 90.3; II-II 60.6, 64.2–3). In each context Aquinas underscores the point that someone in a position of authority acts as an agent of the community whose will is directed to the common good and not to her own private interests. For that very reason, she can exercise authority over free men and women without undermining their freedom, since each participates in the common good and has a stake in sustaining it. Furthermore, because she acts on behalf of the community, she can act toward others in ways that would be forbidden to her as a private individual, executing the protective and punitive functions that legitimately belong to the political community and not to any one individual (II-II 64.3 *ad* 3). By implication, public authority directed toward the common good preserves the equality of private citizens, since under such a regime, no one needs to, or legitimately may, presume to impose penalties on anyone else.

At the same time, there are some things that no one, even someone in a position of authority, can do in defense of the common good. No one is justified in killing the innocent, even in defense of the common good, because "the life of the just conserves and promotes the common good, because they themselves are the principal part of the multitude" (II-II 64.6). More generally, we are told at II-II 68.3 that "no one ought to do harm to another unjustly in order to promote the common good." By implication, the common good and what we might call reasons of state do not set the standards for justice; rather, a community can attain the common good only insofar as it respects standards of justice, including fundamentally the claims of its members to basic kinds of forbearance.

By now it is apparent that, although Aquinas does say that individual interests should be subordinated to the common good, he qualifies this general principle in important ways. Let us consider another such qualification. His claim that general justice directs the activities of all the other virtues might suggest a community in which all the activities of life are directed toward political ends. As we might say, the personal would be political comprehensively and without remainder. Yet when we examine what Aquinas says about the relation between general justice and the other moral virtues, we see that he spells out the terms of this relationship in such a way as to preserve the distinctiveness and individual value of one's private, individual goods. General justice can be said to direct the activities of the other virtues only because the overall good estate of the individual, including her overall perfection as a virtuous agent, contributes to the common good in some way (I-II 60.3 *ad* 2). Hence, if an individual acts out of temperance or fortitude in pursuit of her own private good, or if she aims at the good of some other individual through particular justice, her action is ipso facto directed to the common good, precisely because the latter includes the good of every individual in the community (II-II 58.5). This does not mean that the act in question ceases to be an act of temperance, fortitude, or particular justice, with an immediate orientation to some private good (the agent's or another's). The act retains its character as an expression of the particular virtue that elicits it, while at the same time it is referred to the common good through general justice (II-II 58.6; cf. II-II 32.1 *ad* 2). By the same token, Aquinas observes that, even though justice is the paradigmatic virtue of external operations, through which we are related to other persons, that does not mean that every exterior operation is an act of particular justice (which, as noted above, governs the agent's relations to other individuals), because the other moral virtues dispose the individual rightly with respect to those external acts that affect only herself (II-II 58.2 *ad* 4).

The mention of particular justice brings us to a further point. Aquinas does not just distinguish the common good from the agent's own private good. As we know, he also draws a contrast between the common good and the individual goods of other persons. This is significant because, even though the agent may, and sometimes should, sacrifice himself for the common good, he cannot sacrifice other people in the same way. Once again, we see that Aquinas places clear and explicit limits on the degree to which individuals can be sacrificed in pursuit of the common good. Even earlier, we noted that even a putative law that is genuinely directed toward the common good is unjust, and therefore invalid as a law, if it places inequitable burdens on individuals (I-II 96.5). We might wish for a more extended account of what counts as an equitable division of social burdens, but at least Aquinas recognizes that individual claims to equity and fair treatment set constraints on what can be done in pursuit of the common good.

It would take us well beyond the scope of this project to examine the implications of Aquinas's conception of the common good in any detail. The most significant point from the perspective of this project is that Aquinas understands the common good and the political community in such a way as to give a central place to equality and claims of right. The ideals of particular justice and general justice are thus inextricably linked. Practically, the close connection between these two forms of justice is expressed through the laws of a community, which both express the ideals of equity that are fundamental to political life and enable men and women to live freely in accordance with those ideals. We are once again reminded that the activities of a just judge are paradigms for justice and the right: "This name of right is first imposed to signify the right thing itself; then it is extended to the art through which one knows what is just; and then it is extended to signify that place where the right is rendered. . . . And finally the right is said of that which is rendered by him whose office it is to do justice, granting that he also passes judgment on iniquity" (II-II 57.1 *ad* 1).

From Ideal to Law

In chapter 3 we observed that Aquinas identifies two hallmarks of the right, considered as the formal object of the virtue of justice. That is, the right implies a commitment to a kind of equality, and it is correlated with strictly binding precepts, similar in form to legal enactments (II-II 80). As we saw, Aquinas identifies the ideal of equality pertaining to justice with respect for the equality of status that all men and women enjoy by natural law. This ideal, in turn, implies both norms of nonmaleficence and respect for others' claims of right. On this basis, we are obliged to refrain from harming others in certain specific ways and to honor the claims that others have on us, whether these stem from general considerations or from particular claims of right.

In this chapter we turn to a set of issues raised by Aquinas's claim that the precepts of justice are stringently binding, in a way that is characteristic of justice in comparison to other virtues. Once again, we will see that Aquinas's interpretation of justice is qualified at key points by his claim that the virtue of justice is a perfection of the will. As we know, the will is the principle of the agent's relations *ad extra*, and so the perfection of the will implies right relations with others. This line of analysis, taken together with his commitment to the value of each individual, leads him to give decisive weight to the agent's direct interactions with another. Aquinas accordingly sets out a theory of morality in which strict obligations and binding prohibitions have a central place, even though they do not constitute the whole field of morality.

The critical point to keep in mind is that for Aquinas, the virtue of justice is oriented toward right relations with other people, the community, and God. These are real relations, and although they depend on the intentional actions of the agent, if not both parties, they exist independently of the subjective feelings and perceptions of those involved. Their moral character is determined by objective standards of fairness and equity, and the moral character of the agent is in turn dependent on her stance toward these objective standards, as determined by the kind of action that she chooses. At the same time, these standards are grounded in forms of interrelationship natural to us as social animals, as these are appropriated and transformed through self-reflective reason. In short, the objectivity of justice and its interpersonal character account for the specificity and stringency of its demands. No one can be in a relation with himself alone or can dictate the terms of a relationship by his own subjective perceptions. Our actions express an inner reality, but they also create objective states of affairs that are themselves partially determinative of our inner realities and that shape the social world in which we live.

In chapter 3 we saw that the normative force of the precepts of justice is grounded most immediately and directly in the normative value of the human individual, which is evident to all rational agents through an innate precept of natural right. Aquinas does not need to appeal to any special divine intervention into the normative order of human life in order to account for the binding force of the precepts of justice. For him, the central difficulty raised by the precepts of justice is not their binding force but, rather, what we might describe as the normative grammar of justice. How do we determine, concretely, what it means to render to each his or her right, especially when faced with situations of uncertainty or conflicting claims? Aquinas raises this issue immediately after asserting that the precepts of justice do not allow for any dispensation (I-II 100.8). In response to the objection that God himself seems exempt from the norms of the Decalogue, he responds as follows:

> Killing a person is prohibited in the Decalogue insofar as it has the character of something unjustified, for the precept contains the very rationale of justice. And human law cannot grant this, that a person might licitly be killed without justification. But the killing of malefactors or enemies of the republic is not unjustified. Hence, this is not contrary to a precept of the Decalogue, nor is such a killing a murder, which the Decalogue prohibits. . . . And similarly, if something is taken from another, which was his own, if he is obliged to lose it, this is not theft or robbery, which are prohibited by a precept of the Decalogue. . . .
>
> So therefore, these precepts of the Decalogue, with respect to the rational character of justice that they contain, are unchangeable. But with respect to some determination through application to individual acts, whether, for example, this or that is murder, theft, or adultery or not,

this indeed is changeable; sometimes only by the divine authority, namely in those things that are instituted by God alone, as for example marriage and other things of this sort; and sometimes by human authority, with respect to those things that are committed to human jurisdiction. For with respect to those things, human persons act as the vicar of God, not, however, with respect to all things. (I-II 100.8 *ad* 3)

Any theory of morality needs to address the question of specification, but for Aquinas, this question is especially significant because he places so much emphasis on the stringency of the precepts of justice. In order for a precept to bind stringently, it needs to be formulated in specific terms, or we need to be able to specify it through processes of discernment and judgment. Men and women cannot honor their duties to others and avoid injuring them unless they know concretely what it would mean to fulfill a duty or to inflict an unjustifiable harm.

In this chapter, we focus on a set of issues pertaining to the formulation and application of the precepts of justice in order to get a clearer sense of what it means to describe these as stringently binding. We will accordingly begin with Aquinas's analysis of the moral act, in which he sets out the formal structure of an act of the will. This analysis presupposes that we are in possession of general moral categories, and in the second and third sections we will consider a possible etiology of moral concepts. More specifically, in the second section I will try to show that we can account for the formation of moral categories through processes of rational reflection on the moral emotions, and in the third section I will extend this account to include the strict prohibitions associated with the neighbor-regarding precepts of the Decalogue. Finally, in the last section we will consider the place of discernment in the practice of the virtue of justice.

Norm, Precept, and Act

The core intuition underlying Aquinas's treatment of the precepts of justice is simply that it is always wrong to treat someone unjustly. Expressed in these terms, this claim would hardly be controversial. Yet as Aquinas interprets it, this fundamental claim carries implications that are anything but obvious. It is wrong to treat another *unjustly*, and by implication, we know what it means to harm another person in an unjust way, at least in some paradigmatic cases. An unjustifiable harm implies some distinctive kind of disorder, contrary to the right order of mutual respect and forbearance between individuals that constitutes the object of justice. It is always wrong to treat *another individual* unjustly, and therefore it is always wrong to sacrifice the due claims of one person in order to promote the well-being of another or to promote or safeguard the common good. Finally, it is always *wrong* to act in these ways, implying that someone who voluntarily treats another unjustly is in the wrong, blameworthy, whatever his motives may be.

Seen in this light, Aquinas's interpretation of the precepts of justice is at any rate not obvious. He accounts for the binding force of these precepts through a painstaking analysis of the moral act, which allows him to formulate moral claims and prohibitions in terms that are both precise and stringent. He argues that some kinds of actions are intrinsically disordered and therefore never morally permissible, while at the same time, he limits the scope of responsibility to those things that the agent actually does or negligently fails to do. Both claims would be controversial, but in order to fairly evaluate them, we need to start with some sense of the moral concerns that motivate these claims. Aquinas's overall approach to moral analysis reflects a perspective on morality that is widely shared among those who defend some version of deontological ethics. On this view, as Charles Fried expresses it, "The very *form* of categorical norms (norms of right and wrong) expresses the same conception of human personality as do the *contents* of the norms."[1] He continues,

> To be sure, morality is concerned in some way or another with all the consequences to which we might contribute or which we might avoid. The categorical norms, however, designate what it would be wrong to *do* . . . but their absolute force attaches only to what we intend, and not to the whole range of things which come about as a result of what we do intentionally. The link of intentionality between a moral agent and what he accomplishes . . . is simply another aspect, the procedural aspect, of the substantive contents of the norms. Both aspects express an underlying moral conception of the person. It is respect for persons as the ultimate moral particulars which is expressed by the contents of categorical norms. The mode of application, the procedural aspect, expresses this same certainty of the individual's personal efficacy as a moral agent.[2]

1. Charles Fried, *Right and Wrong* (Cambridge, MA: Harvard University Press, 1978), 14, emphasis in the original.

2. Fried, *Right and Wrong*, 20–21.

I have quoted Fried at length because he clearly expresses the close interrelationship between substantive and formal or procedural commitments that we find in most deontological moral theories. Aquinas's account of moral precepts can best be understood in these terms, which brings us to a critical point. Aquinas believes that the precepts of justice are strictly binding because they are grounded in the claims of others and in the duties that we have toward them. It would be misleading to say without qualification that the binding force of the precepts of justice follows from the structures of the will itself. And yet, taken in one specific way, this observation is true. The values inherent in the ideal of the right are grounded in the claims of others and the agent's duties toward them, but these can inform the will only by shaping its disposition, inclination, and choice in specific ways. The innate structures of the will are not themselves the normative ground of our obligations toward others. Nonetheless, they do determine the form of these obligations, in such a way as to specify just how they are binding. Once we understand what it means to act in certain ways in relation to others, we grasp that these ways of acting count as transgressions, implying that they cannot be justified. By implication, we cannot grasp what the general ideals of justice demand in many instances unless we have some sense of the way in which an agent is related to another through her actions. This sense, in turn, requires an analysis of the structure of the external act that identifies the components of the act as a causal relation and determines the normative significance of each of these. Aquinas provides just such an analysis early in the *prima secundae*, at the end of an extended examination of the concept of the voluntary, the will, and its acts.

For some time now, action theory has been one of the most active fields of philosophical inquiry, and there are currently many ways of understanding the human action, its analytic structures, and its normative significance.[3]

---

3. At the risk of oversimplifying, I would divide Anglophone work on the philosophy of action over the last century into two distinct fields of inquiry. The first of these, stemming from the seminal work of Elizabeth Anscombe and Donald Davidson, focuses on the intentional and causal components of human action. While she wrote extensively on intention, morality, and related topics, Anscombe's most extensive and influential treatment of this topic is G. E. M. Anscombe, *Intention*, 2nd ed. (Ithaca, NY: Cornell University Press, 1963; originally, 1957). Donald Davidson's essays on this topic can be found in *Essays on Actions and Events*, 2nd ed. (Oxford: Clarendon, 2001). The second broad area of inquiry focuses more directly on questions of practical reason and moral theory, and as Elijah Millgram points out, it comprises a number of distinct fields of research that are not always in contact with one another. This comment occurs in his excellent introduction to the current state of these inquiries, "Practical Reason and the Structure of Actions," in *The Stanford Encyclopedia of Philosophy*, ed. E. N.

I will not attempt detailed comparisons between Aquinas's conception of the human act and contemporary views. Nonetheless, in order to avoid misunderstandings, it may be helpful to begin with an overview of Aquinas's conception of the human act.[4] Seen in its most basic terms, human action is a kind of operation, that is to say, an exercise of causal power by the human person, as agent, on some target. As such, human action reflects the same structure as we find in the operations of creatures more generally. It stems from the distinctive form of the human person in some way or other, unsurprisingly, since, as we have seen, a creature's form is nothing other than the principle for its proper operations. It is characterized, moreover, by efficacy and finality. A human action, like any other operation, represents an exercise of the creature's proper causal powers, through which some change is brought about in the terminus of the act. A successful human act is therefore efficacious, that is to say, it brings about some kind of change. At the same time, the change in question should not be understood as if it amounted to nothing more than triggering a process of motion. Causality for Aquinas is always goal-directed in some way, and in the case of human agency, it is directed toward a goal intended by the agent. Hence, a successful human act is marked by finality, insofar as it achieves its aim.[5]

Understood in this way, a human action is an event constituting a par-

---

Zalta, March 26, 2012, http://plato.stanford.edu/entries/practical-reason-action. Christine Korsgaard, Candace Vogler, and Millgram himself are leading figures in this area.

4. The main lines of this account are implied by Aquinas's account of the interconnections among perfection, activity, and form. Human actions, like all other causal operations, are grounded in inclinations that are directed toward sustaining a distinctive form of existence, directly or in relation to the presuppositions or the concomitant effects of the form (I 5.5). Hence, all human beings act for some end—action is characterized by finality—and the human act is successful, insofar as it brings about that end (I-II 1.1–2; cf. I-II 18.1). For a fuller defense of this account of action, including a more comprehensive consideration of relevant texts, see Stephen L. Brock, *Action and Conduct: Thomas Aquinas and the Theory of Action* (Edinburgh: T. & T. Clark, 1998), 49–136.

5. Aquinas's focus on the human action as a causal operation marks the most fundamental difference between him and Christine Korsgaard, who analyzes action in terms of its overall effect on the agent: "Moral standards are constitutive principle of action . . . they are standards that actions must meet in virtue of what they are. . . . Bad actions, actions that are contrary to justice and the categorical imperative, then, are *defective* actions, actions that are bad as actions." A little further, she adds, "The function of an action is to unify its agent, and so to render him the autonomous and efficacious author of his own movements. An unjust or unlawful action therefore fails to unify its agent, and so fails to render him the autonomous and efficacious author of what he does" (*Self-Constitution: Agency, Identity, and Integrity* [Oxford: Oxford University Press, 2009], 160–61, emphasis in the original).

ticular kind of relationship, namely, that obtaining between an agent and the terminus of its active power.[6] As such, a particular action can be individuated from the web of causal interactions within which it is necessarily embedded. It takes place over time, originating with the first moment at which the agent begins to exercise his powers and terminating when the effect of those powers has been communicated to the terminus of the action. So understood, any action *ad extra* will necessarily involve some kind of bodily movement, since that is the only way in which embodied creatures can exercise their causal powers. However, the act will not be identical to any set of bodily movements, but rather, it is properly analyzed in terms of the exercise of causal power taking place in and through those movements.[7] Correlatively, the agent can intend only what he can reasonably expect to bring about through his specific causal powers.[8] We may wish for things that we know we cannot bring about, but such wishes are just that, not voluntary choices directed toward specific acts (I-II 13.5).

The upshot of all this, for the purposes of moral theory, is that the human act, considered as an intelligible exercise of causality, has a certain conceptual and moral primacy. Considered as a causal event, it is an operation of a living creature of a specific kind, which is, as such, oriented toward bringing about certain effects in order to preserve or express a specific way of life. It cannot be analyzed in terms of all the vectors of causation that it may set in motion. Aquinas would say that we can meaningfully distinguish a particular action from all the consequences that follow from it (I-II 20.5). By the same token, he does not consider a failure to act, or an omission, to have the same metaphysical or moral status as an act, although he does believe that omissions are sometimes morally culpable (I-II 71.5). On his view, an agent is morally responsible for those effects of his action that are intrinsic to the kind of act that it naturally is, together with those secondary effects

---

6. On the individuation of actions thus understood, see Brock, *Action and Conduct*, 49–93.

7. Thus, every action will take place in and through what Donald Davidson describes as a primitive action—a configuration of bodily movements, generously construed to include such activities as standing fast, cogitating, and the like—but the object of the act will not (normally) be conceptually tied to any one such primitive action. Rather, it will be tied to the causal efficacy of the act, seen in the context of an appropriately human way of life. There are many ways to kill—with a knife, a gun, strangling, and so forth—but the act of killing is not conceptually tied to any of these primitive actions; rather, it is defined by reference to an exercise of lethal aggression. For further details on Davidson's theory of primitive actions, see his "Agency," in *Essays on Actions and Events*, 2nd ed. (Oxford: Clarendon, 2001), 43–62.

8. As Brock points out in *Action and Conduct*, 139–41.

that can be foreseen, given the situation and the general run of events. He is not responsible for everything that does or does not happen as a result of what he does.

At this point, we turn to Aquinas's analysis of human action as seen from the standpoint of moral evaluation, beginning in I-II 18 with his analysis of the goodness and evil of human actions generally considered. Aquinas believes that our actions fall within morally salient categories that are determined by the objective features of the act, considered as a distinctive kind of causal operation. These determinants, each of which is independently subject to moral evaluation, include the object of the act (I-II 18.2), its circumstances (I-II 18.3), and the end that the agent intends to realize through his action (I-II 18.4). Aquinas recognizes that human actions can be legitimately described from more than one perspective—indeed, as we will see, his analysis of the objective character of morality depends in part on this point. Nonetheless, he also believes that the proper and unqualified description of an action will indicate the kind of act that it is, understood from the perspective of morality. The different components of human action can each be understood in moral terms, and taken together, they determine the moral species of the particular act.

When Aquinas refers to the object of an action, he has in mind what some of our contemporaries would call the act itself, that is to say, the causal operation that the agent voluntarily chooses (I-II 18.2). Understood in this way, as the immediate terminus of a voluntary operation, the object of the act represents the act as an exemplification of a morally significant kind of operation. In other words, the object of the act represents the act itself, described in such a way as to bring out its morally salient and defining features. Some kinds of actions are good or indifferent in kind, while others are intrinsically disordered, in such a way as to render them morally evil. Judging by Aquinas's examples in this article, the kinds of actions in question are inappropriate or they lack due proportion, in comparison to standards of equity and respect for others' claims (again, see I-II 18.2, esp. *ad* 1). To take one of Aquinas's examples, the act of taking what is another's, against the other's will, is objectively disordered and cannot be justified.[9] Correlatively, not every aspect of a particular act plays a role in determining the kind of action that is in question. Some elements of an action are circumstantial, and as such, they do not affect the kind of action that the agent chooses (I-II 18.3).

---

9. This formulation oversimplifies a complex set of questions; see II-II 66, and esp. 66.7, for details and qualifications.

However, they can increase or mitigate the moral quality of a particular act, and so they need to be considered in one's overall moral evaluations. Theft is morally wrong, whether it is carried out by taking someone's wallet or by hacking into his credit card account, but the latter act may be worse morally because it also has the effect of undermining important systems of exchange. Finally, an action is chosen in order to attain or safeguard or exemplify some further aim, which Aquinas identifies as the end of the action (I-II 18.4). This end, again, may be morally praiseworthy or at least indifferent in itself, or it may be in some way vicious. It is generally praiseworthy to give alms to the poor, but this aim, sincerely held, does not justify an act of stealing in order to give alms.

What does this analysis tell us about the overall moral value of a particular act? Aquinas answers this question with a crisp quote from the author he knows as Dionysus, to the effect that goodness implies complete perfection, whereas any defect renders something bad (I-II 18.4 *ad* 3; cf. I-II 18.1). Thus, if any of the components of a particular act is morally problematic, the action taken as a whole is morally evil. In particular, an action that is bad in kind cannot be morally justified by a praiseworthy aim.

But is this really Aquinas's view? In the next question, I-II 19, which considers the morality of the inner act of the will as it chooses a particular act, Aquinas seems to reverse himself on just this point. In the first articles, Aquinas argues that the goodness of the will depends entirely on its object (I-II 19.1–2), which in turn is identified with the agent's overall aim. In that case, what becomes of the distinction between object and end so carefully spelled out in the preceding question? (In addition to the texts cited, see I-II 18.7.) It looks as if Aquinas sets it aside, at least as far as the overall moral judgment of a particular act is concerned. But on closer examination, we see that this is not accurate. He considers action from two distinct perspectives in I-II 18 and 19, and he analyzes the components of the human act in different ways, corresponding to these different perspectives. The distinctions set forth in I-II 18 provide the terms necessary if we are to analyze an action as a unitary whole, taking account both of the operation that the agent directly chooses (namely, the object of the act) and of the state of affairs in view of which the agent chooses (namely, the end; I-II 18.2,4). In I-II 19 Aquinas adapts these distinctions in order to apply them to the distinctive features of the inner act of the will operating through free judgment. The object of the inner act of choice is the concrete action that the agent voluntarily chooses, considered as an action of a specific kind, directed to some further end, in view of salient circumstances. At the same time, Aquinas regards the human act as one unified event, constituted by the agent's inner choice, her exercise of her causal powers, and the exterior act that she performs. Thus, the interior act of the will and the external act are in reality two aspects of one and the same act (I-II 20.3). For this reason, the terms of analysis set forth in I-II 18 can be applied in different ways to the descriptions of the act considered as an interior act of will and as an external performance. These yield two different analytic descriptions of the same action, which track the relevant components of the action from two different vantage points, considering the act an interior operation of the will and as an external operation commanded by the will.

On the one hand, we might consider an action as an operation or process of the agent himself, and in that sense internal to him. Seen from this vantage point, the act is fundamentally an operation of the agent's will. As such, its specific identity is determined by the object of choice, which in this context refers to the concrete act proposed by the reason as good and worth pursuing here and now (I-II 19.1 *ad* 3, 19.3). Hence, the object of the interior act is considered globally, as a concrete whole encompassing everything that the agent knowingly chooses, that is to say, this particular act, chosen in these circumstances as a means to, or constituent aspect of, this further end. For this reason Aquinas says at I-II 19.2 that the goodness of the interior act of the will is determined by the object alone. In this context, the object is nothing other than the particular, fully determinate action that is chosen, and therefore all the components of the act considered as a whole must be considered in this context as complex determinates of one specific choice (I-II 19.2, esp. *ad* 1,2). Nonetheless, these distinctions presuppose a more comprehensive analysis of human action, considered in its integral reality as a free, self-reflective exercise of the agent's causal powers, which originates with the agent's choice and is expressed through an exterior act.

This interpretation is confirmed when we turn to the next question, I-II 20, in which Aquinas considers the morality of the external act. In the first article of this question, Aquinas explicitly raises the question that concerns us here. Are good and evil in human actions constituted fundamentally by the inner act of the will or by the external act? Aquinas replies that it depends. Insofar as the goodness or evil of a particular act stems from the end for which the agent acts, these do depend on the will, and in this respect the goodness of the external act is dependent on the goodness or evil of the interior act of the will. At the same time, "The goodness or evil that an external act has in itself, on account of due matter and due circumstances, is not derived from the will, but rather from reason" (I-II 20.1). Thus, the goodness of the external action adds to, and indeed partially determines, the good of the interior act of the will, precisely because it provides the will with its "terminus and end," and thus, "it adds to the goodness or badness of the will, because every inclination or motion is perfected in this, that it achieves its end or attains its terminus" (I-II 20.4). The external act thus stands in the same relation to the inner act as reason, generally considered, stands to the will. More precisely, the relation between external and inner act is one expression of the overall relation between reason and will. The agent's will in choosing is informed by her rational grasp that this particular act has the rational structure and significance that it does as an act of a specific kind, with a determinate object. Correlatively, considered as a kind of act with an intelligible structure, the external act has a moral significance of its own that partially determines the sinfulness or merit of the agent choosing it.

Why are these distinctions so important for Aquinas's overall moral theory? They are significant, in the first place, because to a considerable extent, moral judgments depend on a clear idea of exactly what the agent is doing. Aquinas holds that certain kinds of actions are objectively disordered, in such a way that the agent who chooses to act in this particular way commits a sin (I-II 18.2, 72.1). This claim presupposes that the act in question is voluntary in the relevant sense, that is, that the agent is aware of those aspects of the act in virtue of which it is disordered (I-II 6.8, 76.2–3). But given that the agent is aware of the morally salient features of an action, it does not matter whether the agent's overall aim or her motivations are good, nor does it matter that the agent chooses on account of the good she pursues, while regretting the disordered act she undertakes. Aquinas holds that anyone who voluntarily chooses an act of a kind that she knows to be disordered is ipso facto guilty of sin, which is tantamount to saying that the overall stance of her will is determined by specific features of her choice (I-II 72.1, 76.1 *ad* 3). Correlatively, in such cases the agent's choice cannot be adequately described or evaluated in terms of her overall aim alone. Her choice is determined by objective features of the kind of act that she chooses, and if the kind of action question is morally wrong, her choice is culpable.

More fundamentally, moral analysis must take account of the agent's immediate act because this is the operation through which she enters directly into relationships with the external world and, especially, with other people. As we recall, human action is essentially an exercise of causality, and given Aquinas's overall account of causal operations, this implies that a successful act relates the agent immediately to the state of affairs that she chooses to bring about (I-II 1.3, esp. *ad* 3). The agent's choice to act in a given way is tantamount to a choice to enter into a relationship of a specific kind, and as such, it qualifies her will in a distinctive way, apart from her overall aims and the motivations behind them.

Once again, we may wonder why Aquinas gives so much weight to the relational aspect of human action, rather than the agent's immediate operations or the effect that the act has on another. Yet this line of analysis is consistent with his overall approach to justice and the other virtues of the will, which dispose the agent to relate rightly to others, to collective entities, and to God. Seen from one perspective, a choice relates an agent to a state of affairs, but if that state of affairs involves some interaction with another agent, the choice relates him to that other as well. Someone who chooses to act in such a way as to harm another unjustly or to slight her in some way chooses to relate himself to that other as one whose claims can be set aside at his discretion. He may think that he has good reasons for doing so, he may be motivated by sincere desire to help many others, but neither the outcome of his act nor the purity of his motives can change what he actually does, namely, inflict an unjust injury on another.

This brings us to a related point. On this line of analysis, objective causal relations do make a moral difference.[10] More specifically, there is a real, objective distinction between bringing something about and allowing it to happen, and this distinction makes a difference morally.[11] Of course Aquinas realizes that failures to prevent harms or to act on behalf of the good can be morally wrong, perhaps even worse than some kinds of direct transgressions (I-II 71.5; II-II 79.3). Nonetheless, he claims that one's direct causal operations have a special moral salience, and for that reason, there is an objective difference between an act of killing, for example, and failing to save someone in mortal

10. Aquinas's realism about causal relations and their normative significance sets him apart from Germain Grisez and John Finnis, who hold that the agent's intention can be specified without any necessary reference at all to the specific form of the causal efficacy behind the intended act; see most recently Finnis, Grisez, and Joseph Boyle, "'Direct' and 'Indirect': A Reply to Critics of Our Action Theory," *Thomist* 65 (2001): 1–44. I agree with Stephen Long that this position is tantamount to collapsing the object of the act into the agent's subjective aim or motive; see his "A Brief Disquisition regarding the Nature of the Object of the Moral Act according to St. Thomas Aquinas," *Thomist* 67 (January 2003): 45–71.

11. This claim is controversial. A number of philosophers have argued that there is no rationally defensible basis for distinguishing among the vectors of causation set up by someone's action, or inaction, in such a way as to mark out a particular set of operations as "the act itself," distinct from side effects, unforeseen consequences, and the like. For an excellent overview of the relevant arguments, together with a frank assessment of their moral significance, see Jonathan Bennett, *The Act Itself* (Oxford: Clarendon, 1995), esp. 143–63.

danger. Again, this claim follows from his overall analysis of human action as a causal relation. The human agent places himself in relation to another in a direct and immediate way when that other is the target of his causal operation. This immediate relation is morally decisive, at least in the sense that, unless the agent gets this relation right, his act cannot be morally justified.

Correlatively, Aquinas rejects the view that the moral quality of the will is determined by the agent's overall stance toward the good or her general commitment to duty or any other general commitment of this kind. Someone may well be disposed toward good ideals or commitments in this way, while still choosing badly in some particular instance. Aquinas holds that someone who voluntarily chooses an objectively disordered kind of action acts in such a way as to incur guilt and reproach (I-II 19.6; cf. I-II 72.1, 78.1 *ad* 2). This is so, even in those cases in which the agent sincerely believes that he is somehow acting for the best, that he is justified by special circumstances, or that he is excused on account of the higher purpose or greater good for which he acts. The orientation of the will is determined by the agent's immediate choice directed toward a specific kind of action, and not exclusively by his overall good aims or general dispositions.

Aquinas is thus committed to the view that some kinds of actions are never morally justified, whatever the agent's motivations or the foreseen consequences of refraining might be. These kinds of actions are correlated with centrally important precepts of justice, for example, the prohibitions against murder, theft, or adultery. For more than half a century now, a wide range of theologians and moral philosophers have debated this general claim, sometimes with reference to Aquinas's moral thought, very often not.[12] It would go well beyond the scope of this book to try to survey these debates, much less to resolve them. Nonetheless, we are now in a position to see why Aquinas takes what many of our contemporaries would regard as an extreme position on this question. He does not regard the relevant precepts as divine commands, which are exceptionless because of God's

---

12. Within the field of Catholic moral theology, the two leading schools of thought on this question are proportionalism and the "new natural law," set forth by Germain Grisez, John Finnis, and their followers. These two schools have generated a staggering amount of literature. For a good overview of the proportionalist approach, see Bernard Hoose, *Proportionalism: The American Debate and Its European Roots* (Washington, DC: Georgetown University Press, 1987). Finnis and Grisez set out the main lines of their theory of practical reason in Germain Grisez, Joseph Boyle, and John Finnis, "Practical Principles, Moral Truth and Ultimate Ends," *American Journal of Jurisprudence* 32 (1987): 99-151, and more recently, Finnis, Grisez, and Boyle, "'Direct' and 'Indirect.'"

authority. He does not appeal to the practical necessity to respect others as rational creatures, as a condition or implication of one's own autonomy. He appeals, rather, to the fundamental claim that each human person has to be treated with respect and forbearance, a claim that follows immediately from the normative significance of human existence itself. The relevant precepts express "the very order of justice," and there can be no justification for setting them aside (I-II 100.8).

Aquinas's theory of the moral act is one part of a more comprehensive account of justice and morality, and we can more readily appreciate its full implications within that context. In particular, Aquinas's claims about the impermissibility of certain kinds of actions should be seen within the context of the commitments to equality and impartiality discussed in the last chapter. It is helpful in this context to consider the law-like character of the precepts of justice, considering these not as enactments, but rather as principles for impartial judgment. The ideal judge pronounces judgment on the basis of rational considerations, setting aside any kind of partiality or aversion. She is impartial, and because she is impartial, she respects the dignity and the due claims of the defendant. Critically, someone who is judged in this way is not subject to another's private judgments but is held accountable by rational considerations.

Similarly, the precepts of justice function in such a way as to safeguard the free status of every man and woman and to ensure that the claims of each are acknowledged. These precepts rule out certain kinds of harms, but at the same time, they preserve anyone from being subjected to the private or partial judgment of another. We are all accountable to one another, but none of us, considered as an individual, has the authority to subject another to judgment. Much less can any one of us justify sacrificing the life or the well-being of another to promote greater goods, however those are understood, in utilitarian terms or in terms of collective well-being. These claims are sufficiently justified by the moral status of each individual, but we have additional reasons for giving special weight to this aspect of morality. Experience shows, all too clearly, that men and women cannot be trusted with unchecked power over others. Prisoners, students, and members of religious communities are notoriously at risk of abuse from those who are supposed to be guarding, teaching, or forming them for just this reason. Strict adherence to objective moral precepts carries its own moral risks, but at its best, a disposition to justice will safeguard the individual from her worst impulses and incline her to respect the claims of all.

This line of argument would be controversial, but many would find it to be compelling, myself included. However, Aquinas's analysis of the moral act carries a further implication that is intuitively harder to accept. That is, he apparently does not acknowledge the possibility of good-faith moral mistakes. The morality of a particular other-regarding act is determined by the kind of relation that it sets up between the agent and another, a relation either of just respect and restraint or of unjust disregard and injury. The agent chooses to act in such a way as to bring about just this kind of relation, and it is this choice, taken together with the agent's aims and relevant circumstances, that determines the moral character of the will itself (I-II 19.1–2). Aquinas recognizes that the agent must be aware of the morally relevant features of an act, or else, if he is not, his ignorance must not be his own fault if it is to excuse a bad act. However, someone who voluntarily acts in an objectively unjust way cannot be said to have a good will, even though his motives are good and he considers himself to be morally justified. For this reason Aquinas claims that an erroneous conscience does not excuse from guilt unless the error is an involuntary error of fact (I-II 19.6).

At this point, we may be tempted to reject Aquinas's arguments out of hand as being too deeply at odds with our moral intuitions to be credible. We value sincerity and general good will more than good conduct, or at least we are quick to excuse those whose bad behavior does not seem to reflect a bad heart. Yet I would suggest that our own relevant intuitions at this point are more complex than we might at first realize. We generally allow for the possibility that someone might do something wrong as the result of a genuine, good-faith moral mistake, and most of us would probably say that in such cases, the mistaken agent is not subjectively guilty or open to reproach. Much depends, however, on the kind of moral mistake in question. For example, many would agree that a doctor who chooses to kill his suffering patient may well do so in good faith, even on the assumption that this course of action is objectively wrong. In such a case, we may well want to say that, even though the doctor did something wrong, he acted well in the sense that he did what he thought was right. Yet we can imagine other situations in which it would be harder to excuse a mistaken judgment, even a sincere mistaken judgment. Until relatively recently, many men and women sincerely believed that African Americans could legitimately be enslaved, and even today, some individuals are prepared to set aside the claims of African Americans to respect and equitable treatment, generally on some dubious pretext. Pretexts are necessary, because no one today wants to admit to outright racism, and most decent men and women are uncomfortable with the distorted relations that go along with these attitudes.

These examples illustrate a key point. Even though we are sometimes prepared to excuse bad behavior on the grounds of sincerely mistaken moral judgments, we hesitate to say that moral mistakes excuse everything. Our moral beliefs and the practical judgments stemming from these beliefs are deeply enmeshed with the background beliefs, attitudes, and sentiments shaping the agent's character, and we cannot regard them in the same light as mistakes about relevant facts. Even though moral beliefs as such may be morally neutral in themselves, they reflect on the individual, they do her credit or they compromise her, and we may question whether certain kinds of mistaken moral judgments can be made "in good faith." In the first example, it is at least plausible that the doctor who ends his patient's life in order to end her suffering does so out of a genuine concern for her and a sincere desire to act in accordance with her claims on him, as her doctor and as a companion in vulnerability and mortality. For this reason it makes sense to say that, in this instance, the agent's objectively bad action, while by definition unjust, is excusable. In the second case, in contrast, it is not so easy to reconcile the agent's beliefs and actions with an overall stance of regard for another. The racist knows in a general way that every other individual is to be loved as oneself—as we have seen, everyone knows this—but she is either incapable of grasping that certain individuals are her neighbors, in the relevant sense, or she simply does not love them in the relevant way, that is to say, she is not inclined to respect their claims on her.

I will not attempt to resolve the problem posed by good-faith moral mistakes. Certainly, some kinds of mistakes are more excusable than others, but the fact remains that even a genuinely well-intentioned unjust act places the agent in a distorted relation to another person. Aquinas, for his part, certainly believes that everyone is capable of grasping at least the fundamental precepts of justice and acting accordingly (I-II 100.1,3; cf. I-II 76.2). Furthermore, he believes that we are naturally disposed to value other people, to wish them well, to want to help them, and to turn from harming them (II-II 114.1, esp. *ad* 2). Of course he is well aware that this disposition is always more or less corrupted, even in the best of us, but his point would be that our malicious tendencies are precisely corruptions of naturally good tendencies. This brings us back to the point with which we began this section. Aquinas could not effectively develop his theory of human action and the will without drawing on precise logical distinctions. However, his theory is not motivated by formal considerations; rather, he relies on formal distinctions in order to express and systematically state what is, at base, a substantive commitment to a particular understanding of justice.

Justice and the Moral Emotions

Aquinas's analysis of the moral structure of the human act offers us a power-ful framework within which to specify just what it is that the agent is choos-ing, and what this implies for the actual disposition of her will. This analysis, as we have seen, depends in key part on the distinction between the object of an action (that is to say, the operation that the agent directly chooses) and the circumstances, on the one hand, and the agent's aim in acting, on the other. His analysis, however, will be usable only if we can identify the object of the act in terms that do not depend on the agent's subjective motives or aims but, rather, draw on normative considerations that can generally be recognized as such. The object of the act is characterized in terms of general moral concepts, including, for example, murder, theft, or almsgiving. Aqui-nas's analysis implies that we can offer substantive, objectively accessible accounts of these kinds of concepts. Can this be done?

In this section and the next, I want to propose that our basic moral concepts are grounded in ways of life and forms of relationship that are central to our lives as social animals, as these are grasped and reformulated through the judgments of reason. Thus, our moral concepts originate in prerational but intelligible ways of relating to one another that provide the necessary starting points for substantive morality. These forms of inter-relationship become salient through moral emotions such as compassion, shame, and anger, which begin to emerge in infancy and are shared by many nonhuman animals. At the same time, these forms of interrelationship become normative in a distinctively human way only insofar as they are grasped, formulated, and transformed through rational reflection. Rational reflection on our initial perceptions of forms of relationships give rise to substantive moral concepts that constitute the core of any working system of morality and, more to our immediate point, fill in the substantive mean-ing of the general precepts of justice. Admittedly, I cannot prove that this is in fact the way in which moral concepts emerge and develop, but I hope to offer a persuasive speculation that takes account of what we know about the moral emotions and moral development, while also doing justice to the distinctiveness of moral concepts.

In this section, I take my starting points from recent research and spec-ulation on the moral emotions, including guilt or shame, compassion, and a preference for fairness, as well as anger and disgust.[13] At one point, scien-

13. For a good introduction to this rapidly expanding field of study, see Joshua Greene

tists and philosophers assumed that these and similar emotions normally emerge in response to rational moral judgments, and for that reason, they did not attract a great deal of interest. Beginning in the 1980s, however, researchers began to identify moral emotions, apparently comparable to those experienced by mature adults, in infants and very young children, as well as nonhuman animals.

Although it can be difficult to interpret the behaviors of nonhuman animals and prelinguistic children, it does seem fairly clear that both are capable of empathy, gratitude, indignation, and other similar responses to the behaviors of others. These emotions are expressed through a range of well-documented behaviors, including comforting those in distress, engaging in reciprocal favors such as grooming or sharing food, refusing to participate in uneven exchanges, or even retaliating for disadvantageous treatment. These kinds of observations are notoriously difficult to interpret exactly, but it is hard to deny that nonrational animals and small children share in a range of emotions that we associate with moral judgments of oneself and others.

For some time, there has been a lively debate among scientists and philosophers over whether the moral emotions of nonhuman animals and young children provide a sufficient basis for moral judgments and practices. According to the distinguished primatologist Frans de Waal, there is at the very least an essential continuity between the relevant responses of nonhumans and human morality. In their introduction to de Waal's Tanner lecture "Primates and Philosophers," Josiah Ober and Stephen Macedo offer a helpful summary of his views: "Emotional responses are, de Waal argues, the 'building blocks' of human morality. Human moral behavior is considerably more elaborate than that of any nonhuman animal, but in de Waal's view, it is *continuous with* nonhuman behavior. . . . Given this continuity of good

---

and Jonathan Haidt, "How (and Where) Does Moral Judgment Work?" *Trends in Cognitive Sciences* 6.12 (2002): 517–23, and Jonathan Haidt, "The Moral Emotions," in *The Handbook of Affective Sciences*, ed. Richard J. Davidson, Klaus R. Scherer, and H. Hill Goldsmith (Oxford: Oxford University Press, 2009), 852–70. For an overview of recent work on the moral emotions of nonhuman animals, see Franz de Waal and Sarah F. Brosnan, "Fairness in Animals: Where To from Here?" *Social Justice Research* 25 (2011): 336–51. In addition, for a detailed account of de Waal's own pioneering work in this field, see his *Good Natured: The Origins of Right and Wrong in Human and Other Animals* (Cambridge, MA: Harvard University Press, 1996). For a comprehensive, and incidentally charming, survey of recent work on the moral emotions of infants and very young children, see Paul Bloom, *Just Babies: The Origins of Good and Evil* (New York: Crown Publishers, 2013).

nature, there is no need to imagine morality being mysteriously added to an immoral core."[14] In his Tanner lecture, de Waal elaborates on this point, arguing that the moral judgments of mature, rational adults are likewise grounded in feelings rather than reasoning:

> People can deliberate as much as they want, but, as neuroscientists have found, if there are no emotions attached to the various options in front of them, they will never reach a decision or conviction. This is critical for moral choice, because if anything morality involves strong convictions. These convictions don't—or rather can't—come about through a cool rationality: They require caring about others and powerful "gut feelings" about right and wrong.[15]

Most scientists and philosophers today would agree that nonhuman animals and humans share a great deal that is relevant to morality, including basic moral emotions and corresponding behaviors. At the same time, there are some key elements of human morality that apparently are not found among nonhuman animals. So far as we can determine, the moral emotions and their corresponding behaviors appear to be elicited only by those within an animal's immediate circle, that is, they do not appear to generalize these responses to include all their cospecifics. Similarly, they do not seem to have a general notion of obligation that would in some way incorporate the more particular kinds of responses into one generalized pattern of action.[16] Again, there appears to be little disagreement about the existence of these discontinuities. The question is, should these count as

---

14. Frans de Waal and respondents, *Primates and Philosophers: How Morality Evolved*, ed. Stephen Macedo and Josiah Ober (Princeton: Princeton University Press, 2006), xiv, emphasis in the original.

15. De Waal and respondents, *Primates and Philosophers*, 18.

16. As Ober and Macedo observe, the former issue is raised in some form by all of de Waal's respondents: "Each commentator asks a similar question: If even the most advanced non-human animals ordinarily limit their good behavior to insiders (kin or community members) can we really speak of their behavior as *moral*?" (*Primates and Philosophers*, xv; emphasis in the original). Among these respondents, Christine Korsgaard emphasizes the latter issue; see "Morality and the Distinctiveness of Human Action," 98–119, in *Primates and Philosophers*, 116–17. Christopher Boehm observes that, although nonhuman animals apparently internalize social norms and associate the violation of these with the threat of punishment, they do not appear to experience self-referential moral emotions with respect to these norms—that is to say, they do not seem to experience guilt or shame. See his *Moral Origins: The Evolution of Virtue, Altruism, and Shame* (New York: Basic Books, 2012), 116–31.

essential discontinuities that reflect a distinctively new element in human morality?[17]

Without doubt, Aquinas would come down on the side of those who identify a fundamental difference between the normative apprehensions and practices of nonhuman animals and human moral judgments and actions. Like most of those who would take this view today, he would claim that the rationality proper to human morality accounts for this fundamental difference. Yet we should not assume that he would relegate the moral emotions of nonhuman animals and small children to the realm of instinct or mindless thinking. On the contrary, Aquinas's moral psychology, and more specifically his treatment of the passions, suggests a more nuanced approach to the moral emotions and their relation to cognition. On this account, the moral emotions can be seen as inclinations of distinctively moral passions, which are elicited by schematic images of a certain kind, and move the creature to act in a specified way. Thus understood, the moral emotions cannot be equated with rational moral judgments, but they do reflect perceptions of others that are veridical, although limited. As I hope to show, this account of the moral passions and emotions has the advantage of accounting for the fact that the emotions are necessary for adequate moral judgments, without reducing moral judgments to emotion. By the same token, this account also advances the aim of this chapter by showing how the particular images that correspond to the moral emotions are transformed, through rational judgments, into moral concepts.

In order to defend these claims, it will again be necessary at some points to go beyond what Aquinas explicitly says and to qualify his claims at some points. Nonetheless, I hope that nothing in what follows will contradict what he says or distort the overall lines of his moral theory. What is more, this line of argument does have substantial grounding in Aquinas's texts. He and his interlocutors did not have our sense of the complexity and richness of the forms of social life exhibited by other kinds of animals, and they do not seem to have been especially interested in early childhood development. Yet they were not unaware of what we would call the moral emotions. They realize

17. As we will see, both Bloom and Korsgaard conclude that there are essential differences between the moral emotions and affect-driven behavior of nonrational creatures and the morality of a rational adult, although Bloom is more inclined than Korsgaard to acknowledge significant continuities as well as discontinuities. In addition, not everyone agrees that recent neurological evidence on the correlation between emotional states and moral judgments proves that morality is dependent on emotion; see Bryce Huebner, Susan Dwyer, and Marc Hauser, "The Role of Emotion in Moral Psychology," *Trends in Cognitive Sciences* 13.1 (2008): 1–6, for an example of the contrary view.

that animals can respond and behave in ways that appear to be kind, brave, or self-sacrificing. In particular, they realized, as Aristotle also did, that the passion of anger appears to incorporate moral judgments. Aquinas himself, following Aristotle, discusses the moral emotion of anger in some detail. Drawing on Aristotle's account, he analyzes the passion of anger in terms of a perception of undeserved injury, calling forth a desire to avenge oneself by inflicting pain on the offender (I-II 46.4). Anger is thus said to be accompanied by reason, in the sense that it presupposes a correlation between a harm inflicted on oneself and a penalty to be inflicted on another, eliciting an inclination of wrath (I-II 46.4). He goes on to say that anger is directed toward some evil, that is, the harm inflicted on one's adversary, under the rational aspect of justice, since it is an inclination directed toward vengeance (I-II 46.6). Anger as Aquinas understands it looks very much like the moral emotions studied by our contemporaries.

Or does it? Aquinas's remarks would seem to imply that anger follows on a moral judgment to the effect that one has been unjustly injured and ought to take revenge. If this is so, the similarities between the moral emotions of animals and small children, and the distinctively rational phenomenon of anger, would be superficial at best. In fact, he apparently says as much. In the course of considering whether the passion of anger is accompanied by reason, he considers the objection that brute animals, who lack reason, also exhibit anger. He replies that brute animals have a natural instinct conferred on them by divine reason, through which they operate in ways that resemble rational judgments, desires, and actions (I-II 46.4 *ad* 2). Aquinas seems to believe that nonhuman animals follow reasonable principles mechanically, operating in accordance with divine guidance.

Yet this conclusion would be too quick. We need to place Aquinas's remarks at this point in the wider context of his analysis of the role of the passions in nonhuman and human animals. As we have seen, he claims that nonhuman animals are moved to act through conscious apprehensions of desirable and undesirable objects, eliciting inclinations of pursuit, avoidance, and the like. They are thus said to operate on the basis of principles of motion internal to them, that is to say, grounded in and dependent on the creatures' conscious awareness and desire. These processes are grounded in God's creative wisdom, but by the same token they express the creature's own intrinsic principles of operation. This would suggest a more nuanced account of anger in nonhuman animals than this text suggests. When we return to Aquinas's remarks on anger, we see that he does in fact go on to qualify his initial remarks in a significant way.

Having established that there is a connection between anger and rationality, Aquinas goes on to ask whether anger presupposes some kind of relation of justice, which implies that we can be angry only with other rational creatures (I-II 46.7). He replies that this is true with respect to anger properly so called, since the passion of anger presupposes a sense of undue injury and aims at vindication, which is, or can be, an act of justice. Yet he is well aware that we do sometimes get angry with irrational objects, like a leaky pen or an unruly horse. In order to account for this fact, he returns to a comparison between nonhuman and human animals. Once again, he reminds us that, through natural instinct, nonhuman animals act as if they had the use of reason. But now he goes on to explain that this instinct operates through the animal's imagination, that is to say, its capacity to form images drawn from its sensory perceptions (I-II 46.7 *ad* 1; cf. I 78.4). Thus, the anger exhibited by nonhuman animals is not simply an unconscious or mechanical response. It functions in the same way as the other passions exhibited by these animals, through affective inclinations elicited by consciously held images of one's environment. Furthermore, Aquinas continues, we too have imagination, in addition to reason, and we are therefore capable of the same kind of anger that we find in the other animals, triggered through a perception or image of being harmed and expressed through an immediate impulse to lash out. This is not the kind of rationally informed anger that is distinctive to us as human beings, but we nonetheless are capable of it.

This text is significant because it indicates a way in which Aquinas's overall account of the passions can be extended to include the moral passions and their corresponding emotions, as these are found in nonhuman animals and young children. I believe that this account could be extended to include the more complex moral emotions of rational adults, including anger properly so called, but I will not at this point attempt to do so. The point I want to underscore is simply that, on Aquinas's showing, the kind of anger that we find in nonhuman animals is an inclination elicited by an image of a certain kind, that is to say, a schematic representation that calls forth a certain kind of response. In this key respect, anger of this kind is essentially similar to the other passions. The same can be said of the moral emotions of nonrational creatures generally. In Aquinas's terms, these passions would be described as inclinations of distinctive kinds of passions, which is the terminology that I will use in what follows.[18]

---

18. We would need to expand Aquinas's analytic list of the passions in order to include a full range of moral passions, but I cannot see that this move would involve any serious the-

We might easily overlook the similarities between the moral passions and the more basic passions that Aquinas discusses because we are inclined to think of the latter in terms of straightforward responses to perceptions of desirable or undesirable objects. It is true that, in the case of anger and other moral emotions, these images are not linked to straightforward targets of desire, aversion, or avoidance. The moral emotions are not directed toward some tangible object, in the way that a desire for a snack might seem to be directed toward a nice piece of fruit. However, as we saw in the second chapter, even the most straightforward inclinations of desire and aversion cannot be understood in such a simplistic way. Nonhuman animals perceive the world through schematic images, which represent the world as it is or might be, in terms that reflect the creature's needs and vulnerabilities. The inclinations elicited by these images are tied to operations in such a way as to move the creature to action. Infants and very small children respond to the world around them in much the same way as other primates do, and it is safe to say that they too apprehend reality through schematic images of this kind. The images that correspond to the passions of rationally mature men and women are shaped by rational reflection, at least to some extent, but human passions operate in response to sensate images in much the same way as has just been sketched out. In every case, passions are characterized by the kinds of schematic images to which they respond, and the kinds of operations that they elicit.

Can we be more specific about the schemata that would correspond to inclinations of the moral passions? The moral emotions are so called, in part, because they elicit interactions with another of such a kind as to imply normative judgments. This experience presupposes a perception of the other as an appropriate target for some kind of interaction, and it also presupposes a schematic representation of the way in which the interaction ought to go. Psychologist Paul Bloom, summarizing the results of extensive research on compassion among nonhuman animals and human infants, notes that newborn babies are distressed at the sound of other babies crying, more so than at other, comparably loud and annoying noises. Other kinds of animals, including monkeys and rats, will avoid behaviors that benefit them in order to avoid hurting a cospecific. Nonetheless, Bloom notes, a cynic might say that monkeys and rats, and perhaps babies, are innately inclined to find the

---

oretical difficulties. They would appear to be associated with the irascible part of the soul, as anger is, since they typically arise through complex inclinations of avoidance and desire; see I-II 23.1, 46.1.

distress of another unpleasant, without feeling anything for the suffering other. However,

> when we look at how babies and young children act, we see something more. They don't just turn away from the person and pain. They try to make the other person feel better. Developmental psychologists have long observed that one year olds will pat and stroke others in distress . . . and you can see similar behavior in other primates; according to the primatologist Frans de Waal, a chimpanzee—but not a monkey—will put its arm around the victim of an attack and pat her or groom her.[19]

So far, we do not need to qualify Aquinas's overall account of the passions in order to account for the moral emotion of compassion as the inclination of a complex passion prompting both sorrow and a desire to comfort. We can account for the infant's or chimpanzee's behavior in these cases without assuming anything other than a straightforward apprehension of a particular object, mediated through perceptions and images informed by an estimative or cogitative sense (I 78.1). In this case, the object in question is not simply a physical entity but a living creature in distress, and this perception elicits an inclination toward an operation, to assist or soothe. This line of analysis does not presuppose that nonhuman animals and infants have any grasp of the other as such, that is to say, an independent entity, similar to and yet distinct from the creature itself. Nor do we need to assume that nonhuman animals and small children bring to mind, as it were, any considerations of the other's situation, any sense of how it would feel to be in the other's place, the appropriateness of responding in one way rather than another, or the like. Nonhuman animals and babies do not need to reflect in these terms at all in order to relate to distressed others in appropriate ways. Their perceptions of others are perceptions of relations, mediated through images that bring together certain patterns of behavior on the part of another with one's responses. These relations, and the responsive operations that they elicit, are as much a part of the living creature's immediate environment and its dynamic interactions with that environment as the ongoing array of edibles and threats, eliciting desire and consumption, or fear and avoidance. A chimpanzee or a baby does not need to think about its fellows as such in order to respond appropriately to them, any more than they would need to think of an orange as fruit in order to eat it.

19. Bloom, *Just Babies*, 48–49.

We have not yet considered a more fundamental objection to extending Aquinas's account of the passions to include moral passions. Recall that for Aquinas, justice is a perfection of the will, specifically considered as the principle for the agent's other-regarding inclinations and choices. By implication, it would seem that the passions are not other-directed in the same way. In fact, Aquinas says so. In the course of explaining why justice does not direct the passions, he observes that "justice pertains to those things that are directed toward another. However, we are not immediately ordered toward another through the interior passions. And therefore, justice does not pertain to the passions" (II-II 58.9). The virtues of the passions, in contrast to justice and the other virtues of the will, perfect them by orienting them toward the agent's own good (I-II 64.2).

These observations would seem flatly to contradict the claim that the moral passions are oriented toward interactions with others. However, a closer examination of both Aquinas's remarks and the phenomena of the moral emotions indicates that this seeming contradiction is not so absolute as it appears to be. Aquinas's comment that we are not directly oriented toward others through the passions suggests that we may be oriented toward others through the passions in a secondary or qualified sense. Moreover, his own analysis of anger presupposes a more complex understanding of what we call the moral emotions than this remark indicates. At the same time, we can make sense of moral emotions in nonhuman animals and small children without postulating that these have a conception of the other *as* another, or much less that this conception is in some way governing the animal's or the child's responses. In these contexts, the moral emotions can best be understood as desires immediately directed toward interactions of a certain kind, elicited by schematic, normatively laden representations of certain kinds of encounters with others. As such, they orient the creature toward a certain way of interacting with another, but they fall short of setting up a relation directly with another, understood as an individual distinct from oneself.

At any rate, Aquinas's overall moral psychology implies that there is a fundamental distinction between the will and the moral emotions, and although we may qualify that distinction in the way just indicated, we cannot erase it while still remaining within the parameters of a Thomistic theory of justice. Nor do we have any good reason for doing so. Aquinas's distinction between the will and the passions, including the moral passions, is correlated with the distinction between intellect and sensate perceptions. By drawing a line between the will and the passions, we underscore the difference, in this context, between acting on principle and acting out of spontaneous feelings of pity, indignation, or the like. While not everyone would agree that morality necessarily presupposes rational judgments, it does appear that the moral emotions, within the context of human life, cannot generate the kinds of principled judgments that we need in order to sustain a human way of life.

Once again, a comparison with nonhuman animals is illuminating. Just as these kinds of animals are naturally oriented to respond to the world in schematic terms, reflecting their needs and vulnerabilities, so they are naturally oriented to respond to others in such a way as to sustain a characteristically social form of existence. Men and women are also naturally oriented to respond to others in ways that fit broadly within a social pattern of existence, and the moral emotions are the most basic and immediately obvious expression of that orientation. Yet even considered on their own terms, these spontaneous inclinations cannot yield an adequate and intuitively persuasive account of moral judgments. Like the passions generally, moral passions are capacities oriented toward particular objects of desire and aversion, and this particularity means that they are limited in a number of ways.

In the first place, as Bloom observes, our innate moral emotions are morally ambiguous, on almost any reasonable showing. Summarizing his very considerable research into the moral emotions of small children, he first observes that "some aspects of morality come naturally to us." But then he goes on to say, "Our innate goodness is limited, however, sometimes tragically so. . . . We are by nature indifferent, even hostile, to strangers; we are prone toward parochialism and bigotry. Some of our instinctive emotional responses, most notably disgust, spur us to do terrible things, including acts of genocide."[20] More specifically, the moral emotions in themselves cannot account for the widespread sense that all persons are equally valuable, or at least worthy of moral consideration. As Bloom notes, we are innately inclined to prefer those in our immediate circle and to respond to strangers with indifference or hostility. Similarly, Frans de Waal, who defends the essential continuities between nonhuman and human morality, admits this point: "It is only when we make general judgments of how *anyone* ought to be treated that we can begin to speak of moral approval and disapproval. It is in this specific area . . . that humans seem to go radically further than other primates."[21] Finally, we simply have too many moral emotions, more specifically, too many contradictory moral emotions, to rely on these as the sole basis for action in relation to others. This problem does not arise for

20. Bloom, *Just Babies*, 5–6.
21. De Waal and respondents, *Primates and Philosophers*, 20, emphasis in the original.

nonhumans, because for them, the moral emotions spontaneously reflect the patterns of relationship appropriate to the group in question. But human perceptions of relations cannot function in this same way for us, in key part because we perceive and relate to other men and women in more than one way, eliciting diverse and sometimes contrary inclinations. King David was angry with Absalom, considered as a rebel against his throne, and he wanted to kill him—yet he also loved him desperately as his son and wanted to protect him. He could not act on both inclinations at once, and he stood in need of some overarching disposition that would have allowed him to perceive and to respond to this individual appropriately, all things considered.

Adult men and women cannot function adequately on the basis of the moral emotions alone. We need criteria by which to evaluate particular perceptions and inclinations, to redirect or even suppress these in some circumstances, and to harmonize what would otherwise be inconsistent inclinations. By the same token, while the moral emotions may appear to offer adequate guidance for action in particular situations, it is more difficult to see how these could sustain consistent, self-directed activity over the course of a lifetime. The moral passions and their corresponding sensate judgments cannot, in themselves, provide these criteria. They are focused on particular types of situations and interactions and do not have the resources, as it were, to generate general criteria for evaluation. In order to direct and integrate the moral emotions, we need to draw on a different set of normative considerations, appropriate to creatures whose way of life is structured around responsibility, accountability, and reasoned judgment.

In her response to de Waal's Tanner lecture, Christine Korsgaard makes this point forcefully. She notes that de Waal admits that apes do not go beyond what he calls ameliorating relations with one another, whereas we try to act out of general principles. She goes on to say that "it isn't a small difference, that ability to be motivated by an ought. It does represent what de Waal calls a saltatory change. A form of life generated by principles and values is a very different thing from a form of life governed by instinct, desire, and emotion—even a very intelligent and sociable form of life governed by instinct, desire, and emotion."[22] This observation seems right, but it raises a further question, or rather, it reminds us of the issues that motivated this debate in the first place. Even if we grant that a distinctively human life is governed by principles rather than emotion, are we committed to saying that the moral emotions have no place at all in the moral life? Apart from

22. Korsgaard, in *Primates and Philosophers*, 117.

being deeply unattractive, this view of the moral life cannot easily account for our experiences of being moved to act by some strong feeling or judging spontaneously that something ought to be done, as de Waal reminds us. Nor can it account for the considerable evidence, to which de Waal refers in the remarks quoted above, that moral judgment is stunted or impaired by deficits in our emotional capacities.[23]

In order to move forward at this point, we need to find a way to explain the distinction between rational morality and the moral emotions, without implying that these have no point of contact with each other. In order to do so, we return to the integral parts of justice, which Aquinas interprets as a precept to respect one's obligations and to avoid inflicting injury. This general precept, which Aquinas alternatively formulates in terms of the biblical injunction to love the neighbor as oneself, is innate and therefore accessible in some form to everyone who is capable of rational thought and action at all. As we recall, this does not mean that the general precept of neighbor-love is analytically or logically necessary, in the sense of depending on our linguistic intuitions or formal considerations of rational consistency. Rather, this precept represents the capacity of the intellect to grasp a fundamental, objective reality, namely, the normative value of each human being.

This is the basis for the saltatory change to which Korsgaard refers. The first precept of justice, like other fundamental principles of the intellect, is a rational principle that apprehends its subject matter through abstract and universally applicable categories. As such, it cannot be derived from the schematic images that inform the inclinations of the passions, even though these images are rich, detailed, and relationally structured. Just as the first principles of the intellect enable us to understand reality in a new way, so the first precept of justice brings something qualitatively new to normative judgments, namely, foundational precepts pertaining to obligation and harm. Because these are correlated with abstract concepts, they provide a general framework within which to bring disparate responses under general categories, to form comparative judgments regarding the obligations that we owe to one another, and to subject inadequate or inappropriate responses

23. This point is amply established by Antonio B. Damasio, *Descartes' Error: Emotion, Reason, and the Human Brain* (New York: Avon Books, 1994). Although there has been considerable work on this subject since this book was published, I do not believe that anyone seriously doubts that there is a strong correlation between organic deficits in the agent's affective capacities and an impaired capacity to form moral judgments. However, there is much less agreement about how this correlation should be interpreted; see Huebner et al., cited in note 17 above on this point.

to critique and reform. In short, the first precept of justice provides the necessary starting points and rational structures for moral reasoning, through which we are able to formulate general moral precepts, values, and ideals, as well as to apply and practice these in a wide range of situations.

And yet, the first precept of justice cannot operate apart from normatively structured images of human actions and relations. As we have already observed, the first principles of the intellect, whether speculative or practical, can operate only through concepts derived immediately from the phantasms, which are tethered to schematic images derived from sensory perception (I 84.7; I-II 51.1).[24] Correlatively, the fundamental act of understanding always takes the form of an apprehension of some perceived or imagined particular thing, not as a bare particular, but as an instantiation of a form, which apprehension is represented through a phantasm as one instance of that general category (I 85.1). The grasp of the universal as instantiated in the particular is necessary in order to come to understand a general concept; furthermore, it remains necessary for continued understanding and reasoning (I 84.7). In speculative matters, this would imply, for example, that I learn what it means for something to be a cat only by grasping that this fuzzy little thing before me falls under this category, and so long as I continue to understand what it means to be a cat, my understanding is tethered to images of real or imagined cats. In moral matters, this means that I can learn what it means to be obliged to someone, for example, only through my experiences of appropriate and inappropriate behavior. I come to see what it means to injure someone by experiencing unprovoked harm or by inflicting it myself. Generally speaking, I cannot really understand what it means to respect the claims of others and to avoid injuring them, apart from a fund of paradigms for respectful or injurious behavior, drawn from my own experiences and what I have learned from others.

It will be clear by now that, although moral reasoning presupposes a grasp of general principles, these principles cannot operate apart from experiences of particular, normatively significant relations. By implication, moral reasoning cannot operate apart from the moral emotions. These are affective responses to an action or a state of affairs that is immediately perceived as appropriate or inappropriate, and as such, they serve as markers for the kinds of relations that fall within the scope of the first principle of justice. But why

24. For a detailed and helpful discussion of Aquinas's theory of cognition, see Robert Pasnau, *Thomas Aquinas on Human Nature* (Cambridge: Cambridge University Press, 2002), 278–95.

should this be the case? The key point is that the first precept of justice and the images associated with the moral passions reflect two ways of accessing the same reality, namely, the normative significance of human existence itself. The experiences and perceptions that elicit responses of compassion, anger, and the like should be regarded as generally reliable indications of the claims we have on one another and the kinds of restraint that we owe to one another. We cannot reflect on these claims and constraints in any systematic way without having recourse to rational principles, but at the same time, rational reflection of this kind presupposes the objective value of human existence, which we grasp through reflection on paradigm cases of respectful, dutiful, or negligent or harmful behavior.

By now, we can begin to see how a Thomistic account of moral reasoning can account for the indispensable role of the moral emotions, while still showing that moral judgments are rational. On this view, moral reasoning is dependent on the moral emotions precisely because it is one kind of human reasoning, and as such, it is grounded in the apprehension of particulars. Strictly speaking, on Aquinas's account the moral emotions as such are not directly necessary for moral reasoning, since these are inclinations of an appetite rather than cognitive capacities. But they are correlated with particular images that form the necessary basis for understanding and reasoning in moral matters, and so long as they are operating properly, they give these images salience and help the agent to discern the morally relevant features presented by new situations. This explains why moral judgment cannot function properly when the capacities for feeling in certain ways are damaged. It is difficult to say, empirically, whether these deficits are primarily intellectual or affective, but whatever the case may be, they make it difficult or impossible for the agent to grasp particular situations as morally significant in some way. She may be able to manipulate the symbolic structures of moral judgment, but she cannot effectively understand the ways in which moral categories are exemplified in particular cases—which is just what Aquinas would predict (I 84.7–8).

We began this section with the aim of trying to understand how we arrive at formulations of the precepts of justice that are specific enough to be applied strictly, as Aquinas would say. He himself has little to say on this topic, beyond observing that the precepts of the Decalogue follow from first principles with only a minimum of reflection, and more specific formulations call for the judgments of the wise (I-II 100.1). We might expect that Aquinas would at some point step back from his taxonomies of moral acts to set out the general principles that determine what counts as obligation, injury, and the like. Yet he does not; and given his overall approach to moral reasoning, he has no reason to do so. Moral concepts are formed in the same way as other substantive general concepts, that is to say, through an intellectual apprehension of some particular—in this context, a particular course of action as a concrete exemplification of a formal category. For example, we come to understand the meaning of injury through repeated experiences of grasping that this act or that negligent failure to act is an instance of a general category of injury. On this basis, we can then begin to develop a sense of the rationale or the point of these distinctions, through which we can relate them to wider contexts of meaning and justification. Nonetheless, abstract thought, in this context as elsewhere, not only begins with the experiences of particulars, but is always inextricably connected to these experiences.

This understanding presupposes that certain ways of relating to others are really, objectively appropriate and respectful, while other ways of relating are not. We may hesitate to ascribe this kind of objective value to natural patterns of relating to others, but at least Aquinas's assumptions at this point do appear to be verified by our experiences. We do perceive some forms of treatment and address as respectful, while others convey disrespect or worse. These perceptions are variable, context sensitive, and changeable, but they are, nonetheless, ineluctably part of our lives. Furthermore, every human society seems to reflect similar perceptions, expressed through patterns of respect, deference, honor, and the like. We may not be able to justify these perceptions by grounding them in abstract principles, and yet Aquinas could plausibly claim that they reflect objective values, intrinsic to our lives as creatures of a certain kind.

Recent work on the moral emotions of nonhuman animals offers further support for Aquinas's approach. We can now appreciate, more fully than Aquinas and his interlocutors could have done, that the lives of certain kinds of animals are naturally structured through patterns of relations that individuals spontaneously perceive as appropriate or not.[25] These patterns of relations look a great deal like the fundamental forms of respect or transgression that we experience ourselves—when a monkey gets less fruit than its mate, we understand all too well why it gets angry. These patterns are clearly

25. For an extended defense of this thesis with respect to the great apes, see de Waal, *Good Natured*; in addition, see Boehm, *Moral Origins*, 89–131, and, with special reference to the processes of self-regulation and communal cohesiveness, see Darby Proctor and Sarah Brosnan, "Political Primates: What Other Primates Can Tell Us about the Evolutionary Roots of Our Own Political Behavior," in *Man Is by Nature a Political Animal: Evolution, Biology, and Politics*, ed. Peter K. Hatemi and Rose McDermott (Chicago: University of Chicago Press, 2011), 47–72.

objective in one sense, insofar as they constitute a species-specific, natural form of life, inextricably bound up with what it means to be, for example, a rhesus monkey or a gray wolf. By the same token, they are normative in the same way that the natural dynamics of living creatures are normative, that is, they sustain and promote the life, well-being, and ongoing existence of the population and its members. Through their participation in these relations, social animals play an active part in promoting their own well-being, or as Aquinas would say, their perfection. While nonhuman animals are not moral agents, they do live in accordance with intrinsic normative principles, which they spontaneously observe, much of the time, and which they also reinforce, through mutual monitoring, punishment, and the like.

Similarly, men and women spontaneously relate to one another in terms of broad natural patterns of interrelationships, often without needing to think much about what we are doing, or why. We perceive that these patterns are natural to us, and we are accordingly drawn to the satisfying way of life that they offer. At the same time, however, we also enter into relations with others as self-reflective agents, freely directing our activities in pursuit of our own aims, while remaining engaged with others who are doing the same.[26] Seen from this perspective, the relational forms of restraint, balanced exchanges, aid, and the like come to be regarded in moral terms as forms of respect, equity, and benevolence, because they now appear in the light of safeguards for individual freedom of action and, correlatively, as ways of expressing one's sense of the independence and value of others. By the same token, ways of relating that place one individual at the disadvantage of another or exclude someone from the shared life of the community are perceived as forms of injury. Generally, these kinds of actions involve inflicting harm or loss on another, but that is not the fundamental reason that they are condemned. Rather, acts of these kinds are problematic because they set up distorted relations in and through an act of harming someone in a distinctive way.

Aquinas offers a good example of this kind of moral discernment in his treatment of the precepts of the Decalogue. In I-II 100.5 he asks whether the precepts of the Decalogue are set forth in an appropriate way. He responds that they are, because they track a certain kind of order. On further exam-

26. Michael Tomasello offers an especially helpful analysis of the processes through which men and women form and sustain cultures through rational interactions, yielding shared conceptions of justifiable and unjustifiable behavior; see *A Natural History of Human Thinking* (Cambridge, MA: Harvard University Press, 2014), 80–123. In addition, see Boehm, *Moral Origins*, 213–66.

ination, we see that the ordering in question depends in key part on what we might call the logic of moral discernment, which takes its starting points from immediate apprehensions of obligation and injury in exemplary cases. Thus, the neighbor-regarding precepts of the Decalogue are correlated with key paradigms of dutiful or injurious behavior, each of which can be extended to other cases once we grasp the essential principle at stake. Thus, the precept to honor father and mother offers the paradigm case of obligation, which provides a touchstone for recognizing other kinds of indebtedness toward benefactors of all kinds. The following prohibitions are all correlated with exemplary cases of harming another, namely, murder, adultery, theft, bearing false witness, and coveting what is another's. Again, Aquinas assumes that everyone can immediately apprehend these as instances of injury, and he briefly explains how each example points to other similar kinds of injury, directed toward the person of another, to those connected to one's victim, or to the possessions or the social standing of another.

By now, it is clear that Aquinas can account for the formation of moral concepts. We arrive at substantive moral concepts in the same way as we arrive at concepts in every other domain, through apprehending formal principles of existence and operation in their particular instances. These concepts provide starting points and touchstones for further reflection, through which we can draw out the implications of our basic insights and develop our capacities for insight as we confront new situations. These capacities for apprehension and discursive reflection provide the necessary connection between the first principles of practical reason in its unrestricted and restricted forms, and the richly detailed ideals and norms by which we live as moral agents.

This leaves us with one question to be addressed. Our aim so far has been to see how Aquinas might account for the concrete content and the stringency of the precepts of justice. We can now see how he can account for the formation of moral norms, but it is not yet clear how he accounts for the distinctive stringency of those norms associated with the precepts of nonmaleficence. We now turn to that question.

Norms of Nonmaleficence

So far, we have been considering how we might move from the first precept of justice and its immediate implications, the precepts of the Decalogue, to more specific precepts, concrete enough to be put into action. If the arguments of the preceding section are sound, we do so through reflection on paradigms for appropriate and inappropriate ways of relating to one another, which are given salience by the moral emotions and understood in moral terms through the application of the first principles of practical reason, operating within the sphere of relations to others. It will be apparent by now that moral reflection at this level will inevitably be bound up with one's own circumstances and social context, in such a way as to limit the possibilities for useful generalizations. Most men and women would agree that they ought to show respect and gratitude to their parents, for example, but just what this means varies considerably from one society to another, and even from one generation to another within the same society. In many societies, these obligations do impose stringent duties, thus fitting one of Aquinas's criteria for strict justice. But in others, these kinds of obligations are considered to be more flexible, operating more like general ideals than strict duties.

In this section, we turn to a consideration of the core precepts of nonmaleficence, those associated with the neighbor-regarding prohibitions in the Decalogue. These precepts too can be grasped only through an apprehension of particular ways of relating to others, and at the level of specific formulations they are shaped to some extent by one's social context. Nonetheless, the central precepts of nonmaleficence are generally formulated in distinctively clear, specific, and exigent terms. They identify kinds of actions that are intrinsically disordered, because they relate the agent to another in some unfair, harmful, or inappropriate way. This kind of action can thus never be justified by either the agent's good motivations or the seemingly greater good at which she aims. The precepts correlated with these kinds of actions fully exemplify the stringency that Aquinas associates with justice, and they lend themselves to the causal analysis of the components of the human act that he sets out in I-II 18–20. In order to formulate and defend the claim that some kinds of actions are never morally justified, Aquinas needs to distinguish the object of the act from the agent's motivations and overall aim.

We have already seen that Aquinas's analysis of the object in terms of the operation that is immediately chosen by the agent provides him with the distinction that he needs (again, see I-II 18.2). Every successful external action consists in a voluntary operation of some kind, chosen by the agent in view of some aim, through which she brings about some intended change. The immediate operation is thus distinct from both the agent's further aim and the circumstances of her act, as we have already seen. The object of the act represents the kind of operation that the agent chooses, defined in such a way as to identify its species, that is, the kind of action that it essentially is.

While particular actions can be accurately described from more than one perspective, the object or species of the action understood in an unqualified sense depends on normative considerations:

> And so, just as the primary goodness of a natural thing is indicated by its form, which gives a species to it, so the primary goodness of the moral act is indicated by an appropriate object. Hence, it is also said by some to be good in kind, for example, to make use of what is one's own. . . . The primary evil in moral actions is that which is from the object, as, to take what is another's. And therefore it is said to be evil in kind, kind being taken for species. (I-II 18.2)

A little further, he adds that "the difference between good and evil, considered with respect to the object, is in itself determined by reason, that is, in accordance with an object that is appropriate or inappropriate to it" (I-II 18.5).

Aquinas thus identifies "the act itself" with the agent's immediate operation, the object of the act, which is either appropriate or inappropriate, in accordance with rational standards.[27] These are very general criteria, of course, but Aquinas's example gives us an idea of what he has in mind. The act of using what is one's own is an appropriate operation, whereas it is inappropriate to use what is another's. Reading further, we see that an act of sexual intercourse within marriage merits praise, while an adulterous sexual act merits condemnation (I-II 18.5 *ad* 3). Aquinas has already offered another example, in a different context, distinguishing between a praiseworthy act of killing for the sake of justice and killing out of anger (I-II 1.3 *ad* 3). In each case, actions that are morally forbidden are correlated with some kind of harm, and they are contrasted with similar operations that are either not harmful at all or that inflict harm in a justifiable way.

These examples thus confirm what Aquinas's overall account of justice would lead us to expect, namely, that the stringently binding precepts of justice that he considers are strictly binding because they involve harming someone in an especially serious way. This claim is certainly plausible. It expresses widely held intuitive aversions to killing and other kinds of assault or harm, which play a key part in the ensemble of moral emotions discussed above. As de Waal observes, "We have strong inhibitions against killing members of our own community, and our moral decisions reflect

---

27. This phrase is taken from Bennett, *The Act Itself*.

these feelings. For the same reasons, people object to moral solutions that involve hands-on harm to another."[28] In any case, we obviously have a stake in defining prohibited kinds of harm with particular care, if only because so much is at stake in maintaining these prohibitions. At the same time, when we turn back to Aquinas's central examples of stringent prohibitions, that is, the relevant precepts of the Decalogue, it is apparent that these precepts do not forbid harmful actions without qualification. Not every kind of killing counts as murder, as we have already seen, and not every appropriation of another's goods counts as theft. The terms of Aquinas's analysis of the moral act imply that these precepts prohibit inappropriate forms of killing, taking, and the like. Clearly, in order to be plausible, not to say practically usable, this view needs to be developed by some further account of the criteria for the inappropriateness, or as Aquinas elsewhere says, the inordinate or disordered character of a given operation.

The so-called Pauline principle, that we ought not to do evil so that good may come, would suggest that a disordered act involves bringing about good ends by inflicting some kind of harm or damage. This principle has traditionally been associated with the doctrine of double effect, which until recently played a central role in Catholic moral theology.[29] As traditionally understood, the doctrine of double effect captures one important aspect of Aquinas's moral analysis, namely, the significance of the causal relation between the agent and others affected by her act. Nonetheless, the claim that it is always wrong to inflict harm is clearly implausible. We cannot live without inflicting some kinds of damage or harm. Every living creature must take the lives of others in order to eat, to maintain bodily health, and to defend against attacks. Some kinds of damage or harm would seem to be clearly justified by a greater good, for example, the sacrifice of a diseased limb to save one's life. Other kinds of harms are bound up with our lives as social creatures, who maintain a common way of life in ways that involve the threat or infliction of coercive force and punishment. The only ways to save the claim that we ought never inflict any kind of damage or harm under any circumstances whatever require either improbable reinterpretations of causality and intention or else a radical redefinition of what it means to do harm, developed along consequentialist lines. Faced with these alternatives,

28. De Waal, in *Primates and Philosophers*, 56.

29. For a good account of the doctrine of double effect as traditionally understood, see Joseph Boyle, "Toward Understanding the Principle of Double Effect," in *The Doctrine of Double Effect: Philosophers Debate a Controversial Moral Principle*, ed. P. A. Woodward (Notre Dame: University of Notre Dame Press, 2001), 7–22.

we have good reason to say that we are justified in inflicting damage or harm in some situations.

Nonetheless, some kinds of actions are likely to strike us as problematic, if not clearly wrong, because they involve inflicting damage or harm in specific ways, tantamount to some kind of unfairness or disregard of the claims of another. Consider those cases in which someone aims at a greater good by inflicting a harm of a specific kind, by injuring another person or depriving her of her property, her freedom of movement, or her good reputation. In these cases, we would at least hesitate to say that these kinds of harms could be justified by appealing to some greater good. Perhaps in some cases they are. We justify conscription in wartime and judicial punishment in these terms, and it is difficult to see how we could maintain a functioning society without doing so. But in other kinds of cases, it is very difficult indeed to see how we can justify injuring someone in a significant way in order to promote some worthy aim. While we may feel justified in punishing the guilty or defending ourselves against attack, we are more reluctant to sacrifice someone who has done nothing to deserve punishment, or to place a person in harm's way through aggressive or reckless behavior. These examples all point to the conclusion that certain kinds of actions are disordered because they are intrinsically unfair in some way. They inflict harm that the victim does not deserve or that ought not to be inflicted on anyone at all.

It might seem that, so far, we have not made any real progress in addressing the question at hand, namely, the difference between harming another and injuring her in some impermissible way. The key to moving forward lies in the examples just cited. No one would disagree that unjust actions are intrinsically disordered. But as these examples suggest, this generalization can be meaningful so long as it is interpreted within the context of widely held paradigms for interacting with someone else in a way that hurts or damages or constrains him. These kinds of interactions are paradigmatic for bad behavior, as de Waal's remark suggests. For that very reason, when we try to distinguish between permissible and impermissible ways of inflicting harm—as, unfortunately, we sometimes must do—we naturally try to identify scenarios in which harms are unmerited, in order to contrast these with other scenarios in which similar harms would be justified. Our moral reflections in these kinds of cases, in which we envision some kind of direct attack on another, prompt us to think in terms of the kinds of harms that might be deserved or the kinds of burdens or losses that we can reasonably expect someone to bear or in some similar terms. Correlatively, our paradigmatic conceptions of just and unjust actions tend to be correlated with one another, in accordance with general, nonmoral descriptions of actions. The concept of wrongful killing, that is to say, murder, has been understood in very many ways, but central to all of these is the idea of homicide, that is, killing a human being. Moreover, substantive conceptions of murder almost always presuppose some systematic distinctions between murder and legitimate homicide.

Aquinas refers to this example, among others, to illustrate the general point that actions can legitimately be described from more than one standpoint (I-II 1.3 *ad* 3; cf. I-II 18.5 *ad* 3).[30] Two actions may be the same in kind, considered from a natural standpoint, while differing specifically, considered from a moral standpoint. Killing someone in anger and executing a condemned criminal are two examples of the natural-action kind of killing. Yet they represent two specifically distinct kinds of actions when seen from the moral standpoint, namely, murder and just execution. Similarly, adultery and marital relations share in the same natural object, sexual intercourse, but differ with respect to the object of the act, seen from a moral standpoint, and enjoying one's own apples and eating someone else's apples are both examples of the use of physical objects, but differ with respect to the moral object.

Aquinas is here drawing on a distinction that was widely held at this time, albeit formulated in different terms, between the natural and the moral description of an act. This distinction is important, because it identifies a class of actions that can be immediately identified in natural terms, and that clearly calls for further analysis and discrimination on moral terms. On this view, at least some kinds of human actions are not identified in terms of the vectors of causality that the agent sets in motion, nor are they identified in the first instance through the agent's subjective aims or intention. Yet

---

30. This is a very familiar point in the philosophy of action. Brock offers a helpful analysis of the relevant issues in *Action and Conduct*, 55–61. The main lines of contemporary discussion of these issues were set by Elizabeth Anscombe and Donald Davidson; see in particular Anscombe, *Intention*, 34–47, and "Under a Description," originally 1979, reprinted in *The Collected Philosophical Papers of G. E. M. Anscombe*, vol. 2 (Oxford: Basil Blackwell, 1981), 208–19; and Donald Davidson, "Actions, Reasons, and Causes" (originally 1963), and "The Individuation of Events" (1969), published in *Essays on Actions and Events*, 3–20 and 163–80. In addition, Anscombe offers an illuminating analysis of action descriptions and intention in Aquinas in her "Medalist's Address: Action, Intention, and Double Effect," *Proceedings of the American Catholic Philosophical Association* 56 (1982): 12–25. Finally, John D'Arcy observes that some kinds of actions, such as killing, are always morally significant and cannot be elided in any description of an action; this is not exactly Aquinas's distinction, but it does reflect a similar concern to describe actions in terms of their salient features. See *Human Acts: An Essay in Their Moral Evaluation* (Oxford: Clarendon, 1963), 18–39.

these kinds of actions are causal operations, they are normally carried out voluntarily, and their moral significance rests in key part on both of these aspects of the act.

In order to follow Aquinas's analysis at this point, we need to keep in mind that his analysis of the moral act presupposes an Aristotelian natural philosophy. On this view, every kind of creature sustains itself through causal operations that stem from its specific form and serve to preserve or develop its existence in some way. If we know what it means to be a creature of a specific kind, we can identify its characteristic operations. These operations are causally structured in specific ways, corresponding to their place in the ongoing systems of responsive activity that are characteristic of all living creatures. For the rational creature, who can choose and act only on the basis of some reasoned judgment, these kinds of operations are immediately understood to be possible kinds of acts, which can be chosen and carried out even apart from reflection on the place of this or that activity in one's overall life. We spontaneously understand what it means to eat something, and we can choose to do so without considering the causal processes involved in taking something edible, consuming it, digesting it, and so forth. Yet this kind of action would not occur as an object of choice apart from its structural dynamics and its place in a wider context of human activity and life.[31]

Aquinas's analysis of the moral act presupposes both a necessary correlation and a real distinction between natural and moral kinds of actions, at least within the context set by the precepts of nonmaleficence that we have been considering. Within this context, the description of an action in accordance with some natural kind is always morally salient, even though not morally decisive, since the natural kind partially determines the agent's grasp of what she is doing and therefore helps to determine her choice. It is always morally relevant that a particular act is an act of killing or sexual intercourse or some other fundamental natural activity. Aquinas's distinction between the moral and the natural description of actions presupposes as much. In any case, he explicitly says that we can distinguish between moral and immoral ways of carrying out these basic natural acts, and furthermore, these distinctions enter into the very definition of the kinds of actions in question. Legitimate homicide and murder are not two variants of the same

31. Matthew B. O'Brien and Robert C. Koons develop a reading of the causal structure of human actions that is similar to the account offered here, in their "Objects of Intention: A Hylomorphic Critique of the New Natural Law Theory," *American Catholic Philosophical Quarterly* 86.4 (2012): 655–703.

kind of action, except in a qualified sense. Rather, they represent two specifically different kinds of actions, considered from the most comprehensive and unqualified rational perspective, that is to say, the moral perspective (again, see I-II 1.3 *ad* 3).

Thus, for Aquinas, the proper description of an act is fixed by its internal structure in two critical ways. It is determined, first of all, by its structure as a natural operation, having a place in the overall patterns of activity proper to human life. Thus, for example, the infliction of lethal force cannot be correctly or adequately described in terms that elide the killing into something else. Second, it is determined by those aspects of its causal and relational structure that are morally relevant. To continue with the example at hand, an act of lethal force that is inflicted as a due punishment for some transgression is an act of justice carried out through the execution of a criminal, whereas an act of lethal force directed against someone who is innocent or who has been judged to be a criminal without due process of law is murder. This is so, because human acts are operations of rational creatures, which are to be evaluated by reference to the normative standards proper to creatures of this kind, that is to say, standards of reasonableness and equity. Whatever else we may say about a given action, we cannot describe it adequately without taking account of its character as a moral act.

This brings us back to the issues raised in the first section of this chapter. Aquinas claims that the object of an act cannot be elided into the agent's overall aim. But why should this be the case? Aquinas's answer to this question can be formulated on two levels. Objectively, the moral character of a particular action depends in key part, although not entirely, on the immediate relation that it sets up between the agent and someone or something else. Those actions that relate the agent to someone else must meet standards of respect and fairness as a necessary, although not a sufficient, condition for judging the act to be morally good. We are already familiar with this point. Subjectively, the moral object of the act that the agent immediately chooses determines (partially or completely) the moral quality of her choice. This is true, in the first instance, because the morality of an act depends on rational considerations that are available to all rationally competent individuals, with slight reflection or with the help of guidance and instruction (I-II 100.1).[32]

---

32. Only partially, because an act that is generically good might still be vitiated by a bad aim or undue circumstances. To take a standard example, almsgiving is generically good, but a particular charitable donation may be vicious if it is motivated by a desire to impress someone the agent wants to seduce.

Rationally competent men and women are thus able to grasp that a particular action involves some kind of unjust or unloving treatment of another. These kinds of considerations identify the kind of action in question, insofar as they determine the moral species of the act (I-II 18.2). Correlatively, this kind of moral disorder will always be voluntary, assuming that the agent knows, in the relevant sense, what she is doing (again, see I-II 72.1).

So far, this line of analysis is incomplete. In order to know that a proposed action is disordered, the agent needs to be aware of the relevant moral precepts. More fundamentally, however, he also needs to know what he is doing, that is to say, he needs to have a sense of himself as a causal agent, interacting with others in such a way as to set up a relationship of some kind with them. In order to account for this level of self-awareness, we need to appeal to Aquinas's notion of the natural species of the human action. Rationally competent individuals are naturally aware of themselves as causal agents, capable of acting in certain basic ways in order to attain fundamental aims. Of course, this does not imply that most men and women need a formal theory of causality in order to function. Rather, they develop a sense of themselves as causal agents through reflection on their experiences of themselves as engaged in the fundamental operations of human life. Given a normal context of observation, experience, and instruction, these operations come to be understood as structured ways of attaining certain basic aims, to be pursued through rationally informed choice.

My point is this: Our concepts of natural kinds of actions, which stem from the fundamental operations of human life, are integral to our sense of ourselves as acting persons. Someone who is engaged in an act of eating or making use of a physical object or killing cannot fail to realize what she is doing. Of course, no one chooses a natural kind of action without further qualifications, including those that determine the moral species of the act. Nonetheless, these kinds of actions are so central to our lives as rational and organic creatures, and so fundamental to our sense of ourselves as agents, that they partially determine the choice of the will. A choice to promote the security of the community or to serve the cause of justice or to exact revenge by killing another is fundamentally a choice to kill. The agent cannot determine what she chooses by selecting one out of an indefinite range of possible act-descriptions.[33] Someone who chooses to kill another cannot help but

---

33. Anscombe makes a similar point with respect to intention: "The idea that one can determine one's intentions by making such a little speech to oneself is obvious bosh" (*Intention*, 42).

choose an act of killing. No level of reflective redescription can render an act of this kind anything other than it is.

But of course, someone may choose to kill in a way that is justified, as well as unjustified. The natural object of the act determines the agent's choice in one way, considered as a living creature of a certain kind, but it leaves it indeterminate in another way, considered from a distinctively moral perspective. The moral perspective, or more precisely, the perspective determined by the ideal of justice, identifies actions in terms of the forms of relations that they constitute. These relations may reflect mutual recognition and respect, equity, and amity, or they may reflect a sense that the natural interests of one may be set aside for the sake of another. Human relations are fundamentally tethered to the natural forms of human interaction, including acts of nurture and care, aggressive acts, sexual intercourse, communicative exchanges of all kinds, and the like. For this reason the natural objects of acts always figure into their moral descriptions. But in addition, these kinds of actions can reflect a disposition to respect the right of others, through appropriate consideration, respect, and fairness, or a contrary disposition to set aside the right of another.

This brings us back to the precepts of nonmaleficence enumerated in the Decalogue, which by Aquinas's time had already been elaborated through centuries of reflection. Each of these prohibitions reflects a way in which the vital interests of one agent can be compromised or set aside, in pursuit of the natural inclinations and interests of another. Through murder, the victim's natural interests are compromised in a final way. Theft and adultery violate boundaries that are necessary if men and women are to support themselves and develop a family life through their own free activities. Dishonesty, slander, and similar activities compromise someone's identity and activities as a free, respected member of one's society, thus undermining her ability to live well, or perhaps to live at all. These kinds of actions are wrong because they harm others in ways that exclude them from the moral community or inflict sufferings that they do not deserve or want. They reflect a will that, in some way and for whatever reason, is disposed to regard others as somehow less than or other than the agent himself, or the collectivity or ideal with which he identifies himself.

At the same time, there are some situations in which one person may legitimately restrain or coerce another, impose some loss on him, or even subject him to violence. A moral theory that refused to draw these distinctions would be too far removed from our initial intuitions to be credible or practically usable. The question is, can we offer a persuasive, systematic account of the relevant distinctions, or do they appear to be ad hoc adaptions to hard cases? Certainly, our moral intuitions and practices will always include ad hoc adjustments, together with unexamined assumptions, inconsistencies, and other lacunae of reason. Nonetheless, the distinctions we draw between justified and unjustified harms do reflect a rough coherence, reflecting an innate sense of what it means to live a natural human life as the social animals that we are. We are naturally oriented to protect ourselves and one another, and for this reason, we are inclined to excuse aggressive attacks when these are immediately required to defend the agent herself or a third party. Similarly, we are inclined to excuse or justify someone who simply takes what she urgently needs in order to sustain her life, even if what she needs belongs to someone else. We recognize that men and women have a legitimate claim to participate in the social life of the community, and so we justify constraints on the free expression of some in order to safeguard the social standing of others.

In the last chapter, we saw that Aquinas interprets the precepts of nonmaleficence as implications of commutative justice, interpreted in terms of ideals of equality, respect, and restraint. His analysis of the moral act provides him with the framework he needs to formulate these ideals in stringent terms. In doing so, he attempts as far as possible to hold on to the intuition that no individual may legitimately act in such a way as to inflict harm on another, as the immediate causal result of a freely chosen act. He recognizes, of course, that we do sometimes need to inflict harm, but as far as possible, he circumscribes the kinds of situations in which this is legitimate. In particular, he analyzes these kinds of situations in such a way as to avoid the conclusion that one person, acting as a private individual pursuing her own interests or judgments, might legitimately harm another. He apparently wants to say that the infliction of harm by one individual on another is always undue and therefore prohibited. Seeming counterexamples to the contrary turn out, in almost all cases, to involve either activities of a public official or an act that, for some context-specific reason, does not violate the due claims of another. Even in the case of lethal self-defense, he is clearly reluctant to say that one private individual can intend harm to another, as we will see.

Aquinas's treatment of homicide and murder offers the fullest and most important example of the first way of accounting for legitimate injury. He begins with the obvious—killing harms someone in the most serious and final way (II-II 64.2). Yet we do generally hold that some kinds of killing are justified, including those inflicted in military conflict, capital punishment, and self-defense (II-II 40.1, 64.2,7). Do these assessments reflect reasoned judgments, and if so, can we connect them to ideals of justice? At this point, we need to set aside the case of killing in self-defense, which, as we will see, is somewhat anomalous on Aquinas's own terms. What can we say about killing on the battlefield or killing as a kind of punishment?

In addressing this issue, Aquinas begins by taking note of the natural values at stake, as he understands them. Men and women naturally desire life, for its own sake and as a precondition for enjoying anything else. On his view, these considerations are enough to rule out suicide, which he regards as an unnatural distortion of the natural desire to live, as well as an injustice toward both the community and toward God (II-II 64.5). They might seem to rule out every kind of homicide. After all, if we are enjoined to love the neighbor as ourselves, we should at the very least permit her to live out her own life. And yet, there are some kinds of situations in which killing is justified, most notably in combat or through capital punishment. At this point, Aquinas once again appeals to considerations of naturalness. More specifically, he observes that the good of the community, or more generally, the common good, is greater and more comprehensive than the good of the individual. Thus, someone who attacks the community or its members can be excised for the good of the community. Aquinas adds that such an individual in some way renounces his humanity by placing himself outside the structures of coexistence that sustain human life (II-II 64.2 *ad* 3).

These claims are disconcerting, but as we read on, we see that these are simply the starting points for a more extended and cautious analysis. We have already seen that he qualifies the priority of the common good to individual goods very considerably, and in other contexts he insists that all men and women share a common human nature, implying capacities and claims that cannot be altogether lost. In this instance, he is led to qualify his initial claims for a specific reason, namely, they do not fit some central elements of our complex moral intuitions about killing. He does not want to say that it is always legitimate to kill on behalf of the common good. On the contrary, he insists in the strongest terms that it is never legitimate to kill someone who is innocent of aggression or crime, even for the most exigent considerations of the common good (II-II 64.6). More surprisingly, perhaps, he also claims that private individuals cannot legitimately kill another, even if the victim is a criminal who has been justly condemned to death (II-II 64.3). Someone who attacks the community or one of its members sets himself outside the relations of trust that sustain human life, but he does not surrender every claim attaching to his human status. Most important, he can claim immunity from the private judgment of another: "The human person who is a sinner is not naturally distinct from just persons. And therefore a public judgment is necessary to discern whether he is to be killed for the sake of the common well-being" (II-II 64.3 *ad* 2). This leaves us with two conditions for justifiable homicide, each of which must be met if the act is to be legitimate. The individual who is killed must in some way have set himself over against the community, through attacking it in a military context or through some grave crime. In addition, only someone who acts by the authority of the community, on behalf of the common good, directly or as the agent of political authorities, can legitimately kill someone. There are many ways in which the act of killing, inflicted by political authorities, might be undue—for example, if the victim has not received any kind of judicial hearing or is innocent. And the infliction of death by one private individual on another, bracketing the case of self-defense, is always an undue act.

Aquinas's treatment of theft and robbery in II-II 66 illustrates a second approach to a seeming case of justified harm inflicted by one individual on another. In this question, he begins with an extended defense of the institution of private property, which is a human invention set up to promote human well-being (II-II 66.1–2). The claims arising from these institutions are conventional rather than natural, but they are nonetheless exigent, and the actions of taking what is another's against her will secretly or by force (theft or robbery, respectively) are gravely harmful to her (II-II 66.4–6). At this point, Aquinas turns to the question of whether it is legitimate to take what is another's in a case of necessity (II-II 66.7). As we saw in chapter 3, he replies that this action is indeed legitimate, because the individual's natural right to claim what he needs to sustain life takes priority over the conventional rights generated by the institution of property. The point I want to underscore here is that Aquinas does not go on to say that this kind of action would be a justified theft or robbery. Since the claims of private property are set aside in such an instance, someone who takes what he needs to live cannot be said to take what is another's at all. The act of taking something held by another in this case is not an injury, because the putative owner does not actually own the goods in question (II-II 66.7 *ad* 2). Again, Aquinas analyzes what seems to be a case in which one private person can harm another, in such a way as to avoid this conclusion.

Finally, we turn to the question of killing in self-defense. Aquinas is not prepared to say that an individual has no right to defend herself, and he acknowledges that self-defense may require killing one's attacker. It is difficult to avoid the conclusion that in this case, one individual can legitimately inflict harm on another. I think Aquinas does admit as much, but he does so in such a way as to argue that in this anomalous case, the choice to kill does not involve a malicious inclination of the will. The key point is that someone who kills in self-defense does not intend to enter into a relationship with her assailant at all. His much-debated remarks on this problem are worth quoting at some length:

> Nothing prevents one act from having two effects, only one of which is intended, while the other is beside the intention. Now moral acts receive their species in accordance with that which is intended, not from that which is beside the intention, as is plain from what has been said above. Thus, from an act of someone's defending himself, a twofold effect can follow, one indeed being the preservation of his own life, the other being the killing of the attacker. Now an act of this kind does not have the formal character of the illicit on this account, that it is intended to preserve one's own life, because it is natural to each thing to conserve itself in being inso-far as that is possible. It is possible, however, that an act proceeding from a good intention can be rendered illicit if it is not proportioned to the end. And therefore if someone made use of more violence than necessary in order to defend himself, that would be illegitimate. If, however, he repels violence moderately, this will be legitimate defense.... Nor is it necessary to salvation that someone renounce an act of moderate self-defense in order to avoid killing another, because each person is more bound to look out for his own life, than the life of another. (II-II 64.7)

On a first reading, Aquinas seems to be saying what he elsewhere denies, namely, that someone's good aims or motives can justify what would other-wise be a wrongful act. But this reading is too quick. He begins by observing that one act can have two effects, only one of which is intended, while the other is not. In the case at hand, the act of defending oneself through lethal force has two immediate effects, namely, the self-preservation of the agent and the death of her attacker. He goes on to say that in this case, it is possible to act in such a way as to intend only the first of these effects, namely, one's own survival, while not intending the other, the death of the attacker. In order to see what Aquinas is getting at here, we need to take account of two points that we have considered earlier.[34]

The first is that, given the terms of Aquinas's analysis of actions, the

---

34. My reading of Aquinas at this point is indebted to Long, "A Brief Disquisition"; Brock sets out a similar interpretation in *Action and Conduct*, 197–208.

intention of an action is correlated with the agent's proximate or ultimate end in acting, that aspect of the overall operation that moves the agent to act (I-II 12.1–2, 18.3). As such, it is distinguished from the agent's choice, which is directed immediately toward the act itself, understood in terms of its morally salient qualities—the object of the act, in other words (I-II 13.1, 18.2). In this instance, Aquinas is saying that in the case of justified self-defense, the state of affairs represented by a dead assailant does not move the agent to act. She just wants to survive this encounter. She does not intend to kill, because the assailant's death is not her end in acting. Nonetheless, this line of analysis does not imply that the act of killing someone in self-defense is anything other than a voluntary choice to kill. I do not see any indication that this is what Aquinas means to say. Critically, he does not say that legitimate self-defense is necessarily limited to some kind of forcible restraint or repulsion, which may mortally injure the attacker, as opposed to an act that stops the agent by killing him, the distinction, anachronistically put, between shooting an attacker and tackling an attacker so forcefully that he dies. Aquinas does say that an act of self-defense carried out through excessive force is illicit, even though the agent's intention is good, but this appears to be only an application of the general point that circumstances can vitiate what would otherwise be an acceptable course of action (I-II 18.10–11). Under some circumstances, lethal force would not be excessive. Not everyone has the muscle mass necessary to stop an assailant through brute force, and resort to weapons may be necessary. Yet even in this kind of situation, the agent can be said to act with the intention of preserving her life, which is an immediate effect of the act that she chooses.[35]

The second point to keep in mind is that Aquinas's remarks on the agent's intention do not presuppose that the agent can determine her intention at her discretion. Intention and choice remain tethered to objective features of the act in question, seen from natural and rational perspectives. He observes that self-defense is not illicit in itself, and not contrary to the virtue of charity. On the contrary, self-preservation is a natural aim shared in some way by all creatures, the first and most fundamental natural incli-

---

35. Compare the way in which Aquinas distinguishes between the sin of scandal and doing something that gives scandal—the sin of scandal, properly so called, implies that the agent is moved to act by the prospect of scandalizing someone else (II-II 43.3). He may well choose just the same kind of sin as another, who acts scandalously without intending to give scandal. In this kind of case, too, intention is decisive, and yet it cannot be formulated without some reference to the agent's actual operation and its foreseen effects.

nation that cannot be regarded as fundamentally disordered or contrary to Christian ideals (II-II 25.4,7; cf. I-II 94.2).

Aquinas is therefore not saying that self-defense is justified because the agent's overall aim is generically good, or even that it is naturally good, but rather, self-defense stems from a kind of self-love that is not contrary to the virtues of the will, especially charity. Moreover, this line of analysis presupposes that the act of self-defense is itself a natural kind of action that can be grasped and pursued directly. In some cases, such an action will also, immediately and indivisibly, be an act of killing. In that case, the action in question can objectively be described in two morally salient ways: as an act of killing and as an act of self-defense. The agent may be moved to act by only one of these two aspects of this particular act, and her intention is determined accordingly.[36]

I will not attempt to determine whether Aquinas's arguments in this article are completely successful, on his own terms or generally. The critical point is that, even at this point, at which Aquinas has strong reasons to allow that a private individual might legitimately harm another in a grievous way, he is clearly reluctant to do so. I believe he is forced by the logic of his analysis to say that, in this instance, a private individual may legitimately choose to kill another, but he takes pains to limit the scope and the significance of that concession. He goes on to say that it is never licit for a private person to intend to kill another. The point is that someone who defends herself through lethal force is not moved to act by the death of the attacker, that is to say, does not intend his death, even if she chooses to kill her attacker in the course of defending her own life.

At this point, it will be helpful to take stock of what we have established so far. Aquinas claims that the precepts of justice are distinctively stringent, and he spells out what that means through an analysis of the moral act. In order to justify this claim, he also needs to explain how we can move from the first principles and the very general precepts of the Decalogue in order to arrive at precepts with enough substantive content to be applied in a stringent way. In the previous section, I argued that, starting from Thomistic principles, we can offer a persuasive account of the way in which our innate

---

36. I have bracketed the question of whether this text represents an early statement of the doctrine of double effect. As is so often the case with these kinds of questions, this debate is almost impossible to resolve without saying a great deal more than would be feasible about what we mean by this doctrine. Boyle argues that Aquinas does anticipate the doctrine in "Toward Understanding the Doctrine of Double Effect," whereas Anscombe, in "Action, Intention, and Double Effect," is more skeptical.

moral emotions are transformed through reflection into substantive norms for respect, obligation, and injury. In this section, I have argued that Aquinas can account for the distinctive stringency of norms of nonmaleficence in terms of distinctions between natural and moral kinds of actions, which are developed and applied through his analysis of the moral act.

Aquinas's analysis of the moral act offers a powerful and cogent way of evaluating our choices and the accepted moral standards that inform them. However, as he himself is well aware, even the most powerful moral theory can go only so far in practice. This brings us finally to a consideration of the place of discernment in the exercise of justice.

The Place of Discernment in the Activities of Justice

Contemporary theories of virtue place considerable weight on the role of discernment in the moral life. In contrast to deontological theories, virtue-oriented theories emphasize that moral rules by themselves are not sufficient to guide moral behavior, and may not even be necessary to the truly virtuous individual. Rather, rules must be interpreted and applied, if not replaced, by a flexible, responsive discernment of the demands of a particular situation. This, at any rate, would have been a widely held view until recently, although recent work in virtue and practical reason has begun to call this dichotomy into question.[37]

Aquinas would not accept an account of moral discernment that claims that the virtuous agent does not need moral rules in order to respond appropriately to situations calling for choice. On his view, moral reasoning, like any other kind of reasoning, is necessarily rule-governed, that is to say, it operates through abstract categories that apply across a range of particulars. This does not mean, however, that there is no place in his theory of virtue for discerning judgment. On the contrary, moral rules are themselves dependent on discerning judgment for their formation and application, as we saw above. The dichotomy between rule-governed and discernment-driven forms of moral reasoning is deeply misleading. On Aquinas's view, this general observation would apply to understanding and reasoning generally, not just to moral reasoning. We form general concepts that enable us to think abstractly and to engage in discursive reasoning, but these concepts emerge

---

37. Julia Annas discusses, and disposes of, this construal of discernment in *Intelligent Virtue* (Oxford: Oxford University Press, 2011), 16–32.

from an intelligent understanding of particulars, and they can be understood only through a continual recourse to particulars, seen as instantiating these concepts.

In chapter 2 I argued that justice and other habits of the will normally develop over time through processes of self-reflective deliberation and choice, leading to the formation of stable dispositions of desire. This line of analysis implies that one's capacities for discernment take shape through the same kinds of processes that lead to the formation of the virtues of the will.[38] Indeed, it makes little sense to separate these, as if they were two distinct developmental tracks. The disposition of justice takes shape through one's engagements with others and one's attempts to respond appropriately to the claims they make on oneself. Through these processes of deliberation and choice, the agent develops her sense of what it means to respect the claims of another, in such a way as to render to each his or her right. As she matures, this sense develops into a comprehensive grasp of the ideal of justice, sufficiently general to apply to a wide range of cases. At the same time, this general conception of justice emerges out of reflection on particulars. Furthermore, like every other general concept, the abstract conception of justice can be grasped only in and through the apprehension of particular instances of just or unjust actions. The stable disposition of justice thus presupposes both a general conception of the ideal of justice and the discernment necessary to apply these ideals to particular cases. The agent develops her capacities for discernment in matters of justice by the same processes through which she develops the habit of justice itself.

At the same time, the virtue of justice is a disposition of desire, not intellect. It presupposes a sound grasp of the ideal of justice and an ability to see how this ideal should be applied in specific cases, but it is essentially a stable disposition to care about the demands of justice, and to incline toward respecting the claims of others in all the affairs of one's life. This disposition takes shape in and through processes of deliberation and choice, through which the agent grasps the claims that another makes on her and desires to respond appropriately to those claims. The agent's desire to behave rightly in

38. This would seem to be Millgram's view as well; see *Practical Induction* (Cambridge, MA: Harvard University Press, 1997), 67-86. Annas similarly emphasizes the role of learning and skilled discernment in the exercise of the virtues. One fundamental difference between her account and Aquinas's is that she gives only a very limited role to the affective side of virtuous dispositions and actions. It would seem that, on her account, all the virtues are reducible to practical wisdom, with desire playing the role of urging the agent to grow in wisdom and to act wisely. See her *Intelligent Virtue*, 16-51.

this or that case presupposes some apprehension, however inchoate, of what it would mean to do so. But this apprehension does not necessarily elicit the corresponding inclination of the will. In order to develop the disposition of justice, the individual must not only form a sound grasp of what it means to act justly in particular cases, she must form and sustain the desire to do so. In practice, someone whose desires are not consistently oriented toward the claims of another will be unlikely to develop the ability to discern what justice demands in particular cases. The experiences, needs, and demands of others will not matter to her, in such a way as to draw her attention and lead her to reflection. Alternatively, she may be so committed to maintaining her own place in society, or so deeply invested in the well-being of her family or her political community, that she is incapable of recognizing the claims of those who fall outside the circles of her immediate concern. These considerations help to explain why certain kinds of moral beliefs appear to be problematic. More to the immediate point, they suggest a starting point for developing a Thomistic account of moral discernment.

We recall that Aquinas formulates the first principle of practical reason as it pertains to the agent's relations with others in scriptural terms drawn from the injunction to love God and neighbor (I-II 100.3 *ad* 1). The kind of love in question, at least in the case of one's neighbor, is what Aquinas elsewhere identifies as the love proper to friendship, a kind of love that can be exercised only by the will (I-II 26.4; cf. 22.3 *ad* 3).[39] This rational love is distinguished from the passion of love because it depends on some grasp of the other as a separate individual, with her own distinctive needs and interests, and it takes the form of inclining toward the good of the other for that other's own sake. It is worth noting that the love of friendship, thus understood, does not imply personal affection or even a direct personal acquaintance. It can take many forms, including those we would associate with personal friendship and romantic love, but in its most basic form, this rational love is simply a disposition to care about the other's well-being, in the same way as the agent naturally cares about herself. The neighbor-regarding first precept of justice can thus be understood as an injunction to take up a particular stance toward other people, characterized by regard for the neighbor for his or her own sake. It calls for a certain kind of affective stance, leading to action, the action of rendering to each his or her right. As Nicholas Wolter-

---

39. Aquinas believes that we are enabled to love God in this way through the theological virtue of charity, but, so far as I can tell, he does not think we are naturally capable of friendship with God; see II-II 23.1.

storff says, "Treating the neighbor justly is not viewed as incompatible with loving the neighbor, nor is it viewed as an alternative to loving him. Treating the neighbor justly is an *example* of loving him, a way of loving him."[40]

It is helpful to compare the first principle of justice with the unrestricted first principle of practical reason, namely, that good is to be sought and done and evil is to be avoided (I-II 94.2). We might assume that this principle does compel the will, since Aquinas claims that the good as discerned by reason is the necessary object of the will. But this way of formulating the relationship between principle and inclination misses the point that Aquinas is making. The will, like every other appetite, is necessarily oriented toward some kind of good, because an appetite is nothing other than a capacity to respond to some good in an appropriate way. From its first incipient operations, the human will is a capacity to incline toward the distinctively human good, as apprehended through reason. The first principle of practical reason thus expresses the rational creature's innate grasp of what might be called the constitutive logic of desire, its orientation toward some appropriate good. This innate apprehension necessarily implies normative categories, in terms of which the agent formulates judgments of value in the terms appropriate to a rational form of existence. In somewhat the same way, the first principle of justice as applied to other persons reflects the rational agent's natural and inescapable awareness of others as separate from oneself and yet like oneself, individuals with their own needs and claims. This awareness takes the form, most immediately, of basic moral concepts that reflect the normative logic of our interrelationships with one another. The rational agent spontaneously thinks in these terms in relating to others and recognizes moral formulations as expressions of something already well understood.

Thus understood, the first principle of justice provides both a starting point for the development of a disposition of justice and a touchstone for sound discernment in one's exercise of that virtue. As the young child begins to develop a sense of herself and other people, she spontaneously perceives them as like herself, and yet not herself, in the way indicated.[41] Normally,

40. Nicholas Wolterstorff, *Justice in Love* (Grand Rapids: Eerdmans, 2011), 85, emphasis in the original. While I do not agree with every aspect of his analysis of justice and right, as indicated above, I believe that Wolterstorff's analysis of the relation of love to justice is cogent and illuminating. He is one of the few moral theorists, perhaps the only one, to make a case for the essential compatibility of love and justice. For the main lines of the argument, see 75–100.

41. For a good general overview of our current understanding of early childhood development, and more specifically of the development for other-identification and morality, see Alison Gopnik, *The Philosophical Baby: What Children's Minds Tell Us about Truth, Love, and*

this sense of the other will elicit inclinations of desire and affection, which develop as the child develops a more extensive and finely grained sense of herself in relation to other people. These feelings are distinct from her intellectual grasp of the separate existence and the claims of others, but normally they will emerge and develop together. The child gradually comes to perceive others as distinct persons, and her natural affections are shaped by the apprehension of distinct others. Without much reflection, she expresses her affections in moral terms, through empathy and responsive care, while also marking her sense of her own individual existence by asserting claims to fairness and entitlement. In this way, immediate responses to others begin to be understood in terms of general categories of obligation and transgression, which can then be generalized in such a way as to apply outside the circles of one's immediate associates.

In chapter 3 we saw that Aquinas connects particular justice, properly so called, with a normative ideal of equality. The first precept of justice expresses that ideal in its most fundamental form, as a kind of practical hermeneutic for evaluating one's relations with others. We naturally share in the same status as free men and women, each of whom has a claim to respect and care that cannot be set aside at someone else's will. At the very least, our fundamental equality implies that the scope of moral concern is unlimited. Each individual counts morally and exercises claims on any other with whom she comes into some kind of relation. Equality also implies that no one's well-being can be compromised or set aside at another's discretion, nor can anyone be denied the fundamental right to freely pursue her own best life, in accordance with her conception of what that means. These fundamental principles are compatible with preferential relations, restraints and qualifications of some claims of right, and liability to harm, in accordance with the exigencies of social life, conflicts among individual claims, and the individual's own malfeasance. But the critical point is that any qualification of the claims of others must be justified in terms of general, impersonal considerations such as these.

Aquinas claims that everyone is capable of grasping the most immediate implications of the injunction to love the neighbor, which he identities with the neighbor-regarding precepts of the Decalogue (I-II 100.1,3 *ad* 1).

---

the Meaning of Life (New York: Farrar, Straus & Giroux, 2009), 202–33. For a more focused examination of the development of concepts of self and others, see Mark R. Leary, "The Self and Emotion: The Role of Self-Reflection in the Generation and Regulation of Affective Experience," in *The Handbook of Affective Sciences*, ed. Richard J. Davidson, Klaus R. Scherer, and H. Hill Goldsmith (Oxford: Oxford University Press, 2009), 773–86.

Through reflection on one's own needs and interests, anyone can identify paradigmatic examples of harming others through depriving them of life, possessions, or communal or family connections. However, these paradigms offer only a rough guide to the practical implications of the ideal of justice. In order to be put into practice, they need to be applied to particular situations, in such a way as to take account of the sometimes conflicting claims of all parties involved in a given situation. In some instances, it will not be obvious which moral concepts are relevant to a situation, or the claims of another may not be immediately apparent. Of course, the agent can draw on many traditions of reflection on the complexities of the moral life, and to a very considerable degree, her moral concepts will come with qualifications built in, as it were. But even the most far-seeing and comprehensive tradition of casuistry cannot anticipate every situation or resolve every practical uncertainty. There will always be some situations that call for an exercise of discernment elicited by the virtue of justice and carried out through practical reason informed by prudence (II-II 47.1,4; cf. 47.10,11). Through processes of discernment, the just individual comes to understand the point and the practical implications of the ideal of justice more fully, to see more quickly how this ideal applies in other situations, and to identify unexpected ways in which to respond to the claims of others.

At the same time, we need to keep in mind that the capacity for discernment associated with justice is a kind of intellectual ability, and as such, it is not itself a form of justice, nor does it render someone just (again, see II-II 47.1,2). As we noted at the beginning of this section, the virtue of justice is fundamentally a disposition toward a certain kind of rational love, expressed through attitudes of care for others, reluctance to violate their due claims, and vigilance lest they be subject to unfair treatment. Someone who loves his neighbor in these fundamental ways will very probably develop a finely honed sense of what the ideals of justice demand in particular situations, and his discerning grasp of the meaning of justice will elicit the corresponding inclinations. But these sensibilities do not, in themselves, make him just. Rather, he is just because he cares about others in this way, and he is moved to reflect on the implications of his care for others.

At the same time, the love proper to justice takes a distinctive form that sets it apart from more personal forms of love, such as the love of particular friendship or romantic love. The love associated with justice is impersonal, in the sense that it extends to all those with whom the agent comes into contact, whether through direct personal encounter or through the agent's images of individuals who will be affected in some way by one's actions. It is elicited by a grasp of the fundamental status of the other as an individual like oneself, apart from any distinguishing characteristics or any particular relation to the agent. In these respects, the love proper to justice may appear to be too detached to really count as a kind of love. Yet experience teaches that men and women can come to care very deeply about others in these ways, so much so that they devote their lives, at considerable personal risk, to promoting the well-being of those who are subject to injustices of various kinds. Some people do seem to have a kind of passion for justice, not unlike the passion that binds spouses in a marriage.

The will is not a passion, and so we must speak metaphorically of a passion for justice. Yet this is an instructive metaphor, as the comparison with romantic love suggests. We are familiar with images of passionate romantic love, especially but not only because this kind of love is paradigmatically linked to sexual desire. Yet whatever the complexities of a particular relationship may be, romantic love cannot literally be a passion and nothing else. In the processes of relating to one another, romantic partners will inevitably experience a range of passions, from affection and sexual desire to anger and tedium. This very common experience clearly illustrates that romantic love cannot be identified with any one passion, and it strongly suggests that it cannot be sustained through an ensemble of diverse passions, either. We can more readily make sense of the love of one partner for another in terms of a disposition of the will, characterized by a commitment to a certain kind of enduring erotic friendship with another. As such, this love is self-reflective and rational, in a way that a passion cannot be. At the same time, we cannot imagine interpersonal love apart from passions, expressed through the full range of feelings that individuals in close relations experience toward each other. These passions elicit the first movements toward a relationship, and they play a key role in developing, sustaining, and expressing it throughout the course of its development. At the same time, an individual in this situation is not just experiencing feelings, but is also acting on those feelings, in ways that are suggested by the feelings themselves. The disposition of the will toward union with another is normally experienced through these passions and the actions that they elicit, in such a way as to generate the impression that love is fundamentally a feeling. Yet apart from some disposition of the will, informed by some reasoned grasp of what it means for oneself to be in relation to another, these feelings would have no coherence and no point.

Most of us would be less inclined to identify justice with a passion, or even a range of familiar passions. The disposition of justice is generally regarded as impersonal and cool, in contrast—generally unfavorable contrast—to the warm personal relations of love, friendship, and care for another.[42] It is true that justice is irreducibly impersonal, in the sense that it is a disposition to render to each his or her right, without regard to the personal qualities or circumstances of the agents involved. At the same time, we should not assume that the disposition of justice is always experienced as a calm commitment to render what is right to each. Like romantic love, the disposition of justice is typically connected with a range of characteristic passions, including anger at the unfair treatment of another, solicitude to act fairly in one's dealings with another, empathetic sympathy with another's sense of outrage, satisfaction at the vindication of someone's claim, and the like. These passions, in turn, prompt the agent to act in specific ways, which are rationally judged to be appropriate and commanded by the will. Justice is not a passion, and yet it is normally experienced through the agent's passions and expressed through choices and actions shaped by those passions.

This line of analysis is relevant to the issue at hand, because it suggests a way of understanding how justice, as a virtue of the will, can be correlated with abilities of discernment that we normally associate with the virtues of the passions. Even though the just will is not a passion, it operates in close conjunction with the passions, which operate in such a way as to shape the agent's immediate perceptions in accordance with his settled paradigms of fairness, respect, and their opposites. The agent thus develops a kind of feel for the right, which enables him to perceive immediately that some kinds of behavior are called for and others are ruled out. These perceptions and sensibilities provide only the starting points for deliberation and choice, but my point is that reason and will do have something to work with, as it were, in the form of an initial discernment of human relationships.

Although he does not discuss discernment in our terms, Aquinas's account of prudence addresses many of the issues we have been considering (see, in general, II-II 47). At any rate, he says enough about the interconnections among reason, will, and passions to indicate that an account of discernment developed along the lines just indicated would not amount to a distortion of his overall psychology. He recognizes that the passions can be shaped and directed by the will and reason to some extent, although they always retain independence as distinct capacities for sensate desire, responsive to immediate perceptions and images (I 81.3; I-II 51.2–3). By the

<hr>

42. The classic expression of this critique is Carol Gilligan's *In a Different Voice: Psychological Theory and Women's Development* (Cambridge, MA: Harvard University Press, 1982); see esp. 26–105.

same token, the passions can influence the will indirectly by shaping the agent's perceptions and judgments, and just as an agent's action confirms the will, it can also elicit further passions (I-II 9.2, 10.3, 77.1). He claims that the will can operate without any motion of the passions, but he would have no difficulty with the claim that normally, passions and will work together in the ways just indicated.

In this chapter we have focused on the formulation and formation of the precepts of justice, with the aim of understanding what it means to say that these bind strictly. As we saw, Aquinas does believe that the prohibitions associated with the Decalogue are strictly binding, and the kinds of actions associated with them are never morally permissible. We are now in a better position to appreciate the point of this claim. Aquinas does not believe that the stringent demands associated with justice reflect either divine commands or the exigencies of rational consistency. He is not legalistic, nor is he especially concerned to maintain social boundaries. He insists on the stringency of the precepts of justice because these express and safeguard the claims of the neighbor, whom we are enjoined to love through the rational love proper to justice. A just man or woman who genuinely loves the neighbor in this way will not want to violate these precepts, but, on the contrary, will take pains not to do so. This stance of respect and forbearance is the cornerstone of the disposition of justice and the way of life that this virtue promotes.

At the same time, justice is only one of a number of dispositions and ideals that go to make up a good human life. In the final chapter, we will return to the question of justice as a perfection of the will, seen in the context of the complementary and competing ideals that enter into our lives.

CHAPTER 5

The Perfections of the Will

In this chapter, we return to Aquinas's claim that justice is a perfection of the will, focusing on a set of questions that arise when we consider justice in relation to other supposed or actual perfections of the will. This may seem to be an abstruse line of inquiry. Nonetheless, we need to pursue it in order to address certain problems that are internal to Aquinas's theory, some of which have been mentioned already. Moreover, as I hope to show, this inquiry opens up new perspectives on the virtue of justice and its place in the overarching structures and central commitments of human life.

In order to pursue these issues, we will need once again to go beyond what Aquinas explicitly says. At the same time, he anticipates the kinds of questions that we will be considering, and he provides a strategy for addressing them. In his initial analysis of habits, Aquinas argues that these dispositions are necessary because the cognitive and affective capacities of a rational creature are innately complex and need to be integrated in some way (I-II 49.4). This general observation applies as much to the will as to the other cognitive capacities and appetites. The will as Aquinas understands it is both the highest and the unifying appetite of the rational creature and the principle for actions *ad extra*. Seen from the first perspective, it is innately oriented toward some comprehensive good, in such a way as to move the rational creature to act and to sustain an integrated course of activity over the course of a lifetime. Seen from the second perspective, it is innately oriented toward others, especially toward other men and women, and it moves the agent to relate to these others in appropriate ways. We would like to think that these two aspects of the will and its operations are integrated, but there is no formally compelling reason why this should be the case. Aristotle famously claims that the best purely human life, comprising virtuous activities in relation to others, is to some extent inconsistent with the best life, absolutely considered, namely, the life of philosophical contemplation.[1] While he does not frame the issue in terms of the diverse potentialities of the will, he does suggest that sometimes an individual has to choose between relating well to others and devoting himself to what is highest and best absolutely.

These may appear to be abstract questions with little practical relevance. Yet conflicts between the claims of individuals and the demands of some greater or higher good are a recurring feature of our moral lives. In contemporary societies, these are most likely to take the form of conflicts between individual rights and the general good of all, or the security and well-being of political society. At the same time, conflicts between personal morality and impersonal ideals or values, for example, artistic expression, are not unknown. We may not feel torn between the political virtues and a life of contemplation, as Aristotle suggests we might, but sometimes we are faced with conflicts between obligations to family, friends, and community, on the one hand, and the consuming demands of an artistic, scientific, or academic vocation, on the other. We will look more closely at some of these conflicts later in this chapter. My point here is simply that the potential conflict between the claims of others and the pursuit of greater or higher goods poses real, practically exigent problems, at least some of which appear to raise questions about the scope and the overriding force of moral considerations. Aquinas's analysis of the will and his overall account of justice as the perfection of the will suggest a persuasive, although controversial, way of resolving these kinds of dilemmas.

Before turning directly to these issues, however, we will begin by considering a basic question that we have not yet addressed, although we have anticipated it at some points. In the second chapter, I noted that, for Aquinas, practical reason is instrumental in form and does not function in such a way as directly to yield moral norms. He clearly does not believe that unjust or immoral actions are irrational, in any straightforward sense. And yet he also says that reason is the proximate principle of human actions, in terms of which they are to be evaluated (I-II 19.3, 71.2, 72.2; II-II 47.6). These observations suggest a need to revisit the question of the place of reason in Aquinas's theory of the virtues, more specifically, in his account of justice. By doing so, I hope first of all to clarify the sense in which practical reason sets the criteria for human action, thus anticipating objections to the claim

---

1. The relevant texts may be found in *Aristotle's Nicomachean Ethics*, trans. Robert C. Bartlett and Susan D. Collins (Chicago: University of Chicago Press, 2011), book 10, chaps. 7-8, 223-29.

that deliberative practical reason is always instrumental for Aquinas. At the same time, this line of inquiry will serve as an introduction to the account of justice as a perfection, to be developed in what follows. Aquinas claims that the virtues perfect the soul by disposing it to exist in accordance with reason. What does that mean, and what does it tell us about justice in particular? We now turn to these questions.

Reason and the Virtues

We have had many occasions to note that for Aquinas, the ideals and precepts associated with justice correspond to objective standards of respect and equity. He does not derive the precepts of justice from considerations of rational consistency, nor does he regard unjust actions as intrinsically irrational. These are not, in Korsgaard's terms, failed actions, that is to say, putative actions that do not meet standards of rationality. On the contrary, Aquinas explicitly says that an immoral action is naturally good and efficacious considered as an action, that is to say, as an exercise of the causal powers of the human creature (I-II 18.1, especially *ad* 3). As Vogler points out, for Aquinas, the operations of practical reason as expressed through our choices and acts are always instrumental, and the criteria of instrumental reasoning can be met through unjust or wicked actions as readily as through just or upright actions.[2]

I believe that this way of reading Aquinas is correct, as far as it goes, and importantly, it locates him properly with respect to ongoing debates about practical rationality and morality. However, this interpretation raises a question that needs to be addressed, if we are to have any confidence that we are on the right track. That is, Aquinas explicitly says, more than once, that reason is the rule and measure, that is to say, the normative standard of the will, or of the virtues (I-II 19.3–4, 64.1–2, 71.1; II-II 47.6, 58.10). This assertion is not inconsistent with the claim that practical reason operates instrumentally at the level of choice, but it does imply that there is more to be said about the normativity of reason.

In order to address this issue, we need to look more closely at what Aquinas says about the way in which reason is the normative standard for

---

2. See, respectively, Christine Korsgaard, *Self-Constitution: Agency, Identity, and Integrity* (Oxford: Oxford University Press, 2009), 160–61, and Candace Vogler, *Reasonably Vicious* (Cambridge, MA: Harvard University Press, 2002), 34–41.

the virtues. He raises this question in the context of the question on the goodness of the interior act of the will, asking whether the goodness of the will depends on conformity to reason (I-II 19.3). He responds that it does, because the goodness of the inner act of the will is derived from its object, and the goodness of the object depends on conformity to reason. He goes on to consider an objection drawn from Aristotle, to the effect that "the goodness of the practical intellect is truth conforming to right desire." He replies: "The Philosopher there speaks of the practical intellect, insofar as it takes counsel and reasons concerning those things that are directed to an end, for thus it is perfected through prudence. With respect to those things, however, that are directed to an end, the rectitude of reason consists in conformity to a desire of a requisite end. But this desire of a requisite end itself presupposes a right apprehension of the end, which comes about through reason" (I-II 19.3 *ad* 2).

Aquinas acknowledges that the virtue of prudence, which is by definition always directed toward good ends, aims at an ideal of sound reasoning directed toward carrying out some morally good desire. Thus, prudential reasoning is instrumental, and its virtuous character presupposes that the agent's appetites are well-disposed through the moral virtues. However, the agent's virtuous desires themselves presuppose a more fundamental act of practical reason, namely, a sound apprehension of the end for which the agent acts. This point is worth emphasizing, because otherwise we might assume that practical reasoning is as such instrumental. The operations of the will through free judgment are always directed toward particular actions, which are chosen on account of some further end (I 83.2–4; I-II 13.1,3). Of course, reasoning in this context will always be instrumental. But by the same token, the apprehension of the end toward which virtuous desires and acts are directed is not itself instrumental but, rather, provides the starting point for all instrumental reasoning.

Aquinas takes this point up again in the *secunda secundae* in his treatment of prudence, which is a virtue of the intellect oriented toward deliberation, choice, and action (II-II 47.1-2). In the course of his initial treatment of the virtue, he asks whether prudence predetermines the ends of the moral virtues. He replies that it does not:

> The end of the moral virtues is the human good. Now the good of the human soul is to exist in accordance with reason.... Hence it is necessary that the ends of the moral virtues preexist in reason. For just as there are certain things that exist in speculative reason as naturally known, with

respect to which there is understanding, and certain things that are known by these, that is conclusions, with respect to which there is knowledge, so in practical reason, certain things preexist as naturally known, and these are the ends of the moral virtues, which stand in relation to things to be done, as principles do to speculative matters, as said above. And certain things are in the practical reason as conclusions, and these are those things that are directed toward an end, to which we arrive through the ends themselves. Prudence is concerned with these, applying universal principles to particular conclusions of things to be done. And therefore it does not pertain to prudence to predetermine the ends of the moral virtues, but only to arrange those things that are directed toward the end. (II-II 47.6)

Practical reason thus determines the ends of the virtues through an intellectual apprehension of the proper ends of action, which provide starting points for deliberating about how to attain these ends. We are on familiar ground at this point. The ends of action to which Aquinas refers are set by the first principle of natural law, which, as we have seen, can be understood in both an unrestricted sense and in the restricted sense associated with justice (I-I 91.2, 94.2; II-II 79.1). At the same time, the innately known first principles of action can be understood and applied only through processes of discursive reflection and instrumental practical deliberation. The central precepts of the Decalogue can be derived from the first precept of justice with minimal reflection, whereas more specific determinations call for extended reflection (I-II 100.1,3).

In the next article, Aquinas goes on to address the question we are considering. What does it mean to say that the good of the human soul consists in existing in accordance with reason? He replies:

This itself, to conform to right reason, is the proper end of each moral virtue. For temperance intends this, lest the human person should be diverted from reason on account of desires, and similarly, fortitude, lest he be diverted from the right judgment of reason on account of fear or daring. And this end is predetermined for the human person in accordance with natural reason, for natural reason says to each that he should act in accordance with reason. But the way in which, and through which means, the human person attains the mean of reason pertains to the disposition of prudence. Granting, therefore, that to attain the mean is the end of moral virtue, nonetheless, the mean is found through the right disposition of those things that are directed toward the end. (II-II 47.7)

This is an interesting text, both on account of what Aquinas tells us, and on account of what he omits. We are told, first of all, that the virtues are oriented toward promoting the functioning of the soul in accordance with overall standards of rationality. Since we have just been told that the good of the human soul consists in conformity with reason, it seems safe to assume that Aquinas is here spelling out what this conformity means. At this level, conformity to reason would appear to be a functional, rather than a substantive category. The human soul attains the good of reason, or as Aquinas elsewhere says, it is perfected through the virtues to act consistently and effectively in accordance with the agent's best standards of rationality (I-II 64.2). In itself, this is a persuasive claim. Romantic fantasies notwithstanding, most mature men and women prefer to live in accordance with their ideals, commitments, and interests, with as little struggle and drama as possible. Moreover, there is an excellent case to be made for the claim that the vices are misfortunes, undermining the agent's own deepest aims and sense of self.[3]

Nonetheless, it is noteworthy that Aquinas does not mention justice in this context. Given what he says elsewhere about the rational standard associated with justice, it is clear that justice does not fit the overall line of analysis that he sets out here. As we know, justice corresponds to a real mean, determined by objective standards of equity and restraint (again, see I-II 64.2; cf. II-II 58.10). It does not pertain to the agent's own inner dispositions, nor is it directly oriented toward the agent's overall good. We might say that in this context, conformity to reason is a substantive, rather than a functional, category. Justice is a perfection of the soul insofar as it brings the agent's will into line with objective normative standards, but, so far, we have no clear indications that justice promotes the agent's own rational functioning.

Once again, we have already had occasion to raise this point. Aquinas's distinction between the rational mean attained by all the virtues and the real mean of justice implies substantive differences among the moral virtues. They all aim at the human good, but in disparate ways; that is, the virtues of the passions aim at the agent's own good, whereas the virtues of the will perfect the agent by bringing her into right relation with others, in accordance with criteria set by human nature generally considered. Aquinas integrates these diverse considerations through an account of the connection of the vir-

---

3. For a cogent and insightful analysis of the traditional deadly vices as destructive of the individual's agency and flourishing, see Gabriele Taylor, *Deadly Vices* (Oxford: Oxford University Press, 2006); the main lines of the argument are summarized at 1–30.

tues, which takes place through the discerning judgments of prudence or the overarching reorientation of the personality brought about by charity (I-II 65.1,3). We are not accustomed to thinking of the virtues in this way; more commonly, moral philosophers focus on what the virtues generally have in common, seen in contrast to some other approach to morality, rather than exploring deep differences among the virtues themselves. Yet there is nothing necessarily inconsistent in this line of analysis. Aquinas in effect makes the case that the human good and the rational ideal corresponding to that ideal are complex, integrating both self-regarding, functional components and other-regarding, objective criteria.

Nonetheless, Aquinas's complex account of the virtues reflects a certain tension. The most immediate indication of this tension comes in the texts on prudence just cited. Aquinas begins the response of II-II 47.6 with the general observation that the good of the human soul consists in conformity to reason, and he then goes on to explain what this means in terms drawn exclusively from the virtues associated with the passions. Elsewhere, he says that the common good, the object of general justice, is the end of individual persons living in community, implying that general justice benefits the individual by bringing her into right relation with that community (II-II 58.9; cf. I 60.5; II-II 58.5). However, he says less about this aspect of general justice than we might expect, and, to my knowledge, he does not ever say that particular justice is good for the agent himself. These omissions leave the impression that, although the virtues of temperance and fortitude are intrinsically connected to the agent's own good, the virtue of justice, considered as a quality of the soul or a way of life, is not. This conclusion is consistent with Aquinas's insistence that the demands of justice stem from the objective claims of others and the community. At the same time, he also says that the practice of the virtues is constitutive of human happiness, at least in the form that is connatural to us, and this position would seem to imply that the cardinal virtues all contribute in some integral way to the perfection of the human agent (I-II 5.5). Aquinas would seem to have at least some stake in showing that justice, as a quality of soul or a way of life, contributes in some way, perhaps only indirectly, to the perfection and flourishing of the individual agent.

Seen from the perspective of contemporary moral philosophy, this distinction between justice and the other moral virtues raises fundamental questions about the motivating force and the cogency of moral considerations, at least insofar as these overlap with the precepts of particular justice. These questions are usually framed in terms of a debate between internalist and externalist accounts of moral motivation, but for our purposes, it is probably not helpful to try to sort out the details of this complex debate.[4] Rather, at the risk of oversimplifying, let me formulate the question as follows: What reasons do we have to observe the precepts of justice, intrinsic to the precepts themselves? Justice is a disposition that takes shape over time, and once it is in place, the agent has the strongest possible motivations for acting justly, without regard to considerations of personal benefit. But why should someone who is not yet disposed to be just, or even someone who is frankly unjust, be moved to respect these norms? On Aquinas's account, the precepts of justice rest on an innate grasp of the normative value and the correlative claims of each human being. Yet he also claims that the will is not necessarily moved by any finite value whatever, including presumably the value of other people. It is entirely possible to know that other people's lives matter morally, and yet not to care. If someone really does not care about others, then it is difficult to see why on her own terms she should want to change. If this is so, then a commitment to justice begins to look like a personal preference, rather than an exigent moral demand.

I believe that Aquinas offers us resources to address this concern, even though we will once again need to go beyond what he explicitly says in order to do so. Before turning to this task, however, it is worth taking note once again of what is at stake for him in the line that he takes on justice and the rational good. Recall, first, that Aquinas makes strong claims about the value of others and the capacity of the agent to grasp that value and to appreciate its normative implications, at least in their broad outlines. Every rationally functional man and woman knows through innate principles of justice that each other person merits equitable treatment and respect, simply in virtue of being a human being. This innate apprehension of the normative value of others is not necessarily motivating, on Aquinas's account, but what it does

---

4. The distinction between internal and external reasons for action was first analyzed by Bernard Williams in 1980 in "Internal and External Reasons," reprinted in *Moral Luck: Philosophical Papers, 1973–1980* (Cambridge: Cambridge University Press, 1980), 101–13. Generally speaking, internal reasons for acting are those reasons that in some way depend on the agent's motivations and desires, whereas external reasons do not. The subsequent debate has been complicated by disagreements over the senses in which reasons can be compelling for someone, connected to preexisting motivations, and the like. Elijah Millgram offers a very helpful brief overview of this debate in "Practical Reason and the Structure of Actions," in *The Stanford Encyclopedia of Philosophy*, ed. Edward N. Zalta, http://plato.stanford.edu/entries/practical-reason-action. For a more extended discussion, developed in the context of a defense of moral realism and externalism, see David O. Brink, *Moral Realism and the Foundations of Ethics* (Cambridge: Cambridge University Press, 1989), 37–80.

establish is the authority of the precepts of justice. On this view, the morally exigent force of the precepts of justice rests directly on the claims of others. There is no need to appeal to motivating considerations or any other kinds of considerations in order to establish that we ought to respect the claims of others, because the authoritative force of the first precept of justice is intrinsic to the precept itself, innately known and fundamental to any kind of moral reasoning within the scope of other-regarding relations. Aquinas cannot admit that we could have cogent reasons for loving the neighbor more fundamental than the first principle itself, without compromising either the overall logic of his analysis or his claims for the normative value of human life.

If the first precept of justice is cogent, then how is it possible that someone might grasp this principle, not only abstractly but in terms of some concrete claim of justice, while still remaining unmoved by that claim? The short answer, from Aquinas's standpoint, is that authoritative force does not necessarily imply motivational force. More precisely, the authoritative force of these precepts does have motivational force, but we cannot adequately account for this motivational force at the level of the motives that any particular individual will necessarily have. Aquinas cannot allow that any consideration of an authoritative or other-regarding kind will necessarily motivate anyone to act accordingly, because in order to do so, he would have to admit that in one respect, at least, the will is necessarily inclined toward some particular, finite object. Such an admission is inconsistent with his theory of the freedom of the will, which for him implies that the inclinations of the will are always contingent, at least in this life.

Any account of the motivational force and reasonableness of justice will need to take account of the innately authoritative force of the precepts of justice, on the one hand, and the radical contingency of the will, on the other, in order to remain within the parameters of an authentically Thomistic account. That being said, I believe we can say more than he explicitly does about the intrinsic value of justice, for the just individual, as well as for those others with whom the agent is engaged. Once again, we recall that justice is a perfection, a full and appropriate development, of the capacity of the will. It does not function in such a way as to promote the agent's own harmonious functioning as an individual, as the other moral virtues do. However, it does function in such a way as to foster the agent's abilities to act in relation to others, in ways that are naturally perceived as appropriate or fitting, and therefore desirable. Moreover, the acts of justice are constitutive of a certain way of life, within which each individual has a respected place, together with the freedom needed to determine the course of her life in a meaningful way. Again, the way of life implied by a commitment to justice is natural to us as distinctively rational social animals, and as such, it is naturally desirable. My point is that men and women naturally admire justice and are naturally motivated to develop and practice it. Naturalness does not entail necessity. It is at least possible that there are some individuals who simply do not admire or desire the values intrinsic to justice at all, and it is certainly possible that these desires and motivations can be overridden by other, competing desires. At the same time, the desires to be just and to live in a just community are not mere individual preferences, either. We might say that they provide internal rather than external reasons for acting, because they are internal to the desires and motives that are natural to us as a kind of social animal, and they play an integral part in sustaining a naturally human way of life. Men and women, considered simply as human beings, always have good reasons for pursuing justice, even if they as individuals are not moved to respect the claims of others.

We return to Aquinas's remark that the good of the human soul consists in existence in accordance with reason (II-II 47.6). While he does not spell out how this general principle can be applied to justice, we can begin to see how he might do so. Justice can be said to bring the human soul into accordance with reason, insofar as it brings the agent's desires and choices into accordance with objective criteria of equity and right. The precepts of justice are authoritative for each individual, whether or not he or she wants to observe them. However, justice and right relations are natural to the human person and to the community, and most people do in fact have some motivation to act accordingly. This sense of the desirability of justice can be overridden, of course, but it is not just a personal preference. We can expect to find it in ourselves and others, and we appropriately count on it as we educate our children, set up communal associations, and attempt to persuade one another in contexts of political deliberation.

Value, Morality, and Perfections of the Will

In this section and the next, we will take up the question of the relation between justice and other comprehensive ideals, both moral and nonmoral, which present themselves as worthy objects of devotion. In this section, we will once again examine Aquinas's eudaimonism, asking whether and, if so, how an ideal of justice can be integrated into the ensemble of activities and aims that constitute a good human life. In the next section, we will look more closely at potential conflicts, especially those generated by the claims of particular justice.

We are by now familiar with Aquinas's claim that the will is necessarily oriented toward the agent's own perfection, or equivalently, his happiness or beatitude, which constitutes the ultimate end toward which all his actions are in some way directed. At the same time, Aquinas also holds that the rational creature, like every other creature, is naturally disposed to love some greater good more than himself (I-II 109.3). This position is not so paradoxical as it might appear, once we take account of Aquinas's distinction between the object, or the objective state of affairs, that constitutes the agent's happiness, and the agent's use or enjoyment of what is sought (I-II 1.8). Seen from the first perspective, the agent's end consists in whatever he regards and pursues as a supremely satisfying object of desire, for example, riches, artistic activities, a stable family life, or God (the classical options are covered in I-II 2). Of course, Aquinas believes that only the last of these really is a fully satisfying and appropriate object of one's ultimate desire, but the point is that all these putative or genuine objects are in some way external to the agent, ways of fulfilling a need or meeting a desire for something beyond the self. In contrast, Aquinas identifies the agent's use or enjoyment of the object of her desire with her perfection, understood in terms of the full and appropriate development of her causal powers. Seen from this perspective, the agent's happiness or perfection takes the form of ongoing activity, through which she develops and expresses her capacities in a fulfilling way.

Aquinas's claims that the will is necessarily oriented toward the agent's own perfection, on the one hand, and naturally inclined to an appropriate love of a greater good, on the other, are therefore not inconsistent. On the contrary, these reflect two aspects of one dynamic process. Subjective perfection through fulfilling activities presupposes that the agent is doing something worthwhile and satisfying, given his natural and individual needs and preferences. Worthwhile and satisfying activities typically involve engagement with something beyond the individual's own immediate satisfactions—enjoyment of nature or aesthetic value, participation in some useful civic project, or the exemplification of ideals of physical power and judgment through athletic activity. These kinds of objects can be said to be or to exemplify or to lead to greater goods, if only the relatively greater good of idealized human perfection of body or intellect. The agent's active love of self thus draws him toward some kind of relation with a good beyond himself.

Correlatively, the agent's love of a greater good will typically move her to do something with respect to that good—to grasp it for herself, to try to foster and contribute to it, to enjoy it through active participation or observation, or just to think about it.

These considerations suggest what Aquinas says at more than one point, namely, that men and women are naturally oriented toward greater goods of some kind (I 60.5; I-II 109.3; II-II 26.4 *ad* 3). More specifically, he argues that we are naturally oriented toward love of a greater good, because we can be regarded as parts of some more comprehensive whole (I 60.5; II-II 58.5). At best, this is an inexact metaphor, and it might seem to imply a devaluing of the individual. As we have already seen, Aquinas qualifies his remarks about the supremacy of the common good by placing strict limits on what can be done to individuals for the sake of the community. At any rate, at this point I simply want to observe that this image does at least illuminate the relation between the individual's subjective perfection and her objective love of a greater good. That is, normally the greater goods in question will consist of wider contexts of meaning and activity within which we are embedded, simply by virtue of our humanity, for example, a natural world, traditions of meaning and activity, and communities and political associations of all kinds. Our individual activities presuppose some kind of relations to these wider contexts, which implies a still closer link between the agent's subjective perfection and her orientation toward what are objectively, although only in limited senses, greater goods.

We can readily see how this line of analysis implies that general justice is a perfection of the will, which promotes human perfection in a distinctive way. The common good of one's political community is a greater good, seen in relation to the individual, and as we would expect, Aquinas says that men and women are naturally disposed to love their political community more than themselves (II-II 26.4 *ad* 3). However, it is important not to generalize too quickly from this point. We might expect Aquinas to conclude, as Aristotle does, that connatural human perfection or happiness consists in a life of political participation, but that is not what he says, at least in the *Summa theologiae.* Rather, he identifies connatural happiness with the practice of the virtues generally considered, a claim that reflects his sense of the complexities of our lives as natural and moral agents (I-II 4.7, 5.5). While Aquinas claims that one's overall perfection presupposes a right relation to one's political community, this is not all that is required.

We all participate in many morally significant communities and associations at once. Every man and woman can be regarded as part of more than one comprehensive reality, each of which reflects distinctive sets of values and structures of interrelationship. These values and ways of relating are not simply absorbed into the life of the political community, although they are qualified and to some extent limited by its overarching claims. Aquinas does not reflect on the complexity of our lives in these terms, but his complex theory of the virtues provides a framework that can accommodate a plurality of values and commitments. It is worth recalling in this context that the demands of general justice do not exhaust the field of morality. General justice is preeminent among the moral virtues because it aims directly at a comprehensive good, that is, the common good of one's political community, and directs the operations of the other virtues toward that object. Nonetheless, the other moral virtues retain their independence, both as distinctive dispositions of the will and the passions and as moral ideals. In order to act morally, in accordance with the ideal of virtue comprehensively considered, the agent needs to discern how to act in accordance with the ideals of all the virtues, insofar as these are relevant to the situation at hand. Practical reason, rightly disposed through the virtue of prudence, enables him to do so by means of a judicious consideration and comparative assessment of diverse considerations, leading to a well-developed free judgment that this or that action is the best option, all things considered.

Aquinas's complex theory of the virtues thus reflects a strong sense of the complexity of our lives as moral agents, called on to integrate diverse and sometimes incommensurable values and claims. By the same token, it points the way toward a fuller account of justice as a personal quality of character, a disposition toward others that is admirable and praiseworthy in itself and that is integrally connected to a worthwhile and desirable way of life, or so I hope to show in what follows. In order to develop this account, I will once again go beyond what Aquinas explicitly says, but in such a way as to develop and extend central elements of his thought.

I take my starting points from his account of perfection or happiness, seen from diverse perspectives as a subjective perfection of one's active capacities, as an objectively desirable attainment, and as a moral ideal. The key point here is that the orientation toward perfection or happiness can emerge and operate only through the formation of stable habits of the will toward one's comprehensive good, in accordance with one's own conception of what that means. These dispositions can be rightly formed only if they bring the diverse subjective and objective aspects of happiness together in the right way, in accordance with boundaries set by the demands of particular justice. Finally, by extending the developmental analysis set forth in

JUSTICE AS A VIRTUE

chapter 2, we can begin to see how dispositions toward justice and related virtues take shape through the individual's self-reflective interactions with others. In this way, we will arrive at a general etiology of the moral life that both lends credibility to the claim that justice is grounded in our natural, socially oriented way of life, and opens up new perspectives on why we admire and value justice and condemn injustice.

In order to move forward, we need at this point to look back to earlier discussions of perfection and happiness as Aquinas understands these interrelated notions. We have already seen that Aquinas does not identify happiness properly so called with feelings of pleasure or delight, nor does he equate it with the satisfaction of someone's actual desires, whatever they may be. He is not an ethical egoist, and he does not deny that we can be motivated by other-regarding considerations. Rather, "happiness" for him is a very general term, equivalent to the perfection of a rational or intellectual creature (I 62.1). Understood in this way, the rational creature's desire for happiness is a distinctive expression of a general metaphysical principle. Every creature aims at its perfection, that is to say, the full and appropriate development of its potential as a creature of a specific kind. Rational and intellectual creatures aim at their perfection in a distinctive way, in accordance with some conception of what it would mean to attain a fully developed or satisfying or admirable life (the key texts include I 5.5; I-II 1.8). But we can no more refrain from pursuing our perfection or happiness through activities than we can choose not to be creatures, and causal agents of a distinctive kind.

Even if we grant all this, however, Aquinas's account of the final end raises a further difficulty that is more directly relevant at this point. That is, it is difficult to see how happiness as Aquinas understands it can be itself a moral ideal, pointing to a way of life that is both praiseworthy and desirable. Keep in mind that Aquinas is not commending ethical egoism, which would imply that a kind of happiness, comprising one's own satisfactions, does have moral value. If this is not what Aquinas means by commending happiness as a normative ideal, then what does he mean? We find it difficult to answer this question because our perspectives have been shaped by an alternative way of thinking about happiness, and ultimately about the will itself.[5] On this alternative account, one's self-interest and happiness are dis-

---

5. For a good overview of the issues raised by eudaimonistic theories, seen from the perspective of a right-focused account of justice, see Nicholas Wolterstorff, *Justice: Rights and Wrongs* (Princeton: Princeton University Press, 2008), 147–79. Those who consider virtue to be instrumental to the attainment of happiness include Rosalind Hursthouse, *On Virtue Ethics*

tinct from one's moral duty, or at least, that is what we should all assume. The leading modern moral theories offer diverse ways of relating happiness and duty, either identifying them, as both ethical egoism and strict consequentialism do, or setting them in opposition or, most commonly, giving priority to duty but allowing a place for self-love. More recently, there have been a number of attempts to establish the empirical claim that a life of morality or virtue leads to subjective satisfaction, thus confirming the view that virtuous practices are instrumental means toward the attainment of nonmoral ends.[6] Each of these theories presupposes that the agent's happiness and her duty represent two distinctive kinds of value, which must therefore be related in some way. The agent's own happiness cannot be regarded as intrinsically valuable, a normative value that can be apprehended as such without reference to an extrinsic principle of duty.

Yet Aquinas apparently does regard perfection or happiness as a moral ideal, implying standards of praise and blame that transcend the individual's perceptions and desires.[7] He identifies connatural happiness with the practice of the virtues, while at the same time denying that these function as means to further, nonmoral ends (I-II 4.7; cf. I-II 2.4, 5.5). He identifies a rightly formed self-love with the highest of the virtues, the theological virtue of charity; furthermore, he identifies vicious dispositions and sinful acts with distorted forms of self-love (II-II 25.4, 26.4; II-II 25.7). While his metaphysical and theological analyses of happiness are distinctive, his overall approach reflects an ancient tradition of moral thought, which we can trace from classical antiquity through the theologians of late antiquity, Augustine especially, to the early scholastics.[8]

(Oxford: Oxford University Press, 1999), 163–91, and John Bolin, *Contingency and Fortune in Aquinas's Ethic* (Cambridge: Cambridge University Press, 1999).

6. For a survey of recent research in this area, see Richard M. Ryan and Edward L. Deci, "On Happiness and Human Potential: A Review of Research on Hedonic and Eudaimonic Well-Being," *American Review of Psychology* 52 (2001): 141–66.

7. In this respect, Aquinas is closer to the Greek and Hellenistic philosophers than to us. As Julia Annas observes, "The ancient concern for virtue occupies in the most important respects the same place in people's thoughts as is occupied today by concerns for morality, and the importance, for the ancients, of determining the place of virtue in one's final end is like the importance, for us, of determining the place of morality in one's life" (*The Morality of Happiness* [Oxford: Oxford University Press, 1993], 47).

8. For an overview of classical philosophical conceptions of happiness, see Annas, *The Morality of Happiness*, 27–47; for a survey of patristic and especially scholastic views, see George Weiland, "Happiness: The Perfection of Man," in *The Cambridge History of Later Medieval Philosophy from the Rediscovery of Aristotle to the Disintegration of Scholasticism, 1100–1600*,

As Julia Annas remarks, the earliest traditions of philosophical inquiry into virtue and morality generally assumed that the desire for happiness is universal, that it can take distorted or legitimate forms, and that, when it is rightly pursued, it leads in some way to the pursuit and cultivation of the virtues.[9] At the same time, the concept of happiness is not necessarily emptied of its usual meaning. As Annas goes on to say, most classical and Hellenistic philosophers would have agreed that any theory of happiness and virtue needs to show that the virtuous life is generally pleasant or satisfying, typically if not always, in order to be plausible. This criterion for a successful theory of virtue may seem like a concession, but at best, it serves as a touchstone for identifying the connections between the virtuous life and the life that is natural to us at a more basic level. These philosophers would have regarded this as a salutary reminder, and so would Aquinas. At any rate, this is the way of thinking that we need to recapture, if we are to understand Aquinas's remarks on perfection or happiness as the final end of human life.

We cannot get a good sense of Aquinas's views on these matters so long as we limit ourselves to the contexts set by contemporary discussions of happiness, even, perhaps especially, those that attempt to establish a causal connection between moral behavior or good character and happiness. We can get a better perspective on his views by drawing on a different set of practical concerns and normative commitments, equally familiar but not so readily divided into neat categories of nonmoral and moral values. In the words of Gabriele Taylor, we can assume that "persons wish to lead a life which they perceive as being by and large worthwhile."[10] Similarly, Ronald Dworkin sets out to defend what he calls a comprehensive liberal theory on the basis of two principles of ethical individualism:

> The first is the principle of equal importance: It is important, from an objective point of view, that human lives be successful rather than wasted, and this is equally important, from the objective point of view, for each human life. The second is the principle of special responsibility. . . . One person has a special and final responsibility for that success—the person whose life it is.[11]

---

ed. Norman Kretzman, Anthony Kenny, and Jan Pinborg (Cambridge: Cambridge University Press, 1982), 675–86.

9. Again, see Annas, *The Morality of Happiness*, 27–47.

10. Taylor, *Deadly Vices*, 3.

11. Ronald Dworkin, *Sovereign Virtue: The Theory and Practice of Equality* (Cambridge, MA: Harvard University Press, 2000), 5.

Success might mean something as basic as desire satisfaction, but that is clearly not what Dworkin means. As he goes on to explain, the ideal of equality rests on a sense of "the importance that their lives come to something rather than being wasted"—in other words, that people live lives that matter, that they themselves regard as meaningful in some way.[12]

Both Taylor and Dworkin reflect, in different ways, a set of ideals and aspirations deeply entrenched in today's society. Men and women very often express a desire to make something of their lives, to live lives of significance and lasting value, to live in such a way as to be useful or to make a contribution or to give back what they believe they have received. They want to live lives that are in some way meaningful or worthwhile. They want to live for a purpose; a recent popular book on this topic quickly became one of the best-selling books in American history.[13] For many men and women, the search for purpose or meaning plays a defining role in their sense of themselves, their self-esteem, and their activities.

We do not usually associate a desire to live in a valuable way with an orientation toward happiness. Given prevalent assumptions, we are more likely to contrast the two. Yet for many men and women, the desire to live with purpose or meaning plays the same general role that the desire for happiness plays, as Aquinas and his interlocutors would understand it. A meaningful life is regarded as supremely fulfilling, and men and women can, and often do, take this aim as the fundamental touchstone for evaluating their particular choices and acts. Furthermore, whatever the specifics of someone's conception of a worthwhile life may be, such a life will usually be understood in terms of both the objective aims or values that she hopes to promote and her activities in pursuit of this aim—that is to say, in terms of the object or matter that is sought, and the agent's own activities in pursuit and enjoyment of that object. Lives are judged to be meaningful or worthwhile by reference to some context, some set of principles or aims or ideals, which extend beyond the individual's own life in some way. Men and women devote themselves to projects that cannot be completed in their lifetime, to traditions of inquiry or artistic excellence that will necessarily always exceed their attainments, to communities that extend beyond them in space and time.[14] Yet the kind of devotion in question cannot be limited to detached

12. Dworkin, *Sovereign Virtue.*

13. The book in question is Rick Warren, *The Purpose-Driven Life: What on Earth Am I Here For?* (Grand Rapids: Zondervan, 2002).

14. For a particularly insightful reflection on this point, see Samuel Scheffler, *Death and the Afterlife* (Oxford: Oxford University Press, 2013), 15–112.

admiration. In order to render one's own life meaningful in these terms, the agent has to do something, to engage in activities that really do further the wider aim in some way. Once again, the image of a part/whole complex offers a useful, though inexact, way of thinking about purpose, meaning, and value in human lives. Men and women want to be a part of something beyond themselves, they want to play their part in civic or family life, they want to take part in artistic or athletic events or communal celebrations.

Finally, a meaningful life is widely regarded as both admirable and a satisfying way to live. In this way, the ideal of a meaningful or worthwhile life resembles the happy life as it was understood in classical and late antiquity. Those who are looking for meaning in their lives are dissatisfied if they cannot find it, and they are likely to hold themselves in low esteem and to find it difficult to motivate themselves to act.[15] In short, they become affectively disinclined to be what they essentially are, active agents in their social and natural world. Those who do regard their lives as meaningful are likely, for that very reason, to regard their lives as satisfying. They feel that they have reasons to live, ideals to orient them in the world, commitments that call forth ongoing activities. They regard themselves as individuals who make a contribution to something beyond themselves, and they respect and value themselves on that basis. We might suspect that some individuals regard a meaningful life as satisfying because it is admirable; in other words, men and women pursue a life of purpose and meaning in order to secure their own self-regard and the admiration of others. No doubt that is true in some cases, but it is not necessarily the case. On the contrary, men and women sometimes choose to live what they regard as worthwhile lives in relative obscurity, or even to contribute to wider aims without the knowledge of others, rather than acting in ways that are more noticeable but less worthwhile from the agent's point of view.

We can generalize this point. Men and women are naturally oriented toward perfection, understood as the full and appropriate development of their native capacities. For many individuals, this orientation is expressed through spontaneous attempts to make connections with ideals, values, or projects that are in some way greater than the individual. Aquinas's remarks about the relation of individuals as parts of some greater whole suggest why this tendency is so widespread. Each of us comes into contact with all kinds of greater goods, which in some cases sustain us directly (for example, one's

---

15. Taylor's perceptive analysis of the deadly sins, and especially the vice of acedia, or sloth, is relevant here; see *Deadly Vices*, 13–30.

family or community) and in others move us to admiration (for example, aesthetic or natural beauty). We are naturally inclined to enter into appropriate relationships with these kinds of goods and to engage in activities that foster and support these relations. Does all this imply that men and women are devoted to these greater goods in order to promote their own perfection? This is the worry behind one common objection to eudaimonism, to the effect that for the eudaimonist, the agent acts morally in order to promote his own happiness or perfection.[16]

This worry is misplaced. The objection assumes that men and women start with a commitment to happiness and then choose to act morally in order to sustain or promote the kind of life associated with happiness. But this way of formulating the relation between the agent's happiness and her commitments or devotions is at best misleading. On Aquinas's terms, every rational agent is indeed drawn to seek her own perfection, and for many, this natural tendency is felt as a desire for some fulfilling or meaningful activity. At this point, the agent's desire for perfection, understood in whatever terms, is self-referential. In Dworkin's words, the agent does not want his life to be wasted; he wants it to count for something. This desire, which at this point is likely to be vague and perhaps not entirely conscious, will lead him to try out various options, including activities that draw him into contact with communities, practices, and ideals of all kinds, each in its way a greater, more comprehensive good. Because these activities are naturally satisfying, the agent is satisfied by them. These experiences, in turn, provide the starting points for considering why some kinds of activities are satisfying, and others not—a line of thought that will ideally tell the agent something about himself, also something about the real worth of the objects of his love. Recall that Millgram identifies experiences of satisfaction through activity as one of the key components of practical induction.[17] The agent experiences certain kinds of activities as subjectively fulfilling, and by reflecting on these experiences, he comes to see what he truly loves and to orient the dispositions of his will accordingly.

The processes of practical induction leading the agent to devotion to greater goods of all kinds are thus grounded in a desire for the agent's own perfection, which is self-referential, insofar as it comes into conscious awareness. Does it follow that a mature agent, who has more or less well-formed

16. Again, see Wolterstorff, *Justice: Rights and Wrongs*, 176–79.
17. Elijah Millgram, *Practical Induction* (Cambridge, MA: Harvard University Press, 1997), 67–85.

conceptions about the communities and ideals that she values and whose will is oriented accordingly, will necessarily pursue the objects of her devotion in the same way? There is no reason to draw such a conclusion. There is a difference between pursuing one's own perfection or happiness or meaning, in a general and abstract way, and pursuing the greater goods that give some content to these abstractions. The rational agent is capable of grasping that the objects of one's devotion are valuable in themselves, and the will is capable of inclining toward these objects out of a love for the goodness that they embody. This love need not be connected to the agent's own enjoyment or participation at all. There is nothing incoherent about a hope that one's family or community or some artistic practice or the rain forests will continue after the individual is dead, even on the assumption that there is no personal afterlife.[18]

At the same time, men and women are naturally drawn to perfecting activity, and in this context, that activity will usually take the forms of participation in one's community, engagement in artistic activities, scientific inquiry, or whatever brings the lover into relation with what he loves. Yet even these activities are not necessarily self-referential, in the sense that the agent necessarily seeks to promote or enjoy some greater good for her own sake or for the sake of attaining her perfection. What she does seek through activity, necessarily, is to enter into appropriate relations with whatever has secured her devotion. Just as human activity is necessarily perfecting, so it is necessarily relational, and it perfects the agent by bringing her into a right relation of some kind. Nonetheless, a relationship is not an individual good but, rather, an impersonal or interpersonal good in which the agent plays a part. Assuming that this relation is genuinely good, it will itself be a kind of perfection for all those involved in it, whether we are thinking of individual persons or of individuals in relation to collectives. Nonetheless, it is entirely possible to intend to enter into relations with others for the sake of those others, whose good one hopes to promote through the relevant activities, or to intend the good of the relation itself.

We turn now to a familiar point. I am arguing that men and women are naturally inclined to seek and pursue a life of meaning, value, or significance. Even if this is so, it does not follow that everyone necessarily does desire this kind of life. This kind of life is natural to the human person, and for that reason, men and women are naturally disposed to seek it and to understand the

18. Again, Scheffler offers a powerful defense of this point; see *Death and the Afterlife*, 15–50.

motivations and concerns of others who are doing the same. Nonetheless, no one is necessarily drawn to such a life. It is not the case that everyone spontaneously pursues a meaningful, worthwhile way of life, if not hindered by false beliefs or bad circumstances. Some men and women simply do not care about anything beyond themselves. They are content to build their lives around their own comfort, security, and satisfactions. They may well take pleasure in intellectual or artistic pursuits, or they may find family life or a life of activism enjoyable and rewarding. But they do not care much about truth and beauty for their own sakes, nor do they have any real stake in the well-being of others or in the common good of the community. Once again, experience confirms that many men and women lead self-contained lives and are content to do so, or content enough, at any rate, to continue indefinitely in this way of life.

These observations might seem to undercut the claim that men and women are naturally oriented toward a meaningful life. But for the rational creature, the naturalness of an aim does not imply that it will necessarily be desired and pursued. As we have already seen, the freedom of the will implies that the inclinations of the will are always in the last analysis contingent, at least with respect to finite goods. Desire and choice could always have gone in another direction, and we cannot finally say why they did not. By the same token, someone who does incline toward a meaningful life, leading to genuine devotion to some greater good, can truly be said to find this kind of life desirable and satisfying for its own sake, not for the sake of some predetermined end. In this sense, those men and women who find a worthwhile life to be desirable and satisfying regard it as such because they incline toward it, shaping their choices accordingly. The inclinations of the will toward one set of possibilities rather than another determine, at least in key part, the way of life that individuals find to be subjectively satisfying.

Because the basic inclinations of the will at this level are ultimately contingent on the will's own motion, they can coherently be regarded as volitional and therefore as subject to normative assessments. It would be misleading to say that we praise or blame men and women for these kinds of fundamental volitions, since the language of praise and blame, with its corresponding categories of right and wrong, might appear to be inappropriate at this level. How can we blame someone for living for herself alone if she really is not wronging anyone by doing so? And yet, we do evaluate these kinds of fundamental volitions in normative terms, carrying strong overtones of moral judgments. We respect and esteem someone who is trying to make something of himself, and by the same token, we are likely to disapprove of someone who has no drive, no desire for anything beyond a comfortable life. We may find ourselves admiring someone who devotes her life to causes that we find repugnant, who may be an opponent in a political contest or a committee meeting. We reject everything she stands for, and yet we admire her courage, we appreciate the fact that she stands for something, when so many others do not.

We have already remarked on Dworkin's observation that "though we must all recognize the equal objective importance of the success of a human life, one person has a special and final responsibility for that success—the person whose life it is."[19] Dworkin does not refer to a theory of the will, but his comment does reflect a widespread sense that human capacities for reasoned judgment and volition imply qualitatively new kinds of normative criteria. We perceive and respond to the free commitments and acts of others, as these are manifested in the agent's particular acts and patterns of activity. These kinds of judgments fit awkwardly with what we take to be typical moral judgments, and yet they are not clearly nonmoral judgments, either. This is the sphere of admiration, sympathy, and self-esteem, or contempt, distaste, and shame. Our sense of others, and of ourselves, as committed, active, and responsible, or as irresolute, passive, and irresponsible, plays a central role in our lives as social beings and in our sense of personal self-esteem or shame.

At the same time, our normative judgments at this level are likely to be qualified and ambiguous. It is all too possible to admire commitment, courage, and devotion, while wishing that these were directed to a better cause. Sometimes people devote themselves to unworthy ends. For example, someone may structure his life around his commitments to the athletic successes and general reputation of his alma mater, not just as a college student, but throughout his lifetime. In such a case, we may feel both admiration for such steadfast loyalty and a bit of disdain for such a whole-hearted devotion to one's college, years after moving on to adult life. Sometimes people commit themselves to what are clearly worthwhile aims, but they pursue these in problematic ways. We may admire someone who devotes the best part of his energies and time to attaining an ideal of artistic perfection, while at the same time we are dismayed at his neglect of his young children.

Aquinas's theory of the will suggests a way to think about those normative judgments that reflect admiration and approval for someone's devotion and yet may be morally qualified or ambiguous in various ways. Once again,

19. Dworkin, *Sovereign Virtue*, 5.

we can usefully draw on the image of the agent as a part of a greater whole, naturally oriented toward a more comprehensive good. Responsiveness to something beyond oneself reflects a kind of qualified perfection, which is perceived and valued as such. By the same token, self-oriented dispositions, reflected in self-seeking or narcissistic self-preoccupation, reflect vicious distortions of the will, and they tend to call forth contempt or disdain, even when someone is, as we say, harmless. These kinds of judgments reflect a sense of someone's overall dispositions of the will, seen in relation to the natural orientation of the will toward the agent's comprehensive good. Of course, men and women do not think in terms of a metaphysical theory of the will, but my point is that we naturally perceive and respond positively to someone's dispositions in ways that that theory would lead us to expect. We admire those who are committed to something beyond themselves, and we disdain those who live only for themselves, and these responses reflect our sense of what it means to express and fulfill, or distort and stunt, the natural orientation of the will toward some comprehensive good.

We can thus account for the pervasive sense that commitment and devotion are admirable and praiseworthy in themselves. But can Aquinas's theory of the will account for the ambiguities of commitment, as reflected in our conflicted judgments? I believe that it can. We might best frame the analysis in terms of necessary and sufficient conditions for judging someone's dispositions to be praiseworthy in an unqualified way, that is to say, a fully moral way. Recall that the will is necessarily oriented toward the agent's own perfection, understood subjectively as perfecting activity and objectively, in terms of some aim that the agent pursues and enjoys through these activities. Although this general statement needs to be qualified in the ways indicated earlier, for Aquinas it reflects the necessary structure of causal agency generally, as exemplified by causal agents of the kind we embody. Every mature, functionally normal man and woman will be inclined to develop some kind of disposition to the individual's own perfection or happiness, and this tendency as such is neither praiseworthy nor blameworthy—it is just part of what it means to be human.

This disposition, however, can be developed well or badly, in such a way as to promote the agent's full perfection or to undermine it. Men and women are naturally oriented to devote themselves to some more comprehensive good, an orientation that is often reflected in a desire to find meaning or purpose, to live a life of value in terms that extend beyond individual lives. At the same time, this natural orientation toward some more comprehensive good is not compelling. Individuals can and do freely incline toward a life of self-seeking and self-preoccupation. We can leave it as an open question whether this kind of life is subjectively satisfying for those who incline toward it. At any rate, such an orientation reflects a fundamental distortion of the natural orientation of the will toward a greater good, and as such, it cannot be admirable or praiseworthy, even in a qualified sense. It is worth noting that this kind of disposition is also contrary to the fundamental stance of justice, in both its particular and its general forms. Someone whose overall stance can be summed up as "me first" cannot simultaneously develop a perpetual will to render to each that which is his or her right, for the obvious reason that the rights of another may conflict with one's own immediate needs and desires. Similarly, someone whose highest concerns center around the self will not place the demands of the common good ahead of her own interests.

In contrast, we admire someone whose life reflects a disposition to orient herself toward some ideal or aim more comprehensive than herself. This disposition represents the distinctively human expression of a universal natural tendency, and as such, it elicits the kind of admiration that we reserve for excellence of mind or will. Yet, normative responses at this level may still be qualified in various ways. Men and women may devote themselves to unworthy or even perverse aims, or they may pursue worthy aims in ways that are inappropriate or illicit. In these kinds of situations, we may well admire someone's devotion, while wishing that it were directed to a better cause. Or we might praise someone for her commitment to her political community, while condemning her for safeguarding the community in an unjust way, for example, approving the torture of prisoners in order to extract useful intelligence data. Unqualified admiration for someone's disposition toward a more comprehensive good, in contrast, presupposes that the agent is devoted to a genuine and worthy aim that she pursues in an appropriate way.

What counts as genuine aims, and what counts as appropriate or inappropriate ways of pursuing those aims? Aquinas's account of the virtue of justice suggests answers to both questions. The ideal of general justice, which orients the individual toward the more comprehensive good of the political community, appears to set out an obvious object for individual devotion. The ideal of particular justice, and especially the precepts connected with that ideal, place constraints on what anyone can legitimately do in pursuit of even the most comprehensive aims. Both answers would seem to be straightforward, and yet each raises difficulties.

Consider first the claim that we are naturally oriented toward the common good of the political community to which we belong. Not every political community is worthy of devotion, and in our globalized context, we may well wonder whether even the best political community represents the highest connatural good that we can envision. Moreover, we can readily think of comprehensive goods that are not political, and yet are at least good candidates for worthy and appropriate devotion. Aristotle himself suggests one such aim, namely, philosophical inquiry, which he describes as a life that is more than human. Many men and women today devote themselves to scientific inquiry with the same whole-hearted enthusiasm, and others similarly devote themselves to ideals of artistic attainment, athletic perfection, and the like. It is hard to believe that these aims are unworthy objects of devotion, simply because they are not directly political.

Aquinas recognizes that supposed political authorities, laws, and judicial judgments are sometimes unjust, and he holds that in these cases, individuals are not bound to observance and indeed may be justified in overthrowing a ruler through force of arms (I-II 96.4; II-II 42.2 *ad* 3). Clearly, he does not hold that general justice implies obeisance to whatever political regime happens to be in power. Nonetheless, he is committed to the view that individual men and women ought to love the common good of their community more than themselves. This love may take the form of ongoing commitments to resistance and reform, in the name of the true common good that the community could achieve. But general justice is inconsistent with a stance of indifference or hatred to one's community. Each individual is sustained by her community, both physically and as a part of a culture and a tradition of rational discourse. Furthermore, the community, especially its legal structures, sustains the way of life and the safeguards necessary to preserve the fundamental equality of all individuals. For this reason, general justice promotes the central ideals of particular justice. I repeat—a political regime may be unjust, and furthermore, the community itself may be corrupt. The individual may have little reason to feel gratitude or respect, much less love, for her homeland. But so long as a community is functioning at all, and assuming that it stays within the outer limits of forbearance for the lives and freedom of its members, it will in some way merit the individual's gratitude and regard.[20] Even bad parents deserve some gratitude and consideration, and by the same token, even bad communities merit at least a minimal, critical loyalty and commitment.

---

20. The outer limits are set by practices such as genocide or slavery, both of which reflect not only indifference or hostility but a malicious will to eliminate the other from the community altogether. No one is bound to love an association of persons that is actively seeking his destruction, or that of other individuals, whose true claims he is bound to respect.

Similarly, one's community makes a kind of moral claim that other sorts of ideals do not. By no means does this distinction imply that artistic pursuits, scientific inquiry, and the like are unworthy objects of pursuit. Nor do we have any reason to suppose that each individual should devote more time and energy to promoting the common good than he gives to other pursuits. As we saw earlier, Aquinas assumes that private citizens will devote only minimal time to promoting the common good directly, since that is the task of political officials. Nonetheless, the common good makes a moral claim that other kinds of general goods do not. No one can be blamed for preferring action movies to the opera, but we do blame someone who has no commitment at all to the common good of his community.

We turn now to the claim that the precepts of particular justice set constraints on what individuals can do, even in pursuit of the highest and most worthy aims. Once again, we need to address a potential tension in Aquinas's account of justice, in this instance, the tension between the claims of individuals and the relative priority of collective over individual goods. Here is what I have in mind. Aquinas's theory of the will implies a way of understanding the perfection of the will by reference to the natural orientation toward some greater good, which is further analyzed in terms of apparent and real, lesser and greater forms of comprehensive goodness. Thus, we can make sense of the claim that someone who lives for a purpose, devoting her life to worthwhile aims, is more admirable than a self-centered egoist, and someone who lives for the community or art or science is more admirable than someone who lives for his alma mater. So far, normative analysis runs along a continuum, in accordance with the generally straightforward criteria of greater and lesser, more and less worthy.

However, the ideals of particular justice introduce a qualitatively new set of criteria. It is true that particular justice, like general justice, is said to perfect the will by disposing it to pursue its proper object in an appropriate way. Nonetheless, there are significant differences between the two. General justice disposes the will directly toward a comprehensive good, the common good of a political community, and for this reason it would seem to be directly linked to the natural orientation of the will toward the agent's final end of perfection. Particular justice, in contrast, depends on ideals and norms pertaining to one's relations to a good, so to speak, that is equal to oneself. Aquinas formulates the relevant part of the first precept of justice in terms of the scriptural injunction to love the neighbor as oneself. That is, one's neighbor, any other man or woman, is not to be regarded as a lesser good whose claims give way to the individual's desires, but neither is the other to be regarded as a greater good, an appropriate object for comprehensive devotion.

As we saw in chapter 4, Aquinas holds that each individual is, in certain key respects, inviolable, and he places strict constraints on the kinds of harms that can be inflicted in defense of the common good. His views on the legitimacy of sacrificing individuals to the political good or to other more comprehensive goods are not open to question. We may, however, question whether this strict commitment to the claims of the individual is fully consistent with his overall position on justice, morality, and the will. As we have seen, it makes sense, on Aquinas's terms, to speak of greater or more comprehensive goods, relative to the individual. He uses the language of part and whole to justify the subordination of individual interests to the common good. Following this line of thought, it would appear that individuals are capable of dedicating themselves to communities, associations, and ideals. Someone might even sacrifice his own fundamental interests, or perhaps even his life, for the sake of his commonwealth or for the sake of some demanding commitment. While our assessment of these sacrifices will vary from case to case, they are very often rational and admirable.

This brings us to the question at hand. If it makes sense to speak in terms of goods that surpass the individual's own good, then why is it never permissible to sacrifice individuals to the common good or to some other more comprehensive good? If men and women can rationally sacrifice themselves for a greater good, why can't they sacrifice someone else? We might even say that the logic of the first precept of justice pertaining to others supports this conclusion. We are enjoined to love the neighbor as oneself—but we are also told that we ought to love some greater good more than ourselves. If we can and should set aside our own interests for the sake of a greater good, why are we not allowed, and perhaps even required, to do the same for one whom we love—not more than, but as ourselves?

We cannot sacrifice others for the sake of a greater good for the same reason that we are not obliged to sacrifice our own life to an attacker, or to compromise our relation to God for the sake of another (II-II 64.7; II-II 26.4). There is a fundamental asymmetry between the individual's relation to herself and her relation to others. Men and women are naturally capable of self-governance in accordance with each person's best judgments about the way of life that best suits the individual. Each individual can, and indeed must, make some judgments about the way he or she ought to live, and to act accordingly. No one can make these judgments for someone else. In the first place, none of us has the perception to know how someone else should relate to greater and more comprehensive goods. Furthermore, no one has the moral power to impose these kinds of judgments on someone else. This conclusion follows, again, from the ideal of equality that is central to justice. No one can be subject to the private judgments of another, even when those judgments are motivated by high ideals and benevolent aims.

Similarly, none of us is in a position to judge and act from the perspective of the universe, or to act on behalf of impersonal goods, without reference to the claims of others. The normative structures of human life reflect the natural limits of our capacities for understanding, judgment, and effective action. We are naturally suited to live together on a basis of mutual respect for one another's claims, and the normative structures of our lives are grounded in this specifically human way of life. I do not mean to suggest that we are not able to act on behalf of more comprehensive goods in significant ways. Of course we can, and in many cases we should do so. We clearly have individual and collective responsibility to try to safeguard the environment, for example, and arguably we are also responsible for preserving our artistic heritage and promoting intellectual inquiries of all kinds. My point is simply that the claims of others put constraints on the ways in which we carry out these responsibilities.

At the beginning of this chapter, I noted that the will is a complex faculty, and its natural inclinations can potentially come into conflict. Justice and the other virtues of the will function in such a way as to resolve these conflicts by integrating diverse inclinations into a unified, dynamic orientation toward the good. We are now in a better position to see why this observation is relevant to our central commitments and our moral concerns. On Aquinas's view, the perfection of the will implies a disposition of love and commitment to some greater good. At the same time, he also holds that men and women are moral creatures, implying not only capacities for moral action but stringent claims on others to certain kinds of respect and forbearance. These two aspects of human perfection, and by implication the perfection of the will, are not obviously linked together; on the contrary, they apparently can come into practical conflict with one another. Aquinas believes that in cases of conflict, the claims of the other override any seeming claims stemming from greater goods. But this line of argument in itself does not resolve the paradoxical tension between these two aspects of perfection. In the next section, we will ask whether and, if so, how we might offer a positive resolution to this seeming paradox.

Commitment and Regard, Two Aspects of Justice

At this point, it will be helpful to review what we have established so far. On Aquinas's account, the disposition of the will toward a more comprehensive good represents a perfection of the will, although perhaps only in a qualified sense, depending on the appropriateness of the object of one's devotion and on the specific ways in which this orientation is expressed. The virtue of particular justice, which disposes the individual toward right relations toward others, is also a perfection of the will, but it pertains to a distinct aspect of the will and introduces considerations of a qualitatively different kind. Yet the unqualified perfection of the will, and by implication the coherence of the moral life, presupposes that these perfecting dispositions can be integrated in such a way as operate harmoniously together. How might this be done?

These may appear to be theoretical worries far removed from actual experiences, but by now, we are in a position to appreciate their practical significance. The conflicts that arise between obligations to the community or one's devotion to general ideals, on the one hand, and our responsibilities to other individuals, on the other, are central to our moral lives and especially salient today. Furthermore, these conflicts appear to be intractable, precisely because they represent two alternative approaches to morality and virtue, or as Aquinas would say, two ways of understanding what it means to attain one's perfection as a rational and free agent. We are naturally drawn to collective goods of all kinds, and seen from certain perspectives, the claims that these place on us can appear to be overriding—because they involve the well-being of so many people, or alternatively, because they present us with ideals that appear to be impersonal, off the scale of the normative evaluations that we apply in our relations to one another. And yet, we are also naturally responsive to the claims of others and are disposed to respect their freedom and independence.

Thus, the orientation of the will toward the comprehensive good is potentially inconsistent with its orientation toward right relations with other individuals. The key word here is "potentially." If we could show that the natural operations of the will necessarily generated an antinomy of this kind, then it would indeed follow that the moral life on Aquinas's account is fundamentally incoherent, or else that his theory of the will is flawed. However, the potential for inconsistency, in itself, does not raise problems for Aquinas's theory of the will or his theory of the virtues. On the contrary, Aquinas acknowledges that the complex, innately unformed appetites of rational creatures can potentially develop in badly integrated, inconsistent ways (I-II 49.4). That is precisely why these appetites need well-formed habits, that is to say, the moral virtues—namely, to develop and integrate the appetites so that they are consistently inclined toward appropriate goods, in such a way as to elicit orderly activities directed toward genuinely good ends.

In the case of the will, the potential for inconsistency reflects its complex orientation toward diverse elements of our natural lives as social animals and rational beings. These innate inclinations can develop in such a way as to be at odds with one another, but they can also develop in tandem, in such a way that each shapes and promotes the other. If the different aspects of the will were naturally linked in such a way that they could never come into conflict with one another, the will would not need virtuous dispositions in order to function. But by the same token, we can develop justice and related virtues because these aspects of the will can be brought together in an appropriate way.

In order to move forward, we need to go back to a point that was developed in chapter 2. Aquinas sometimes gives the impression that the will emerges spontaneously and in fully functional form as soon as the agent is capable of rational thought. But when we take account of the wider context of his psychology, it appears unlikely that this is his view. The will is a human capacity, and like the other capacities of intellect and desire, it cannot function properly without the formation of stable habits, orienting it toward its innate objects in some relatively determinate way. These habits presuppose some kind of developmental process, which involves the engagement of the capacity in its immature or incipient form, and therefore it normally takes time to unfold. Aquinas himself says very little about what a process of this kind would involve, but by drawing on recent work in practical reason and the formation of desires, we can do so. Briefly, it unfolds through the agent's reflective experiences on his own activities, through which he begins to build up a sense of the kinds of activities that are in some way satisfying to him, and to generalize from these experiences. Recall that this process engages both the will and the intellect, working in tandem. The agent reflects intellectually on what he desires and enjoys, but these considerations presuppose that he actually does desire and enjoy some things. Initially, these desires may operate through the passions alone, as they probably do in small children, but as soon as the child begins to know what he likes and to act accordingly, his will is engaged, albeit in incipient forms.

In chapter 4 we saw that we can account for the formation of moral concepts in a similar way, through the development of the child's reflective grasp of the principles informing his relations to others. Through these processes, the child abstracts from his experiences of the moral emotions, such as we share with the other animals, to form fundamental concepts of obligation and injury. We might usefully frame these developmental trajectories as two ways of specifying the first unrestricted principle of practical reason and the first principle of justice. These two principles are formally similar, and they are developed through experience in similar ways. The agent's orientation toward the comprehensive good takes its starting point from the self-evident proposition that what is good is to be done, and what is evil is to be avoided. This formal principle is filled in, so to speak, as the agent develops a substantive conception of the good, comprehensively considered. In just the same way, the first principle of justice becomes meaningful only as the agent grasps what it means to be a human person, what this implies normatively, and what it means to relate appropriately to others. This level of comprehension implies a grasp of the other as a moral agent, a bearer of both rights and responsibilities. Thus, both the agent's disposition toward the good and her disposition to relate in a certain way toward others presuppose some development from formal conceptions of the good, to a substantive notion suited to a domain of activity.

There is nonetheless a relevant difference between the first principle of justice and the first unrestricted principle of practical reason. Considered as principles of the intellect, these are formally similar. However, they differ with respect to what we might think of as volitional significance. The first unrestricted principle represents the intellectual foundation for the inclination of the will toward a comprehensive good, or indeed, toward anything at all. To put the point in another way, the principle that good is to be pursued and its contrary avoided is always, so to speak, engaged. The will necessarily does incline toward some actual or perceived good, both in its fundamental commitment to a comprehensive end and through its particular choices. The first principle of justice similarly provides the will with the necessary starting points and structural principles for relating to others in appropriate ways. However, the will is not necessarily inclined to love the neighbor, appropriately or not, and the first principle of justice in itself cannot elicit that inclination. Rather, this inclination, like every other inclination toward a delimited good, is ultimately contingent on the will itself.

This dissimilarity between the first principle of practical reason in its unrestricted and restricted forms helps to explain how the paradoxical tension we are considering might arise. Every functional adult is necessarily oriented toward a comprehensive good that she regards as constituting her happiness or perfection. The inchoate conception of the good as formulated in the first unrestricted principle is always going to be specified in some way. Exactly how this conception is developed will depend to some extent on the agent's contingent inclinations and commitments, which is why almost any attractive pursuit or compelling ideal can be developed into someone's idea of his comprehensive good. Of course, someone can also incline toward her own interest and comfort as her comprehensive good, formulating this in terms of some sense of what it would mean to live an undisturbed, pleasant life. But in one way or another, whether well or badly, everyone who is capable of coherent activity at all will develop a rough comprehensive conception of the good through reflection on what he most truly and consistently desires.

However, no one is necessarily inclined to love the neighbor, appropriately or at all. Aquinas believes that everyone necessarily thinks of human relations in moral terms, but it does not follow that anyone is necessarily inclined to behave in accordance with the corresponding precepts. Even psychopaths seem to think of their relations to others in terms of moral notions of injury and entitlement, in the limited sense that they see themselves as entitled in various ways, and injured by those who do not meet their expectations. More typically, men and women are aware of the basic norms of fairness and respect as these are inculcated through their society, and if they are at all well-disposed, they will observe these most of the time. However, something more is required for the stable commitment to render to each that which is his or her right, in every case and without subordinating this aim to another. The agent must want to do this, consistently and as a matter of policy, and must also develop a sense of what, practically, this commitment might mean. This step is by no means inevitable. Indeed, the very pervasiveness of morality, as a set of conceptual categories and social practices, can obscure the extent to which someone is really committed to observing the claims of others. Men and women can lead lives of irreproachable fairness and consideration for others, only to discover in a moment of crisis that there is, after all, something that matters more to them than the claims of others.

At the same time, this line of analysis helps to clarify the processes through which the agent's commitment to a comprehensive good can develop in tandem with a disposition to respect the claims of others. These dispositions stem from the innate structures of the will, and while they need not emerge together in one individual, we can readily see how they might do so, through the same developmental processes through which the innate orientation of the will is focused on substantive objects.[21] As we have already seen,

21. In addition to the authors cited in chapter 4, see Barbara Rogoff, *Apprenticeship in*

these processes are intrinsically social and relational, involving continual interactions between the child, her caregivers, family members, peers, and the community to which she belongs. Her dispositions are formed through the active training and discipline of those closest to her, in accordance with communal ideals and paradigms of good behavior. She experiences pleasurable activities through work or play with family members and friends, and those around her introduce her to communal, religious, or aesthetic ideals that she may regard as inspiring or attractive. Thanks to their social character, these processes of formation elicit and shape the child's awareness of herself and others as free, morally significant agents. Practically speaking, her grasp of herself as one person among others and her emerging sense of the comprehensive good to which she is committed will initially be interconnected, in such a way that each qualifies the other.

We can easily think of examples illustrating this point. Children grow up as observers and active participants in the work, the social and religious lives, and the enjoyments of their families. Their earliest and best memories will often be tied to participation in the active life of the family—helping out with cooking or cleaning, working alongside a farmer in the fields, playing with mom's laptop and hoping not to crash it. If a child is involved in artistic or athletic activities, he is likely to practice at home, and then when he plays or performs the whole family will come to watch. As he matures, the adolescent begins to develop a sense of a satisfying life out of his memories and experiences of communal activities, which are pleasurable in part because they are communal. At the same time, his emerging sense of what it means to be a moral agent will be practically qualified by his sense of what it means to be an active, responsible participant in shared values and ideals. His paradigms for responsibility and accountability, his ideals for admirable or noble behavior, his sense of what others can claim from him and he can claim from them—all these will be practically bound up with the practices and values informing a particular way of life. A child who grows up in a farming family is likely to think of good men and women, initially, as good farmers, to admire someone for her patience and her responsive sympathy to nature, to think

---

Thinking: Cognitive Development in Social Contexts (Oxford: Oxford University Press, 1990), for a good discussion of the ways in which cultural factors shape cognitive and moral development. In what follows, I am also indebted to Alasdair MacIntyre's account of the ways in which the virtues are shaped through participation in shared practices; see *After Virtue*, 2nd ed. (Notre Dame: University of Notre Dame Press, 1984), 181–225. For a similar, more recent account, see Julia Annas, *Intelligent Virtue* (Oxford: Oxford University Press, 2011), 16–51.

of his own responsibilities initially in terms of his first experiences of caring for an animal or maintaining a garden, and the like.

I do not mean to imply through these examples that one's moral sense is necessarily defined or limited to the ideals and practices inherent to a given way of life. Much less would I claim that the fundamental precepts of non-maleficence and obligation are dependent on, or justified, in terms of the instrumental role that they play in sustaining a community or a way of life. These precepts stem directly from the moral character of human existence, which is why they are both general and stringently binding. My point, rather, is that our understanding of these precepts is initially bound up with particular claims and obligations, which are generally informed by more comprehensive ideals proper to some valuable way of life. This represents a critical first stage in the development of a sense of oneself, as someone who cares about others, and as someone who cares about the kinds of ideals that give meaning and direction to life.

As we have seen, our general moral concepts are necessarily grounded in concrete paradigms for right and good behavior, which will draw extensively on our initial paradigms for that which is good, worthy of commitment and choice. This same observation also applies to the agent's grasp of the comprehensive good, seen in relation to fundamental moral categories. The commitments and the moral sensibilities of young children and adolescents draw on concrete paradigms of all kinds, but that is not the end of the story. Mature adults likewise think of their central commitments and their responsibilities to others in concrete terms, bound up with practices, routine interactions with others, recurring conflicts, and in short, all the activities and interactions that go to make up a human life. No one wills the comprehensive good as an abstraction or commits herself to Beauty, or even to Music as embodied in performance. Rather, she wills to live in a certain way, implying certain choices and patterns of activity, in order to pursue a career as, for example, an opera singer. The general commitment of the will is inextricably bound up with the agent's grasp of what it would mean, concretely, to live out such a commitment, and with her ongoing inclinations toward the kinds of activities that go to make up a way of life.

Seen from this perspective, the potential tension between the agent's commitment to a comprehensive good and his commitment to particular justice is in one way easier to resolve than we might have thought, and in another way more difficult. It is easier to resolve because these commitments are practically integrated through the agent's commitment to a way of life that he envisions in terms of specific patterns of activity and forms of interrelationships. To the man or woman committed to an ideal of right relations with others, this way of life will be structured in accordance with the precepts of particular justice and the boundaries that these precepts set. At the same time, the agent's dispositions toward right relations will be focused by her particular commitments, in such a way as to give salience to the claims of others engaged in the same pursuits. In these contexts, the ideals of an objective way of life and the ideals of fairness in accordance with objective standards can come together in such a way that each reinforces and extends the other. Practically speaking, the impersonal ideals to which men and women commit themselves are never just impersonal ideals. They imply a collective way of life, structured in accordance with the demands of a common pursuit. Men and women formed in these communities will find it easy to love their fellows in the appropriate ways, valuing them as partners in shared commitments, and willingly rendering to each one the respect and consideration that is his or hers by right.

In this way, someone's commitments to an ideal will naturally—although not necessarily—lead toward a disposition toward others that looks a great deal like particular justice. But of course, this kind of situational regard is not justice. The scope of particular justice is limited to the sphere of interpersonal relations, but within that sphere, it is general and unrestricted. In order to move from a good disposition toward one's fellows to justice properly so called, the individual must make a further conceptual and volitional leap. She must generalize from the paradigms for appropriate behavior toward colleagues or community members in such a way as to fill in, so to speak, the innate moral conceptions of obligation and harm, and she must want to relate to all others in the same general ways as she relates to those in her circle. Furthermore, she must both understand and willingly accept that right relations to others generate claims that can be stringently binding and overriding, even in the face of conflicts with her most cherished ideals and commitments. I remarked earlier that, seen from the perspective of the kinds of rich, concretely grounded commitments by which most of us live, the potential conflict between these commitments and the disposition to respect the claims of all appears more difficult than we might have thought. The more keenly someone feels the claims of a splendid ideal or a cherished way of life, the more she may be tempted to set aside the rights of other individuals when they conflict with that claim.

Before proceeding, let me address a potential misunderstanding. Individual aspirations can come into conflict with others' wishes and interests in all kinds of ways. I do not want to imply that, in these kinds of conflicts, individuals should always be prepared to sacrifice their ideals and commitments simply because someone else asks them to do so. Wishes may be unreasonable or selfish, and interests may be limited or may be met in more than one way. In any human relationship or community, there will always be considerable scope for balancing the competing desires and needs of individuals in equitable ways. What I am talking about, in what follows, are conflicts between clear and serious moral claims and aspirations toward some comprehensive ideal, which cannot easily be resolved through ordinary processes of negotiation and mutual deference. These are the kinds of cases that seem to present a dilemma.

Nonetheless, this seeming dilemma is not, in fact, necessary. Comprehensive goods are comprehensive because they can be instantiated in many different ways. Someone might be faced with a hard choice between respecting the claims of others and pursuing one particular way of relating himself to an ideal of some kind. But it is difficult to imagine a situation in which someone would be forced to completely forgo active commitment to a comprehensive good in order to fulfill his obligations to another or to avoid injuring the other in some way. It is important to keep in mind that the ideals and impersonal goods to which we devote ourselves are themselves sustained through communal activities of all kinds, which offer many different ways of devoting oneself to a cherished ideal. If the agent's will is really oriented toward the impersonal good that he loves, and not toward an image of himself as exemplifying this ideal in a particular way, he can find ways in which to act on and express his love, while at the same time staying in right relationships with those around them.

Bernard Williams, in a much-discussed essay, poses what he believes to be an example of moral luck in a case based on the life of the painter Paul Gauguin.[22] Gauguin, as imagined by Williams, deserts his wife and family in order to become a great painter. He succeeds, and his success justifies his action, but if he had not succeeded, his action would not have been justified—that is the moral luck to which Williams refers. This line of analysis is not persuasive. The most immediately relevant objection is that Williams assumes that Gauguin is justified retrospectively in abandoning his family if he succeeds in doing what he sets out to do, namely, becoming a great painter. Aquinas would reply that Gauguin is not justified at all, at the time of his act or retrospectively, whether he succeeds or fails in his artistic aims.

22. Williams, "Moral Luck," in *Moral Luck*, 20–39.

This does not mean that Gauguin was faced with a choice between moral obligation and his love of art. It does mean that he was morally obliged to forswear his desire to relate himself to his ideals in one specific way. That undoubtedly would have been a great sacrifice, and no doubt the artistic world would have been poorer for it. We should not take these sacrifices and losses lightly. But the alternative view would imply that the lives and the appropriate claims of Gauguin's wife and children can be set aside for the sake of someone's desire to pursue an ideal in a particular way. Aquinas could not admit that, and neither should we.

Conflicts between the claims of individuals and the common good of a political community raise a different set of issues, because, as we noted above, the community itself exerts moral claims on its members. The community, acting through authorized representatives, can ask certain things of its members that no one individual could ask of another, and it can act aggressively to punish wrongdoing and to protect the community from external threats. Nonetheless, it does not follow that the community is morally justified in doing anything whatever, even in defense of communal security or in pursuit of serious social goods. While the limits of legitimate state power are currently under debate, we still see a wide international consensus that some kinds of actions are never legitimate; in legal terms, the associated norms are nonderogable, that is to say, they cannot be set aside, even in the most serious emergencies. Examples would include torture, enslavement, and genocide.[23]

Of course, people do question whether there are any limits to the legitimate exercise of communal power, especially under circumstances of conflict.[24] Many are persuaded by the claim that the political community has

23. For a definition of nonderogable norms as understood in current international law, see Mary Ellen O'Connell et al., *The International Legal System: Cases and Materials*, 7th ed. (St. Paul: Foundation Press, 2015), 457. Jeremy Waldron discusses the implications of these kinds of norms seen in relation to recent legal debates over torture, in "Torture and Positive Law," in *Torture, Terror, and Trade-offs: Philosophy for the White House* (Oxford: Oxford University Press, 2010), 186–260.

24. This debate has a very long history. Michael Walzer offers a powerful defense of the view that moral constraints can be set aside in situations of supreme emergency in *Just and Unjust Wars: A Moral Argument, with Historical Illustrations* (New York: Basic Books, 1977), 251–68. On the other side, see John Ford, "The Morality of Obliteration Bombing," *Theological Studies* 5.3 (1944): 261–69, 289; Thomas Nagel, "War and Massacre," in *Mortal Questions* (Cambridge: Cambridge University Press, 1979), 53–74; and Charles Fried and Gregory Fried, *Because It Is Wrong: Torture, Privacy and Presidential Power in the Age of Terror* (New York: Norton, 2010). Finally, for an extensive account of the development of public, academic, and

not only a right but a positive duty to do whatever is necessary to preserve its continued existence. These considerations may seem to present a dilemma for someone who is committed to respecting the claims of the individual, while at the same time being realistic about the exigencies of national security. Yet, once again, there is no dilemma here. The claim that communities are justified in doing whatever is necessary to preserve themselves is mistaken. It is true that a political association has an obligation to defend itself, because it acts on behalf of its members and the way of life that they share. This obligation sets political communities and their representatives apart from private individuals, who are not similarly obliged to defend themselves. Nonetheless, the moral considerations, and especially the exigent claims of individual men and women, set limits on the legitimate use of military force and state power. Each individual enjoys certain claims over against other individuals and the community itself, some of which can be set aside only through his own transgressions, and others that cannot be set aside at all. At the end of the day, these claims have to trump even the most serious questions of national security, if we want to take the moral significance of individual lives with the seriousness that it deserves.

To those who remain unconvinced, I would suggest a thought-experiment as a way of testing moral intuitions. Suppose that, through some dreadful circumstances, we were forced to preserve a vital national security interest through torturing a terrorist. If this seems acceptable, then consider whether it would also be permissible, in exactly the same circumstances, to torture the terrorist's child, who is perhaps innocently in possession of his father's secret? And if not, why not? This suggestion may seem shocking and unfair, but my point is that very few of us really believe that, in extremity, we are not bound by any moral constraints at all. Men and women of good will can disagree about where, in unusual and desperate circumstances, we should draw the line between what is acceptable and what is not. Nonetheless, the fact that we recognize the need for drawing some such line is itself an indication that we are aware of a first principle of justice, which provides a shared starting point for communal, as well as individual, discernment.

If the arguments of this section are sound, we may conclude that there is no necessary antinomy between the demands of particular justice and the agent's love of greater goods of all kinds. At the same time, it is clear that

---

legal views on the permissibility of extrajudicial use of force, indefinite detention, and torture in the wake of the terrorist attacks of 2001, see Joseph Margulies, *What Changed When Everything Changed: 9/11 and the Making of National Identity* (New Haven: Yale University Press, 2013).

these are stringent demands that call on us to sacrifice serious interests and to assume risks and losses that we might otherwise avoid. We may well question whether the stringent demands associated with justice can themselves be justified. Strictly speaking, this demand cannot be met. As we know, Aquinas claims that the moral status of the individual is built into the very meaning of what it is to be human—for this reason the relevant part of the first principle of justice is said to be self-evident. Thus, the moral status of the individual and the distinctive evaluative concepts implied by that status reflect necessary starting points and categories for thought within the domain of human relationships. We cannot prove or justify these claims and categories, because they themselves provide the necessary starting points for argument in this domain.

Yet the foundational status of the first principle of justice does not rule out a dialectical defense, which attempts to bring out the central role that it plays in the relevant field of beliefs and practices. This same general observation applies to all the foundational principles of speculative and practical reasoning. We cannot prove the law of noncontradiction, and yet we cannot envision a kind of reasoning that disregards this principle completely. Of course, we can imagine a succession of contradictory propositions, but, on reflection, we find that these cannot intelligibly be regarded as discursive reasoning. Similarly, we cannot prove that every causal operation is necessarily directed toward some goal, broadly identified with what is good, but we cannot make sense of the claim that movements without any kind of goal could count as causal operations. On reflection, it appears that our fundamental conceptions of what it means to reason and to act presuppose the first principles of speculative and practical reasoning.

It may appear that we cannot defend the first principle of justice in this way, because it would seem that men and women can and do disregard this principle. I am not so sure that rational agents can function in relation to others without drawing on this principle in some ways, even apart from any desire to respect the claims that it implies. At any rate, even if individuals can disregard the first principle of justice, communal associations cannot do so. It is difficult even to imagine a cohesive human society that has no norms of right relations at all. Unless individuals can relate to one another on a basis of shared expectations, grounded in fundamental concepts of obligation and injury, it is difficult to see how they could attain even the minimal levels of mutual trust and shared purpose necessary to sustain any kind of cooperative activities at all. Other social animals spontaneously observe the structuring principles of their association through the inclinations of moral passions, but men and women can relate together only through a shared conceptual sense of what it means to relate rightly to others. We do have examples of societies in decay that come very close to sheer anomie, but these serve only to illustrate the point—this kind of catastrophic breakdown of social relations occurs only under extreme duress, and the resultant associations are no longer viable communities.[25]

So far, we have reason to believe that normative commitments are necessary for communal life, but why these commitments in particular? Once again, we proceed by way of offering an account of what it would mean to integrate the claims of individuals and communal and general ideals into an overall way of life. We cannot prove that individuals have the moral status that they do, but we can spell out what this perspective implies for our moral practices and our overall way of life, in such a way as to bring out its compelling force. The thought is that a commitment to the claims of particular justice goes beyond the scope of one's relations to individuals; it implies a distinctive way of construing communal and general ideals, and it extends further, to envisioning a way of life. This way of life is intrinsically desirable in itself, in key part because it is structured around a sense of the limitations of human judgment and the need for collective solidarities. It is only through a commitment to particular justice and to the ideals of communal life implied by that commitment that we have even a possibility of living with others on a basis of mutual respect and forbearance.

Well-meaning men and women may well feel justified in overriding, or even obliged to override, the claims of other individuals in order to promote collective security or to promote the greater good, or even for the sake of those others themselves. The difficulty with taking up this stance, however, is that it carries with it an implicit commitment to an alternative way of life, one in which men and women cannot relate as equals. In a community of equals, each individual enjoys sufficient security and command over material resources to live a natural human life, enough freedom to act as the self-governing agent that he or she is, and enough respect to participate in processes of communal deliberation.[26] These claims will be qualified in

25. The classic example would be the Ik of northeastern Uganda, as described by anthropologist Colin Turnbull in *The Mountain People* (New York: Simon & Schuster, 1972).

26. This observation reflects, in a drastically condensed form, John Rawls's account of a decent society, structured through a consultative hierarchy, and Joseph Raz's analysis of the social conditions for individual freedom. See John Rawls, *The Law of Peoples* (Cambridge, MA: Harvard University Press, 1999), 62–77; and Joseph Raz, *The Morality of Freedom* (Oxford:

accordance with the exigencies of communal life, but only in such a way as to subordinate the individual to the community itself, not to the judgments or whims of any individual. Aquinas would say that this is the only kind of community in which authority and rule are consistent with the free status that men and women naturally enjoy, simply by virtue of shared humanity. The alternative would be a community in which the claims of some may be subordinated to the interests of others—to a community structured in accordance with principles of dominion and servility.

While more could be said in defense of Aquinas's commitment to the overriding claims of individuals, I hope I have at least indicated why so many, myself included, find it to be compelling. It will be apparent by now that Aquinas's conception of particular justice implies something more than the claims and obligations of individuals, important though these are. It implies a commitment to a way of life that is integrally bound up with a certain conception of human society at its best. In this way, the object of particular justice, the right, is connected to the object of general justice, the common good. The virtue of justice implies a commitment to a way of life, and we can grasp what justice means only when we have at least the outlines of that way of life before us.

Conclusion

This project began with a contrast between Aquinas's approach to justice as a virtue and the theories of virtue developed by John Rawls and his interlocutors. The differences do not run, as we might have expected, along the lines of a familiar distinction between ideals of virtue and rules of justice; on the contrary, Aquinas associates justice with overriding, strictly binding precepts of nonmaleficence. The differences between these two perspectives are more fundamental. For Rawls and his interlocutors, justice is embodied in social and institutional systems, insofar as they operate in accordance with norms of equality, respect for and promotion of personal autonomy, or the like. Justice thus understood can be said to be a virtue, but only in an extended sense, much as truth can be said to be the first virtue of an intellectual construct. For whatever reasons, Aquinas does not offer a theory of justice in this sense. What he does offer is an account of justice as a personal virtue, a praiseworthy disposition of the will that places the individual in

---

Clarendon, 1986), 217–44, 369–430. Of course, I do not claim that either would endorse the way in which I develop their views.

right relations to all those around her. It may appear that Aquinas and our own contemporaries are, in effect, talking past one another in their respective inquiries into justice.

Yet these differences, fundamental as they are, should not be overstated. The personal virtue of justice cannot simply be equated with justice as embodied in social arrangements, and yet the term "justice" is not simply used equivocally in these contexts, either. In each case, justice is identified by reference to overlapping sets of ideals, normative concepts, and expectations, including an ideal of equality, concepts of right, claim, and wrongful harm, and an expectation that the demands of justice are in some ways overriding. Furthermore, each of these ways of thinking about justice captures some aspects of this comprehensive ideal in a way that the other does not. In this book, I have focused on justice as a personal virtue, but a fuller treatment of justice as ideal and practice would need to be extended to institutional arrangements as well. But by the same token, theories of justice developed along contemporary lines and focused on, if not limited to, social and institutional systems are also incomplete, seen from the perspective of justice considered as a virtue. Not everyone will find both of these claims persuasive, and some further comment on each is therefore in order.

First, it is important to recognize that contemporary theories of justice are addressed to practical concerns that present themselves inescapably to all of us, especially—but not only—in the urban, mobile, and complex communities spreading throughout the world today. Our societies cannot function without extensive, complex, and impersonal institutions, bureaucracies, and social systems of all kinds. Most men and women today understand quite well that these systems are precisely that—impersonal systems of interlocking roles and functions, which do not depend fundamentally on the personal dispositions and judgments of the individuals occupying those roles. The impersonal character of institutional structures goes a long way toward explaining why institutions of all kind, and especially large bureaucracies, are so generally despised. Men and women are naturally oriented toward interpersonal associations, which offer them a respected place and are responsive to their individual needs. Bureaucracies cannot provide anything of the sort. Nonetheless, they play an indispensable role within any human society, and they necessarily play a very considerable part in contemporary life. It would be sheer irresponsibility on the part of a moralist to ignore them or to try to envision a world in which they did not exist. We create these systems because we cannot live without them, and we have an exigent responsibility to set them up in such a way as to express and promote our best social ideals of justice, respect, and sufficiency.

At the same time, Aquinas's account of justice as a virtue focuses on some aspects of justice that contemporary theories do not address, except perhaps in cursory ways. Most fundamentally, Aquinas's account of justice is grounded in a normative analysis of a specific kind, displaying the many ways in which justice both presupposes and goes beyond the values intrinsic to our natural life, and to the more restricted ideals of the other moral virtues. In the process of developing this account, he sets out a cogent and attractive account of justice as a disposition and a set of practices that we ought to pursue and that we might plausibly regard as a key part of an admirable and satisfying way of life. He grounds his account of particular justice in an ideal of a natural equality of status, and through his detailed analysis of the precepts associated with that virtue, he offers an extended account of what it means, conceptually and practically, to regard the individual as one's peer, one's neighbor, someone whose claims and needs place obligations on oneself. He offers us good reasons to regard justice as a moral claim and not simply a social desideratum, while at the same time offering enough by way of context and explanation to indicate what a commitment to justice would practically entail.

This brings us to a further aspect of Aquinas's account of justice. That is, justice as a moral ideal is grounded in natural values, and yet it goes beyond these—or perhaps it would be better to say that the moral virtue of justice reflects the self-reflective appropriation of inchoate natural values, through which these are integrated into distinctively rational normative ideals. The same can be said about all the moral virtues, each of which both presupposes natural values and transforms them in such a way as to generate a qualitatively different normative claim. We are now in a position to appreciate more fully what this general observation means with respect to justice. We are, after all, social animals, naturally drawn to a communal, structured way of life. To a very considerable extent, the practices that sustain our lives together emerge spontaneously, and they take forms analogous to those found among other primates. These fundamental structural forms provide us with a basic grammar, as it were, for deference, recognition, and respect, as well as all the normative claims that sustain us in right relations with one another. So far from setting the right and the good in opposition to one another, Aquinas grounds the right in the good without compromising its overriding force.

Aquinas's account thus has the further advantage of confirming a widespread intuition that there is such a thing as a natural justice, which is in some way prior to the specific practices, enactments, or institutional structures of a given society. Without some kind of preconventional standards for fairness and equity, we would have no basis for critiquing our particular social arrangements or addressing claims that emerge outside the boundaries of any one community. That, at least, would seem to be one basis for our intuitive sense of natural justice. Yet it is difficult to account for this intuition, or even to express it, within the framework of many contemporary theories of justice, which are fundamentally and almost exclusively focused on institutional structures and social systems. Correlatively, the institutional focus of these theories goes together with a degree of uncertainty about the scope of one's own claims. Do the norms and structural forms of fairness and equality embodied in just institutions reflect generally accessible ideals that ought to be generally observed, even if practically they must sometimes be approximated? Or should we take these to be pragmatic accounts of the normative claims intrinsic to our own communally specific political ideals and way of life?

For both Aquinas and his interlocutors, the claims of natural right and natural justice do not generate an alternative social and legal system of their own, standing alongside the conventions of particular societies and the customary practices constituting the law of nations. Rather, natural principles are expressed in and through these conventional forms, which represent alternative and, to some degree, incompatible construals of natural social practices and values. We cannot expect Aquinas's account of justice, or medieval conceptions of natural right more generally, to provide a practical ideal of communal justice that is at once universally binding and concrete enough to be put into practice. The natural law is not a charter for a world society. However, Aquinas's account of justice as a personal virtue, grounded in and therefore responsive to natural values, does imply that the contingencies inherent in our institutional and social ideals of justice do not go all the way down. These conventional forms can be understood as expressions, or perhaps distortions, of a kind of natural justice that is grounded in the values intrinsic to our socially structured way of life.

Aquinas's account of justice and contemporary theories of justice thus represent two distinct, yet potentially complementary, ways of thinking about this complex moral and social ideal. We have good reasons to try to bring these perspectives together. The disposition of justice, by its own inner logic, draws the agent to create and support certain kinds of social conventions, an inclination that is mediated through a basic disposition to love the neighbor and an informed grasp of what that means.

The virtue of justice is only one among many virtues, and for Aquinas, it is not even the highest virtue. That place is reserved for charity, the theological virtue of the will that brings men and women into friendship with God. Even within the scope of the connatural virtues, the virtue of religion, which is directed toward paying due homage to a deity, is considered to be a higher virtue than justice properly so called. Seen from our contemporary perspective, we face serious moral questions that cannot readily be fitted into the framework of justice, pertaining to our responsibilities for the environment and the nonhuman world.

Yet even if justice is not the only or the highest virtue, it sets the moral boundaries of our lives. It provides the framework for the exercise of religion and charity, and it places limits on what we can do in defense of any more comprehensive aim. If we cannot love the neighbor whom we can see, we will not be able rightly to love God, whom we do not see; and by the same token, we will not be able to love and serve the many greater goods that invite our devotion. No matter what else we may or must do, we are always obliged to render to each that which is his or her right. Morality and religion may demand more, but we can never do less.

Bibliography

Primary Sources

Aquinas, Thomas. *De malo*. In *Quaestiones disputatae*, edited by P. Bazzi, M. Calcaterra, T. S. Centi, E. Odetto, and P. M. Pession, 2:439–699. Turin and Rome: Maretti, 1953.

————. *In Aristotelis librum de anima commentarium*. Edited by P. F. Angeli M. Pirotta. 4th ed. Turin and Rome: Maretti, 1959.

————. *Summa theologica*. In *Opera Omnia iussa edita Leonis XIII P.M.*, vols. 4–12. Rome: Ex Typographia Polyglotta S.C. de Propaganda Fide, 1888–1906.

————. *Super Librum Dionysii De divinis nominibus*. In *Opera Omnia*, vol. 29. Paris: Apud Ludovicum Vives, 1871–80.

Aristotle. *Aristotle's Nicomachean Ethics*. Translated by Robert C. Bartlett and Susan D. Collins. Chicago: University of Chicago Press, 2011.

————. *Aristotle's Politics*. Translated by Carnes Lord. 2nd ed. Chicago: University of Chicago Press, 2013; originally 1984.

Cicero. *De Inventione*. Loeb Classical Library. Cambridge, MA: Harvard University Press, 1940.

Secondary Sources

Annas, Julia. *Intelligent Virtue*. Oxford: Oxford University Press, 2001.

————. *The Morality of Happiness*. Oxford: Oxford University Press, 1995.

————. *Platonic Ethics, Old and New*. Ithaca, NY: Cornell University Press, 1999.

Anscombe, G. E. M. *Intention*. 2nd ed. Ithaca, NY: Cornell University Press, 1963; originally 1957.

————. "Medalist's Address: Action, Intention, and Double Effect." *Proceedings of the American Catholic Philosophical Association* 56 (1982): 12–25.

————. "Under a Description." In *The Collected Philosophical Papers of G. E. M. Anscombe*, 2:208–19. Oxford: Basil Blackwell, 1981; originally 1979.

Bartlett, Robert C., and Susan D. Collins. "Interpretative Essay." In *Aristotle's Nicomachean Ethics*, translated by Robert C. Bartlett and Susan D. Collins, 237–302. Chicago: University of Chicago Press, 2011.

Bejczy, István P. "Law and Ethics: Twelfth-Century Jurists on the Virtue of Justice." *Viator* 2.3 (2005): 197–216.

———. "The Problem of Natural Virtue." In *Virtue and Ethics in the Twelfth Century*, edited by István P. Bejczy and Richard G. Newhauser, 133–54. Leiden: Brill, 2005.

Bennett, Jonathan. *The Act Itself*. Oxford: Clarendon, 1995.

Bisson, Thomas N. *The Crisis of the Twelfth Century: Power, Lordship, and the Origins of European Government*. Princeton: Princeton University Press, 2009.

Bloom, Paul. *Just Babies: The Origins of Good and Evil*. New York: Crown Publishers, 2013.

Boehm, Christopher. *Moral Origins: The Evolution of Virtue, Altruism, and Shame*. New York: Basic Books, 2012.

Bolin, John. *Contingency and Fortune in Aquinas' Ethics*. Cambridge: Cambridge University Press, 1999.

Boyle, Joseph. "Toward Understanding the Principle of Double Effect." In *The Doctrine of Double Effect: Philosophers Debate a Controversial Moral Principle*, edited by P. A. Woodward, 7–22. Notre Dame: University of Notre Dame Press, 2001.

Brandt, Richard B. *Morality, Utilitarianism, and Rights*. Cambridge: Cambridge University Press, 1992.

Brink, David O. *Moral Realism and the Foundations of Ethics*. Cambridge: Cambridge University Press, 1989.

Brock, Stephen L. *Action and Conduct: Thomas Aquinas and the Theory of Action*. Edinburgh: T. & T. Clark, 1998.

———. "Causality and Necessity in Thomas Aquinas." *Quaestio* 2.1 (2002): 217–40.

Brundage, James A. *The Medieval Origins of the Legal Profession: Canonists, Civilians, and Courts*. Chicago: University of Chicago Press, 2008.

Bushlack, Thomas. *Politics for a Pilgrim Church: A Thomistic Theory of Civic Virtue*. Grand Rapids: Eerdmans, 2015.

Cates, Diana. *Aquinas on the Emotions: A Religious-Ethical Inquiry*. Washington, DC: Georgetown University Press, 2009.

Chenu, M. D. *Toward Understanding St. Thomas*. Translated by Albert M. Landry and Dominic Hughes. Chicago: Regnery, 1964.

Coleman, Janet. "MacIntyre and Aquinas." In *After MacIntyre: Critical Perspectives on the Work of Alasdair MacIntyre*, edited by John Horton and Susan Mendes, 65–90. Notre Dame: University of Notre Dame Press, 1994.

———. "Property and Poverty." In *The Cambridge History of Medieval Political Thought, c. 350–c. 1450*, edited by J. H. Burns, 607–48. Cambridge: Cambridge University Press, 1988.

Constable, Giles. *The Reformation of the Twelfth Century*. Cambridge: Cambridge University Press, 1998.

Coons, John E., and Patrick M. Brennan. *By Nature Equal: The Anatomy of a Western Insight*. Princeton: Princeton University Press, 1999.

Cronin, Kieran. *Rights and Christian Ethics*. Cambridge: Cambridge University Press, 1992.

Damasio, Antonio B. *Descartes' Error: Emotion, Reason, and the Human Brain*. New York: Avon Books, 1994.

D'Arcy, Eric. *Human Acts: An Essay in Their Moral Evaluation*. Oxford: Clarendon, 1963.

Davidson, Donald. *Essays on Actions and Events*. 2nd ed. Oxford: Clarendon, 2001.

De Caro, Mario, and David MacArthur, eds. *Naturalism and Normativity*. New York: Columbia University Press, 2010.

Decosimo, David. *Ethics as a Work of Charity: Thomas Aquinas and Pagan Virtue*. Stanford: Stanford University Press, 2014.

De Sousa, Ronald. "Emotion." In *The Stanford Encyclopedia of Philosophy*, edited by Edward N. Zalta. Last revised January 21, 2013. http://plato.stanford.edu/archives/spr2014/entries/emotion.

De Waal, Frans. *Good Natured: The Origins of Right and Wrong in Human and Other Animals*. Cambridge, MA: Harvard University Press, 1996.

———. *Primates and Philosophers: How Morality Evolved*. Edited by Stephen Macedo and Josiah Ober. Princeton: Princeton University Press, 2006.

De Waal, Frans B. M., and Sarah F. Brosnan. "Fairness in Animals: Where To from Here?" *Social Justice Research* 25 (2012): 336–51.

Dworkin, Ronald. *Law's Empire*. Cambridge, MA: Harvard University Press, Belknap Press, 1986.

———. *Sovereign Virtue: The Theory and Practice of Equality*. Cambridge, MA: Harvard University Press, 2000.

Engstrom, Stephen, and Jennifer Whiting. Introduction to *Aristotle, Kant, and the Stoics: Rethinking Happiness and Duty*, edited by Stephen Engstrom and Jennifer Whiting, 1–18. Cambridge: Cambridge University Press, 1996.

Finnis, John. *Aquinas: Moral, Political, and Legal Theory*. Oxford: Oxford University Press, 1998.

———. *Natural Law and Natural Rights*. Oxford: Clarendon, 1980.

Finnis, John, Germain Grisez, and Joseph Boyle. "'Direct' and 'Indirect': A Reply to Critics of Our Action Theory." *Thomist* 65 (2001): 1–44.

Flannery, Kevin. *Acts amid Precepts*. Washington, DC: Catholic University of America Press, 2001.

Foot, Philippa. *Natural Goodness*. Oxford: Oxford University Press, 2001.

Ford, John C. "The Morality of Obliteration Bombing." *Theological Studies* 5.3 (1944): 261–309.

Frede, Michael. *A Free Will: Origins of the Notion in Ancient Thought*. Berkeley: University of California Press, 2012.

Fried, Charles. *Right and Wrong*. Cambridge, MA: Harvard University Press, 1978.

Fried, Charles, and Gregory Fried. *Because It Is Wrong: Torture, Privacy, and Presidential Power in the Age of Terror*. New York: Norton, 2010.

Gilligan, Carol. *In a Different Voice: Psychological Theory and Women's Development*. Cambridge, MA: Harvard University Press, 1982.

Gondreau, Paul. "The Humanity of Christ, the Incarnate Word." In *The Theology of

Thomas Aquinas, edited by Rik van Nieuwenhove and Joseph Wawrykow, 222–51. Notre Dame: University of Notre Dame Press, 2005.

Gopnik, Alison. *The Philosophical Baby: What Children's Minds Tell Us about Truth, Love, and the Meaning of Life.* New York: Farrar, Straus & Giroux, 2009.

Greene, Joshua, and Jonathan Haidt. "How (and Where) Does Moral Judgment Work?" *Trends in Cognitive Sciences* 6.12 (2002): 517–23.

Grisez, Germain. *The Way of the Lord Jesus.* Volume 1: *Christian Moral Principles*; volume 2: *Living a Christian Life.* Chicago: Franciscan Herald Press, 1983–93.

Grisez, Germain, Joseph Boyle, and John Finnis. "Practical Principles, Moral Truth and Ultimate Ends." *American Journal of Jurisprudence* 32 (1987): 99–151.

Haidt, Jonathan. "The Moral Emotions." In *The Handbook of Affective Sciences*, edited by Richard J. Davidson, Klaus R. Scherer, and H. Hill Goldsmith, 852–70. Oxford: Oxford University Press, 2009.

Hause, Jeffrey. "Aquinas on Aristotelian Justice: Defender, Destroyer, Subverter, or Surveyor?" In *Aquinas and the Nicomachean Ethics*, edited by Tobias Hoffmann, Jörn Müller, and Matthias Perkams, 146–64. Cambridge: Cambridge University Press, 2013.

Hermann, Barbara. *The Practice of Moral Judgment.* Cambridge, MA: Harvard University Press, 1993.

Hoose, Bernard. *Proportionalism: The American Debate and Its European Roots.* Washington, DC: Georgetown University Press, 1987.

Huebner, Bryce, Susan Dwyer, and Marc Hauser. "The Role of Emotion in Moral Psychology." *Trends in Cognitive Sciences* 13.1 (2008): 1–6.

Hursthouse, Rosalind. *On Virtue Ethics.* Oxford: Oxford University Press, 1999.

Kent, Bonnie. "Losable Virtue: Aquinas on Character and Will." In *Aquinas and the Nicomachean Ethics*, edited by Tobias Hoffmann, Jörn Müller, and Matthias Perkams, 91–109. Cambridge: Cambridge University Press, 2013.

———. *Virtues of the Will: The Transformation of Ethics in the Late Thirteenth Century.* Washington, DC: Catholic University of America Press, 1995.

Korsgaard, Christine. "Morality and the Distinctiveness of Human Action." In *Primates and Philosophers: How Morality Evolved*, edited by Stephen Macedo and Josiah Ober, 98–119. Princeton: Princeton University Press, 2006.

———. *Self-Constitution: Agency, Identity, and Integrity.* Oxford: Oxford University Press, 2009.

———. *The Sources of Normativity.* Cambridge: Cambridge University Press, 1996.

Kovesi, Julius. *Moral Notions.* London: Routledge, 1967.

Kuttner, Stephan. "A Forgotten Definition of Justice." *Mélanges G. Fransen, Studia Gratiana* 20 (1976): 75–109.

Leary, Mark R. "The Self and Emotion: The Role of Self-Reflection in the Generation and Regulation of Affective Experience." In *The Handbook of Affective Sciences*, edited by Richard J. Davidson, Klaus R. Scherer, and H. Hill Goldsmith, 773–86. Oxford: Oxford University Press, 2009.

Lisska, Anthony J. *Aquinas's Theory of the Natural Law: An Analytic Reconstruction.* Oxford: Clarendon, 1996.

Long, Steven A. "A Brief Disquisition regarding the Nature of the Object of the Moral Act according to St. Thomas Aquinas." *Thomist* 67 (2003): 45–71.

Lottin, Odon. "Le concept de justice chez les théologiens du moyen âge avant l'introduction d'Aristote." *Revue Thomiste* 44 (1938): 511–21.

———. "Les premières définitions et classifications des vertus au moyen âge." In *Psychologie et morale aux XIIe et XIIIe siècles*, 3:100–150. Louvain: Abbaye du Mont César, 1948.

———. "Les vertus cardinales et leurs ramifications chez les théologiens de 1230 à 1250." In *Psychologie et morale aux XIIe et XIIIe siècles*, 3:154–93. Louvain: Abbaye du Mont César, 1948.

———. "Libre arbitre et liberté depuis saint Anselme jusqu'à la fin du XIIIe siècle." In *Psychologie et morale aux XIIe et XIIIe siècles*, 1:11–389. Louvain: Abbaye du Mont César, 1942.

MacDonald, Scott. "Aquinas' Libertarian Account of Free Choice." *Revue Internationale de Philosophie* 52 (1998): 309–28.

MacIntyre, Alasdair. *After Virtue*. 2nd ed. Notre Dame: University of Notre Dame Press, 1984.

Margulies, Joseph. *What Changed When Everything Changed: 9/11 and the Making of National Identity*. New Haven: Yale University Press, 2013.

Mattison, William, III. "Can Christians Possess the Acquired Virtues?" *Theological Studies* 72 (2011): 558–85.

McInerny, Ralph. *Aquinas on Human Action: A Theory of Practice*. Washington, DC: Catholic University of America Press, 1992.

———. *Ethica Thomistica: The Moral Philosophy of Thomas Aquinas*. Rev. ed. Washington, DC: Catholic University of America Press, 1997; originally 1982.

———. "Grisez and Thomism." In *The Revival of Natural Law: Philosophical, Theological, and Ethical Responses to the Finnis-Grisez School*, edited by Nigel Biggar and Rufus Black, 53–72. Sydney: Ashgate, 2000.

Millgram, Elijah. *Practical Induction*. Cambridge, MA: Harvard University Press, 1997.

———. "Practical Reason and the Structure of Actions." In *The Stanford Encyclopedia of Philosophy*, edited by Edward N. Zalta. Last revised March 26, 2012. http://plato.stanford.edu/entries/practical-reason-action.

Miner, Robert. *Thomas Aquinas on the Passions*. Cambridge: Cambridge University Press, 2009.

Nederman, Cary J. "Aristotelianism and the Origins of 'Political Science' in the Twelfth Century." *Journal of the History of Ideas* 52 (1991): 179–94.

Newman, Joseph P., and Amanda R. Lorenz. "Response Modulation and Emotion Processing: Implications for Psychopathy and Other Dysregulatory Psychopathology." In *The Handbook of Affective Sciences*, edited by Richard J. Davidson, Klaus R. Scherer, and H. Hill Goldsmith, 904–29. Oxford: Oxford University Press, 2009.

Nozick, Robert. *Anarchy, State, and Utopia*. New York: Basic Books, 1974.

Nussbaum, Martha C. *Love's Knowledge: Essays on Philosophy and Literature*. Oxford: Oxford University Press, 1990.

————. *Women and Human Development: The Capabilities Approach.* Cambridge: Cambridge University Press, 2000.

O'Brien, Matthew B., and Robert C. Koons. "Objects of Intention: A Hylomorphic Critique of the New Natural Law Theory." *American Catholic Philosophical Quarterly* 86.4 (2012): 655-703.

O'Connell, Mary Ellen, Richard F. Scott, Naomi Roht-Arriaza, and Daniel Bradlow. *The International Legal System: Cases and Materials.* 7th ed. St. Paul: Foundation Press, 2015.

O'Grady, Paul. "Philosophical Theology and Analytical Philosophy in Aquinas." In *The Theology of Thomas Aquinas,* edited by Rik van Nieuwenhove and Joseph Wawrykow, 416-43. Notre Dame: University of Notre Dame Press, 2005.

O'Neill, Onora. *Towards Justice and Virtue: A Constructive Account of Practical Reasoning.* Cambridge: Cambridge University Press, 1996.

Pasnau, Robert. *Thomas Aquinas on Human Nature: A Philosophical Study of "Summa Theologiae" Ia 75-89.* Cambridge: Cambridge University Press, 2002.

Perkams, Matthias. "Aquinas on Choice, Will and Voluntary Action." In *Aquinas and the Nicomachean Ethics,* edited by Tobias Hoffmann, Jörn Müller, and Matthias Perkams, 72-90. Cambridge: Cambridge University Press, 2013.

Porter, Jean. *Ministers of the Law: A Natural Law Theory of Legal Authority.* Grand Rapids: Eerdmans, 2010.

————. *Moral Action and Christian Ethics.* Cambridge: Cambridge University Press, 1995.

————. *Natural and Divine Law: Reclaiming the Tradition for Christian Ethics.* Grand Rapids: Eerdmans, 1999.

————. *Nature as Reason: A Thomistic Theory of the Natural Law.* Grand Rapids: Eerdmans, 2005.

————. "Reason, Nature and the End of Human Life: A Consideration of John Finnis's *Aquinas." Journal of Religion* 80.3 (2000): 476-84.

Proctor, Darby, and Sarah Brosnan. "Political Primates: What Other Primates Can Tell Us about the Evolutionary Roots of Our Own Political Behavior." In *Man Is by Nature a Political Animal: Evolution, Biology, and Politics,* edited by Peter K. Hatemi and Rose McDermott, 47-72. Chicago: University of Chicago Press, 2011.

Rawls, John. *The Law of Peoples.* Cambridge, MA: Harvard University Press, 2001.

————. *A Theory of Justice.* Rev. ed. Cambridge, MA: Harvard University Press, 1999; originally 1971.

Raz, Joseph. *The Morality of Freedom.* Oxford: Clarendon, 1988.

Reid, Charles J., Jr. "The Canonistic Contribution to the Western Rights Tradition: An Historical Inquiry." *Boston College Law Review* 33.1 (1991): 37-92.

————. *Power over the Body, Equality in the Family: Rights and Domestic Relations in Medieval Canon Law.* Grand Rapids: Eerdmans, 2004.

Rist, John. *Augustine: Ancient Thought Baptized.* Cambridge: Cambridge University Press, 1994.

Rogers, Eugene. *Thomas Aquinas and Karl Barth: Sacred Doctrine and the Natural Knowledge of God.* Notre Dame: University of Notre Dame Press, 1995.

Rogoff, Barbara. *Apprenticeship in Thinking: Cognitive Development in Social Contexts.* Oxford: Oxford University Press, 1990.

Rorty, Amélie. *Essays in Aristotle's Ethics.* Berkeley: University of California Press, 1980.

Ryan, Richard M., and Edward L. Deci. "On Happiness and Human Potentials: A Review of Research on Hedonic and Eudaimonic Well-Being." *American Review of Psychology* 52 (2001): 141–66.

Sahaydachny, Antonia Bocarius. "The Marriage of Unfree Persons: Twelfth Century Decretals and Letters." In *De jure canonico medii aevi: Festschrift für Rudolf Weigand,* edited by Peter Landau, 483–506. Studia Gratiana 27. Rome: Libreria Ateneo Salesiano, 1996.

Scheffler, Samuel. *Death and the Afterlife.* Oxford: Oxford University Press, 2013.

Schneewind, J. B. *The Invention of Autonomy: A History of Modern Moral Philosophy.* Cambridge: Cambridge University Press, 1997.

Slote, Michael. "Agent-Based Virtue Ethics." In *Virtue Ethics,* edited by Roger Crisp and Michael Slote, 239–62. Oxford: Oxford University Press, 1997.

———. "Justice as a Virtue." In *Stanford Encyclopedia of Philosophy,* edited by Edward N. Zalta. Last revised July 22, 2014. http://plato.stanford.edu/archives/fall2014/entries/justice-virtue.

Southern, R. W. *Scholastic Humanism and the Unification of Europe.* Volume 1. Oxford: Blackwell, 1995.

Stump, Eleonore. *Aquinas.* London: Routledge, 2003.

Taylor, Gabriele. *Deadly Vices.* Oxford: Oxford University Press, 2006.

Tierney, Brian. *The Idea of Natural Rights: Studies on Natural Rights, Natural Law, and Church Law, 1150–1625.* Atlanta: Scholars Press, 1997.

———. *Religion, Law, and the Growth of Constitutional Thought, 1150–1650.* 1982. Reprint, Cambridge: Cambridge University Press, 2008.

Todd, S. C. "The Language of Law in Classical Athens." In *The Moral World of the Law,* edited by Peter Coss, 17–36. Cambridge: Cambridge University Press, 2000.

Tomasello, Michael. *The Cultural Origins of Human Cognition.* Cambridge, MA: Harvard University Press, 1999.

———. *A Natural History of Human Thinking.* Cambridge, MA: Harvard University Press, 2014.

Torrell, Jean-Pierre. *Saint Thomas Aquinas: The Person and His Work.* Volume 1. Translated by Robert Royal. Washington, DC: Catholic University of America Press, 2005.

Tuck, Richard. *Natural Rights Theories: Their Origin and Development.* Cambridge: Cambridge University Press, 1979.

Turnbull, Colin M. *The Mountain People.* New York: Simon & Schuster, 1972.

Urmson, J. O. "Aristotle's Doctrine of the Mean." *American Philosophical Quarterly* 10.3 (1973): 223–30.

Vera, Luis. "Tablets of Flesh: Memory, Media, and the Perfection of the Image in Digital Societies." PhD diss., University of Notre Dame, 2015.

Vogler, Candace. "Aristotle, Aquinas, Anscombe, and the New Virtue Ethics." In *Aqui-*

nas and the Nicomachean Ethics, edited by Tobias Hoffmann, Jörn Müller, and Matthias Perkams, 239–57. Cambridge: Cambridge University Press, 2013.

———. *Reasonably Vicious*. Cambridge, MA: Harvard University Press, 2002.

Waldron, Jeremy. *Torture, Terror, and Trade-Offs: Philosophy for the White House*. Oxford: Oxford University Press, 2010.

Walzer, Michael. *Just and Unjust Wars: A Moral Argument with Historical Illustrations*. New York: Basic Books, 1977.

Warren, Rick. *The Purpose-Driven Life: What on Earth Am I Here For?* Grand Rapids: Zondervan, 2002.

Wawrykow, Joseph. *God's Grace and Human Action: "Merit" in the Theology of Thomas Aquinas*. Notre Dame: University of Notre Dame Press, 1995.

———. "Hypostatic Union." In *The Theology of Thomas Aquinas*, edited by Rik Van Nieuwenhove and Joseph Wawrykow, 222–51. Notre Dame: University of Notre Dame Press, 2005.

Wedgwood, Ralph. *The Nature of Normativity*. Oxford: Oxford University Press, 2007.

Weiland, George. "Happiness: The Perfection of Man." In *The Cambridge History of Later Medieval Philosophy from the Rediscovery of Aristotle to the Disintegration of Scholasticism, 1100–1600*, edited by Norman Kretzmann, Anthony Kenny, and Jan Pinborg, 673–86. Cambridge: Cambridge University Press, 1982.

Wenzel, Siegfried. Introduction to *Summa Virtutum de Remediis Animae*, edited by Siegfried Wenzel, 2–12. Athens: University of Georgia Press, 1984.

Westberg, Daniel. *Right Practical Reason: Aristotle, Action, and Prudence in Aquinas*. Oxford: Clarendon, 1994.

Williams, Bernard. "Internal and External Reasons." In *Moral Luck: Philosophical Papers, 1973–1980*, 101–13. Cambridge: Cambridge University Press, 1981; originally 1980.

Wolterstorff, Nicholas. *Justice: Rights and Wrongs*. Princeton: Princeton University Press, 2008.

———. *Justice in Love*. Grand Rapids: Eerdmans, 2011.

Name Index

Albert the Great, 163
Annas, Julia, 8n13, 11n19, 11n20, 15n27,
    33n47, 60n1, 119n8, 219n37, 220n38,
    243n7, 243n8, 244, 261n21
Anscombe, Elizabeth, 175n3, 208n30,
    211n33, 218n36
Aristotle, 2, 4, 8–9, 10n18, 16–17, 18,
    26–27, 36–37, 38, 47, 51, 53, 57, 64–65,
    67, 69n11, 117–19, 120–21, 122, 126,
    129, 131, 132, 134, 139–40, 143, 191, 209,
    229–30, 232, 240, 253
Augustine, 18, 54, 59–60, 63–64, 243

Bartlett, Robert C., 8n14
Bejczy, István P., 18n33
Bennett, Jonathan, 182n11
Bisson, Thomas N., 121n11
Bloom, Paul, 188n13, 190n17, 193–94, 196
Boehm, Christopher, 189n16, 201n25
Bolin, John, 243n5
Boyle, Joseph, 206n29, 218n36
Brandt, Richard B., 132n18
Brennan, Patrick M., 118n6
Brink, David O., 236n4
Brock, Stephen L., 13n24, 79n17, 83,
    176n4, 177n7, 208n30
Brosnan, Sarah F., 188n13, 201n25
Brundage, James A., 122, 136n23
Bushlack, Thomas, 3n6

Cates, Diana, 67n8
Chenu, M. D., 52n59

Cicero, 15, 42, 49–50, 53, 117, 125, 127, 131
Coleman, Janet, 143n30, 154n38
Collins, Susan D., 8n14
Constable, Giles, 121n11, 122n12
Coons, John E., 118n6
Cronin, Kieran, 135n22

Damasio, Antonio B., 198n23
D'Arcy, John, 208n30
Davidson, Donald, 175n3, 177n7, 208n30
Deci, Edward L., 243n6
Decosimo, David, 15n27, 19n34
de Sousa, Ronald, 68n9
de Waal, Frans, 188–89, 194, 196, 197,
    198, 201n25, 205–6, 207
Dionysus, 179
Dworkin, Ronald, 33n47, 56–57, 118n6,
    132n18, 244–45, 247, 250
Dwyer, Susan, 190n17

Engstrom, Stephen, 4n7

Finnis, John, 51, 148n35, 182n10, 183n12
Flannery, Kevin, 51n57, 79n17
Foot, Philippa, 5n8, 24
Ford, John, 265n24
Fried, Charles, 174–75, 265n24
Fried, Gregory, 265n24

Gauguin, Paul, 264–65
Gilligan, Carol, 226n42
Gopnik, Alison, 222n41

Greene, Joshua, 187n13
Grisez, Germain, 51, 148n35, 182n10, 183n12

Haidt, Jonathan, 188n13
Hause, Jeffrey, 47n55
Hauser, Marc, 190n17
Hermann, Barbara, 12n23, 109
Hoose, Bernard, 183n12
Huebner, Bryce, 190n17
Hume, David, x–xi
Hursthouse, Rosalind, 5n8, 8n11, 9n15, 10n17, 11n19, 11n21, 24, 242n5

John of Damascus, 123
Justinian, 1, 45, 117, 139

Kant, Immanuel, x–xi, 4, 23, 26n41, 57, 109
Kent, Bonnie, 14, 84n23, 88n25, 119n8
Koons, Robert C., 209n31
Korsgaard, Christine, 4n8, 25–27, 55, 60, 157, 176n3, 176n5, 189n16, 190n17, 197, 198, 231
Kovesi, Julius, 33n47
Kuttner, Stephan, 117n2

Laurentius, 137–38
Leary, Mark R., 223n41
Lisska, Anthony J., 149n35
Long, Stephen, 182n10, 216n34
Lorenz, Amanda R., 159n39
Lottin, Odon, 7n9, 18n33, 63n6, 79n17, 80n18, 117n2

MacDonald, Scott, 82n20, 95n28
Macedo, Stephen, 188–89, 188
MacIntyre, Alasdair, 261n21
Macrobius, 50
Margulies, Joseph, 266n24
Mathison, William, 31n44
McInerny, Ralph, 51, 149n35
Millgram, Elijah, 90n26, 100–101, 175n3, 220n38, 236n4, 247
Miner, Robert, 67n8

Nagel, Thomas, 265n24
Nederman, Cary, 18n33
Newman, Joseph P., 159n39
Nozick, Robert, 132n18, 133
Nussbaum, Martha, 10n18, 56–57

Ober, Josiah, 188–89
O'Brien, Matthew B., 209n31
O'Connell, Mary Ellen, 265n23
O'Grady, Paul, 51n57, 52n57
O'Neill, Onora, 8n11, 10

Pasnau, Robert, 14n26, 19n35, 34n48, 66, 79n17, 82n20, 95n28, 199n24
Perkams, Matthias, 77n15, 79n17, 84n23, 102n32
Peter Lombard, 18
Plato, 26n41, 59–60
Porter, Jean, 19n35, 117n3, 144n31
Proctor, Darby, 201n25

Rawls, John, 1–2, 8, 12, 32, 33, 132n18, 268n26, 269
Raz, Joseph, 268n26
Reid, Charles, 122n12, 133, 135n22, 138
Rist, John, 60n1
Rogers, Eugene, 51n57
Rogoff, Barbara, 260n21
Ryan, Richard M., 243n6

Sahaydachny, Antonia Bocarius, 122n12
Scheffler, Samuel, 245n14, 248n18
Schneewind, J. B., 160n40
Slote, Michael, 10n16, 60n1
Southern, R. W., 53n59, 121n11, 136n23
Stump, Eleonore, 3n6
Suárez, Francisco, 160

Taylor, Gabriele, 234n3, 243, 245, 246n15
Tierney, Brian, 2n5, 133–34, 135, 136–38, 143
Todd, S. C., 120n9
Tomasello, Michael, 67n8, 69n11, 86n24, 202n26
Torrell, Jean-Pierre, 79n16
Tuck, Richard, 133

Turnbull, Colin, 268n25

Urmson, J. O., 37n51

Vera, Luis, 31n44
Vogler, Candace, 4n7, 61, 90n26, 92n27,
    176n3, 231

Waldron, Jeremy, 265n23
Walzer, Michael, 265n24

Warren, Rick, 245n13
Wawrykow, Joseph, 55n60
Wedgewood, Ralph, 23n36
Weiland, George, 19n35, 243n8
Wenzel, Siegfried, 32n46
Westberg, Daniel, 14n26, 101n32
Whiting, Jennifer, 4n7
Williams, Bernard, 236n4, 264
Wolterstorff, Nicholas, 12n23, 16, 55,
    106–7, 108, 160, 221–22, 242n5, 247n16

Subject Index

Act, 173–86
  and end, 178–89
  and intention, 110–11, 203–6, 216–19
  natural and moral descriptions,
    204–10
  and object, 39–40, 178–79, 204–12
Anger, 190–92
Animals, nonhuman, 66–68, 74–76,
  83–86, 182–203
Appetite, 20–23, 64–72, 86–88
  relation to form, 20–21, 64–66

Charity, 4, 54–58, 163–69
Choice
  as a capacity or exercise of will, 13–15,
    63–69, 77–78, 83–85
  and the formation of habits of the will,
    97–104
Common good, 161–69, 240–41, 252–54,
  265–66
Commutative justice, 47–48, 126–27
  and precepts of nonmaleficence,
    48–49, 126–27
  restitution as the object of, 47, 126
Constitutional model of agency, 60, 157

Decalogue, 152–53, 172–73, 202–3
Discernment, 9–10, 219–27
Distributive justice, 3, 47, 124–25
Double effect, 206, 215–18
Duties between unequals, 49–50, 127–31

Equality, 116–31, 131–45

and the common good, 161–69
and exchange, 117–18
and neighbor-love, 221–27
Eudaimonism, 11, 106–10

First principles of practical reason, 49,
  55, 146–61, 233, 258–60
  as pertaining to justice, 152–61,
    221–27, 267–69

General justice, 3, 45, 161–69, 240–41

Habit, 3–4, 19–23, 85–96
  defined by object, 32–36
  necessity for, 20–23, 85–88
Happiness, 73–74, 96–104, 106–10,
  238–56
  and a meaningful life, 245–56

Internalism and externalism, 235–36

Judge, judicial proceedings, 46, 124, 142,
  167–69

Killing, 117, 213–15
  in self-defense, 215–18

Legal justice. *See* General justice
Liberum arbitrium. See Choice
Love of neighbor, 157–60, 221–27,
  254–56
  and first principles, 153–56

Moral luck, 264–65
Moral mistakes, 184–86

Natural law, natural right, 136–37,
    146–51, 156
    and equality of status, 121–22, 144–45
Normativity, 23–31, 68–69, 71–72

Obedience, 129–31

Particular justice, 3–4, 45, 115–45,
    254–56
Passions, 66–70, 93–94
    and love of neighbor, 224–27
    and moral emotions, 182–203
Perfection, 15, 19–20, 27–31
    happiness as a kind of perfection,
        73–74, 96–104, 238–56
    and specific form, 64–71
Political authority, 165–69
    limitations in conflict situations,
        213–15, 265–67
Potential parts of justice. See Duties
    between unequals
Practical induction, 100–104, 247–48
Practical reason, 231–38
    and discernment, 219–27
    not inconsistent with immoral acts,
        61–62, 91–93
    in relation to the will, 70–71, 80–83,
        89–93
Property, 140–41, 215
Prudence, 43, 232–33
Precepts, 126, 173–86, 203–9
    consistent with virtuous discernment,
        219–27

relation to virtue, 38–42, 151–52
stringency/exceptionless force,
    171–72, 183–85, 266–69

Right
    the object of justice, 17, 44–45, 115–16,
        116–31
    the right and the good, 12–17
Rights, human or natural, 16, 131–45
Rules. See Precepts

Theft and robbery. See Property

Virtue, 7–30, 31–43
    cardinal and theological, 42
    infused and acquired, 18, 29–31
    mean as standard, 36–38, 151–52,
        234–35
    parts of a virtue, 43–44
    relation to precepts/rules, 38–42,
        151–52
Voluntariness, 74–76, 83–85

Will, 14–15, 59–114
    as a causal principle, 63–72
    exercised through choice, 13–15,
        63–69, 77–78, 83–85
    formation of, 95–104, 222–23, 247–64
    freedom of, 78–83
    principle of relations ad extra, 12–13,
        95–96, 120
    relation to reason, 70–71, 80–83,
        89–93
    subject of habits, 85–104, 257–58